The Changing Face of Economics

THE CHANGING FACE
OF ECONOMICS

Conversations with Cutting Edge Economists

∾

*David Colander, Richard P. F. Holt, and
J. Barkley Rosser, Jr.*

UNIVERSITY OF MICHIGAN PRESS

ANN ARBOR

ॐ Dedicated to our wives
Pat, Lorna, and Marina

Copyright © by the University of Michigan 2004
All rights reserved
Published in the United States of America by
The University of Michigan Press
Manufactured in the United States of America
⊗ Printed on acid-free paper

2007   2006   2005   2004   4   3   2   1

A CIP catalog record for this book is available from the British Library.

Library of Congress Cataloging-in-Publication Data

Colander, David C.
   The changing face of economics : conversations with cutting edge
economists / David Colander, Richard P. F. Holt, and J. Barkley Rosser.
   Includes bibliographical references and index.
      p.   cm.
   ISBN 0-472-09877-2 (cloth : alk. paper) — ISBN 0-472-06877-6
(pbk. : alk. paper)
   1. Economists—Interviews.   2. Economists—Biography.
3. Economics.   I. Holt, Richard, P. F., 1953–   II. Rosser, John
Barkley, 1948–   III. Title.
HB76.C65   2004
330'.092'2—dc22   2004007728

Contents

Preface

∾ This book was initially conceived by Ric, who cornered Dave and Barkley at a Post Keynesian conference and told them of an idea he had for a book. The idea was to expand upon some of the ideas that Barkley and Dave had put forward on the PKT-NET, of which Ric is moderator, in a debate about the importance of new work being done within the mainstream. Barkley had strongly argued that Post Keynesians needed to take seriously the new complexity work and that it was not more of the same "mainstream" drivel, which many on the PKT-NET saw it as being. Dave agreed with Barkley, but that wasn't surprising since he was seen by many on the PKT-NET as "one of them mainstream guys." Based on that interchange and previous discussions, Ric suggested that the three of us do a book that would convey to heterodox economists the exciting work that was being done in the mainstream, as well as to let the mainstream know that many heterodox economists were concerned about the same issues.

The initial idea was kneaded and reworked again and again. The conception of the book vacillated chaotically as we argued out the main points of what we believed and how we believed heterodox economics interfaced with mainstream economics. The introduction went through revision after revision. There were almost weekly debates among us, with the introduction going from one to the other, and back to the first, and each time being changed to reflect the views of the last person who had it. But ultimately the process converged, and the three of us remain friends.

Much of the debate concerned what was meant by *heterodox, orthodox,* and *mainstream,* with each of us considering ourselves to be on the edges of these categories, but our perceptions of ourselves differed. Dave saw himself as mainstream, whereas Barkley and Ric saw themselves as heterodox, even though all our views were almost identical. In one of those discussions Dave told Barkley that Barkley was no heterodox economist, as he had always pictured himself, but instead just another mainstream economist. The reason why Barkley fitted into mainstream economics wasn't that he agreed with a neoclassical orthodoxy—he was rather disdainful of that—but because the arguments he was making were ones that the mainstream was willing to engage, both because his book on chaos theory had established him as a legitimate modeler and an economist to be taken seriously and because the arguments that he was making fit nicely into a broader conception of mainstream that Dave argued was the real mainstream.

The three of us continued to argue and to explore what we meant by *mainstream, orthodox,* and *heterodox,* and how one distinguishes them, and that exploration finally gelled into an introduction to the volume. In it we argue that the old neoclassical orthodoxy, which we describe as an approach based on a holy trinity of rationality, greed, and equilibrium, is in the process of being replaced with a new orthodoxy, which can be described as an approach based on a holy trinity of purposeful behavior, enlightened self-interest, and sustainability. This movement to this new trinity is broadening the mainstream enormously and making it inclusive of a much wider range of economists—economists who are not neoclassical but who are still mainstream.

☙ *The Evolution of the Book*

Having clarified our thinking, we next had to choose what we were going to write in the book. Ultimately we decided that the most interesting book would be a set of interviews that showed the issues in particular case studies. It would be economists telling their story firsthand, rather than us telling a secondhand story. After much discussion and debate we chose a list of interviewees who were working within this broader mainstream, who were pushing the edges of theory, and who were geographically possible to interview. There were many we could have chosen, and the debate about whom to include was heated. Ultimately we chose a set of interviewees who we felt were representative of the many dimensions on the edge of economics and who also had interesting stories to tell.

The initial conception we had of the book was that it would show heterodox economists the exciting work that was being done within the mainstream and the mainstream the exciting work within the heterodox camps, but the book evolved into one written for a broader audience, showing people the changing face of economics. We came to the conclusion that, intellectually, it didn't matter whether an economist was heterodox or orthodox; all that mattered was whether he or she had good ideas and could express those ideas. We also found that new work in the profession depended not only on the ideas but also on the sociology of the profession. Heterodox economists were those economists who were shut out of the conversation, and they consisted of two types. The first type was those who were discussing the same set of ideas that the mainstream was addressing but which the mainstream was not willing to listen to for a variety of sociological reasons. The sociology of the profession narrowed the conversation and required conformity in language and approach in order for someone to take part in the mainstream conversation. Individuals in this group who conformed to the mainstream language and approach could go in and out of the mainstream. They were arguing about the same issues. The second group of heterodox economists was those whose ideas fell outside even this widened holy trinity and who therefore could still be defined as heterodox. But this was a much smaller group than is normally considered heterodox.

We then went out and did interviews—whenever possible having all of us there, but always having two of us at the interviews. We transcribed and edited the interviews and sent them back to the interviewees, who corrected our transcription and cleared up a number of confusions. Finally we talked with editors about publishing the book, and in that discussion a friend, Ken MacLeod, suggested that we include reactions to the interviews of some top economists. We followed his suggestion and conclude the book with interviews of both Paul Samuelson and Ken Arrow. In these interviews we asked them not so much about their work but about how they viewed the work at the edge that the interviewees were doing.

∾ People to Thank

There are many people to thank. We presented the introduction at a number of conferences and workshops, each time getting helpful comments, leading us to more rewrites, but in the process clarifying our thinking. Ken Koford, Larry Moss, Richard Kerry, and Marina Rosser come particularly to mind, but there are many others. A variation of the introduction was published in the *Review of Political Economy,* and we thank the editor, Steve Pressman, and reviewers for helpful comments. We also thank reviewers for the University of Michigan Press, who made a number of helpful comments. The interviewees also deserve enormous thanks for their willingness to spend a large part of a day in front of a tape recorder answering our questions. They also took our transcriptions and reworked them, making sure that the responses to our questions were clear. There were numerous people who helped with production. Marcia LaBrenz guided the book through production, and Mary Meade helped with a number of questions. Finally, Betsy Hovey did a nice job of copyediting. We thank them all. Pam Bodenhorn transcribed some of the interviews and did an excellent job. Helen Reiff prepared the index and was as helpful as ever. At the University of Michigan Press, Ellen McCarthy took the project under her wing and was very supportive. She is a great editor.

Introduction

∾ This book is about the economics profession or, more precisely, the process by which economic thinking changes. We believe that this process is important because economics is currently at a turning point: it is moving away from a strict adherence to the holy trinity—rationality, greed, and equilibrium—to a more eclectic trinity of purposeful behavior, enlightened self-interest, and sustainability.

The change is ongoing and has many dimensions, most of which have not coalesced to a level that has reached the lay public. But anyone involved in economic research recognizes the change, although it is not clear how all the new pieces will ultimately fit together. This book tries to give the reader some sense about what the changes are and the process through which they are influencing the profession. The changes are not new; in fact they have been going on for decades. What is new is that we are now arriving at the point where the changes are recognizable to individuals outside the profession. Thus, we are seeing more and more articles in the popular press on aspects of the new economics—behavioral economics, agent-based modeling, evolutionary game theory, and experimental economics.

∾ The Story We Tell

The story we tell here is of economists who have been, or who are currently, involved in this change. It is a story of how they have pushed and tested the boundaries of the profession in ways that eventually change how standard economics is done. To understand our story, it is helpful to think of the profession as a complex system. Complex systems cannot be understood from assumed first principles; they can only be understood through the process of change that underlies them. In the same way, the economics profession can best be understood by the process of change that characterizes it. Most previous studies of the economics profession have tended to take a static view of the profession as an unchanging entity in equilibrium. That's not the way we see it: we see it as a dynamic, constantly changing entity, seldom in any state that could reasonably be called a steady state equilibrium. We see the economics profession as a self-reproducing, evolving, complex system of interacting individuals and institutions that is continually testing and reinterpreting old ideas, developing new ones, and trying to relate those ideas to a changing reality. Most of it is done locally, with individuals working in their small area, with little concern about the global changes taking place. But globally the sum of those local changes represents a major change in what economics is.

Getting a handle on such a dynamic entity and conveying its essence to others often requires giving it static classifications and organizing it into distinct periods. Historians of economic thought must do this to provide structure for their consideration of past economists. But these classifications are crutches, not characterizations of reality. They are imposed by the observer and are not necessarily part of the essence of the profession at any point in time. Any static classification hides the dynamic change occurring underneath it. For this reason the classifications used by historians of thought, such as classical or neoclassical, while useful and perhaps even necessary, are nevertheless confining and miss important dimensions of the profession.

Our focus on dynamic changes in the profession explains our interest in work at the edge of economics.[1] It is innovative and successful work at the edges of the profession that signals the future direction of change in economics and how the profession eventually comes to be viewed and understood by its elite. The very concept of an edge of the profession is designed to suggest a profession in which there are multiple views held within it, and this goes against the standard classifications of economics. Those standard classifications convey a sense of the profession as a single set of ideas. In our view, that is wrong; it is much more useful to characterize the economics profession as evolving, made up of diverse economists who hold an evolving set of ideas. The profession is loosely held together by a shared approach to economic problems, but it is seldom static or fixed in its views.

Standard classifications tend to miss the diversity that exists within the profession, as well as the many new ideas that are being tried out. They miss the important insight that one can be part of the mainstream and yet not necessarily hold "orthodox" ideas. Standard classifications also emphasize a fairly narrow orthodoxy or core to the profession and convey a picture of all conventional economists accepting this core. The reality is more complicated; conventional economists often hold a variety of views simultaneously. If the variance of views increases, while the core remains relatively unchanged, the static characterization of the profession will not change, but its dynamic characterization will.

A large variance in acceptable views, such as has emerged in the profession over recent decades, signals that changes are likely in the future. In our view the interesting story in economics over the past decades is the increasing variance of acceptable views, even though the center of economics has not changed much. For example, mainstream economists today such as William Baumol, George Akerlof, Thomas Schelling, Truman Bewley, and Paul Krugman, in important aspects of their thinking, are working outside of what is generally considered the orthodoxy of the profession. Yet their ideas are widely accepted and discussed within the mainstream of economics. It is such work that has increased the variance of acceptable views in the profession.

To capture that variance of acceptable views, static classifications must be seen for what they are—useful fictions that are meant for beginning students. These classifications are backward-looking and must be supplemented with a discussion of the variance of ideas acceptable to the mainstream. At any point in time a successful discipline will have hundreds of new ideas being tried out, as new methods, new technology, and new information become available. That is what happens at the edge of economics.

This edge of economics has both intellectual and social elements. The intellectual aspect of economics at the edge fundamentally involves originality. This does not mean that all ideas at the edge are totally new. Ideas have origins and grow better in some environments than in others. The history of economics is full of instances in which old ideas are rehabilitated or revived and found to be useful and advantageous within the new context that is emerging.

In the work at the edge, ideas that previously have been considered the holy trinity in economics—rationality, greed, and equilibrium—

are being modified and broadened, and the process is changing the very nature of economics. What is making it possible for these ideas to take root now, but not in the past, are advances in analytic technology that have made it possible to study much more complex models than before, developments in computing capabilities that have allowed one to study problems that do not have analytic solutions, and advances in other disciplines relevant to economics. The combination of these advances has opened up completely new ways of integrating those ideas into the core beliefs of the field and has often changed the core beliefs in important ways.

As the process unfolds, sociological issues impinge upon and constrain what is possible intellectually. This impingement occurs because the reproduction of ideas involves the social, political, and economic structures of the academic and policy-making establishments in which ideas are developed and transmitted. Ideas, however original and possibly wonderful, that do not become accepted by some of the elite of the profession, and which do not eventually get funded, will not be accepted and transmitted within the profession. To internally move the discipline to a new position, some of the profession's elite must accept these ideas.

In our view what is occurring in economics today is a modification of the standard view of paradigm shifts proposed by Thomas Kuhn (1970), at least as it relates to the economics profession. Kuhn argued that the driving forces of change are those ideas that challenge the very system of thought in a way that puts them outside the mainstream and that ultimately are only introduced, "funeral by funeral," by a paradigm shift. This makes it easy to recognize that a paradigm shift has occurred.

We see this view as not quite fitting the economics profession for two reasons. First, it downplays the multidimensionality of the profession at any point in time, and second, it downplays the role that an elite, open to innovation and change, plays in the process of change. From our dynamic perspective an alternative channel exists that allows for significant changes to occur within the mainstream of the profession. These changes do not lead to sudden paradigm shifts but instead lead to cumulative evolutionary changes that ultimately will be recognized as a revolutionary change. The changes that lead to this ex–post revolution were initially accepted within the profession gradually, more along the lines suggested by Imre Lakatos (1978). This alternative channel is the following: When certain members of the existing elite become open to new ideas, that openness allows new ideas to expand, develop, and integrate into the profession. In that case change within the profession can be accepted gradually, being introduced "data set by data set" and "new technique by new technique," as well as "funeral by funeral." In some cases these new ideas will originate from outside the mainstream, from those who consider themselves heterodox, even if the acceptance of such ideas leads to their "normalization" and removal from being identified as heterodox.

These alternative channels allow the mainstream to expand and evolve to include a wider range of approaches and understanding. Eventually, sufficient change is made so that future historians of thought will consider the orthodoxy of the period changed. This, we believe, is already occurring in economics. Mark Blaug, one of the most distinguished current historians of economic thought, has pointed out that beginning as early as the 1950s the classification "neoclassical economics" was no longer appropriate to characterize modern economics (1998, 2), an argument further developed by Colander (2000a).

The difference between Kuhn's view and ours is in how changes generally come about in a profession. We suggest that changes, even ones that will eventually be considered revolutionary, often come from within and will not be noticed for years. Kuhn's view suggests that they can only come from outside and are quite apparent when they occur. The dynamic approach of change within the profession that we are introducing here involves stealth changes, in which advocates of new ideas may gain acceptance among the elite of the profession and even achieve positions of power and prominence within at least some leading academic institutions of economics. The change, however, is so gradual that the profession often does not notice that it has occurred.

The reason for the difference is the multiple dimensionalities that we see in the mainstream profession. The ideas that the profession holds are a complex maze of evolving ideas. Individuals in the profession see minute change upon minute change but do not have a perception of the aggregate of the changes. Only when historians of thought look back, after sufficient time has passed to gain some historical perspective, does the larger change become apparent.

∾ The Process of Change

Both the social and intellectual aspects of change must be understood to understand the evolution of ideas. The work at the edge is generally begun by younger researchers and in some cases those who are doing heterodox work. But their ability to do that work, and to have their work affect the profession, is dependent on the existence of crucial persons in the leading academic establishments who represent the mainstream of economics and are open to seriously considering new ideas. These crucial people may be the ones who have developed what was considered the old orthodoxy, but their having developed it doesn't mean that they aren't open to change and new ideas. There is nothing inconsistent with being one of the originators of a theory and simultaneously being a critic of that theory. Good economists simultaneously recognize the strengths and limitations of a theory and are open to new approaches and ideas. A good example of a person that fits this category is Kenneth Arrow. Although he is associated with what is considered modern neoclassical orthodoxy, he was instrumental in the introduction of the complexity approach into economics.[2]

The consideration and ultimate acceptance of a new idea by a certain portion of the elite becomes a key to the process of how the conventional foundation of the discipline evolves. It is not crucial that those developing the ideas initially be at leading establishments. But they must be able to attract the attention of influential individuals at those institutions in order for their ideas to be published in venues that will receive attention and for research along those lines to get funded. This allows students and advocates of those ideas to get hired at those institutions and thus to establish themselves within the mainstream of the discipline, even when the originators of these ideas remain somewhat outside the mainstream elite, or even from the zone of the heterodox.

ᴑᴕ Orthodoxy, Heterodoxy, and the Mainstream of Economics

It is helpful in making our argument to carefully consider the terms *mainstream, orthodox,* and *heterodox,* how they are used, and how they relate to our idea that the dynamics of change in a profession is at the edge of the profession. Let's start with mainstream economics. In some sense *mainstream economics* is the easiest of the above terms to define, although it may be the hardest to identify in practice. It is in large part a sociologically defined category. Mainstream consists of the ideas that are held by those individuals who are dominant in the leading academic institutions, organizations, and journals at any given time, especially the leading graduate research institutions. Mainstream economics consists of the ideas that the elite in the profession finds acceptable, where by *elite* we mean the leading economists in the top graduate schools. It is not a term describing a historically determined school but is instead a term describing the beliefs that are seen by the top schools and institutions in the profession as intellectually sound and worth working on. Because of this, mainstream economics usually represents a broader and more eclectic approach to economics than is characterized as the recent orthodoxy of the profession.

In our view *orthodox* is primarily an intellectual category. It is a backward-looking term that is best thought of as a static representation of a dynamic, constantly changing profession and thus is never appropriately descriptive of the field of economics in its present state. Orthodoxy generally refers to what historians of economic thought have classified as the most recently dominant "school of thought," which today is neoclassical economics. In our view modern mainstream economics is quite different from this neoclassical concept of orthodox economics. Having the two terms is important for us because it allows us to make intertemporal comparisons between the most recently dominant school of thought, in this case neoclassical economics, and today's evolving mainstream economics.

To help us get a grasp of what we mean by neoclassical orthodoxy and how it relates to mainstream economics, it is important for us to first define what neoclassical economics has been viewed as being. Neoclassical economics has been viewed as considering the central core of economics to be the theory of equilibrium, based on the optimizing behavior of fully rational and well-informed individuals in a static context. It is particularly associated with the marginalist revolution and its aftermath. Léon Walras and Alfred Marshall can be viewed as its early and great developers, with John Hicks's *Value and Capital* (1939) and Paul A. Samuelson's *Foundations of Economic Analysis* (1947) as its culmination. When a dynamic context is assumed, individuals understand the probability distributions of possible outcomes over the infinite time horizon at the moment of decision. The neoclassical orthodoxy tests the results of that model by using conventional econometric techniques that are based upon a foundation of classical statistics. Perhaps the most important characteristic of the neoclassical orthodoxy is that axiomatic deduction is the preferred methodological approach.

Orthodox neoclassical economics is generally seen as having two main branches. One is the Paretian-Pigovian branch that is willing to accept the possibility of market failures and that governments might be able to improve welfare and efficiency through careful interventions. In terms of policy it is generally considered a liberal approach and has been strongly based in the United States at MIT and Yale. The other branch, associated with the University of Chicago, strongly emphasizes the efficiency of market outcomes. In terms of policy this branch is generally considered a conservative approach, but many Chicago-leaning economists would argue that classical liberal would be a better description of their school. The Chicago branch of neoclassical orthodoxy has other important elements that distinguish it. Specifically, it emphasizes the superiority of economics and its methods and ideas over those of other social science disciplines, as exemplified in the work of Gary Becker.

The difference between mainstream and orthodox becomes clearer when one recognizes two other aspects of the term *orthodox*. The first is that the name and specification of what is orthodox usually comes decades after the time period has existed. Thus, orthodox specifications inevitably are backward-looking, not current or forward-looking. Second, in economics at least, the name for the orthodox school has usually come from a dissenter, who opposed the orthodox ideas, not from a supporter of these ideas. For example, Karl Marx (1847) coined the term *classical economics,* even though the classical school is seen as starting back in the late 1700s. Before Marx's general classification there was no name for the classical orthodoxy.

Similarly the term *neoclassical economics* was coined by Thorstein Veblen (1900), referring to the economics of the last part of the nineteenth century as he tried to tie this period of economics to classical economics so as to make the argument that both are unscientific (Aspromourgos 1986). In each case, the classification was made by an economist to create a better target for his criticism. Defining orthodoxy, and giving a name to it, gives a critic an easy target; it implies a static unchanging dimension of thought. But this static view is an inappropriate characterization of the economics field. At any point in time, and especially by the time that the term becomes generally used, a large part of the mainstream profession disagrees with important dimensions of what is then thought of as orthodoxy.

Finally, let's consider the term *heterodox.* It is defined in reference to orthodox and hence has meaning only in relation to orthodox. It tends to be "against orthodox" and is defined in terms of what it is not, rather than what it is. An economist who sees him- or herself as heterodox does not subscribe to the current orthodox school of thought, as defined by the historians' classifications and has also defined him- or herself outside of the mainstream. Heterodox economists are highly unlikely to get funding through normal channels such as the National Science Foundation, although they might receive alternative funding from a variety of sources. Thus, heterodoxy involves both sociological and intellectual aspects. Since many mainstream economists also do not accept important aspects of the orthodoxy, the additional feature that determines a heterodox economist is social: heterodox economists refuse to work within the framework of mainstream economics, or their ideas are not welcome by the mainstream, either because of failure to communicate or lack of acceptance of a common methodology.

In the economics profession various schools, many of which have long histories, comprise heterodox economics. These schools have their own networks and organizations and journals and academic institutions where they dominate. Often the fundamental intellectual content of a heterodox school is rejection of orthodoxy, or at least major elements of orthodoxy. In economics, at least, beyond this rejection of the orthodoxy there is no single unifying element that we can discern that characterizes heterodox economics. In fact, it is well known that many varieties of heterodoxy have more disagreements with each other than they do with orthodoxy. But it should also be said that many of the ideas that are now on the edge of economics were previously emphasized by different heterodox schools, and these schools can play an important role in developing new critiques of the orthodox. Among the most established of the heterodox schools with reasonably full systems of institutional support are Marxists, Post Keynesians, feminists, Old Institutionalists, and Austrians.[3]

If the field of economics were static and one-dimensional, these two classifications, orthodox and heterodox, would be sufficient, but it isn't and they aren't. The economics profession is dynamic, constantly changing. Since these classifications usually lag developments in the field by decades, the terms *orthodox* and *heterodox,* when used in a current setting, tend to be backward-looking, describing beliefs that have long since been discarded, or at least significantly diminished, by a large number of members in the profession.

To understand the dynamic aspect of the profession and the role of economists working at the edge, the distinction between mainstream and orthodox is central. The edge of economics is that part of mainstream economics that is critical of orthodoxy and that part of heterodox economics that is taken seriously by the elite of the profession. Our argument is that modern mainstream economics is open to new approaches, as long as they demonstrate a careful understanding of the strengths of the recent orthodox approach and are pursued with a methodology acceptable to the mainstream.

For economists working at the edge, attacking the profession is not sufficient; they must be developing new methods and ideas. In this approach the difference between mainstream and heterodox becomes far less important than whether they are doing work at the edge. Both mainstream and heterodox economists are working on issues that challenge the neoclassical orthodoxy because that orthodoxy is no longer descriptive of what the mainstream elite believes. The elite's vision of economics is forward-looking—its ideas are exciting today, and here is where they may lead; the static classifications of economics are backward-looking, emphasizing where economics has been.

This concept "elite of the profession" is elusive but is understood by those in the profession. It is those mainstream economists who have made important contributions to thought in the past. It includes some (but not all) Nobel Prize winners and most economists who have major chairs at top graduate programs. If one has standing offers from a number of top schools to come and teach, and if one receives calls from NSF about who to put on its panels, one is in the elite of the profession. Examples of well-known mainstream elite are Paul Samuelson, Kenneth Arrow, Robert Solow, Thomas Schelling, Amartya Sen, Joseph Stiglitz, Chris Sims, Michael Woodford, George Akerlof, Richard Thaler, Anne Krueger, and Jagdish Bhagwati. As you can see, it is a very diffuse group.

Recognizing that there is an elite element in the mainstream that plays a crucial role in what new ideas will prove to be part of the acceptable edge of economics raises two problems—one of how open the elite will be and another of how these ideas then disseminate throughout the rest of the mainstream and the profession more generally. Currently, in regard to the openness question, our view is that the elite are relatively open minded when it comes to new ideas but quite closed minded when it comes to alternative methodologies. If it isn't modeled, it isn't economics, no matter how insightful. It is here where the heterodox and mainstream elite normally collide. Specifically, it is because of their method, not their ideas, that most heterodox find themselves defined outside the field by the elite.[4]

We certainly are not claiming that the mainstream is always pluralistic and open minded, willing to accept heterodox views with open arms. Far from it. They are human and become fixed in their ways of looking at things and often reject alternative views without giving them serious consideration. That's part of human nature. This means that in many ways, which we consider unfortunate, the mainstream elite can suppress the views of heterodox economists (and when they accept them, they often do so without properly citing the heterodox sources of those ideas). Moreover, they often use their method as a tool to protect views that don't fit nicely into their way of thinking. What we are claiming is that their closed-mindedness is generally unconscious and representative of almost any group that has the power to be that way, including, in their own smaller spheres, many heterodox economists. What we are also claiming is that the worst types of heterodox suppression and narrow-mindedness are not carried out by the elite but instead by economists whose professional credentials are mediocre for the very reason that they are not as imaginative and creative as the elite.

Our view regarding the second issue, how ideas are disseminated, is that the process is a long and drawn out one that works along the following lines. Work at the edge usually shows up first in working papers that are presented at graduate seminars and workshops that are the incubators of new ideas in economics, although sometimes these ideas were initially generated by persons outside of those seminars. The ideas in these working papers will generate discussion among professors at graduate schools—some will be panned; others will be tentatively accepted and mentioned to professors at other schools. Some ideas will generate a buzz and, when they do, will attract intense interest. (This generally occurs before publication.) Eventually the ideas will be published in top journals, but that publication is often a tombstone process demarking ownership of the ideas more than it is a spreading of them. The diffusion of the ideas throughout the elite of the profession will have already occurred, although sometimes an idea will be published and not get noticed until sometime later.

As this process is occurring, the working papers or articles will show up in core graduate program reading lists and eventually make their way into graduate textbooks. This process from conception of an idea to graduate textbooks can take up to ten years. Intermediate-

and upper-level undergraduate textbooks usually take another five to ten years to include the idea, although it may show up as a supplemental box or an added paragraph earlier than this. Principles books take another five to ten years to actually incorporate the idea as a central element, although, like their undergraduate upper-level counterparts, they may add them as addenda so that they look modern.

There is a paradox in this diffusion process. The more central the idea, the less likely it is to be included in a central way in the texts. For example, complexity suggests the whole conception of equilibrium in an economy needs to be reconsidered, and experimental economics suggests that the entire approach to thinking about the appropriate mix of induction and deduction needs to be rethought. Such a reconsideration and rethinking would likely change the entire way textbooks are structured and the way the courses are taught. Such major changes are unlikely to show up even with the long lags discussed. Instead they will be simply added as an addendum to the existing core. (For a discussion of these issues, see Colander 2000b.) Such changes resemble more the kind of changes that Kuhn discussed in his analysis of paradigm shifts, even if the shifts have occurred in the more gradualist manner that we have been describing.

Why the enormous lag? The reason is that the professors who actually teach the majority of the courses are most comfortable teaching what they have studied, and the publishing industry writes for that majority. Since the average undergraduate professor has been out of graduate school for a long period of time, this professor (the audience textbooks target) will generally be most comfortable teaching older material as the core of the course, with new material scattered throughout. The material shows up in higher-level courses first because the higher the level of the course, the more likely a specialist in the area is teaching the course and that specialist is more likely to feel comfortable including new developments.

This long lag should not be seen as a complete waste; it also serves a useful function in that it provides a filtering process that eliminates those ideas that seemed wonderful but turned out to be just fads. For example, the Keynesian IS/LM model has remained the core of many undergraduate macro texts even after it has all but been excluded from what is taught in graduate schools. New books reflecting the new graduate school approach have been published, but they have not been generally adopted at the undergraduate level.

This lack of acceptance by the undergraduate texts reflects the uncertainty with which many in the mainstream profession both at the undergraduate and graduate level saw the rational expectations revolution in macro. While it was a logical extension of microeconomic reasoning, it did not seem reasonable to many, suggesting that something was wrong with the models that were based on it in its strong form. For that reason the rational expectations revolution led to the work in what we call the complexity revolution, which is striving to provide a stronger underpinning for macro models generally. This work begins from the assumption of rationality but seriously considers the problems of defining rationality in a complex environment and, when there are problems, accepts the complex environment as its reference point, rather than taking a simpler environment.

The lags in this process can lead to situations where an idea that has come to be viewed as somewhat old hat at the elite mainstream level may only finally be appearing at the principles textbook level. What this means is that textbooks, especially lower-level texts, often do not reflect the diversity of views acceptable to the mainstream but instead reflect an older orthodox position.[5]

Another important difference between the mainstream and orthodoxy is that economists working within the mainstream can find their views evolving. For example, they might be working with a particular approach but then change. Consider rational expectations and the New Classical revolution in macroeconomics. One of the early developers of rational expectations, Leonard Rapping, modified his views significantly and became a leading heterodox economist before his untimely death. Another example is Thomas Sargent, also one of the leading figures in the application of rational expectations to macroeconomics. As a result of visiting the Santa Fe Institute he came to abjure a strict rational expectations view (Sargent 1993). His more recent work with Lars Hansen and others (Hansen and Sargent 2000) has attempted to provide quantitative approaches to dealing with Knightian uncertainty, and thus he has moved out of orthodoxy but has remained mainstream and is on the edge of the edge of economics. We don't include him as a researcher at the edge of economics because in his work he is trying to deviate as little as possible from orthodox views, whereas, in our view, researchers at the edge of economics are open to letting the results of their research lead to whatever result they may. Our point is that mainstream economists are open to change if they can see a way to bring their skills and knowledge to bear on developing that change.

As should be clear from this discussion, in our view the edge is where the action is in the profession. Whether that work at the edge is considered heterodox or mainstream is primarily a matter of the individual's proclivity to fit within the existing mainstream and the degree to which he or she directly attacks, rather than softly criticizes, the work of the elite. Our set of interviewees includes economists who are in different categories, with some of them having moved from category to category over time. Thus, Herbert Gintis began as clearly heterodox with an announced Marxist orientation. Over time both he and the mainstream have moved toward each other. Some, such as Deirdre McCloskey, started out as quite mainstream and have moved into heterodoxy. Duncan Foley started from near mainstream, moved to heterodoxy, and turned back somewhat toward the mainstream as he struggled to answer questions about the foundations of the economic system. Others, such as Buz Brock and Ken Binmore, have pushed against the boundaries of economics while constantly remaining in the mainstream. Often we find economists in different categories working on the same issues, but with all providing challenges to the economics profession.

Working at the edge does have its problems, especially for those whose proclivity is toward attacking, rather than working within, the existing field and hence finding themselves in heterodoxy. They face significant sociological problems of achieving acceptance from the established mainstream. Economists considered heterodox often find it difficult gaining funding for their work, and they will likely be squeezed out of the decision-making process at their universities. We see some of these problems in the careers of some of our interviewees. Those involved in working at the edge who are in the mainstream lack this sociological problem but also often find themselves at odds with those around them to some degree as they press against the boundaries of the mainstream.

༶ The Edge of Economics in Historical Perspective

While our focus is on modern work at the edge of economics, a brief historical discussion of the work at the edge may be useful. Let's start with classical economics, which, in history of thought textbooks, is usually presented as beginning with Adam Smith.[6] The existing orthodoxy before Smith is usually presented as mercantilism, a school of thought with a belief in protectionism to achieve balance of payments surpluses and in gold as the basis of the wealth of nations.

But economic reality during that time was far more complicated than presented by this orthodoxy. It was later mercantilists, like Thomas Mun and David Hume, who developed more sophisticated views of balance of payments that influenced Smith's writings. Another important economist of this time was Richard Cantillon, whose ideas also influenced Smith. He was joined by French physiocrats such as François Quesnay and Anne Robert de Turgot. Using our terminology, Cantillon, the later mercantilists, and the physiocrats would be the economists of their time who worked at the edge. What Smith did was to bring together and publicize their work. Smith's justly famous *Wealth of Nations* (1776) amounts to a well-formulated presentation of ideas largely developed by others. Thus his role was to pull together ideas from an already developing literature and to put them together in a package that would be widely accepted and be looked upon as the mainstream economics of his time.

Another important dimension of classical economics during its one hundred years of prominence was the large variance of acceptable views in its mainstream. The economics of David Ricardo is fundamentally different from the economics of Smith in its formalist method, as is the economics of Thomas Malthus in policy implications. The economics of John Stuart Mill is yet quite different from that of either Ricardo or Malthus. Different theories of value were used at various times by different people. But now it all goes under the general heading *classical* and is usually presented as more fixed in its views than it actually was. Eventually, an increase in variance of views among the mainstream undermined the classical orthodoxy. This led to an evolution in economic thought from classical to neoclassical economics. The evolution is seen as occurring in the 1870s with the work of Carl Menger, William Stanley Jevons, Marshall, and Walras.

The reality is, again, more complicated. Cournot, Jules Dupuit, and the German proto-neoclassicals developed many of the ideas, which we now consider part of neoclassical economics, decades earlier. Coming from an engineering background, as did Dupuit, Cournot stood completely outside of the orthodoxy of his day and became the father of neoclassical orthodoxy, as well as game theory. Among other things, he was the first to draw supply and demand curves and to formally posit their intersection as representing equilibrium. He was also the first to use calculus to explicitly solve for optimization outcomes with implied marginal conditions.

If we were writing this book back in the 1840s, Cournot and

Dupuit would represent work at the edge of economics in their time. Menger, Jevons, and Walras were working at the edge while also being mainstream.[7] They pioneered the ideas that undermined the previous orthodoxy of the time based on labor or cost theories of value. Marshall and Walras, in his later years, represented the mainstream that consolidated what would later be perceived to be the orthodoxy. They were the elite economists who were needed for those new ideas to be accepted into the mainstream that finally changed the orthodoxy.

The mainstream of this period was open to accepting new ideas and modifying its own. Although Marshall is known as a founder of the neoclassical school, his work contains much discussion of the problems with the approach. He knew he hadn't solved the general equilibrium problem and that he had not correctly integrated time into the analysis. He was open to new ways of solving these problems, but he saw no way of doing it with the mathematics available to him during that time.

With Walras, recent discussion (Walker 1996) makes it clear that with the fourth edition in 1900 of his *Élements d'Économie Pure* he shifted his views considerably and presented a simpler and more static version of his theory. This was the edition that was translated into English and became the Walras whom most modern Walrasians know and follow. The earlier editions contained many discussions of dynamics and complexity, but he recognized that it was beyond him to capture this complexity in his models. The point is that these economists, whom many see as orthodox economists, generally knew the limitations of their analysis and had many dimensions to their thought. Calling them orthodox implies close-mindedness; calling them mainstream captures their open-mindedness.

❧ The Revolutions of the 1930s and Their Aftermath

The 1930s demonstrate the degree to which beliefs can change in a short time period within the mainstream. John Maynard Keynes and his macroeconomic revolution responded to the external stimulus provided by the shock of the Great Depression. Keynes did not identify his object of attack as being neoclassical economics but as classical economics. Indeed, he invoked Malthus against Ricardo as his model and always showed admiration for the work of Marshall, if not always his immediate follower A. C. Pigou. But his questioning of the efficient functioning of markets and his doubts about the accuracy of expectations undermined many of the beliefs of the neoclassical orthodoxy, and his work swiftly changed the content of mainstream economics. In fact, during the 1960s it was supporters of classical ideas such as Milton Friedman who would be seen as working at the edge against the entrenched neo-Keynesian orthodoxy.

From 1937 to the mid-1950s, Keynesian economics was sweeping the top graduate schools despite political opposition both within and outside the profession. During this period Keynesian economics was considered work at the edge, but by the mid-1950s, Keynesian macroeconomics was old hat. Mainstream macroeconomics was amended to include the formal integration of money into the Keynesian model with IS/LM analysis. By the mid-1960s monetarism was appended to Keynesianism along with neoclassical microeconomics in the neoclassical synthesis, and Keynesian economics lost much of its edginess.[8] In the 1970s the edge of macroeconomics changed to a microfoundations approach that led to a New Classical rational expectations model and in the 1980s a new Keynesian model that emphasized microeconomic explanations for wage and price rigidity. But since this time there has been much chaos in modern macroeconomics, and the current work at the edge is exploring areas, such as complexity theory and computer simulations, as ways to redefine model building in macroeconomics.

Modern microeconomics also has become more diffuse. From the 1930s to the 1960s, Pigovian microeconomics was considered the work at the edge. It explored formally the general equilibrium conditions for efficiency and acknowledged the government role in correcting market failures. In the 1960s the focus changed to issues of tradeoffs between equity and efficiency. This was also a time when deductivist formalism, as seen in the work of Gerard Debreu, reached a peak.[9] Since that time work at the edge has become very diffuse, covering areas like evolutionary game theory and psychological economics while still using highly technical model building.

The current state of affairs in mainstream economics is that its content is not as focused as mainstream researchers might like but it is connected by its methodology of technical model building. For this reason most of our interviewees do highly technical work. Those economists working at the edge of economics who don't are far less likely to influence the mainstream of the profession directly. They may, however, do it indirectly by influencing others who then translate their work into more technical and acceptable methods. The two exceptions that we include are Deirdre McCloskey, whose work challenges the modeling and methodological foundation by challenging mainstream economics, and Robert Frank, whose clarity of writing and insights have spread ideas at the edge to a broader audience.

❧ Modern Work at the Edge of Economics

We emphasize complexity as a defining factor of the new work at the edge of economics because it appears to us to be the vision behind this work. But the actual work involves a number of fronts, and the people working on those fronts have varying degrees of connection to the broader complexity approach. Along with this, and interacting with it, is a new openness to ideas from other disciplines. The new complexity economics is also increasingly a transdisciplinary economics.[10] More specifically:

- ❧ Evolutionary game theory is redefining how institutions are integrated into the analysis.
- ❧ Ecological economics is redefining how nature and the economy are viewed as interrelating.
- ❧ Psychological economics is redefining how rationality is treated.
- ❧ Econometric work dealing with the limitations of classical statistics is redefining how economists think of empirical proof.
- ❧ Nonlinear dynamics and complexity theory are offering a way of redefining how we conceive of general equilibrium.
- ❧ Computer simulations are offering a way of redefining models and how they are used.
- ❧ Experimental economics is changing the way economists think about empirical work.

These changes in turn have led to a broader set of changes in how mainstream economics sees itself. It is much more willing to accept that the formal part of economics has limited applicability, at least as currently developed. It is also far more willing to question the special status of economics over the other fields of inquiry and to integrate the methods of other disciplines into its methods.

Each of the economists we interview represents at least one of these dimensions of what we see as work at the edge of economics. From the interviews, we hope that the reader will get a sense of the importance and influence of these different dimensions on the profession.

In reviewing modern work at the edge, one individual stands out as a precursor in its development. That person is John von Neumann. Although his work in economics received limited attention during his life, partly because of the mathematical esotericism of his work and having it appear in German instead of English in the 1920s and 1930s, John von Neumann is, in our view, the most important precursor of modern work at the edge of economics. He helped start game theory, and his work on cellular automata (1966) prefigured much of today's work in the area of computer simulations of heterogeneous and autonomous agents.[11]

Although the new work at the edge of economics draws on many ideas that have long been around, such as bounded rationality, the importance of evolutionary processes, and the heterogeneity of agents, the willingness of the mainstream to accept these ideas has varied with time. Sometimes it takes external events for work at the edge to be considered. For example, the more than 20 percent decline of the U.S. stock market on October 19, 1987, for no obvious reason led many economists to be more open to models that allowed such an aberration to occur (the standard models did not). Financial economic theory had previously been a bastion of a strong neoclassical perspective emphasizing rationality and efficiency of markets. This event challenged that perspective significantly. Sometimes it is simply just a process of time before the ideas are accepted, as was the case with the experimental economics that started in the 1950s but has taken several decades to be accepted into the mainstream.[12]

Another event that furthered the openness to ideas at the edge of economics was the collapse of the Soviet Union and of the socialist bloc. It revealed how fragile and nonresilient economic systems may be. Thomas Sargent (1993, 2) has indeed cited this particular event, along with his discussions at the Santa Fe Institute, as having undermined his faith in the rational expectations assumption. The modern economic world has proven to be a place given utterly to unpredictable and surprising events. The search to explain this has opened up many economists to new ways of thinking and approaches that involve work at the edge.

This change can be seen in the reaction of economists to two conferences held nearly a decade apart at the Santa Fe Institute. The first, held in 1988, generated a book entitled *The Economy as a Complex Evolving System* (Anderson et al. 1988). According to M. Mitchell Waldrop (1992), this conference featured a set of largely mainstream economists and defenders of general equilibrium orthodoxy, assembled by Kenneth Arrow, and a set of physicists assembled by others. The economists mostly attempted to defend an orthodox approach while they faced sharp challenges and ridicule from the physicists for holding relatively simplistic views. Although models using nonlinear dynamics and other complexity approaches have been developed for some time (Rosser 1999), such approaches at that time remained outside the mainstream camp.

The second conference saw a very different outcome and atmosphere than the first (Arthur et al. 1997a). No longer were mainstream economists defensively adhering to general equilibrium orthodoxy. Now they were using methods adopted from biologists and physicists, many suggested at the earlier conference, in innovative ways.[13] They were much more open to complex economic analysis. These two Santa Fe conferences are representative of the change that occurred throughout the profession during this time. It was as if the ideas planted by earlier researchers in many areas, such as experimental economics, behavioral economics, and nonlinear dynamics, were taking root. Thus, by 1997 the mainstream accepted many of the methods and approaches that were associated with the complexity approach. What it had not accepted was the broader complexity vision. (For a discussion of that broader vision, see Colander 2000c). That broader vision is held by a much smaller group of economists, and it may or may not be held by the individuals working on the edge of economics. But as the work at the edge progresses and accumulates, it shifts the center of economists' approach and, in our view, eventually will create a new orthodoxy centered around a broader complexity vision.

✺ The Interviews

In this book we provide a glimpse of the ideas that are slowly changing the profession. Our key expository approach is a set of interviews. Nine of the interviews are with economists whom we see as playing a part in working on the edge that is causing change in the profession, and who have interesting stories to tell. They are not unique; they are simply representative of hundreds of leading economists who have been involved with economics at the edge.

In making our selection of whom to interview we tried to pick economists who have interesting histories and who represent different elements of the composite change that we see currently taking place in economics. Our focus on economics at the edge means that we do not focus on other economists who are significantly advancing economics by improving existing techniques and ideas or who are working within more standard approaches. For example, we do not include economists such as Alan Krueger, James Heckman, or Thomas Sargent, despite their innovative and important work. We see their work following more standard lines; they are deepening rather than broadening and expanding the profession.

The final two interviews are with Ken Arrow and Paul Samuelson, the two economists who have probably done most to shape modern economics. In these interviews we ask them not about their work but rather to reflect on the other interviews and on the changes that are currently going on in the profession.

With the exception of the final two interviews the economists being interviewed are, for the most part, not household names—economists at the edge seldom are. In fact one can even argue that if they become so, they lose their ability to influence the profession—writing for the public takes time and pulls one away from the type of research that can change the profession. Fame tends to wear the edge down, at least in the eyes of economists. At the same time, it will be the better-known economists who popularize the changes and make them well-known. Thus we included Robert Frank in our selection as representative of economists who walk the fine line between research and popularization of that research.

Each interviewee was chosen for a variety of reasons: originality, influence, history, geographic proximity to us, and because we saw them as representative of a particular line of thought. They provide what we believe is a good representation of how economists doing work at the edge of economics think and how they influence the profession.

We do, however, want to emphasize that the geographic proximity of our choices led to our leaving out an important dimension of work at the edge of economics. While it is true that modern economics is in large part centered in the United States, and thus our focus on U.S.-based economists might be justified, it is far less true of economists working at the edge. There are significant clusters of economists at the edge who work abroad. Thus, we would have liked to have had more economists from outside the United States. We didn't simply because we are located in the United States and it was much easier for us to interview economists who live here. As seen in the interviews, many of these individuals have spent time abroad, and their working groups are often internationally, rather than U.S., based.

The interviews represent four different aspects of work at the edge of economics. The first is the broadest and constitutes methodological changes and the introduction of evolutionary game theory as the core theory for thinking about the economy. The first interview is with Deirdre McCloskey, whose work is probably the broadest of all the individuals we have interviewed. We see her as representative of the changing methodological foundations of modern economics and how developments in other fields as far away as literary criticism have influenced economic thought. She comes as close as there is to a postmodernist influence in economics. McCloskey also represents how individuals can change their views significantly, in her case from a Chicago economics approach to a much broader approach. The second interview is with Ken Binmore, who has been a leading developer of evolutionary game theory. His work is representative of the importance that game theory has in modern economics—it is indeed the core of the underlying theory—and the way in which work in game theory has influenced policy. Binmore is also representative of how modern economics is interacting with other disciplines, such as evolutionary biology and philosophy. The third interview is with Herb Gintis, whom we chose as representative of the experimental work that is accompanying the game theory work, although he is also doing important work on game theory. Gintis also shows how the views of economists can change over time—in Gintis's case how he moved from a radical Marxist approach to an approach much more within the mainstream.

The second set of interviews is with Robert Frank and Matthew Rabin. We chose both as representative of work being done in behavioral economics. We also chose Frank because his work has been influential in popularizing new approaches to economics, which shows a different element of work at the edge than that seen in many of the other interviews. Another reason we chose Rabin is because of his youth. Whereas the preceding four interviewees are well along in their careers, Rabin is much younger. The reality is that most of the work at the edge of economics is being done by younger researchers who start from the foundation of where the older researchers leave off. But, with each successive generation, the edge moves, and the previous work at the edge is simply seen as the way economics is done.

The third set of interviews, with Buz Brock and Duncan Foley, were chosen as representative of the modern work in complexity. Complexity work in economics is often associated with Santa Fe, but what we are calling complexity work actually has a longer history and is being carried out at many other locations. For example, Foley has played an important role in developing complexity ideas apart from the Santa Fe Institute, and that alone made him a nice choice for us. But we also chose him because his unique career shows how the search for an answer to a particular problem—how to find the microfoundations of macroeconomics—can lead one to move between the mainstream and heterodoxy as one explores various approaches. His interview also shows how events in the world, such as the Vietnam War, can influence the path of research. Brock was chosen because he has been a leader in the development of complexity economics both theoretically and in econometrics. His work is representative of how nonlinear techniques are being integrated into economic thinking and changing the way we think about stability and equilibrium in the economy and also the way in which empirical work is thought about.

The fourth set of interviews, with Richard Norgaard and jointly with Robert Axtell and Peyton Young, shows another dimension of the way in which the complexity revolution is affecting economics. Norgaard was chosen because he has been a crucial developer of the new ecological economics. He represents how modern economics is interacting with other disciplines and is influencing the way economic reasoning is used in policy.

Axtell, a student of Herbert Simon, was chosen because he has been a leader in the application of simulation methods in the study of complex models of interacting heterogeneous agents. His work shows how young researchers are introducing computational and simulation techniques into the toolbox of economists as the natural way to handle complexity. If analytic methods don't yield results, computational methods might; analytic tractability is no longer a reason not to explore an issue. Young is a leading evolutionary game theorist who showed how to analyze large-scale models with persistent stochastic perturbations and who has helped to establish a foundation for agent-based modeling.

As stated, the individuals we interviewed are not all that unusual in their research interests or approaches, and they do not see themselves as revolutionaries. They see themselves as economists doing what economists do. There were many other economists we could have chosen as representative of each of the approaches we are describing. But that is precisely our point. Modern mainstream economics is different from neoclassical economics; it involves exploring a variety of issues with a variety of new techniques. Anyone who is interested in understanding modern economics must take that into account.

NOTES

1. This introduction went through numerous drafts as we refined our arguments in response to critical responses both by interviewees, outside readers, and reviewers. The term *edge of economics* refers to work challenging the previously considered "orthodox" ideas. Initially, we described it as cutting edge work, but some of our interviewees pointed out that cutting edge work can only be defined historically as work at the edge that has panned out. Comments by Larry Moss and Ken Koford and by early interviewees were very helpful in redirecting us in our terminology.

2. Philip Mirowski (2002, 432–36) argues that an important influence on Arrow in his change of view was a former student, Alain Lewis (1985), whose work continues to be little known by most of the profession.

3. We recognize that this characterization oversimplifies the state of heterodox economics. Not only are there many subcategories and schools within these main branches of heterodoxy but there are many other schools or approaches as well.

4. See Colander 2003 for a development of this point in reference to the Old Institutionalists.

5. This lag of textbooks in mainstream thinking can be seen in earlier times as well. In his writings John Stuart Mill gave up the wage fund doctrine but retained it in his principles book. He states that these new developments "are not yet ripe for incorporation in a general treatise on Political Economy" (Mill 1929, xxxi).

6. We focus upon developments within the English-language history of economics. Arguably there were separate national mainstreams in at least the French and German languages, and some others with their own mainstreams, orthodoxies, and heterodoxies. From time to time work at the edge of one these language's tradition would influence the English language's mainstream, with the French-language economists Augustin Cournot and Léon Walras being especially important examples. And, of course, the German-language Karl Marx was certainly the most important figure in the development of heterodox economics in all the language traditions. Arguably in the latter

half of the twentieth century, the domination by English-language economics became so great that these separate traditions have mostly disappeared.

7. Now viewed as the father of the heterodox Austrian school, Menger can also be viewed as the culmination of the German-language proto-neoclassical school that came to understand such neoclassical concepts as opportunity cost, diminishing marginal productivity, and diminishing marginal utility during the mid-1800s. A member of this latter school, Johannes Heinrich Rau, first produced a modern supply and demand diagram with price on the vertical axis in 1841. For further discussion of this largely forgotten school, see Streissler 1990.

8. Post Keynesians, such as Paul Davidson, argue that this synthesis view should hardly be considered Keynesian.

9. See Debreu 1991 for a discussion and defense of this period. See also Weintraub 2002 for an interesting discussion of this period.

10. There is much discussion now regarding how one is to describe research that involves more than one discipline. The oldest term is probably *multidisciplinary*. However, this is now usually applied to situations where persons get together and contribute ideas from their separate disciplines in ways that maintain the distinct identities of their disciplines, as in separate chapters within a book. A more recently used term is *interdisciplinary*, which involves more integration of the ideas of different disciplines. However, this is often used in the sense of dealing with ideas that exist in the intersection of two disciplines, leading to particular specializations, such as "water economist," which focuses on relevant aspects of both hydrology and economics. Following the lead of the ecological economists, we favor the term *transdisciplinary* to describe the new developments at the edge, which implies a more thoroughgoing and profound interaction between the disciplines leading to some kind of new synthesis and transcendence.

11. See Colander 2000c for a discussion of von Neumann's role. The argument that von Neumann was the most important figure in the development of twentieth-century economics is strongly made by Mirowski (2002). He argues that much of the influence of von Neumann's work came through economists involved with military work in World War II and in the immediate postwar era at the RAND Corporation. The major strands of these influences in the United States would work through the Cowles Commission, first at Chicago and then at Yale, through MIT from its radiation lab, and through Chicago from the Statistical Research Group at Columbia.

12. Vernon Smith (1992) argues that during the 1950s infant experimental economics coevolved closely with early game theory.

13. One sign of the change is that there were only two economists who participated in both conferences, Brian Arthur and Buz Brock. They were clearly among those at the first conference who were least involved in defending orthodoxy and most open to newer approaches. Not surprisingly, Brock is among those interviewed for this volume.

CHAPTER 1

Deirdre McCloskey

Distinguished Professor of English, History, and Economics,
University of Illinois at Chicago, and Tinbergen Professor,
Erasmus Universiteit Rotterdam.

∾

The interview was conducted at the Park Plaza Hotel in Boston, March
16, 2002.

How did you get interested in economics?
When I was in high school in 1959–60, I read Steinbeck's *Grapes*
of Wrath and thought of myself as being on the Left. I was a Joan
Baez socialist. I went to college intending to be a history major and
found that you had to work an awful lot, you had to read all these
books, it was really quite tedious; that's not because I didn't have
good teachers, I had excellent teachers. I wanted something easier
and something that would satisfy the adolescent desire of doing
something good in the world. I couldn't do political science, or government as they called it at Harvard, because my father was chair of
the department. So I said, how about economics? And somebody
suggested looking at Bob Heilbroner's book. So in the summer
before my sophomore year I read Heilbroner's book and instantly
became a convert to economics, as has happened to hundreds of
other people with that book.

∾

How were your first classes in economics? Did you enjoy them? Did you enjoy your teachers?

I took Otto Eckstein's Ec-1, and he did an excellent job. In it we had some superb visiting speakers. I remember John Dunlop coming; he stunned those smart-ass Harvard undergraduate guys. (Almost all of us were guys, because in those times the proportion of females was quite small, so we were tough.) But overall it wasn't a stimulating first course. As a sophomore I had a seminar with Eric Gustafson, who was for a long time at the University of California at Davis. He was terrific; he charmed us into this field. It was a weekly meeting where we produced a paper. Then in my junior year I had Lars Sandburg, the economics historian, as my tutor in my macroeconomics course. The microeconomics course was one of the very last times Edward Chamberlin taught, and he did, as always, an extraordinary job despite the fact that he was ill. It was gripping stuff.

In the spring we had Arthur Smithies, who had a bemused view of macroeconomics. I have never gotten over my bemusement of macro. It still sticks with me. What happened with Arthur was very interesting. At the time I didn't quite grasp it. He would keep trying to explain the multiplier or something like that, and he would screw it up because he was drunk. He would come to class drunk, or at least hung over. He'd get confused, and in a self-deprecating way he would say that he couldn't understand why something wasn't working out. I think he was actually, in a subtle way, criticizing the whole field. The reason I can't get it clear to you is because it is not clear, but perhaps it was just his hangover.

You decided to stay at Harvard to go to graduate school.

Unfortunately. I could have gone to MIT, but John Meyer, the transportation economist, was supporting me. He was at Harvard, so I decided to stay. They didn't offer me a big fellowship at MIT because I didn't graduate summa cum laude. And I did a terrible senior dissertation that will go down in the annals of how not to do a senior dissertation. It was a boring input-output model; the title was "Road and Rail in India."

Did your background with your intellectual family significantly influence how you thought of economics?

I always thought of economics as being very much a social science, as being part of intellectual activity in general. That's natural for the son of a political scientist and the son of a very intellectual, if not formally educated, mom. I still have intellectual conversations with my mom; she's about eighty. We might do a book some day called *My Daughter the Economist,* which has a lot of ironies in it, where we'll have a conversational format where she'll ask about economics and try to get me to predict the interest rate.

What did your father think about economics?

Well, he had a course with Alvin Hansen when he was a graduate student at Harvard in 1945 or 1946. He had gotten an A in the course because he was a smart guy, but he told me once that he had skipped over all the diagrams and equations because he had a math phobia. Even in 1945, that was difficult to do. It's impossible now. So he was amazed that his son had some mathematical ability. The economists he knew at Harvard, and he knew them all since they shared the same building, were the more broad and cultivated ones because that's how economists were at the time. He was a close friend of Ed Mason, an older man at this time. He was a friend of Alex Gerschenkron, who turned out to be quite important in my career. He was friendly with Carl Kasen. At this time these were the type of people in economics. Down the street at MIT they were the same kind of people. They were people who read books. If they had been like economists are now, I think my father would have been really worried about me.

You were at Harvard during the Vietnam War and everything else. What was your position on that? We have heard you described as the one conservative at Harvard. Would that be correct?

I certainly was not a conservative on the war. There's a famous photograph, one of those shots that appear in all the histories of the period, which is a photograph of McNamara at Harvard, surrounded by Harvard students around his car. We hated the guy. I'm in the front row. I was not violently against the war, and I didn't really do anything about it, and I was ashamed about that. During that time I was in favor of ending segregation, but unlike some of my classmates who were down in Mississippi and South Carolina in the summer of 1963, I didn't do anything about it. After a while there were women's rights and gay rights. I was in favor of those, but I didn't do anything about it.

So when it came time for me to stand up and ask myself, "Should I stand up as a gender-crosser or just say no that's a private affair and I won't speak to anyone?" I thought that I had to stand up because it was my last chance. So, in any case, I was not a conservative. I don't know who's telling you those things. I was not a socialist at that time but a middle-of-the-road enthusiast for planning, as we all were. We thought we were so smart.

You did your thesis in economic history, and then you went to Chicago. Did this middle-of-the-road person feel comfortable going to Chicago?
I steadily changed. My joke is that I've been everything. I was a communist, I was a man, I was a mathematical economist. I was all these things; now I'm not. My political views were steadily developing in a Chicago direction. In fact as an undergraduate, as a junior, I did these Harvard-type Chamberlin attacks on the Chicago view of industrial organization. Then I figured out through "Road and Rail in India," and other episodes, that if you didn't apply economics, there wasn't anything there. Since you could apply the stuff of George Stigler and Milton Friedman, I started to wonder if this is how you should go. And then, when I started to do my dissertation, it became obvious to me that if you want to talk about the competitiveness of the iron and steel industry, you've got to have some crystal clear mathematical idea of what competition means.

What was your dissertation on, and were people supportive of, the topic?
Yes, people were supportive. It was on "Economic Maturity and Entrepreneurial Decline: British Iron and Steel, 1870–1913." The point was, as a title of another paper of mine put it, "Did Victorian Britain Fail?" which was a theme of socialists for a long time. They wanted it to fail because they wanted capitalism to be a failure right from the beginning, or at least as early as they could make it fail. I was opposed to this, but I didn't really finish the dissertation until well after I got to Chicago. I started at Chicago in August 1968, around the time of the Democratic National Convention, and I didn't finish the dissertation until the following year, late in the fall. People liked it, and it got the Wells Prize. I graduated in June 1970.

When you were at Chicago, you also visited LSE and Stanford, right?
Yes, I did. Not LSE in particular. I visited Birkbeck College. Eric Hobsbawm was there, and I was in the history department not in the economics department. The economics department in Birkbeck was a famous location for Marxists. That was in 1975–76. I visited

Stanford in 1973, they offered me a job, and I turned them down. That so annoyed them, especially Paul David, that in 1980 when I wanted a job there they wouldn't extend it.

Were you comfortable with the Chicago position?

Yes at first, because the Chicago position at that time was exemplified by people like Friedman and my main man Bob Fogel, whom I of course had a lot of contact with. There were also Al Harberger and George Schultz. But by the time I left Chicago, it had come to be exemplified by people like Bob Lucas and Gary Becker. Lucas in particular changed the character of the Chicago School. He made it a freshwater pond, and a small pond at that.

So by the time I left in 1980, I was very uncomfortable there. I had been there for a long time, twelve years. Leaving Chicago was one of the big decisions of my life. It was a great place to be an assistant professor, but if I had stayed, I would have been doomed to a life of 22–1 votes. I didn't think the way they were going was right; it would have been horrible.

I don't know what would have happened to me emotionally because they would have been hammering away at their stupid attempt to turn economics into a branch of, not the engineering department, but the math department, and it wouldn't have worked. Furthermore, I ate lunch every day for twelve years with the economists from the Business School. They were the ones who met "downstairs." There were some people from the economics department who would come. But it was mainly from the Business School like Merton Miller, Fischer Black, Myron Scholes, George Schultz, etc. So it was the Business School economists I hung out with.

Why was I with the Business School economists? Partly it was because they were more social. The upstairs economists would be off conspiring. Recently, it occurred to me, a few months ago actually, that the reason I was so comfortable with the Business School people was because they didn't have control of my tenure. So I learned a gigantic amount from these guys. It occurs to me now, twenty years after the event, that I was wary with my colleagues. In 1974 I got tenure.

One of your reviewers wrote that sometime around 1976 you underwent a profound and controversial life change. "You stopped doing economics and instead devoted yourself to telling the rest of us how to do economics." What brought about the change? How would you respond to him?

To say that I stopped doing economics is a stupid statement. I've produced more economics between 1976 and 1977 than that guy has produced in his life. I didn't stop doing economics. I continued to do economics, but I got very dissatisfied with the positivist anthology at Chicago, the so-called positivism. I'm kind of stupid, I don't grasp things quickly, but I do keep thinking about things. I do change my opinions. It's scandalous in some parts of economics to admit that you change your opinions, but I did. Being a Chicago School economist, recall if you can that in the early 1970s it was not a good idea to be a Chicago economist; it was not popular in the rest of the profession. When I went to Stanford, they didn't like Chicago economists, which was shown clearly in the great debate over Stan Engerman and Bob Fogel's *Time on the Cross* in 1973. I was in this beleaguered minority. I was all for it because I was for the underdog; I was always for the underdog, which means I am always the underdog.

I grew to understand how the Chicago School argued, and I can do it myself, but they were lying about how they arrived at their conclusions. I could see that they were obviously lying, but I was just annoyed and shocked that they continued to lie about how they got to the questions that they got to. And then it gradually occurred to me that if this is true, then maybe the whole profession is lying, and that belief has gotten stronger as I have gotten older. People say, "We do econometrics, and that tests our hypotheses." Baloney. We do theory. I was just rereading last night Paul Krugman's famous article where he tries to introduce geographical considerations into economics, and it is a very skillfully done article. It's rhetorically very skillful. I can show you how it works rhetorically, but it is complete nonsense scientifically, not because it is wrong but because it is arbitrary. There are a zillion other ways of formalizing geography in economics that would come to opposite conclusions to those he comes to, and yet he's kind of airily saying that this is a contribution. Then there are a thousand other articles modifying that. It doesn't get anywhere: they modify it and get completely different conclusions. If you change your assumptions, you get different theorems. So the whole exercise, it gradually dawned on me, was complete nonsense, so that's what turned me. But it is unfair and kind of stupid to say that I stopped doing economics.

*You continued in economic history, correct? Your 1981 book on enter-
prise and trade in Victorian England is seen as a landmark.*

Yes, and I kept doing other books. I did my price theory book.
The problem with the book is that I don't have as much faith as I
had, even in 1985 when I did the second edition, in blackboard exercises. If I redid it today, I'd have to introduce so much empirical
material the book would be many inches thick.

*Do you feel that you have received a lot of resistance from the
profession on your rhetorical work?*

Oh, yeah. Resistance isn't the word; blankly uninformed opposition is how I'd describe it. An awful lot of economists only read the
titles of most of my articles, if that. Economists don't read very
much, and they're not too curious, which, I think, is our main fail-
ing as a science, in the way that the best anthropologists or historians are curious and want to know more about things. An awful lot
of economists, and I keep getting this, think that I am advocating
rhetoric. Many seem to think that what I'm saying is that we use too
much math or statistics and that's boring and we should have more
flowery speech and just pour more of it into an article.

I finally figured that the first edition of the *Rhetoric of Economics*
was badly organized and it gave the impression that it was a philosophical book. It's not; it's a rhetorical book. It's not from the
department of philosophy but from the department of English, and
that's the point. So in the second edition I turned the whole book
around. I threw out some chapters and added some new ones and
turned the whole thing around. It now starts with examples and
exercises: here's how you do this stuff, here's how you find out
where the metaphors are and how they work and how the stories
work. I have a bunch of stuff about Ronald Coase. I take to pieces
an article by Coase, and then at the end I throw in some of the philosophy. For a while I thought I was doing philosophy. I am a professor in philosophy, but I am also mainly a professor of English.

*You went to Iowa in 1980, and they had a whole group of people
working on rhetoric.*

Absolutely, as I discovered after I got there.

Is that where you were introduced to rhetoric?

No. Wayne Booth at Chicago introduced me to it. In the fall of
1979 Wayne asked me if I would like to give a talk to his undergrad-

uate class on the rhetoric of economics, and I said, "Oh sure, but what's that?" He said that I may want to examine a few books like his and some others, which I did over the Christmas break of 1979—the experience is all very vivid to me. It was in my father-in-law's house. I saw that all science was rhetoric, though I don't know if I would have expressed it quite as clearly as this in December 1979. After all, science is meant to persuade other scientists. So it's not just announcing your findings to the universe; it's directed at other human beings.

Like all speech, the words coming out of my mouth have intent. It doesn't mean some subterranean evil intent; it just means they are intentional, if only to clearly inform, that's an intention, or to change one's politics or to change one's economic policy. My interest in rhetoric was just beginning. Then I went to Iowa and wanted to form an intellectual community to carry on this work, to think about it more. I found a guy in political science, John Nelson, and we became a team.

It turned out that they had a great group of rhetoricians in the communications studies department, as it was called then. We had these small seminars, which developed into a conference in 1984. Kuhn, Toulman, and Rorty were there and a whole bunch of famous folks. We formed an institute, but unfortunately it was always poorly funded, and in the end that's why I left Iowa. For years I was trying to persuade the deans of what an unusual situation they had at Iowa, and they couldn't understand it because they think in terms of regular departments.

What's the connection with postmodernism? How do you see yourself relating to postmodernism?

I'm a postmodernist. I describe myself as a postmodern, free-market, quantitative, English professor, Chicago School, feminist, Episcopalian female. Which I say is why I have no friends. All my friends are annoyed by at least one of my descriptors. My mom, who likes everything about me, has no trouble with my gender change—it took her five minutes to adjust—but she really dislikes that I am an Episcopalian. We argue about this all the time; she's not any kind of a believer.

People sometimes have argued that as soon as they push you and you moderate your position they ultimately agree with you. But when you first write something, you seem to push the issues too hard—you push them over the edge to get a reaction, and then you moderate it. Is that a rhetorical style you have?

It's a style of thinking I have, which is a more genial way of saying it. I don't ever intend to say false things. I am extremely earnest about that, and I know it sounds implausible because I say lots of outrageous things, but at least at the time, as you noticed, I keep shifting, and you could make this hypothesis that this protects me. But I confess to you that I am earnestly focused on the truth with a small *t*. So are most serious people.

Sometimes the truth isn't the best way to convince people. Which way do you come then?

I'm a rhetorician, I know a lot about this economic stuff. I've read many books; I go to all the conferences; I know how to do it, and I love to do it. I've been interested in it and all their theories, and I can't do it any more. I can't do the tricks. I mean obviously the way to succeed in economic life is to write in this oracular way, and that's the way Krugman's article is. It's kind of the Bob Solow version of this new technique. You're kind of self-deprecating, but you are oracular—it's a mysterious truth that you are stating. St. Augustine, in a famous passage, says that God made the Bible hard to understand in order to inflame the young men with more passion to know. If it had been easy, if God had said, "Look it's really simple: there are three of us, one, two, three. Is there something about three you don't understand?" If he made it all very simple, he wouldn't have attracted the respect of the young men, and that's true. So these silly articles that adopt this technique win, and mine don't. That's life; I can't bring myself to do it.

Did you find Iowa to be a good place? Did you find support there?

I had a lot of support in that a lot of people in other fields, not economics, were interested in what I was doing and I was interested in what they were doing. What we were doing is well captured in the title of our rhetoric group; it's called the Project on Rhetoric of Inquiry, which is to say the study of how persuasion takes place in academic life and in policy matters. We had a couple of guys from the math department; in law school, obviously in law; in English, lots of people from English; but then also engineers because every field, as I discovered in the summer of 1979, is concerned with persuasion. That doesn't make it some advertising flake who decides how science is to be perceived. As I said, the way Bob Lucas writes is perfectly tuned to what young men want. Men want to see the mysterious, that there is much more going on here than I can now reveal.

Why do you think you received so much resistance from the profession against your work?

Economists are very hierarchical. They are very easily fooled by these rhetorical techniques because they don't see them; they don't know that they are putty in the hands of Bob Solow for all these years. Not that he's a bad guy—he's a fine guy—but he is very good at it, even though he says these awful stupid things about axioms and proofs being the heart of economic science. Nonetheless, he gets away with it because he is able to clothe it, because they don't see the point. For most people most assertions are hard to believe. You would have to be that way, or science would zig and zag off here, and then someone else would send it over there.

Let's go specifically to significance testing.

That's my most important substantive criticism.

How do you go beyond attack? Here's some economists who really want to do it right—how would you explain to them here's how to do it?

Go to any journal of any other science and examine it. Go to the *Physical Review* and look at how these scientists make quantitative arguments. They make them in the entire annual issue of the *Physical Review,* and you'll never find a significance test. You won't ever find a theorem. Now guys, you say you are the physicists of the social sciences? Have you ever looked in a physics journal? What has happened is that there are some of our colleagues who have been trained in physics, but ordinarily as undergraduates, ordinarily from textbooks. They haven't gotten to the frontier of physics. On the frontier, physicists don't do theorems, and they don't do statistical significance. So you talk about the magnitude of the coefficient, and you have discussions with your colleagues of how big is big. Does the minimum wage cause unemployment? That's an ill-formed question to start with because it's always a question of how much. If it causes 1/10 of 1 percent of unemployment that's one thing, and if it causes 80 percent of unemployment, that's quite another. We would want to know how much and what's big. T-tests don't tell you about how big something is.

What the t-tests do is just like what the existence theorems do: they turn us to thinking about on/off propositions. It's what I am coming to call Samuelson economics. That's what's wrong with modern economics. As long as we call it the mainstream, it's never going to change. We have to have a name for it, and Paul is at the heart of both of these developments in modern economics. Qualitative theorems, as he explicitly urged in his dissertation 1941, published in 1947. Then he was Klein's thesis adviser; Klein was his first Ph.D.

Someone can make the argument that at the frontier you are quite right, but most of the people doing t-tests are not at the frontier. They're doing applied policy stuff.

They're making dramatic mistakes in policy, and they are hurting millions of people. Steve Ziliak and I have a whole bunch of examples of this from the *AER*. You have policy conclusions of how to help the unemployed in Illinois that are nonsense, which are contrary to the welfare of the taxpayers and the unemployed of Illinois, that are done on the basis of t-tests. The short statement of my point is that the t-test is neither necessary nor sufficient for importance.

There is a lot more work being done in nonparametric econometrics.

That doesn't help as long as they use tests. When they use tests to run their stuff, whether they're parametric or not, it doesn't matter.

You have to have some tests, and tests are part of the rhetoric of how you convince people.

You have to have real tests. Look, we could use the numbers in the Boston phone directory to decide whether or not a scientific hypothesis is true. Open to any page at random and if it is odd that hypothesis is correct; if it is even then you can choose any degree of skepticism you want. You can say, "Okay, if the last two digits of the phone number are between 0 and 4, we accept it; if they're higher than 4 up to 99, we reject it." You can do whatever you want, but it's random, and no one would think that would be a good procedure. My claim—and if you read this stuff carefully and slowly, it will change your life, I'm not exaggerating—is that this stuff is no better than that. It's identical to it. It's not an approximation of an ideal procedure. It has nothing to do with an ideal procedure; it's completely arbitrary. No one understands this point except a few leading statisticians.

$\mathcal{D}$EIRDRE MCCLOSKEY

Most people are looking for some alternative tests. What do you see as the alternative?

There is no mechanical alternative. Thinking is thinking; thinking is not the application of formulas. Now if you want a formula, I can provide a procedure that is to focus on the magnitudes. Announce the magnitudes in meaningful units, in contexts that matter for policy.

There is this amazing dispute about mammograms. Under the surface of the current dispute is a misuse of statistical significance. Some people say, "Oh, don't bother over age fifty." We are saying that the number of people saved is, at the sample sizes we have, statistically insignificant. You mean you're concerned about the embarrassment you might have if it turns out that fewer than this number are actually saved, yet you agree with the over-forty people that lives are saved? Yes. Wait a second; the purpose of medical science is to save lives. This procedure saves lives. Yeah, but it is statistically insignificant.

These people are killing people; it's not a minor matter. And it's in that context you talk about it. You say, look, if there are risks to mammography that offset the lifesaving-on-average effect, however fuzzily perceived, however God in her mercy hasn't arranged things to have a nice clean fit, sorry that's life. If exposure to X rays of the thing itself doesn't cause more cancer than it cures, or the false positive problem, and then you do operations that might kill people. If there's that problem, that's cost-benefit; that's what we do as economists. But if the only reason to reject this policy is that the sample size isn't large enough so you're not sure you heard the person outside the door now crying, "help, help"—she may have been saying, "kelp, kelp"—if we heard "kelp, kelp" outside the door, all three of us would jump up and go outside the door, even though at the 5 percent level of significance we could clearly reject the hypothesis that she said, "help, help." The signal was not clear.

How much would Bayesian econometrics help?

I don't want to get into that because then people start talking about theology. I don't want to admit that this is a Bayesian point. Yeah, I'm a Bayesian; you're all Bayesians. But it doesn't matter because that's not the point. To drag it over to the Bayesian point is to get people all confused. If you are a pure-as-driven-white-snow classical statistician, if you didn't think that hypotheses have probabilities, it's still nonsense.

Do you find some of the procedures that Ed Leamer is developing helpful in giving directions to younger people in what to use?

I do, but what Ed's stuff says is, take a look at the various trade-offs in the data. That, in essence, is what it means. He's not providing tests. Maybe he does provide them but that's a corruption of his basic point, which is look at the data. He has been saying that for thirty years now. Look at the data. I'm an economic historian; I believe in looking at the data. There's some people who think that I'm against quantification, against econometrics. That's ridiculous. I'm in favor of it. But it's become completely dominated by arbitrary tests that are rubbish.

In 1995, you announced that you were having a sex change.

I prefer to call it a gender change. The problem with "sex change" is that what *s-e-x* means in our culture is pleasure, and I didn't do it for pleasure.

Is it true that the chair of Iowa said he was relieved when you said that. He thought you were doing something serious like turning into a Marxist?

It was actually the dean of the College of Business, where economics is located. That's exactly what he said. He said, "Oh, thank god, I thought you are going to confess to converting to socialism." And I knew from the moment he said that he was going to treat me as a friend. And he did. Then he said, and these are the consecutive sentences that came out of his mouth, after everyone stopped laughing, he said, "This is great for our affirmative action program." Then he said, "Now hold it, I pay you a lot. I can cut your salary to 70 cents on the dollar."

Do you think your gender change affected how you did economics?

Oh, yes it did. Although my choices fit pretty well with my ultimate identity, being an economic historian. I did not go into transportation economics or economic development, though both of those have lots of females. But it mainly affected my view in that I was a guy, not that I was a guy wanting to be a girl, but I was a guy and I thought like a guy. When I was a child, I thought like a child, but now that I am a woman, I'm putting away childish things. I thought like a guy, and economics is very much a guy science.

Another story I heard was that you were riding in a taxi with Arjo one time and somebody cut the two of you off, and you started cussing, and Arjo said to you, "Careful, Deirdre, that's your old personality."

I have changed. The guys want it to be that way because it makes them feel more comfortable. This is Don in drag—that's how a lot of guys think of it. That's not how any of the women who know me think about it. As soon as they talk to me for five minutes, they say this is a woman.

But does it still come out, those aggressive behaviors?

Of course it does, as it comes out of my mom, who's an XX chromosome person. If you met my mom, you'd see that my personality now is very similar to hers. She talks the same emphatic way—the way some people think is the male side of Don. But it's not: it's the McCloskey side of Don. I am more like my mom in this sense. My father was much more soft-spoken.

You were anathema to feminist economists. You went out there, and they attacked you more than anything else.

There was this famous episode, famous in our little world of feminist economics, where we had this incredible flame war that went on for about two months. I have it all, and some sociologist at Minnesota did a study of this dispute. This happened in 1994, and he found that my interventions were 9 standard deviations above the mean in length and frequency. Maybe it was 6, but it was a tremendously large outlier. I was way off, egregious even in the modern sense. I was so ashamed of that. Now I have been very careful not to get into arguments of whether it's possible to be a free-market economist and a feminist at the same time, which is what the issue focused on.

You still hold the view that you can be a feminist and a free-market economist.

Absolutely.

Can you explain the argument on how you can be both?

Yes. The market is the great liberator of women; it has not been the state, which is after all an instrument of patriarchy. It's been the marketplace, the local fruit and vegetable stall, that [was] always staffed by women. The market is the way out of enslavement from your dad, your husband, or your sons. This path out of enslavement has been the standard sequence in lots of countries. The enrichment that has come through allowing markets to operate has been a tremendous part of the learned freedom of the modern women. I could go on and on. I have a full argument worked out. I am not the only person believing this. There are a few others, Joan Taylor Kennedy is an example. As you see, I am always for the underdog.

One of the things that some economists worried about when you announced your gender change was that you have been a strong, force-ful voice for change within the profession and that your gender change would take the focus away from your attack on the profession.

I'm sorry; I can't arrange my life to suit the economics profession, though I've done a good deal of that.

Do you think that your Aunt Deirdre persona that you sometimes use is always helpful?

No, as I've seen with the enraged reaction of Doug North. As I said before, I am who I am. I'm not just doing stuff. The times when people just do things to annoy after adolescence are rare. Most adults mean it when they say something. It's not just for show. Since so many men objected to the Aunt Deirdre stuff, I have toned it down in some of the places where it would be used. I just finished an essay, a pamphlet for Marshall Sahlins, an anthropologist, in a new series called Prickly Paradigm Pamphlets. It's going to be published by Chicago; it's called "The Two Secret Sins of Economics." In it I think I used the Aunt Deirdre figure only once.

Some people have looked at your work and said, "Here's the person who is writing and saying there is no methodology, and then she becomes probably the strongest moral voice for what people should do."

I think I have changed my opinions from earlier times. You notice I change my opinions a lot, like Keynes. His famous reply, "When I get new information, I change my mind, what do you do?" I seem to go into ten-year cycles on everything. I think if I were to redo my earlier papers around 1983 and after, the ten years after that when I was actively involved with this stuff, I would say that the mistake that the methodologists like my friend Mark Blaug [make] is that they think that there is an epistemological argument for certain methodologies. I don't think that makes any sense. But there are ethical arguments for having certain procedures, and in a way that's consistent with what I say because I say that there was a high-

sprachethiklich kind of rules, that you should try to tell the truth with a small *t*. You should try to be open to other people's arguments. You should try to hear what they are saying and actually allow them to influence you if possible.

Then there is much lower-level technical advice, such as the statistical significance part, although I have discovered that there are ethical failures that support the technical error, and it's clearly an error. I could show you how absurd it is in math. I think, in a way, my point is that there is no middle ground, that it's just empty. There's no place where it's not quite all the way to ethics, and it's not quite the technical things that only economists are interested in. Mark Blaug and the rest think there are philosophical Rules for Scientific Method that apply to economics. I guess I still think that's nonsense because scientists are humans and that science is persuasion of humans. End of story. You are not going to find any distinction between science and other forms of serious inquiries.

Of the three vices, the Samuelsonian, Kleinian, and Tinbergenian, a number of people have claimed that the Tinbergenian is the weakest of the vices.

I agree. At the time I thought so and probably shouldn't have included it, but I was a Tinbergen Professor. Tinbergen in fact was at the heart of a lot of this stuff. Klein was not the Satan, he was the Beelzebub of econometrics; he was the junior devil because the main devil was Tinbergen. Statistical significance came from him, as I claim in the book, as did an engineering attitude that, as you recall, came to its height in the 1960s. At that time we all were quite clear that we could fine-tune the economy.

What would you consider to be your current research agenda?

I have two very clear projects. I'm working on a book called *Bourgeois Virtue*, which I hope will be a major public intellectual book. It is a consideration of the history and psychology of the middle class since 1600, and the philosophy of ethics for a commercial society. It is Adam Smith's project, and I am trying to get that project started all over again.

What I want to do in the long term, as kind of my last substantive work before I go into the grave, is a book (I always think in terms of books, which by the way is a big mistake, but I like that scale) on language in economics. There are eerie homologies between linguistics and economics, and there always have been. I think that on the ground economies operate through language, and we don't acknowledge it in economics. We say, look, it's private, it's the profane, it's all the *p* variables, price, profit, property, whereas we talk about the sacred all the time. I politely informed the maid outside my room that I was going to be leaving my room at 11:00, and I didn't have to be polite with her. There was no substantial subinterest in that. It was just how we use language. So I feel that there is some very deep connection between speech and the economy, and I think ultimately that's the way forward for economics because we keep trying to make prudence work exclusively.

How does that fit in with the work on evolutionary norms?

It fits reasonably well except the trouble with evolutionary norms is that there's still another attempt to make everything fit into the profane. There's this interesting book by Alex Field on this stuff that asks why is it that we don't kill people as we drive around in our car if they are in the way—just knock them down. When I was trying to get out of Amherst, which is not easy, there was a woman who was walking the wrong way along the highway, that is, her back was turned to the traffic. There was a perfectly good sidewalk, and she was walking in the street. I don't think she was simpleminded because I saw other people doing the same thing. I thought, "What the hell is wrong with these people—get on the sidewalk." And I had a fleeting impulse to kill her. You know how one is in traffic: the raw monster comes out of us. But then I checked the impulse because I am a human and not a bear. A bear would have killed her. So I didn't kill her.

You have recently moved to the University of Illinois at Chicago. How has that changed your research at all?

I've been thrilled to go to the UIC. As to why I moved there—as with all these things there was a push and pull. The push was that the Department of Economics at Iowa was so determined to be a fourth-rate imitation of MIT, as every department in the United States wants to be. They are in the process of destroying the department at Notre Dame this way. We who care about economics being something other than Samuelsonian ought to form a committee and go speak to their president. I could have stayed at Iowa, obviously, but I have been there for nineteen years. I had this large house that I loved, but it was too big. So I decided to come back and be an urban girl. I've got this loft downtown that is marvelous. It's so much fun to be back in the city again. Of course when I was in Hyde Park, I didn't ever go downtown because it's isolated. If I was going to go back to Hyde Park, I thought, I might do that and went back and took a look at it and said, "God, this is a depressing place," and decided not to.

You have been over to the Netherlands. How did you find that different?

It's made me more aware, but I was fairly aware of this before, that there's a heterodoxy of economics in Europe. On the other hand, it has made me alarmingly aware of the spread of Samuelsonianism and how the mainstream becomes the only stream. I don't think our science can advance if we stay Samuelsonian. I don't think it's very much advanced despite all the articles.

In terms of your current view of the profession is there much hope for it? Where do you see it going?

I'm an optimist; you can't have the life I've had without being an optimist. To abandon tenure at Chicago was one brave thing I did, and then changing gender was another. I think we're all courageous in our lives.

I'm an optimist, so I am hopeful. I don't think Samuelsonian economics can be the long-run equilibrium of such an important field such as economics. I think that because of the two secret sins of Samuelsonian economics, the qualitative theorems and significance testing in the absence of the loss function, we can't make scientific progress. We can do a lot of other stuff. We can take a look at tables and see how large schooling is in the national economy; that kind of thing is science. So I'm sure we can make some progress, off the center of the scientific stage of so-called mainstream Samuelsonian economics.

An interesting concrete example of this was a presentation Ken Arrow made when he came to Iowa, where he was trying to make the obvious point that we shouldn't spend all of our time in undergraduate economics preparing people for graduate school. This is a point that I have made over and over again, that we should be preparing students for life, for business and law school. Arrow said, "Look, the main argument for this is not very complicated: as we all know, half of 1 percent of our students, if that, go on to graduate school in economics, end of argument." The argument is not special to Arrow, but the fact that it came from Arrow was very interesting. He didn't come and say there is an existence theorem proof that there doesn't exist some social welfare function such that blah blah blah. He didn't do that. He said, "Look, here's the number that shows obviously that the policy of making undergraduate programs into junior graduate programs is a mistake."

Where do you see the economic profession going in the next twenty-five or thirty years?

I think it's obvious. Like a lot of other fields it's going to go in a computational direction. It has already started. It happened in architecture, for example, quite interestingly. Now large and even small projects are designed entirely by computer, instead of by artwork. So I think that's the way it's going to go, and econometrics defined as this absurd idea that the only empirical method we have in economics is the fitting and then significance testing of hyperplanes is going to shrink and shrivel up.

Existence theorems are going to go by the wayside because I think all economists now are so good at math department math they've finally twigged to the thought that you can prove existence theorems until the cows come home and you haven't accomplished anything. I am hopeful that the falling cost of computation is going to save us. It hasn't yet though. Ziliak and I are doing a study of the 1980s in the *AER,* the same method we had in the 1996 paper called "Standard Regression," and the bad news is that it hasn't improved; still 96 or 95 percent of economists are misusing statistical significance.

Why do you think somebody like Jim Heckman misuses it?

I've got to find out. Jim has been very courteous toward me. He's been very amiable toward my gender change, and since I've been at Chicago, he's the only one of my former colleagues who's been socially friendly to me. When I get home, I am going to send Jim an e-mail and ask him what he thinks he's doing because someone told me something he said about my criticisms that got me very excited. According to somebody else he said that my program is nihilism. I detect that same sense in the form of your question. If we don't do this stupid procedure, what are we going to do? Which I think is a bad question. It's not nihilism at all, though I am postmodern, but that doesn't make me a nihilist. I don't think those necessarily follow from each other.

DEIRDRE MCCLOSKEY

We chose a limited number of people to interview, Bob Frank, Herb Gintis, Dick Norgaard, Matt Rabin, Bob Axtell, Buz Brock, Duncan Foley, Ken Binmore, and you. Is there an area of new work that you believed we missed?

When you gave the list, I thought of Bruno Frey, but I think he's covered pretty much by Bob Frank. Though I think Bruno's work is just excellent, and he's kind of, in the same way as Bob, but even more so, inside the horse, inside the wooden horse, and he is undermining the p-only economics, price, prudence, the profane. That's all we do. Bob Lucas says that as soon as we exhaust those kinds of arguments economics stops. I don't think any of these people think that's true. I think they all say, what all your interviewees are saying, is that there's more than p's—there are the s's, solidarity, speech, society, in short the sacred against the profane. It doesn't have to be nonmathematical, as Buz shows; it doesn't have to be nonquantitative, as Bob Frank shows; it doesn't have to be airy-fairy in any way. It's real science. It's complete science, instead of being incomplete.

Deirdre McCloskey

Distinguished Professor of English, History, and Economics, University of Illinois at Chicago, and Tinbergen Professor, Erasmus Universiteit Rotterdam.

INFORMATION ON THE WEB ABOUT DEIRDRE MCCLOSKEY
http://tigger.uic.edu/%7Edeirdre2/index.htm

EDUCATION
B.A. Economics, Harvard College, 1964
Ph.D. Economics, Harvard University, 1970

SELECTED PUBLICATIONS
"Does the Past Have Useful Economics?" *Journal of Economic Literature* 14 (1976).
Enterprise and Trade in Victorian Britain: Essays in Historical Economics. Aldershot: Ashgate, 1993.
"The Rhetoric of Economics." *Journal of Economic Literature* 21 (1983).
The Rhetoric of Economics. Madison: University of Wisconsin Press, 1985.
The Vices of Economists; The Virtues of the Bourgeoisie. Amsterdam and Ann Arbor: University of Amsterdam Press and University of Michigan Press, 1997.

SPECIAL HONORS AND EXPERIENCE
Also taught at Stanford University, University of Chicago, and University of York, England
Guggenheim Fellowship, 1983; National Endowment for the Humanities Fellowship, 1984; and May Brodbeck Fellowship in the Humanities, University of Iowa, 1987–88
John F. Murray Chair in Economics, University of Iowa, 1984–99
Research Fellow: University of Manchester (Honorary Simon Fellow), Bellagio Study Center, Rockefeller Foundation, Birkbeck College, and University of London (Honorary Research Fellow)
Member, editorial boards of *Explorations in Economic History, Journal of Economic History* (Coeditor), *Economic History Review, Economics and Philosophy, Journal of British Studies, Economic Inquiry, Reason* (Contributing Editor), *Journal of Economic Method, Feminist Economics, American Economic Review, Queen: A Journal of Rhetoric and Power, Critical Review* (Contributing Editor), *Journal of Economic Perspectives* (Associate Editor), and American Economic Association: Executive Committee (1994–97)

CHAPTER 2

Kenneth G. Binmore

Professor of Economics, University College, London

∾

This interview took place on November 30, 2001, in Princeton, New Jersey, at the residence of David Colander.

How did you get into economics?

I didn't intend to be an economist when I set out. I began by studying chemical engineering at the University of London, but my adviser assured me it would only get duller and duller, and so I switched to mathematics, which was good for me. We were mostly taught applied mathematics, which proved useful in a bread-and-butter kind of way when I eventually became an economist, but what I wanted to be at the end of my undergraduate career was a pure mathematician.

The big guns at my college were into classical analysis, and so this is the kind of stuff my early papers are about. In the paper I am still proudest of, I solved one of the lesser problems left over by the great mathematicians Hardy and Littlewood. It was from Littlewood that I first learned about common knowledge. His *Mathematician's Miscellany* of 1937 already has the story of the three ladies with dirty faces that people keep reinventing all the time (Littlewood 1986).

I was never very good at plowing a single furrow, and I switched

∾

fields several times, working on both real and complex analysis, approximation theory and functional analysis. But the big jump came when an unpleasant new chairman persuaded those of us active in research to look for jobs elsewhere. I ended up at the London School of Economics, which was then in the thick of the big Vietnam demonstrations of the '60s. But I still had no intention of becoming an economist. I was hired to be part of a new mathematics group in a large department of statistics and computing because I had written some papers on probability theory. I continued working in pure mathematics for ten years or so after the move, eventually becoming chairman of the department. I still get royalty checks from some of the mathematical textbooks I wrote during this period.

I used to attend the LSE mathematical economics seminar to see what mathematics I should be teaching. At first I didn't understand very much, but one day, I found myself thinking that I could do better than yesterday's speaker on the subject of Arrow's impossibility theorem, and that was the start of the slippery slope (Binmore 1975).

How did you get into game theory and bargaining?

I was always interested in games. I loved to play and invent board games as a kid. When I was a student, I foolishly used to play poker for immensely more than I could afford to lose.

One of my duties at LSE was to organize the teaching of mathematics to social scientists, including economists. So I got one of the mathematicians who knew something about it to put on a game theory course. When he left suddenly, my colleagues said that I had to teach the course because it was my idea in the first place. So I took von Neumann and Morgenstern's book (1944) with me on a sailing trip during which we were trapped in Cherbourg harbor for a week by gales. Having very little money to get out and around with, there wasn't much for me to do but read the book. I suspect I am the only person who has ever read the whole book from cover to cover. When I got to the poker models, I just couldn't believe that so much bluffing could be optimal. Nor could I understand von Neumann's mathematics. So I worked it out for myself. And he was right! How could von Neumann be wrong? This hooked me on the subject, and I went back to teach the game theory course feeling enthusiastic about it.

Because I was completely new to the subject, I didn't know where game theory had gone astray. So, instead of writing more and more axioms for cooperative solutions as people were doing in the '60s, I went off in another direction. I returned to Nash's papers of the early '50s. His bargaining papers were particularly fascinating. So I started working on bargaining, and that's when I was finally captured by economics.

But nobody was interested in bargaining in those days. At one seminar I gave, someone stood up and said that he didn't understand why I was talking to them because "bargaining is not part of economics." Can you imagine? But that was a commonly held view at the time. Von Neumann and Morgenstern said that the bargaining problem is indeterminate. The view was therefore that bargaining was a problem for psychologists rather than economists, all this in spite of Nash's work, which was known only to a small group of specialists. Perhaps the most useful thing I did in those days was to popularize Nash's theory.

When did bargaining theory start to catch on?

Perhaps four or five years after I began thinking about it. At first, of course, there were only a few of us, including Roger Myerson and Ariel Rubinstein—about whom I have a good story.

By this time, I was running the economic theory workshop at LSE, and I invited Rubinstein to visit since people said he was something special. On arriving, he told me that he had tried to work on bargaining but hadn't got anywhere. Rather patronizingly, I asked what he had been trying to do. He then told me the Rubinstein bargaining theory—as published in 1982! The reason he thought he hadn't got anywhere was that he believed that the real problem in bargaining is coping with incomplete information—which, of course, is perfectly right insofar as it goes. Anyway, I looked at what he had done and wondered whether it could be correct. That evening, I saw that he was almost certainly right and that his argument would also work in the convex case—so generating the Nash bargaining solution. I think Rubinstein was rather pleased the next morning with my enthusiasm.

I made no great discoveries in bargaining theory, but I think my contribution was valuable—although I still don't believe that some labor economists know how to use the Nash bargaining solution properly, which can be quite frustrating. Outside options are often built into models in quite the wrong way, although the right way is very simple. The disagreement point in Nash's theory shouldn't be identified with the outside option point. Outside options should appear only as constraints on the range of validity of Nash's solution. Shaked, Sutton, and I even ran experiments to check that outside options work like this in practice, and they were very supportive of the theory (Binmore et al. 1985).

You don't need all Rubinstein's apparatus to see how it works. Imagine that you and I have agreed to split a surplus. Your outside option now increases but still remains less than your previously agreed payoff. You now claim more, but I refuse to budge. You therefore threaten that you will take up your outside option, but I say that your threat is not credible because I am already offering you more than your outside option. In the tape recordings of some face-to-face experiments, we sometimes heard subjects actually telling each other this story.

Don't the ultimatum game experiments suggest that may not work sometimes?

But our experiments show that the piece of theory I just described does work! One of these days, we will perhaps understand why it is that some pieces of economic theory work well in the laboratory and other pieces don't work at all. But behavioral economists overreach themselves when they seek to discredit all economic theory by only quoting the cases where it doesn't work.

What of the work of Charlie Plott or Vernon Smith? Or my experimental papers on bargaining? It doesn't seem very scientific to me when behavioral economists respond to this literature by pretending that it doesn't exist.

It appears you first discussed evolutionary game theory in print in 1984 in your paper on extensive games in the Economic Journal. *How did you become aware of this approach? What were the roles of the biologist Maynard Smith and the game theorist Reinhard Selten?*

I didn't know anything about biology then, although I am very interested now. I don't think I even knew that Selten was into biology at the time I started saying that trial-and-error adjustment processes were the way to think about equilibrium selection.

In fact, the idea goes back to 1838 since this was how Cournot first thought about equilibrium. Part of the reason that we speak of a Nash equilibrium rather than a Cournot equilibrium is perhaps that people thought that Cournot's dynamic process wasn't realistic—so why bother with its end product? Much of the impact of

Nash's 1951 paper introducing Nash equilibrium was ironic because it allowed economists (temporarily) to put the problem of how an economy gets to an equilibrium on a back burner while they got on with exploring the implications of being at an equilibrium. (Interestingly, Nash's paper is a carbon copy of his thesis, except for a passage on the evolutionary interpretation of equilibria that the editors insisted on removing.)

But now it seems that we have gone as far as we can go without worrying about how people get to equilibria, so this issue has now come off the back burner and is the subject of really serious research that is beginning to show signs of getting somewhere at last. Note, incidentally, that I don't identify evolutionary game theory only with its biological applications. I think cultural evolution in economic systems is just as important.

But you do cite Maynard Smith (1982)?

You circulate a paper, and then people draw attention to references that you should include. That's how I discovered Maynard Smith. Of course, I was delighted with his work. We had him give one of our economic theory workshops at LSE, which was a huge success. Since then, I have always tried to foster links between biology and economics.

When did you become aware of Selten's work? He seems to be one of the economists who had it early (1975, 1980)?

Selten was into lots of things before other people. But cutting edge guys, like Nash, Harsanyi, or Selten, are seldom part of the mainstream. I recall it being thought an odd choice when I proposed we try and hire him in Michigan. It turned out that he had never had a previous approach from an American university!

We had Selten visit in London for a week many years before the Michigan story, when I learned many things from him: not only his ideas about biology and much else but also the ultimatum game. In retrospect, this conversation was perhaps the foundation of the ultimatum game industry that continues to flourish. When we were talking about Rubinstein's bargaining model, Selten told me that I shouldn't be too enthusiastic about subgame-perfect equilibrium because the experiments carried out at his suggestion by his student, Werner Güth, on the ultimatum game didn't yield the subgame-perfect outcome. At the time, I didn't think that the experiments addressed the anonymity issue adequately, and so I proposed to my

Kenneth G. Binmore

colleagues, Shaked and Sutton, that we run an experiment of our own.

I think this was the very first networked computer experiment. We borrowed a psychology laboratory at LSE and bored holes through the walls between cubicles to pass wires through. There was no networking software in those days, but we found a computer whiz who made our amateur system work by the seat of his pants. The experiments confirmed that Güth et al. (1982) were right about the ultimatum game, but we found that the outcome in a two-stage ultimatum game was much closer to the subgame-perfect equilibrium.

The original paper of Güth et al. was largely ignored at the time, but our paper in the *American Economic Review* (Binmore et al. 1985) generated enormous interest, which continues to this day. At one time, my social citation index was colossal because it was the fashion to denounce us as authors who manipulate their experiments to fit their favored theory. Nowadays, our work is usually not quoted at all, although our data are entirely in line with that from all the other experiments on two-stage ultimatum games. More recently, I have run a whole batch of two-stage ultimatum games to see whether the data is consistent with behavioral models in which people have a taste for fairness. The leading "fairness" models at the time (they are always changing) didn't fit the data at all. Nor does backward induction do well, except when the parameters of the game are close to those of our original experiment.

The latter consideration doesn't worry me at all these days since all the hassle over backward induction led me to question the rational foundations of the idea. So all the time I was being denounced by behavioral economists for defending backward induction, I was simultaneously in trouble with game theorists for attacking it!

What of refinements of Nash equilibrium?

I felt very strongly, right from the beginning, that game theory isn't just an entertainment for scholars. Either it's eventually going to predict the behavior of real people under appropriate conditions, or we're just wasting our time. I'm not saying that abstract game theory isn't fun, but I wouldn't devote my life to it if that was all it was.

It was for this reason that I wrote a paper called "Modeling Rational Players I" (Binmore 1987), in which I argued that the refinement literature was dead. The urge to write the paper came during a talk in which the speaker was applying game theory to a three-stage model of advertising. The model had vast numbers of equilibria, which could be represented as the points in a square. When all the refinements then current were marked in different colors on the square, the whole square was covered! So every equilibrium was defensible according to somebody's theory. But when these refinement theories are examined, they turn out to have very flimsy foundations. As I said earlier, not even backward induction is always safe.

But interesting games commonly do have many equilibria, and so the equilibrium selection problem isn't going to disappear because refinement theory failed to solve it.

It seems that you've posed evolutionarily stable strategies (ESS) as a method for doing this. But isn't it true that you can have multiple ESSs and cases where there is no ESS at all?

This is a misunderstanding of my position. I advocate looking at the adjustment dynamics that take real people (or animals) to equilibria. An ESS is an attempt to capture more about the idea that an equilibrium is the end product of a dynamic process than a Nash equilibrium, but Maynard Smith would agree that it is not very successful in this role. Aside from the drawbacks you mention, we know that the limit points of a simple adjustment process like the replicator dynamics need not be ESS. Moreover, as soon as you get into extensive games, you have whole stacks of connected components of Nash equilibria to worry about. Evolutionary drift within these components then puts paid to any idea that ESS will be an adequate notion. In brief, ESS is just a first stab at a hard problem. Sometimes, one stab is enough, and so one wouldn't want to throw the idea away, but nobody is claiming that ESS solves all our problems.

In 1992, you and Larry Samuelson argued for a modified ESS, or MESS. In that technique, you use a metagame in which you have utility-maximizing agents who select boundedly rational finite automata to play the game under study. Aren't you just bringing back the pseudorational refinements approach as alleged by Sugden (2001) in another context?

It is good that you mention Larry since all my evolutionary work has been done in tandem with him. We know that MESS is just another stopgap like ESS, but one does one's best with what tools are available.

KENNETH G. BINMORE

However, it isn't the MESS idea that critics like Sugden dislike but the metagame story of Abreu and Rubinstein's (1988) path-breaking paper on modeling bounded rationality using finite automata. In fact, Larry and I introduce evolutionary ideas in order to *dispense* with Abreu and Rubinstein's metagame with utility-maximizing agents (in much the same way that some papers remove the fiction of a Walrasian auctioneer by actually modeling the price adjustment mechanism in a market explicitly). So we aren't guilty of smuggling pseudorational refinements back into the action—we are guilty of the opposite.

When you talk about evolutionary drift, you describe an ultralong-run solution, which consists of a probability distribution over a bunch of possible equilibria. Aren't you then running, in some sense, a metagame on a metagame? Is the door being left open for an infinite regress of metagames on metagames: the evolution of the evolutionary process?

The questions about metagames are a red herring, but there are layers upon layers in our approach, although no infinite regress. The layers relate to expected waiting times.

Larry and I distinguish the short run, the medium run, the long run, and the ultralong run. We don't think that subjects in the laboratory or people in real life figure out how to play games by thinking hard. They learn by trial and error. In the short run, what matters most is not the strategic structure of the game they play but the way it is framed. The framing triggers responses that are adapted to the games they are accustomed to play in real life that have similar frames. (These real-life games are seldom one-shot games, and hence the strong tendency of subjects to cooperate a lot.) In the medium run, the subjects' behavior begins to change as they gradually adapt to their new circumstances. In some games, subjects adapt quickly. In games like the ultimatum game, they adapt slowly. In the long run, they are likely to find their way to the neighborhood of an equilibrium of the learning process, which will commonly correspond to a Nash equilibrium of the underlying game if the learning dynamics aren't too noisy.

But if the learning dynamics are noisy at all, the system won't stay at the first equilibrium that is reached. If we wait long enough, the system will be bounced out of the basin of attraction of the original equilibrium by a conjunction of unlikely events. If we wait a great deal longer, we will be able to determine the frequency with which the system lies close to each Nash equilibrium of the underlying game. It is this ultralong-run probability distribution that forms the focus of the work of Young (1993a) and of Kandori, Mailath, and Rob (1993).

Larry and I think that the expected waiting times for ultralong-run theories to be relevant are often too long to make economic sense. We have therefore studied long-run equilibrium selection. People think of equilibria as lying at the bottom of pits in a landscape determined by the learning dynamics. But we find that Nash equilibria in extensive games commonly come in connected components lying on the floor of a hanging valley—one with a precipice hanging over another valley down below. It is when the system falls into such a valley that evolutionary drift becomes relevant.

Once the system is on the floor of a valley, evolutionary pressures exerted by the learning dynamics disappear. All that now matters is the residual noise. This may or may not tend to push the system towards the precipice. If it mostly pushes the system away from the precipice, then the system may get trapped in the hanging valley for very long periods of time—although it will eventually escape in the ultralong run.

We explain this theory in "Musical Chairs" (Binmore et al. 1995b) and "Muddling Through" (Binmore and Samuelson 1997). One application is to the ultimatum game. Behavioral economists commonly assert that "game theory says that people will play the subgame-perfect equilibrium"—as though there were only one theory of games on which everybody was agreed. However, the ultimatum game has an infinite number of Nash equilibria, each of which is a possible solution of the equilibrium selection problem. Larry and I show that plausible assumptions about the noise in the learning dynamics can result in the system being trapped for a very long time close to a Nash equilibrium that isn't subgame-perfect and in which the proposer offers the responder a substantial share of the pie. In Learning to Be Imperfect (Binmore et al. 1995a), we illustrate the idea with a simple 2 x 2 game we call the ultimatum minigame. (Behavioral economists have taken to calling this the miniultimatum game, but it is the game that is small, rather than the ultimata.)

In brief, one can't have a realistic theory of evolutionary equilibrium selection that ignores expected waiting times. Sometimes being more realistic about the way that noise enters a model can reduce the expected waiting times in an ultralong-run theory to something plausible, but Larry and I think that we more frequently

KENNETH G. BINMORE

need to turn to long-run theories. It is often true that the ultralong-run theories confirm intuitions left over from refinement theory, but the same isn't true of long-run theories. If we are right, game theorists therefore still have a lot of work to do.

In your 1999 paper with Larry Samuelson, you talk about "hanging valleys" as in an Escher print, in which people keep walking downstairs but end higher up?
The landscape metaphor is dangerous in game theory for this reason. For example, the three-legged centipede game has only one hanging valley, but when you fall over the precipice, you fall back into the same valley from which you came. Limit cycles exhibit the same phenomenon in a simpler form. You keep "falling" but end up back where you began.

Does reducing waiting times cause more people to die?
This is a reference to our paper with Richard Vaughan in which we identify the payoffs in a biological game with death probabilities (Binmore et al. 1995b). This is one way of being more realistic about how noise enters a model. More noise helps speed up the transition to the utralong run. For example, we were able to reduce the expected waiting time in a model of Kandori, Mailath, and Rob (1993) from 10 to the power 72 iterations to about 5,000 iterations. But you don't need to kill people off faster to make this happen!

In complex models with heterogeneous agents, a key parameter is how often people are willing to switch strategies. Do you agree that this parameter is crucial?
This is our experience with evolutionary models. Some inertia must be built in, or the system can behave wildly. But people can't be thinking of everything all at once, and so some inertia must surely be realistic.

What's your view of chaotic dynamics?
Do you believe that chaotic dynamics is a great new science? I think it is just another fad, like catastrophe theory some years back. Both are correct theories that have useful applications, but the idea that they are about to displace orthodox mathematical models is just hype. For example, I am often told that game theory's obsession with equilibria has been rendered out-of-date by chaos theory, but

the subjects in my laboratory don't seem to have noticed. Nor does the fact that the planetary motions are theoretically chaotic seemed to have altered the way astronomers go about things.

You seem to believe that game theory and economics can become an engineering tool in some contexts. Can you expand on that?

I think that some parts of economic theory already are engineering tools in some contexts. Auction theory is the leading example. We can predict what kind of auction design will work best in a given economic environment and then test the design in the laboratory with a good deal of confidence that it will work as planned. This is what my team did when we designed the $35 billion telecom auction for the British government.

I think the areas in which similar techniques can be used successfully are much wider than is generally supposed. Our chief problem is that we are not allowed to get on with it—partly because economists traditionally promise more than they can deliver and partly because vested interests act to block reforms.

This is quite a different perception of economics than most people have.

I am not claiming that all of economics should be regarded as a branch of engineering. Only the small part of microeconomic theory that turns out to work well when tested in laboratories. As for the rest, one can't stop giving policy advice because the theory isn't perfect. One does the best with whatever tools are available.

But you probably mean more than this, and it is probably true that my belief that one should approach the social sciences in the same way that we approach the physical sciences used to be unusual. But my impression is that this attitude is quite common nowadays.

But you also like philosophy?

Yes. I like lots of things. I'm not very good at taking a particular thing and just following and following it up.

You have criticized the widespread use of the concept of common knowledge in game theory. What underlies your criticism? Is it a logical problem with Gödel's incompleteness theorem?

I don't criticize common knowledge as such. It is rather the pointless ritual of claiming that everything in sight is to be assumed to be common knowledge. If that really needed to be true, we wouldn't ever be able to apply the theory because all that stuff is never common knowledge. Milgrom (1981) has shown that something is common knowledge if and only if it is implied by a public event—something that can't happen without our all observing each other observing it.

Like the minister coming in with the ladies with dirty faces?
Yes, that's right. If that's the only way common knowledge can be attained, then it won't be attained very often.

But the fact that things that are usually assumed to be common knowledge in models that aren't usually common knowledge in practice isn't the disaster it is usually said to be. For example, the philosopher David Lewis is widely believed to have shown that coordinated action is rationally impossible without common knowledge of the joint agreement to act, but this is just wrong. The way computer scientists tell the story involves two Byzantine generals who need to coordinate an attack on the enemy occupying a valley between them. They send messengers back and forward confirming the last confirmation of the plan to attack, but the agreement can never become common knowledge in this way. Rubinstein's e-mail game is a formal version of the same story.

But Larry Samuelson and I (2001) show that with a more realistic model, coordinated action is indeed possible, even though the agreement to act never becomes common knowledge. Indeed, the only equilibrium of our model that doesn't survive an evolutionary analysis is the unique equilibrium of Rubinstein's model, in which all communications are ignored.

Is this related to your argument (1997) with Aumann (1995) about backward induction? You seem to argue that people might not behave irrationally because they might do something unexpected?
I think that common knowledge is a red herring here. The real issue is whether we should accept Aumann's definition of what rationality should mean. I think that such a definition can't possibly be right because it fails to take account of what people would believe if someone were to deviate from rational behavior. It is not that a rational person might do some irrational thing unexpectedly. Since he is rational, he won't do something irrational. But the reason he won't do something irrational is because of what would happen if he did.

We therefore can't ignore counterfactual events or subjunctive conditionals as Aumann thinks. This isn't a deep issue. I don't touch a hot stove because I would burn my hand if I did. It is therefore counterfactual that I will touch the stove, but it would be pointless to try and analyze why I don't touch the stove without taking into account this counterfactual.

I plan to explain all this in the second edition of my book *Fun and Games*, which I am just finishing up.

Isn't Aumann's response that if people have common knowledge of each other's rationality, they won't behave stupidly?

Nobody is suggesting that rational people will behave stupidly. What keeps you on the equilibrium path is your assessment of what would happen if you were to deviate. But if you were to deviate, what would the other players deduce about your mode of reasoning? And how would this affect their future behavior? Aumann seems to say that we needn't worry about such counterfactual events. However, I am tired of this fruitless debate.

Why has the debate been fruitless?

It resolved nothing. Aumann's students defended him loyally, and the rest of the world continued as before. However, at least nobody takes backward induction for granted any more as God's gift to rational choice theory.

What is the relevance of this debate to financial economics?

When financial economics becomes an engineering discipline, nobody will use backward induction. Agents won't be modeled in a way that makes them impervious to opportunities to exploit bad play by their rivals. The final outcome will be determined using evolutionary equilibrium selection. I don't imagine that Aumann thinks any differently on this issue. He would be displeased if his defense of backward induction under impossibly ideal circumstances were to encourage the dinosaurs who think that rational expectation theory is the cat's whiskers.

Where does Gödel come into this?

Gödel's theorem isn't relevant to the debate over backward induction in finite games of perfect information. But elsewhere, I have argued that his theorem shows that there can't be such a thing as "perfect rationality." I think the argument is watertight, but I

Kenneth G. binmore

made it to urge more serious consideration of the importance of models of bounded rationality rather than because I thought it had deep significance for how we study economics.

You have taught introductory economics, and so you have gone through the standard principles book. Does your approach fit into that or not?

I don't have any philosophical problems with the content of principles books, but I would scrap the standard Principles of Economics course if given the opportunity. What freshmen need to learn is when and how markets work and when and how they don't work. I think the best way to do this is with classroom experiments in the manner pioneered by Ted Bergstrom's book. I would also teach the students how to read and comment intelligently on the financial pages. Perhaps they wouldn't then be so bored when they get taught serious microeconomics at a later stage.

When don't markets work? When bubbles crash?

And all the other reasons that textbooks give. My consultancy work has made me particularly sensitive to the abuse of market power. Before I got my hands dirty looking at the details of particular cases, I had no idea how much society lets the fat cats get away with. Nor is there any excuse, because much of the necessary regulatory stuff ought to come under the heading of economic engineering.

You have proposed Bayesian approaches to deal with problems arising from the failure of common knowledge and backward induction. Is it not the case that there can be a failure to converge using Bayesian methods in infinite-dimensional space?

Bayesian decision theory is just a tool that one uses when writing a model. It isn't something that could somehow substitute for common knowledge or backward induction.

On this front, I am sometimes accused of inconsistency because I forget myself every now and then by denouncing the evils of Bayesianism. I remember being more or less laughed off the platform at a finance conference when I let my views slip out. (How come Selten escapes ridicule when he says similar things?)

Economists have forgotten that Savage (1954) says that it would be "ridiculous" and "preposterous" to apply his theory in a *large* world because Savage's consistency axioms only make sense in a small world, where people can survey in advance how they would react to all possible pieces of information they might receive in the future. Only then can they be sure that they won't want to change their prior after being taken by surprise by something totally unanticipated.

Consistency is only a virtue in a small world in which players can be sure of not starting out with a mistake. What's the point of being consistently wrong? That's why scientists aren't Bayesians. When a theory is refuted, they throw it away.

But none of this applies to game theory. When you formulate a game, you *create* a small world. So, of course, Bayesian updating applies when the players are modeled as being rational. I have done my share of this. But the lack of realism involved in modeling real human beings as Bayesian updaters is one of the reasons why it is important that we develop evolutionary game theory at a faster pace.

As for convergence problems in infinite-dimensional spaces, they trouble me not in the least. One doesn't choose a theory because it has nice mathematical properties.

You talk positively about experimental economics, but you have also said that it is a lot like chemists mixing reagents in dirty test tubes.

I use the chemistry metaphor to criticize bad experiments—especially those designed to show that economic theory doesn't work. What could be easier? If I want to show that chemistry doesn't work, I simply mix my reagents in dirty test tubes. We should learn from the physicists, who put a lot of effort into training their graduate students to run experiments in a properly controlled way—otherwise physics would always be refuted.

My own view is that we can't reasonably expect economic theory to predict at all in the laboratory unless

1. The problem we ask subjects to address is reasonably simple (and isn't made complicated by its framing).
2. The subjects are properly motivated by receiving adequate payments.
3. There is ample time for trial-and-error learning.

Making sure that these and other considerations apply to cleaning your test tubes. Our biggest success from keeping test tubes clean is the experimental triumph of equilibrium theory. I can remember

KENNETH G. BINMORE

63

when it was said that Nash equilibrium doesn't predict at all in the laboratory. But who says that now?

So we have a lot of work to do in experimental design?
Yes—each new topic requires the development of new experimental techniques, just as in physics. Right now, I think the most important topic should be the attempt to draw a line between the domain where neoclassical economics works and the domain where it doesn't. I know it isn't very exciting, but that's normal science. What we need less of is all the sensation mongering—with people inventing supposedly data-driven theories that are going to change the world but disappear from view after being almost immediately refuted by the next experiment.

Remember all the theories of unexpected utility that were fashionable a few years ago? Where are they now? It turns out that all the theories are bad at predicting laboratory behavior, but the least bad is ordinary expected utility theory.

Your three principles, are they the only source of dirt in the test tubes?
No. They are only the principles that seem most relevant to game theory experiments. But I don't want to give the impression that I think one only has to keep the test tubes clean and then economic theory will be confirmed. Theory is sometimes wrong. For example, I think backward induction and Bayesian updating often fail to predict in the laboratory because the theory behind them isn't always right.

How do you decide that the theory is wrong?
It would be great to know the answer to that question! In the absence of a definitive answer, I think we should muddle along like the physicists do. My own approach is to try and make the theory work in the laboratory by keeping scrubbing the test tubes. If it still won't work, look at its philosophical underpinnings. If they are suspect, that's probably why the theory won't work.

What is the core theory we should be testing?
That equilibrium works. Economists often don't realize how hard the concept is for layfolk. My colleagues and I just did some work for the British government on incentives for senior medics in the National Health Service. The incentives proposed were intended to persuade medics to work fewer hours in private practice. But the

proposers neglected to consider that fewer patients would then be treated privately. A simple equilibrium model showed that all the incentive schemes under consideration would actually have the effect of lengthening waiting times for treatment—the opposite of what was intended. Our arguments proved persuasive, but I would have been much happier if I were able to quote laboratory studies in defense of models like ours.

Something that seems to come out of this experimental debate is that you think fairness needs to be seen as a product of evolution. The critical response is, why not just accept that a taste for fairness was just washed up on our evolutionary shore? Why are you so skeptical about these "exotic preferences"? What is so exotic about them? Aren't they just preferences?

I am skeptical because the claims aren't consistent with the data. It is true that human behavior in laboratory settings can sometimes be summarized by fitting exotic utility functions to the subjects using revealed preference theory. There is no harm in this. The harm arises when it is implicitly claimed that such exotic preferences are stable and portable.

To say that preferences are stable means that they don't change over time. But the subjects' behavior does! Sometimes subjects learn very rapidly indeed. When Al Roth switched sides because of the overwhelming evidence of this phenomenon, I thought that the debate was over, but I was naive. To say that preferences are portable means that the preferences found using one game also apply to other games. But they don't! Even awarding some players a meaningless gold star changes behavior in the ultimatum game.

Behavioral economists do their best to save their theories by adding in more and more parameters—rather like Ptolemy with his epicycles. I really don't understand why they can't face up to the fact that people often seem to behave irrationally because they are irrational, rather than inventing more and more complicated utility functions for them to maximize.

I think that the current behavioral approach—that people somehow just have an intrinsic taste for fairness—is not only unsupported by the data but is downright dangerous when its advocates start trying to influence policy. Welfare economics needs individual preferences to be the same before and after a reform, but the behavioralists offer no evidence that the exotic utility functions they attribute to people are stable in this sense. What evidence there is

KENNETH G. BINMORE

actually supports the contrary view—see, for example, John Ledyard's (1995) survey of the enormous experimental literature on the private provision of public goods.

As for the evolutionary connection, I don't think anyone denies an evolutionary origin for our sense of fairness. My difference from the behavioral school on this issue is only that I think this fact can be useful in formulating a theory of fairness. The theory to which I subscribe is that fairness evolved as an equilibrium selection device for the repeated games that we commonly played as prehuman hunter-gatherers. My two-volume book *Game Theory and the Social Contract* gives the details.

Norms that evolved for equilibrium selection in repeated games get triggered by the way one-shot laboratory games are framed. We then have to learn by trial and error that the norm is being applied in a situation to which it is not adapted. And we do, slowly in some games and fast in others.

None of this is to deny that people have some built-in regard for others. Why else do I give a small fraction of my income to charity? A small fraction of people seem to be all warm glow, and we call them saints or give them medals. But the data doesn't support the claim that most people feel a lot of warm glow all the time.

Is your work with Larry Samuelson on the ultimatum game relevant here?

Yes. We think it explains why learning can be so slow in games like the ultimatum game. In one of our simulations, it took 60,000 iterations to move significantly away from a system started near one of the many Nash equilibria of the ultimatum game. The simulated subjects didn't stay there because they had exotic preferences that made them like staying there. They stayed close because it is hard to move away from a Nash equilibrium, whatever dynamics you may be using.

Was it fun writing Fun and Games *(1991), and how was it received?*

I wrote *Fun and Games* for money, to put my youngest child through college. It's always hard work to write a book, but it is always fun too if you love the subject. As for how it was received, I don't seem to be able to write anything at all that doesn't generate hostility from some quarters, but I occasionally get e-mails from people who liked the book a lot and want to tell me about their enthusiasm.

I am now finishing up a very substantial revision, which really is a labor of love since I don't need the money any more. I hope people will enjoy all the puzzles and paradoxes I've worked into the text.

In many ways, your two-volume Game Theory and the Social Contract *(1994, 1998) is your magnum opus. How did you come to write it?*

I have always been interested in philosophy but had never attempted to do anything original until invited to talk at a mammoth social choice conference in Canada. I hurriedly put together a bargaining analysis of John Rawls's (1972) original position, but when I presented the paper, I didn't expect to find John Rawls himself in the audience. When he introduced himself afterwards, I felt like sinking into the ground at the thought of all the books I should have read but hadn't before talking on such a subject.

Afterwards I began to do the homework I should have done before. In particular, I started to worry seriously about the problems of interpersonal comparison of utility that both Rawls and Harsanyi (1977) finesse in their pioneering work. This led me to abandon the Kantian perspective they adopt for a Humean approach, in which fairness norms are seen as equilibrium selection devices whose origin is to be sought in our evolutionary history, both social and biological.

I found that anthropology, biology, and psychology were as important as philosophy in the syntheses I attempted, but I don't regret all the effort that went into trying to get a grip on all these disciplines. I only regret writing at such length. I have just written a shorter popular version of the book to be published by Oxford University Press with the title *Natural Justice.*

How did Rawls respond to the work?

Rawls was extremely positive about my work. His disciples tell me that I don't really understand Rawls's *Theory of Justice,* but I think they make too much of irrelevant matters of detail that Rawls himself didn't think worth fussing about. I think the same is true of economists who criticize his models. It is true that his formal analyses are not up to the standards expected in economics journals, but that isn't where the interest of his work lies.

You suggest that the later Rawls moved to a new position that is less distinctive than in his original theory of justice. Is it perhaps more sophisticated but grayer?

𝒦ENNETH G. BINMORE

Rawls knew that there were things wrong with his original theory and sought to correct them in later work. But there was a tendency to proceed by qualifying earlier claims, rather than starting from a firmer base. I prefer the earlier, clearer vision—warts and all.

You suggested that the main audiences for Game Theory and the Social Contract *were economists, political scientists, and philosophers. How do people from each of these disciplines react?*

I had hopes that the book would gain me acceptance as a philosopher, but moral philosophers—especially American moral philosophers—are usually quite hostile. They see me as an outsider with no respect for their way of doing things. Making fun of Immanuel Kant goes down particularly badly. So does denying that the Naturalistic Fallacy is a fallacy. On the other hand, I get a good reception from philosophers of science, among whom I have become quite well-known. Only in Germany do I get a good reception from moral philosophers, but I think this is because they have had so much Kant from an early age that they welcome anything a bit different.

How about political scientists?

I haven't made much impact with political scientists. Perhaps my work is too mathematical for their taste. On the other hand, I have done well with scientists and biological anthropologists. I guess I am happier to have biologists aboard than philosophers or political scientists.

And how about economists?

Most economists continue to dismiss theories of fairness as irrelevant to their subject. But welfare economists are commonly supportive. I haven't faced any hostility from economists, except from the behavioral school defending the simplistic idea that fairness should be modeled as something that people just happen to have a taste for.

What about Robert Sugden?

Bob Sugden isn't hostile to my basic approach—I learned some of what I say in my book from him. But he lives in a world in which there is a grand conspiracy run from Chicago, of which I am a part, the aim of which is to prevent the tenets of neoclassical economics from being challenged.

Sugden has published an Economic Journal *essay (2001) that argues that your use of von Neumann and Morgenstern utility and your argument about the origin of morals is a recovery program for the superrational refinements approach to equilibrium selection. Are you being accused of being orthodox when you are not?*

Accusing me of being orthodox on refinement theory is like accusing Samson of being a Philistine. However, Sugden objects to a lot more than refinement theory. I don't know what would become of economics if we followed Sugden's advice and threw utility theory and the like out the window.

But the real point here is that Sugden doesn't see that the models in the book are only parables that are intended to illustrate that the logic of the theory holds together properly. It never occurred to me that people would think that my simplistic stories were intended to capture all the richness of human behavior.

What do you think of Rabin and Thaler's (2001a) attack on marginal utility as an explanation of risk aversion?

They don't understand what they are attacking.

A key part of your argument in Game Theory and the Social Contract *is that Adam and Eve bargain over the equilibrium they will operate in the Game of Life they play in the Garden of Eden. You call the larger game that includes the bargaining the Game of Morals. Is this new game a metagame? Isn't this new set of rules in the Garden of Eden a fundamental contradiction to the evolutionary approach?*

The mention of the Garden of Eden signals that we are in parable mode here. When you questioned the metagame approach before, I gave the example of the Walrasian auctioneer who doesn't really exist. What really exists in most markets is an adaptive dynamic process whose end product is the same *as if* there were a Walrasian auctioneer. Similarly, Richard Dawkins's genes aren't really selfish. How can a molecule be selfish? But the end product of an evolutionary process is *as if* the genes were selfish players of a game.

In the same way, there isn't really a Game of Morals. Our prehuman hunter-gatherer ancestors didn't really bargain over which equilibrium to operate in their Game of Life. How could they bargain before language evolved? However, I give reasons (chap. 2 of vol. 2) why it is plausible that evolution might have generated an outcome, which it is *as if* they had bargained over which social contract to operate.

KENNETH G. BINMORE

69

I think this *as if* issue is very important for economics in general. I don't believe people do much figuring out of anything. If they behave as if they had, some evolutionary process—biological or socioeconomic—must be responsible.

What about coevolution?

You mean simultaneous social and biological evolution, as in the evolution of language? I argue that the evolution of fairness norms has a similar character.

If I am right, the deep structure of all fairness norms is biologically determined, as with language, and hence is universal in the human species. Like language, it would then also be unique to the human species. But, just as the particular language used in a particular locality is culturally determined, so the standard of interpersonal comparison used in a particular context is culturally determined.

I therefore agree with the many authors who have pointed out that what people count as fair differs with the context, but I differ in my explanation. It seems usually to be taken for granted that the standard of interpersonal comparison is universal and so the deep structure of the fairness norm differs between contexts. I suspect the reverse.

You identify four different political ideologies: utilitarian, neofeudal, libertarian, and whiggish. Is the last the one you favor?

These are fancy names for what one might otherwise call *planned centralization, unplanned centralization, unplanned decentralization,* and *planned decentralization.* I am very keen on the latter, and I think that the new discipline of mechanism design allows us to make a start on moving in this direction.

I see the left-right paradigm as a mistaken attempt to decide between the utilitarianism of socialism and the laissez-faire attitudes of libertarians. But this isn't a choice that is open to us since neither of these utopian models is genuinely workable. I think that the political organization of all modern societies is *neofeudal*—a word I made up before George W. Bush inherited his father's mantle. The debate should be about whether we should move from a neofeudal social contract to a whiggish social contract. This isn't a very original thought since the founding fathers of the American Republic had much the same idea.

You argue that the tit-for-tat solution is not as general a solution to the Prisoners' Dilemma as Axelrod (1984) argues.

You are talking about Axelrod's evolutionary simulations of the *repeated* Prisoners' Dilemma.

Axelrod is usually credited with having discovered that cooperation can be supported as an equilibrium in the indefinitely repeated Prisoners' Dilemma, but the folk theorem of repeated game theory had been proved more than thirty years before his *Evolution of Cooperation* appeared. What he deserves credit for is drawing attention to the importance of evolution in selecting among all the equilibria that the folk theorem shows exist.

But more careful computer simulations show his claims that evolution will choose strategies like tit-for-tat to be mistaken. We shouldn't expect nice strategies, that are never the first to defect, to be selected in the long run. Nor should we necessarily expect evolution to select forgiving strategies. For example, the grim strategy does very well when the initial population consists of all one- and two-state finite automata. Nor should we expect that the selected strategies should be simple. However, the big mistake is that the selected strategies will necessarily be retaliatory—reacting to cheating by another player with some kind of punishment. This is true in two-person games, but three-player games are a whole new ball game.

The important claim that does seem robust is that evolution will eventually select a Pareto efficient outcome.

You recently had a paper in which you talk about the breakdown of social contracts (Binmore 2001).

I think the human species has two equilibrium selection devices. One is fairness, and the other is leadership. Leaders who fail to nominate equilibria that are close to those that their followers perceive as fair risk creating rebellious coalitions who are able to coalesce because they have fairness as a common coordinating principle. One of these days I intend to write something more solid on this subject.

You were made a Commander of the British Empire by the Queen of England for your work in designing telecom auctions for the British government. Is the English clock auction the solution? What do you think of the English clock auction?

I guess you mean an ascending-price auction in which the price rises automatically and bidders keep their fingers on the button until they wish to stop bidding. I am used to calling this a Japanese auction! As for my somewhat absurd honor, although I led the team that did the work, I would have liked to see Paul Klemperer recognized as well.

What is your preferred auction solution? What is the solution that saved $35 billion for the British government?

Klemperer and I believe it is a bad mistake to think in terms of an auction design that is optimal independently of the economic environment in which it is to be used. We think that a new design has to be engineered for each new environment.

In the case of the big British auction, the original problem was that only four licenses were to be offered to a market in which there were four incumbent operators. So who else would bid? We therefore came up with a sealed-bid design intended to promote entry. When it unexpectedly turned out that there was enough spectrum for five licenses, I fought hard to persuade the British government to abandon all the hard work that had gone into the old design and to switch to the ascending-price format that was eventually used. Shortly after, the Dutch government copied this design for their very much less successful auction, but they should have copied our *first* design because they were trying to sell the same number of licenses as they had incumbents. I later faced the same problem in Denmark—after the NASDAQ had collapsed and so circumstances were as adverse as possible—and there a version of the sealed-bid design did rather well.

In any case, the important thing is that you shouldn't buy auction designs off the shelf. Each design must be carefully tailored to the circumstances. This is why all of the telecom auctions that I masterminded—in Britain, Belgium, Denmark, Greece, Israel, and Hong Kong—are different in significant ways.

What is the key to making $35 billion?

Owning something in short supply for which the demand is very large! All the designer of an auction then has to do is not to screw things up. But events around the world show that it is easy to screw up if you don't know any game theory and so are not attuned to strategic issues.

Are there other people we should have interviewed?

You seem to have concentrated on eccentrics. It is true that Einstein provided this image for scientists supposedly at the cutting edge, but I suspect that eccentricity just gets some people talked about more. As for others who might have been on your list, what of Peyton Young and Jim Heckman?*

If we look at the profession over the last twenty years, what has really developed as most important?

I don't pretend to be able to give an overview for the whole profession, but I'll go for game theory, experimental economics, and microeconometrics. Within economic theory, I continue to think that models of learning and evolution are the way forward. Like all new things, there was hostility to this approach at first, but now sociologists and anthropologists have climbed aboard.

You see yourself more as a social scientist than an economist. Do you see philosophy and political science merging again?

I don't see any strong need for us to hang labels on ourselves. However, I am sold on the idea that the methodology of economics can be applied just as successfully in other disciplines. It has already had a major influence in evolutionary biology, and it looks to me as though biological anthropology and sociology are in a very receptive state.

As for political science and philosophy, I don't see any prospect of their getting back together. Why should they?

Do you disagree with how Matthew Rabin is approaching the introduction of psychological ideas into economics?

I don't disagree with his aims. We certainly need to melt the boundaries between economics and psychology. This is why a third of the research fellows at the research institute ELSE that I founded in London are psychologists. But they don't have much time for armchair theorizing, and I think they are right. Psychology needs to be driven by data. I am not saying that there should be no theorizing at all, but any theorizing should be accompanied by rigorous testing in the laboratory.

*Editors' Note: We interviewed Ken Binmore before we had included Peyton Young as an interviewee.

KENNETH G. BINMORE

Is it your training as a mathematician that pulls you across disciplinary boundaries?

I guess a sound training in mathematics is a good basis for a career in almost anything. On the other hand, I know top-class mathematicians who have no curiosity at all about anything but their own specialty.

Do you have to be mathematically trained to be at the cutting edge?

I think you have to have some mathematical training to count as being educated at all, let alone to be at the cutting edge of research! But in retrospect, the exaggerated respect for mathematical skills that was typical of the times in which I was getting started in economics was a bad thing—especially since it coincided with the Bourbaki phase in pure mathematics, in which formal, axiomatic mathematics was much overvalued compared with problem-solving, algorithmic mathematics.

Even more than other learning, I suspect mathematical learning needs to be worn lightly if it is to be really useful.

Is game theory the answer to everything?

Yes. All of social science is just a branch of game theory. Unfortunately, we don't know much game theory yet, and so this insight doesn't get us very far!

Game theory made two earlier attempts to get into economics. This last time, it seems to have made it. Is that because experiments allow us to apply it better?

I don't think game theory's success in some experiments had much to do with its gaining acceptance. In the first wave of excitement, people tried to apply two-person, zero-sum game theory, but what economic situations are zero-sum? At the second wave, people tried to apply cooperative game theory, but we know now that cooperative theories need to be supported by noncooperative models before they can be reliably applied. In other words, game theory didn't get imported into economics at the first two attempts because the theory wasn't good enough. Economists bought game theory only when game theorists started selling something worth buying.

Where do you see economics going in the next fifty years?

In fifty years' time, I think that economics will be classed as a science, like physics and chemistry. People will regard the present as the golden age of economic theory. All the petty backbiting and squabbling will be forgotten. Only the von Neumanns of this world will be remembered by name, but the rest of us will have done our bit if our contributions turn out to survive the test of time.

KENNETH G. BINMORE

Kenneth G. Binmore

Professor of Economics, University College, London

INFORMATION ON THE WEB ABOUT KENNETH G. BINMORE
http://else.econ.ucl.ac.uk/index.php

EDUCATION
B.Sc. Mathematics, Imperial College, University of London, 1959
Ph.D. Mathematics, Imperial College, University of London, 1962

SELECTED PUBLICATIONS
Foundations of Analysis: Logic, Sets and Numbers. London: Cambridge University Press, 1980.
Fun and Games. Lexington, MA: D. C. Heath, 1991.
Playing Fair and *Just Playing.* Vols. 1 and 2 of *Game Theory and the Social Contract.* Cambridge: MIT Press, 1994 and 1998.
"Equilibrium Selection and Evolutionary Drift," with Larry Samuelson. *Review of Economic Studies* 66 (1999).
"The Biggest Auction Ever: The Sale of 3G Telecom Licenses," with Paul Klemperer. *Economic Journal* 112 (2002).

SPECIAL HONORS AND EXPERIENCE
Fellow Commoner of Churchill College, Cambridge University, 1980–
Fellow, Institute of Mathematics and Its Applications, 1980, and Econometric Society, 1988, British Academy
Member, Academy of Social Science, 1999–
Commander of the British Empire, 2001–
Visiting Fellow, Institute for Advanced Study, Princeton University, 2001
Member, American Academy of Arts and Sciences, 2002–

CHAPTER 3

Herbert Gintis

External Faculty, Santa Fe Institute, Emeritus Professor,
University of Massachusetts

∾

The interview was conducted on March 15, 2002, at his home in
Northampton, Massachusetts.

Can you tell us how you got into economics?

In college I knew nothing about economics. I was in a special
program at the University of Pennsylvania for students who had
scored high on their SAT tests. In this program we didn't take normal courses. I took only one history course as an undergraduate,
and no English courses. I studied mostly math, French, and Spanish
language and literature. I was in the program from 1958 to 1961, and
one of those years I was in France. I also taught Calculus I, a regular
undergraduate course, my last year there, which paid my tuition.
The bottom line is that I never had a social science course, and so I
knew nothing of economics. I didn't know what "income" was
when I went into graduate school in economics; I did know what an
"income tax" was, however, because my dad always complained
about paying it.

After graduating from the University of Pennsylvania I went to
Harvard to get a Ph.D. in math. I was very political, and as I was

∾

writing my dissertation in mathematics; it seemed like I was schizo-
phrenic. I spent hours and hours writing a dissertation, but what I
really was doing was spending time organizing for social change in
poor communities around Boston and participating in the antiwar
movement. So I decided to switch out of math with just a master's
degree. A friend of mine owned a sandal shop that he ran in Harvard Square. I took over his shop and became a sandal maker and
hired some young women to make handbags. It was okay, but I
wasn't really into feet, so after doing it for a while I decided to go
back to school. I asked a friend of mine, Chuck Levenstein, who's an
economist, what should I do. He asked me if I were a Marxist. I said
yes, although I didn't really know what that meant. I had read
C. Wright Mills, and some writings by Marxists, so we were radical
Marxists. So he said, "Well then you should do economics because
the economy determines everything."

So I took off from making sandals one day (I told my assistant to
mind the shop), and in June of 1963 I went to Littauer Center (the
Harvard University economics department) in my leather work
clothes—a bearded, long-haired hippy if there ever was one. I wandered about, but nobody was around since it was summertime. One
door was open, there was a guy named James Duesenberry, so I
walked in and said that I wanted to study economics. He asked me
why, and I told him the story about Marxism and the economy. He
said that he could get me into the department with no problem
because it was a transfer from one department to another and the
economics department loves mathematicians. But he told me to
read an introductory textbook before I started graduate school to see
what I was getting into. I asked which one, and he said Samuelson.
So I read Samuelson and came back. He asked if I still wanted to do
economics, and I said sure. He said that he thought I was going to
find out that studying economics is different than what I was thinking it was going to be, but okay. And that's how it happened.

At first I was very hostile to becoming an economist. I felt like I
was not one of these people. How could I tell my artist and hippie
friends that I was studying to be an economist? No way. My attitude
was that I'm not really an economist because I care about consciousness and culture and all of that. Then I got totally socialized—
to the point where I prided myself in being able to read the national
income accounts and knowing what "errors in variables" means. It
took me some time, however. Now I am at the point of bristling
when people bad-mouth economists. Who would have believed it?

What graduate courses do you remember?

Harvard teachers were not well-known for caring very much about teaching. They were better than my teachers in the Harvard mathematics department, however. Howard Raiffa taught me game theory; he was very good. I was so naive; I got straight A's my first year when I was a graduate student, and then I got B's my second year. I realized later that in my second year I really understood what was going on and I wouldn't give the profs the answers they wanted. I was obstreperous, even then, and haven't changed much since.

To show you how naive I was, in my first year, I took International Trade with Gottfried Haberler. I took it because I wanted to study imperialism, so we were halfway through the course, and we had read all these abstruse general equilibrium models, and I could throw around all these input-output tables. But we hadn't gotten to imperialism yet. So I raised my hand in class and said, "Professor Haberler, when are we going to study imperialism?" He looked at me and said, "This is not a course in nineteenth-century British history." Everybody in the class laughed. I hadn't a clue why.

Who else was in classes with you at Harvard?

Deirdre (then Donald) McCloskey and Tom Sargent were in classes with me. I was on the Left, though, so I didn't have many friends in the department. My fellow graduate students were more traditional, but they didn't dislike me, for the most part. For instance, they elected me president of the graduate economics club, where I could stir up a lot of trouble. During the Vietnam War, because of the popularity of the antiwar movement, almost everybody was on my side. But I didn't have anyone to bounce ideas off of. Sam Bowles was in Nigeria, so he wasn't around when I was a graduate student. He came back my last year. We got to be good friends right away, and then we formed this group to teach a radical economics course, Soc. Sci. 125. The group of teachers included Tom Weisskopf, Arthur MacEwan, Stephan Michelson, and Richard Edwards. But all except Edwards were all older than me; they were assistant professors.

You entered the department already radicalized, so the department didn't radicalize you at all. Did you have friends in other departments?

My friends were SDS (Students for a Democratic Society) people, political people, and counterculture people, but some were students, graduate and undergraduate, at one of the many colleges and universities around Boston and Cambridge.

What was your dissertation topic on, and how did you pick it?

My dissertation was called "Power and Alienation." It was a critique of the principle of exogenous preferences in neoclassical economics. I said that preferences are created by the system, and then the system satisfies the preferences; so you couldn't justify the institutions of capitalism solely on the grounds that they satisfy preferences. It explored first how the system works and, second, how one can possibly justify, in a normative sense, the satisfaction of needs if the needs are created endogenously to the system. A lot of it was about preference change and preference analysis. It was very abstract general equilibrium analysis. When Sam Bowles came back from Nigeria we started working together. He was a big shot—a professor who had a grant with labor economist John Dunlop. Sam put me on his grant and said that I should focus on how I could prove my hypothesis.

Talk about the way people change over time! At the time I wrote my dissertation, I just wanted to do theory. Now I am totally the opposite. I still do theory, but mostly I want to see the evidence, and I spend 99 percent of my time gathering evidence and supporting people who want to gather evidence. How can you have decent theories without good evidence?

Clearly, it seems to me now, the Achilles heel of the social sciences is their inability to perform controlled experiments, making it virtually impossible to formulate and test sophisticated theories. But at that time my interest was theory. Sam wanted me to at least *think of* how I would prove my radical theory of endogenous preferences. He also argued that it would be good for me in the job market.

He said, "Why don't you do something about the educational system?" At the time he had been writing extensively on the subject of educational resources. Sam gave me some topics to think about. But I came up with one on my own, which was to show that you could not account for the contribution of education to earnings by looking at the cognitive performance of students, so personality variables must really be what the schools are producing for the capitalist workplace.

This also was a focus of our book *Schooling in Capitalist America*, which we published in 1976. It's docility and the punctuality that really affect wages, we argued. That's why people pay more for educated workers, and not just the cognitive stuff. We argued against people who said skills are unimportant (e.g., Harry Braverman and Ivan Illich), but we said skills are produced in such abundance that their shadow price is virtually zero (no longer true, probably). I analyzed empirical studies of grades and cognitive test scores and wages for my dissertation, which I finished in 1969.

Arthur Smithies was the head of my committee; I chose him because I wanted a guy who wasn't going to interfere with me. Sam Bowles wasn't around when I finished. I don't think Smithies ever read my dissertation, but he gave me a few pep talks.

My dissertation was very fruitful work for me; it came out nicely. And it's still on the mark. Sam and I have a paper in the *Journal of Economic Literature (JEL)*, that was recently published with Melissa Osborne (this is thirty-three years later), substantially vindicating our earlier analysis, and in many cases more strongly than even we believed at the time. The data is much better now. We even have something like a smoking gun on what the personality traits are that affect wages, but we still don't have a lot on how education affects wages. We need a lot more data.

Were you heavily involved with the Review of Radical Political Economy *(RRPE)?*

Definitely. I don't remember a lot about how *RRPE* started, but I was part of it. I was there all the time. There were a huge number of people involved. I used to go to the conferences all the time, and I was on the editorial board. But professors weren't the only ones—it had a broader base. The *RRPE* journal was not "peer reviewed"; any *URPE* (Union of Radical Political Economy) member could run for the board of the *RRPE,* and many did.

Then you moved to the School of Education at Harvard? Did you think of other places?

Since I was a radical, I was precluded from getting jobs in many economics departments. In fact, the head of my department, Richard Caves, sent out an unsolicited letter to the schools I applied to saying that I was a dangerous radical. One of those letters went to a friend of mine who was on the faculty at SUNY-Stonybrook, and he gave me a copy. Once in a very vituperative confrontation with the faculty, when the Harvard Visiting Committee, which included Andrew Brimmer and other big shots, was there, we graduate students complained about the rigidity of the economics department.

At the appropriate point, Zvi Griliches (someone I really liked, who unfortunately died last year) was saying how the department is unbiased. At that moment, Rick Edwards, who was a graduate student then, gets up and says, "How can you say that? I am going to read to you this document that Richard Caves, head of the department, sent unsolicited," and then read the letter about my being a dangerous radical to the Visiting Committee.

So I didn't receive any job offers from economics departments. I did not consider departments outside the top ten. I received offers from education schools like Berkeley. At one point James Duesenberry, who was on my dissertation committee, told me that he thought he could get me a job at one of the SUNY schools. I told him to forget it and, indeed, acted offended. I was a total elitist. There was no way I was going to teach at an un-Harvardlike place.

Harvard makes a list of its so-called good students who are on the job market that year and passes them out to the top ten departments, and I was not on that list. So I didn't get any good job interviews, much less offers, in economics. I'm very pissed about that. They didn't treat me fairly. I was a bit unruly, but a really mature department would have acted differently.

I was very pissed at the Harvard department. I did not like those people. In fact, I did not know that academics could be pleasant until I went to Princeton. I was at the Institute for Advanced Study in 1977, and the Princeton faculty members would invite me to dinner or lunch and say, "Let's talk," and they were very friendly. It hit me like a ton of bricks that not every university was as bigoted as Harvard. I am sure it was because of the Vietnam War. We were occupying buildings, and a lot of them were working for the CIA. That included Arthur Smithies, my adviser, who was doing a crop analysis for the CIA in Vietnam (this was discovered when antiwar protesters "liberated" University Hall).

Did you have any supporters at Harvard? How about Ken Arrow?

Ken Arrow wasn't around a lot, but he's always been a big supporter, then and now. He is one of the most completely wonderful people I have known. When I was on the faculty later, he was at Harvard. I was eventually an assistant professor and an associate professor at Harvard in the economics department. But he was not there then. Albert Hirshman and Kenneth Galbraith were there. It has certainly been a privilege to know these great men. They were supportive, but they are nobodies—zeroes—as far as the Harvard economics faculty was concerned. Galbraith has no power whatsoever. Albert Hirshman and I became very friendly, and my wife became friendly with his wife, but those would be the only two who were supportive. Even Duesenberry never supported me, though he was always friendly and engaging. It was extremely difficult for Harvard faculty members in that period. They lived through the '50s, and they never heard of anybody doing stuff like we were doing. It was totally unheard of. In the 1950s nobody even had a beard, so it was very hard to accept people like me.

How was your experience in the School of Education?
It was great. Sandy Jencks was there, and I worked with him. I'm still friendly with him. He's now at the Kennedy School. David Cohen was also there. They were both very nice, and they gave me a lot of room. They were tolerant of my idiosyncrasies—probably thinking I'd grow out of them. Sandy did a great book on inequality and made me a coauthor. I was the one who tipped him off about path analysis, but I certainly didn't deserve to be a coauthor of *Inequality*.

Did you keep contact with the economics department during this time?
I tried; I still wanted to be an economist. I didn't think of myself as an education person at all.

How did you move back into the Harvard economics department in 1973–74?
The year Sam Bowles came up for tenure, I was appointed assistant professor in the economics department, and that was because there were, by that time, strong pushes by four people—Ken Galbraith, Albert Hirshman, Ken Arrow, and Wassily Leontief. Richard Caves told me the year before that I would be a member of his department "over my dead body" (yes, his very words). But he lost. This Gang of Four argued that Sam was a good economist, and while one may disagree with him, it was ridiculous not to reappoint him for political reasons. I think the department threw Sam's supporters a bone by giving me an appointment. When Sam didn't get tenure, they threw the four of them a bone again, and they promoted me to Associate Professor. The view was that Sam's gone, so we'll promote Herb.

At that point I had a very agonizing choice to make, which is that I could have stayed there for another six or seven or eight years as

Associate Professor of economics until they threw me out, or leave. Meanwhile Sam was working out an alternative, which was to come up to the University of Massachusetts and make a radical department. I was always conflicted by the choice because I really did not want to leave Harvard. I did not like most of the professors (besides the Gang of Four, I thought Duesenberry was wonderful, and I liked Robert Dorfman a lot).

Basically, I saw the department as a pusillanimous bunch. I didn't get along with them, but I really liked being there: it was intellectually great, the students were totally marvelous. I just last week gave a lecture at Harvard in the biology department. The audience was mostly undergraduates, but after about five minutes I forgot they were undergraduates—they were just fellow intellectuals. So I was very conflicted, but I chose the University of Massachusetts.

How did the opportunity to set up a department come about?

The University of Massachusetts used to be an agricultural extension college. In the late 1960s and early 1970s it received a lot of money, and they hired like crazy. The economics department was just this backwater. One day Hugo Sonnenschein, a recent Ph.D., wandered into the office of the dean and said: "I want to set up my own department, and if you allow me to do this, I'll wipe out the dead wood." The dean said okay since that's what they were doing with a lot of departments. So Sonnenschein hired a bunch of hotshots, really good economists, including Vernon Smith, Ron Ehrenberg, Ron Oaxaca, and Jim Cox.

There was one young guy there among the old guard, named Mike Best, who was an SDS person. The students loved Mike and couldn't bear the mathematical types Hugo brought in. Hugo and his crowd tried to get Mike Best fired since they were cleaning out all the old guys. That was a mistake, and the students were up in arms about it. This caused so much trouble for the deans that they got pissed off at Hugo and they took over the department.

They then hired Sam Bowles, me, and some others without consulting the department. So we came into a bad situation. We didn't really know the story until we got here. We tried to keep the good people, but without much luck. Hugo was gone before we got here. We really wanted to keep Vernon Smith and Ron Ehrenberg and their colleagues. They stayed around for a few years after we got there, but then they moved on. The deans were happy. We were the ferrets that had come to clean out the mice in the barn.

They brought in three of you right?

They brought in me and Sam Bowles, Rick Wolff, Steve Resnick, Len Rapping, Jim Crotty, and Rick Edwards, so that's seven. We soon hired a few more, until we were about half the department.

Did you get along with everyone in that group?

Yes. We had two major problems at the beginning. One was that we had a ton of work to do to run the department, and the second was to develop a working relationship with the nonradicals. They didn't appoint us, and they were scared of us because they thought we were a bunch of commies. Eventually, we worked it all out and had a nicely running department for a long time.

How did your research focus change during this period?

Well, Sam and I spent several years trying to shore up Marx's labor theory of value. We called it "Sites and Practices," and we tried to make it work. Alfredo Medio, who made the labor theory of value an analytical device, inspired our work on this topic. But later we realized we faced two problems. One of them was pointed out to us by Geoff Hodgson, who said, "After you make the labor theory of value look pretty and work it out so that it is intellectually credible, you no longer have the labor theory of value, but something quite different. So why call it the labor theory of value?"

The other thing that happened was we seriously, at some point, started studying what non-Marxist economists were doing. We were doing analytical model building, so we started reading the journals. I had done an article called "Capitalism and the Labor Exchange" for *RRPE* in 1976, which basically laid out the view that Marx says that labor is not a commodity and that labor and labor power are different. This was before Stiglitz did his paper on labor and the principal agent model, which was 1984. It said the reason labor is different is that although you buy and sell it on a market, you can't enforce the relationship through a contract—there is no contractual enforcement. The worker comes to work, and you pay him a wage, but there is no quid pro quo. All he gives you is a promise. So this was really a basis for an alternative theory of the firm—the idea that there's a market failure, a nonenforceable contract. We took this ball and ran with it, giving up Marxism.

So we started doing that at the same time that Joe Stiglitz et al. were doing it, but we didn't know that they were doing it also. Sam and I were separated at that time too. I was at Princeton's Institute for Advanced Study and then at Harvard while Sam was at Berkeley for a year. Sam did a paper on this, and I had worked with Tsuneo Ishikawa, who was an economist at Harvard. We wrote some papers on the labor exchange in which we used the basic principal agent model. We got scooped on that because Stiglitz published it first. I still say that if you look back at my article in 1976 on the labor exchange, it said what the problem was quite clearly and laid it out properly.

So once we figured out that we could model the nature of conflict between capital and labor in the work process using a principal agent model and incomplete contracts, we just gave up on the labor theory of value. At one point I remember Sam saying to me that in a year we're not going to be doing the labor theory of value at all, and he was quite right. We totally moved away from that. Then we got into doing capital theory.

Didn't this cause fights between you and other Marxists, where they no longer saw you as a Marxist?

The change in our theoretical tools didn't provoke much hostility, but at the same time Sam and I changed our politics. Our new approach appeared in *Democracy and Capitalism,* in 1986. By 1990 I was irate that the traditional Marxist Left in the USA hadn't seen that their politics had failed, both for the advanced and developing countries. I went on a quixotic mission to convince my old Marxist friends that it was time to rethink their political positions and analysis. This caused lots of fighting, and it was quite fruitless. It took me about two years to realize it was time to stop arguing with Marxists and just move on.

Duncan Foley said that his interest in Marxism wasn't necessary political. What he was interested in was developing a Marxian model of the economy, just like a Walrasian model of general equilibrium theory. Did you take that approach?

I love Duncan. We've always been good friends, but I am very different from him. I never liked general equilibrium theory. I always thought it was really the wrong way to go. The modeling approach to Marxism that Duncan loved is what I call mechanistic Marxism—you take people out of it, and you put in a bunch of equations. He had a book he loved that I hated, by I. I. Rubin. It was Arrow/Debreu for the Marxist. I never bought that view, and today he doesn't either. His statistical mechanics stuff is much more to my liking. Ironically, I have recently fallen in love with general equilibrium theory and am working on some dynamite dynamic general interdependence models, using agent-based computer modeling.

I wouldn't say politics are central to my economics, but the only reason that I do what I do is because I think it's important in the real world. I'm not a shining moral light. I'm just a normal, everyday person; I don't make any claims about my moral or political insights being anything special. But I can assure you that there is not a moment when I do economics, or whatever I do, that I'm not thinking about how this is going to make a better world. That's the only thing that I care about. Even when I read math and physics, all I care about is how it helps us better understand and hence change the world.

One of the reasons I got out of math was that I was surrounded by people who never ever thought about whether things were useful or not. I love to study physics, and I study general relativity for fun, but I can't stand math when it's irrelevant to the sciences. I never had the view that intellectual life is somehow a tool of politics. That's why I could never get along with the Italians like Garegnani. For them, intellect is just a tool for communist revolution or something. It's a Talmudic exercise, and I've never treated it that way. For me, ideas must be true, and truth must be useful.

Things were evolving in Russia and the socialist systems over this time. How did that change or affect the way you approached economics?

I never had any sympathy for Russian-style communism or for centrally planned economies. I had a deep horror of the apparatchik way of life. When I read George Orwell, I totally bought it, so I was never a friend of the Soviet Union. I refused to have my stuff altered for publication there—they said they wanted to publish my articles in Russian but would have to make certain cuts. I said, no way. Maybe they did it anyway, but I did not give my approval. One of the happiest days of my life was when the Berlin Wall came down and when communism was overthrown. These were distinctly happy days for me, and I thought the Soviet Union was the biggest albatross for making social change in the West. The reason was that whenever you tried to do anything, they would say, "Oh you're just a communist." So yes, we liked Euro-communism; that was great because it wasn't communism. We were always very strong on democracy and civil liberties. When Amnesty International came around, we were right there saying that civil rights are the tools of workers and peasants, which people can use to make a better life for themselves, and that's what really counts.

Our book in 1986, *Democracy and Capitalism,* said that the Marxists were right in that history is the history of struggle, but not just class struggle. It's not about the means of production. It's about freedom; it's about having the dignity and freedom to pursue the things you want to pursue in life—collectively and individually. I can't say that we foresaw the overthrow of the Soviet system— nobody foresaw that. What we published in 1986, which was really written in 1984, said that we were totally into the democratic revolutions in Latin America and in the Philippines. We saw democratic revolutions as the wave of the future, and the overthrow of the Soviet system would be part of that. Thank God it was.

Weren't the radicals of the 1960s Marxists? They fought for civil rights.

They were mostly not Marxists at all. Marxists were not in the forefront of the struggle for civil liberties. Marxists hated that stuff. I remember saying liberty and freedom are important, and to Marxists those were fighting words. That's bourgeois crap, they would say. The civil rights struggle, for them, was just a step towards socialist consciousness.

Was that always part of your thinking?

No. I went though a period when I believed that it was bourgeois crap, too. It didn't last very long. I never wrote anything that said anything like that. I tried it out. I tried a lot of things. I wrote an article in 1978 in *Socialist Review,* which was a long defense of what we are doing now, which is that the Marxists have this view of culture, which is the same the liberals have, like in sociology, which is that culture is this seamless web of ideas that fit together functionally to make society run a particular way. So the idea behind liberalism is that you have these ideas of due process with civil rights and individualism and all of these fit together seamlessly to make the ideology of capitalism work. So when you say you believe in liberty or freedom, then you are buying into that whole seamless structure of liberal ideology.

I totally disagreed. At that time I was reading a lot of Wittgenstein, and the article I wrote was very Wittgensteinian. It talked about tools of discourse, and it said culture is not a body of thought at all. It's a set of discourses that people use to communicate and to organize themselves and their tools. When the worker says, "We want our freedom," they are not buying into something. They didn't read John Locke, and they don't know any ideology. All they're saying is that they're using a tool of discourse to get something they want in their struggles. Culture is this web of contradictory intersecting discourses that people use to their own advantage.

The whole Marxist thing that ideology is the ideology of the ruling class is totally wrong because culture is internally contradictory. Sam and I developed these ideas in *Democracy and Capitalism* where there are sites like the patriarchal family, the capitalist economy, and the liberal state. They all have their own discourses, but they interpenetrate, and people transport discourses from one place to another, where they disrupt the system. So the way you overcome patriarchy is by applying the discourse of the state, which is due process and equality before the law. In short, we were very strongly pushing for using the liberal discourses because they can lead to emancipation when applied to the economy and to the family.

Reading Democracy and Capitalism, *you get the impression that was the time you and Sam were breaking away from the Marxists. Was that your statement of breaking away or did you consider yourself to be a Marxist at that time?*

I don't remember. I think at that time we said we weren't Marxists and we weren't liberals. Things just happened very gradually. Where does it get you if you call yourself a Marxist or a non-Marxist? It's just a bunch of words. You don't get anything out of doing it, so I don't think we ever did so. I don't think Sam Bowles has ever said, "I am not a Marxist." Maybe he has—I don't know.

With the development of postmodern Marxism, Sam and I basically stopped doing Marxism. We were now doing principal agent models; we were perfectly happy as clams doing neoclassical economics, or what we called "nongeneral equilibrium neoclassical economics with endogenous enforcement and information." We were the left wing of the Joe Stiglitz camp.

After the fall of the Soviet Union the whole Third World socialist movement totally fell apart. We found that the countries that were doing well were capitalist, like South Korea, Costa Rica, and those in the Pacific Basin. We read all of this and read *Monthly Review,* which was the organ of Third World socialist development. It all failed; it totally failed. Cuba is a disaster; it's a joke. So how can you go on and write the same stuff? How can you have the same politics you did before?

Some people just write the same stuff again. They don't care. They're really interested in the intellectual stuff. Other people, like Rick Wolff and Steve Resnick in my department, go into this postmodernism. I am a serious intellectual enemy of postmodernism in any form. I think it is an abdication of our scientific responsibility to find out how the world works and use it to make it a better world. The postmodernists hate science, and they can't do math. All they know is words. People who want to understand the world have to be able to do both math and words. I may not be the smartest person in the world, but I do both math and words.

I was very upset at the takeoff of postmodernism. All of a sudden the Leninists have become fuzzy-wuzzies. That's when I went off and said: "Okay we have to stop being Marxists because it's not getting us anywhere." It lost, and if you lose, you go home and try something else. What these guys do is that they lose and then they gather their wagons in a circle and they lick their wounds until they die, like the old IWW (International Workers of the World). They get together every year with banners and hats and become totally irrelevant to real politics. They simply make themselves happy. It upsets me that these smart people, who were so dedicated to social change, just opted out and started doing what was fun for them. That's when I said, "Besides not being Marxist, this stuff you are doing doesn't get you anywhere."

Your approach to problems has to fit the times. Consider unions; the Left is in favor of unions as if it's 1920 again. Social change is probably not going to come through unions. The union movement in the U.S. has had its day. Thinking that you are going to bring about social change by supporting the teachers' unions, the AFL, and the Teamsters and other labor aristocracies is way off base. Luckily, I think the new Left in the United States is not like that. Younger people on the Left now have a very different attitude towards politics. Politics is a personal moral statement: we don't like inequality, and we are going to protest it, and we are going to try to be on the side of the poor and the weak. I think that's a fine thing to do.

I can't do that because I still have in me the old Marxist idea that what we are looking for is a systemic change. We're looking for new ways to organize systems, and we want a better world for everybody, and it doesn't come about by just fighting on the side of the weak. You have to have new ideas for reorganizing social institutions. I'm radical in that sense. I still believe that devising alternative institutions is the only thing that is really interesting to do, but I'm conservative in the sense that I realize often that it is hard to do that. Let me put it this way: there are so many things that we know would make a better world for most people that it's easy to be optimistic, even if my goal of institutional alternatives should not pan out.

After you left your Marxist period, and made your peace with the mainstream, you moved to what you once called a post-Walrasian period. What does that mean?

No name has ever caught on. I don't know what to call it. First of all, Sam and I do not consider ourselves heterodox. We don't like the idea of heterodox; we like the idea of homodox, which is if you are a scientist you believe that there is a truth and you should work out what that is and that people who have legitimate disagreements with it should be listened to. You should adjudicate that, and economists shouldn't say more than they know. By the way, most "mainstream" economists consider me a shocking radical. They are wrong, however. I'm just a scientist doing his work.

The hypothesis we have in the introductory chapter of this book is that the profession has become more open since you first entered the profession. When you started, the reality was that if you were outside of a framework that would be called neoclassical, you were heterodox, but now there is much more exploration. Is that consistent with your view?

Yes I think so. Things change. People that were, I wouldn't say enemies, but certainly way far away from us in 1975, are really good friends now. I recently told Joe Stiglitz how much I admire him. I really think he's so exemplary, not just because he's smart but because of what he did in the Clinton administration and what he did at the World Bank. When he won the Nobel Prize, all he talked about to any reporter who asked him questions was that the real problem is world poverty.

When I first met him, Dunlop insisted on the young radicals getting together with the real smart guys who were not the radicals, and Stiglitz was one of them. So we got together for lunch at the Harvard Faculty Club. It was a little strained at first, but we had a nice talk, and I finally said to Stiglitz, "Listen Joe, do you really believe that the interest rate is the intersection of the supply and demand for capital?" I said exactly that, and he said, "Yes, I believe that." So twenty years later I said to him, "Listen Joe, you really threw me a curve ball when you told me you believed this." I thought if this is what the smartest people in the profession believe,

I'm not going to even talk to them; meanwhile he totally revolution-izes capital theory along the lines that supply and demand don't determine interest rates! Either his views changed, or he was being "in your face" to me.

I would say the same thing about George Akerlof, who is a much calmer person than Joe. We weren't really friends when we were younger, but now we are really quite close. George is in my research group, and I think the world of him. Sam and I have gotten closer to the profession, and the profession has gotten closer to us. They totally accept the work we do. But there's still a lot of tension when we complain that the profession isn't moving fast enough in what it teaches undergraduates and graduate students.

When the MacArthur grant I have with Rob Boyd, an anthropol-ogist, came up for renewal, they sent our proposal to three econo-mists and one noneconomist to evaluate whether it should be renewed. All the reviews were unbelievably superlative. This was a dream—reviewers are always SOBs. They said that the work that we did, and the work that we were going to do, was totally outstanding work. However, they were angry at the tone that I took in writing the proposal. Three of the four were angry because I said economics believes in rational actor models, which they vehemently denied. One called my description of the economics profession "snake oil salesman" tactics. They said that the economics profession is totally open to new ideas. MacArthur didn't ask me to rewrite the pro-posal. In fact, most noneconomists agree with my position, which is not that economists are closed minded—they emphatically are not. But they consistently choose textbooks that teach material that they know is false and/or completely out-of-date.

That's one of the reasons we are doing this book, because we don't think people have the right view of where economics currently is.
You can't write all economists off as ideologues because they're not. They're open to new ideas. However, there's still this incredible tension in what we teach. I am so displeased at the way undergradu-ate and even graduate economics is taught. Undergraduate econom-ics is a joke—macro is okay, but micro is a joke because they teach this stuff that you know is not true. They know the general equilib-rium model is not true. The model has no good stability properties, it doesn't predict anything interesting, but they teach it. The pro-duction theory that is taught is also a joke. They use this old Mar-shallian production with long-run average cost curves and the like

to determine firm size. This doesn't determine firm size; it determines plant size. Totally different things determine firm size. So why do we teach undergraduates this? Why do you teach income and substitution effects and Giffen goods when there are so many interesting things to discuss? So I am so upset by what they teach. I am retiring from U. Mass. this year (Sam is, too), so I won't have to deal with this anomaly any more.

If this were physics or astronomy, when they get new ideas at the forefront, they immediately teach them, but in economics they teach the stuff that even thirty years ago people didn't believe. My view is that economists should not be so tolerant of teaching out-of-date ideas. Micro is a total disaster. So I think there's still a tension and that there will be one for a long time. I guess sometimes people treat Sam, me, and all these people who do behavioral work like they treat the dentist: it hurts but you should go do it.

Is the reconciliation with people you shared tension with twenty years ago because you changed or they changed or some combination? What has allowed you to feel more comfortable with these people?

If you dispassionately and seriously study the world, you should come to similar conclusions about how the world works, whatever your values or political commitments. So when Joe Stiglitz looks at the world over a period of years, he comes to see it more the way it is. And when we look at it more and more, we come to see the way it is. So it is not surprising that we have come together.

What's surprising is in the social sciences it appears to be acceptable for different disciplines and different branches of disciplines to have totally different ideas and not be bothered by it. Sociology has one way of teaching the theory of the firm, and economics has another, and psychology has another. They all have different theories about the individual, and they seem perfectly happy with that. Well that's totally scandalous, absolutely unacceptable.

Why would a sociology department teach things with a very different model of the human actor from an economics department? That's crazy. Of course, everybody has their own expertise—if you are an anthropologist, you know a lot more about the organization of simple societies than if you're an economist—but if we study the same thing, we should have the same theory. If we disagree, we should look at the evidence and let that decide. I think a lot more social scientists are doing that today. They're not so much ideological today: people are much more driven by the facts; they are more

HERBERT GINTIS

humble about the strength of their theories. So there's a lot more ways for us to agree about stuff.

You might be seeing that change within the top twenty schools, but there's really a major demarcation between that and lower-level schools, isn't there?

Absolutely. I think if you are real smart, you can get away with being deviant. If you get a job at Princeton or Stanford, you can be a deviant because you have a good job and you're smart. If you're at a second-rate school, you can't be a deviant. They'll kick you out. No one listens to you because you are not at Stanford, and you're probably not as smart as the guy at Stanford anyway.

But it is also true that the way they teach economics at all the schools is pretty bad. There was no behavioral economist in an economics department before David Laibson got his job at Harvard, and now Sendhil Mullainathan at MIT. So now maybe it's okay. And they hired Al Roth to teach game theory, who is a great experimenter and who started out being the least behavioral game theorist you can imagine but now is doing behavioral experiments himself.

Outside of a few places, people are afraid to do dissertations on behavioral or evolutionary topics because they are concerned where are they going to get hired. They go and give a talk somewhere, and people never heard of this stuff. I think only now experimental economics has cracked through. The great experimenter Vernon Smith and the stellar psychologist Daniel Kahneman (a member of my research group) won the Noble Prize recently. Who would have expected that ten years ago?

You are our representative for experimental economics in our set of interviews. Can you discuss where you see experimental economics fitting in?

My research concern, starting from my dissertation, has been to figure out a decent model of the human actor—how people make decisions and how they strategically interact. What we had up until recently, with the experimental economics of Vernon Smith et al. at Arizona (now at George Mason), was just a bunch of statements without any empirical evidence. The reason we tend to lack evidence is that we can't do controlled experiments on humans. You can't set up a world and run it one way and then set up another one and run it a different way. You might be able to do that with monkeys, but you can't do that with humans. Experimental economics is to allow us to see how human beings behave in controlled environments, in ways that are scientifically replicable.

Game theory gives you the intellectual apparatus for describing a controlled environment for strategic interactions. You have who the players are, what the strategic choices open to them are, what the information symmetries and asymmetries are, and what some of the payoffs will be, especially the material payoffs.

One of the things we've found in experimental economics is that there is not a lot of disagreement about what the experimental findings are. In other words, if someone does an experiment in one place and someone else does it in another place, they find the same thing. So these experiments can be replicated. Also, there's a possibility of changing the parameters to get better variance. This allows us to model human behavior. So we can change the payoffs; we can change the information; we can add stages to games. It's a very flexible tool for finding out how humans behave.

The implications are that sometimes they appear to behave exactly the way theory tells you. For example, in a market-type setting, they almost always fit neoclassical theory. Indeed, with demand and supply, humans behave even more efficiently than the theory tells you. But whenever you have real strategic interaction, so people can affect one another's behavior by their strategic choices, we find people are much more complex than standard economic theory predicts. They don't conform to the standard paradigms.

I should say that the weakness of experimental economics is that we have to be able to correlate what people do in experiments with what they do in daily life. If someone behaves altruistically in an experiment, does that mean they behave altruistically in daily life? We don't know; we haven't studied it, and that's what we are beginning to study now. If people are very sharing in a public goods game, do they vote for income redistribution at the ballot box? How about survey materials? When people say that they are very tolerant of other ethnic and racial groups, that doesn't translate into their trusting them when they play a trust game. We have evidence of that. So there are all sorts of things that we don't know. But as far as I'm concerned, the way we are going is the way we should go.

A very long time ago, Steve Marglin said something in a talk that I never forgot. He said that first of all we should be humble in the social sciences because we don't know a lot. He said a lot of the reason we have these divergent theories is simply that we don't have the evidence to say any of the things either side is saying. So of course we will disagree because there's no evidence that it's either right or wrong. That really hit me.

In my recent game theory book, *Game Theory Evolving*, the first quote is from Wittgenstein, and it says, translated into English, "that which you do not know, you should shut up about." People are willing to talk about all sorts of stuff that they know little or nothing about. So I think experimental economics is giving us almost a Hubble telescope into human behavior. It's a way of studying something that's never been studied before.

Now we're also trying to mend our fences with social psychology because social psychologists get very upset with economists' recent entry into experiments. They've been doing this stuff for years, but we say that there's a big difference. The only way to move forward, as far as we know now, is to have a model where you think of agents optimizing subject to constraints, which is what game theory does. You then vary the constraints to see what it is they optimize. That's not what they do in social psychology. They have hydraulic models or identity models, and they never vary the payoffs. They don't even use payoffs usually—it's all implicit in their models. So we say to them that you've got to get your act together; there are a lot of interesting things that should be redone.

For instance, we have a whole project on so-called insider/outsider behavior, which is the study of how human beings tend to make arbitrary distinctions of who are the good guys and bad guys. Then they are partially altruistic in that they will sacrifice on the part of whom they consider the good guys and hate the bad guys. The social psychologists figured this out in the '60s. They did some wonderful experiments that are quite suggestive, but again we're doing it now where you have real monetary payoffs. We think this will be as important as the reciprocity work that we've been working on.

The point I'm trying to make is that what we need is data. We need data in order to adjudicate among theories. All the talk in the world, and all the theorizing in the world, is not going to substitute for having good data to build good theories on. Social scientists have to recognize that they're scientists. Whatever your politics are, and I have very strong political ideas and very deep commitments, they shouldn't affect your work. Politics don't affect the work I do, except to the degree that I work on some things as opposed to others. I never talk about my politics with the people I do research with. I don't care, and they don't care, and we get along just fine.

People who are making love don't talk about politics while they are making love; people who play tennis don't talk about politics when they are playing tennis. We don't have to talk about our politics when we do economics. The people who do aren't playing by the rules, and they probably don't know how to play by the rules. They're probably cheating because they can't play by the rules. If you can't make your argument on the basis of evidence, and you say, well, politically this and that, you are not playing by the rules. That's why I think experimental economics is so important.

So will game theory catch on this time, though it has tried a few times before to become the organizing framework, because it is associated with experimental economics?

Game theory is so central to everything in the behavioral sciences that without it experimental work would be of little use. The auctioning off of the airwaves by the FCC was more important than experiments for game theory. The fact that game theory is used in biology is also very important. The fact is, game theory is not something that is unique to economics; the way it developed in biology is as interesting as the way it developed in economics—and very different because it wasn't associated with economists' notion of rationality. You don't think of pond scum as rational or irrational.

Do you believe now that your work has been drawing from game theory and experimental economics even though you weren't aware of it?

No. I studied game theory with Raiffa, and loved it; his book with Luce was great. I still remember some intellectual experiences I had. I remember being in class with him, and he would say something that blew my mind. But I gave up on game theory. It didn't appear to be going anywhere. If you look at Luce and Raiffa now, it doesn't move you. The reason why is that it's mostly cooperative, not noncooperative, game theory. The real people who brought game theory back were the Gang of Four: Kreps, Wilson, Milgrom et al., and other people of the Stiglitz generation, my generation.

Sam Bowles and I came to game theory from Marxism. We started talking about sites and practices. Well, that's the rules of the game and the strategies people use. In our 1986 book, *Democracy and Capitalism,* we never attached it to game theory. One day we got the idea that somehow this is game theory. I started reading all about game theory, and I started teaching game theory; no one had ever taught game theory in the Pioneer Valley. So I developed the first undergraduate game theory course in the Connecticut River valley; it may still be the only one. So we came from Marxism.

We never liked classical game theory; we never thought the economy reduced to being self-interested. One of the first things we read was the biologist Maynard Smith's book *Evolution and the Theory of Games,* which of course is a totally evolutionary book. So I had no problem thinking evolutionarily about game theory right from the beginning. It allowed me to integrate cultural and genetic evolution into my models. So we came to it from a very different place than most people did.

When I was doing my early work, I had never heard of experimental economics. I found out about it in 1992 when I was reading *Scientific American.* I'm a total scientist. I read *Scientific American* and *Nature, Nature Genetics, Science, Trends in Evolution,* and other science journals and magazines. I get important ideas from them. It was there I read an article by Vernon Smith on experiments. Now we had thought we knew what experiments were—you had pigeons operating on supply and demand, and you prove Adam Smith was right. Vernon did this article in which he said just the opposite. He said that if you do auctions, and you change the rules for the auctions, you get very different results. I was totally blown away. So that's when we decided that it was important to do experiments.

We had a friend, a younger Austrian colleague, Ernst Fehr, who was kind of a disciple of Sam and mine. He started doing stuff on fairness. I remember seeing him and asking what he was doing these days. He said he was working on fairness. I thought it was just brilliant. What he has done with experiments has really affected us very seriously. Ernst is on the forefront; he's the leader. Similarly, when I got to work with Rob Boyd, the anthropologist, when I read his 1985 book *Culture and the Evolutionary Process* with Pete Richerson, I was delighted. The evolutionary game theory approach they use is a wonderful way to think about culture scientifically. It fits with a lot of other stuff. What we are doing now is bringing all of these things together into one unified behavioral framework. But thinking about how it comes together, it's important to recognize that we're learning a lot from younger people.

We also interviewed Ken Binmore, Matt Rabin, and Bob Frank. How would you differentiate yourself from them or see similarities with each of them?

Well, Binmore shares our stress on evolutionary game theory and on evolution itself—the belief that humans have evolved as a species. If you look at his magnum opus, you see this idea as being pervasive. What the original position was for Rawls or Hobbes, or the state of nature for Rousseau, he takes as a historically understandable fact about the nature of human environment. It is a summary of the social and environmental situation that humans were in for their whole species of evolution up until ten thousand years ago. So we agree totally with that. However, he's been one of the few people to really hold out for the self-interested actor model, where everybody else has said no. He almost has to take this position because he uses it so centrally in his books. In my view there is almost no evidence that his position is correct; he shores it up in really weird ways.

Bob Frank did some of this stuff before anyone else. I used his book *Passions within Reasons* in my undergraduate classes before I even knew anything about this stuff. I think he's very important. I find him to be a bit dilettantish; that is, he does something, and then he moves on and does something else. He doesn't stick to one thing long enough for it to make an impression on the field. The way you make an impression is to do the same thing over and over for six or seven years until you get it right. That's what Ernst does, and that's what Danny Kahneman did with his stuff on loss aversion and prospect theory. You just do it over and over, taking care of every objection, and going back and doing it again because you are never right the first time. Bob Frank doesn't seem to follow that approach; he writes this great book but then moves on and does stuff about inequality and big ponds and little ponds. Matt Rabin is a friend and a member of our research group. It is a privilege to know and work with him.

Could you see the two approaches as working together: one sows the seeds for people to go in, and others do the tilling?

Sure, absolutely. Matt Rabin is one of us. He doesn't like evolutionary models. He keeps away from that completely, but he's a real innovator on a lot of this stuff. He thought about justice and fairness early on; he takes psychology as being important, and he's brilliant.

What do you see as really going on over the next twenty years in terms of the profession? If we revisit you in twenty years, what do you think you'd say?

I would not venture to answer that, but I can tell you what I'd *like* to see happen. I'd like to see a better integration of the behavioral sciences from biology to psychology to economics, politics, and anthropology. I'd like to see all the behavioral sciences integrated in an intellectually satisfying way, instead of being fragmented, hostile, antagonists. It's very hard; there's a lot more to do, but I think that's really where we are going to figure out more about humans and how they work.

What do you see as the most important changes in the economics profession in the last twenty years?

The big thing is the abandoning of the neoclassical general equilibrium model as the basic way you think about the economy. Economists tend to use it as a crutch because it's a big whole grand theory, and it gives them peace of mind not to reject it. But nobody does it, so they use it for ideological reasons. People are fond of saying, "Let the market decide." Well, yeah, if you have a good theory; if there's unique solutions or stable solutions, you can do that. But there aren't.

So I think the big thing is doing more strategic interaction studies of particular institutional settings with labor markets, capital markets, consumer goods markets. In theory we are replacing the general equilibrium model with some notion that what happens is a game theoretic model. You have Nash equilibria that aren't necessarily market clearing or don't have the optimality properties of Walrasian general equilibrium. What's really hard for people to accept is a theoretical construct from another field. They can accept empirical results from another field, but not theoretical results. Game theory is fine because that's economics, but not other theoretical ideas.

One battle that Sam and I lost that I don't think we should have lost is our interpretation of the weakness of neoclassical general equilibrium theory and our sketch of an alternative, which we actually published a couple of times, once in the *Journal of Economic Perspectives* and once in the *Quarterly Journal of Economics*. Sam is now working on a book (Princeton, 2004) that argues that the major markets in a capitalist economy are not quid pro quo markets; they're markets with money on one side and something on the other side that cannot be guaranteed but can be cautiously enforced by a contract. So we have labor markets: we have the wage and then labor, whatever that is.

We also have capital markets. A guy lends you money, and you give him a promise to repay it. But that promise is not enforceable in a court of law unless you already have collateral. In consumer goods markets, I give you money, and you give me a product. Why is it a good product? Our work provides a general approach to answering these questions. There is a quid pro quo on one side, but the other side requires money.

You have to have money be on the short side of the market. Money is power, and the people on the short side of the market have power. In labor markets the boss has the power over the worker. In consumer markets the consumer has the power over the producer in the sense that consumer sovereignty means that the producer is always running around trying to satisfy your needs. In capital markets the lender has power over the borrower because they are all on the short side of the market. These markets do not clear; price is higher than marginal costs. If they weren't, the firm wouldn't want to sell you more stuff. But we really haven't developed an acceptable model that incorporates all these issues.

In my view a very real problem is that these issues involve *power*, and talking about power is not something economists like to do. Game theory allows us to integrate power into the model. When you say the person on the short side has power, it's something very simple. If you're on the short side of a market, you have many options because you have the possibility of choosing them versus choosing somebody else. So you can hurt and help. In a clearing market you can't hurt or help anybody.

So we have what I think is a really nice theory here, but economists don't buy it. I'm sure it's our fault, but I tend to say that it's not our fault; it's really that economists don't like the idea of power. They're so wedded to market clearing that if you say that in equilibrium markets don't clear, you're sounding like John Maynard Keynes or something.

I think basically people don't like to take paradigmatic structures and constructs from other parts of the discipline. My comparative strength is to recognize the core controlling ideas in a discipline and recognize their validity and the importance of including them in any final theory of how society works. So, for instance, for most of my life I hated the sociologists' approach that people are socialized to behave in certain ways because that goes counter to the idea that people make strategic choices, that they evaluate and can change their beliefs. But there is something right about socialization theory, which is the whole idea that human beings have this capacity to *internalize norms,* meaning that certain types of behavior become not constraints on actions but become goals of action. We internalize them unless we are sociopaths. An example is empathy towards others—the desire not to hurt others who don't warrant it. That's something we really learn and we really internalize it. Many of us would rather die than violate that norm by hurting someone egregiously. But it's not present in economics, and it's not present in biology. I just wrote an article for the *Journal of Theoretical Biology* which uses the concept of the internalization of norms, and it's probably the first time that anything like that has happened. It's still hard because biologists really hate sociological theory. My point is that people tend not to understand the core ideas of another discipline, and that's sad because we have to bring them all together.

How did you become involved with the Santa Fe Institute? What's your view of its evolution?
Sam and I became involved with the institute through some friends: Larry Blume and Steve Durlauf and Ken Arrow, who is a mentor-friend. Ken Arrow was involved with the Santa Fe Institute from its beginning. He is one of my heroes because he's a guy who does something and then moves on. He's moved on from general equilibrium to complexity. Larry and Steve ran the economics program quite successfully for a number of years, and they got us involved in the Santa Fe Institute. We went there a lot.

What would you say is the approach to economics at Santa Fe?
There's no one approach. They started out doing econophysics but have since branched out. Brian Arthur emphasized path dependency. Steve Durlauf did statistical mechanics. Larry Blume is more of a traditional economist, but he has worked creatively to expand the range over which you do your theorizing. When their tenure came to an end, Ken Arrow asked Sam and John Geanankopolos to be the new economics program directors, and they trade off. John is one of the few creative neoclassical general equilibrium people around. His approach is fundamentally different from Sam's and mine.
What Sam has brought to the Santa Fe Institute is more of a

notion of the behavioral science rather than physics or pure economics, and they have been very supportive. Sam is just an amazing person—an amazing organizer. He's indefatigable. I run a really large research project, but he runs a big research project like mine plus he does the Santa Fe Institute and more.

At first, many years ago, I was hostile to the hype surrounding the Santa Fe Institute, with their talk of "complex nonlinear dynamics," "genetic algorithms," and the "edge of chaos." I said, "Give me a break—isn't that just differential equations?" But then I realized that's exactly what I do, complex nonlinear dynamics. I have all the problems everyone else has. I do not do chaos, and I have not found that useful for what I do, but I use Mathematica, and I program agent-based models all the time because you can't solve these complex nonlinear dynamic things just using closed form analytical expressions. It's not just economics: there's good stuff going on in chemistry, in computer science, in biology. We get along very well with people at the institute. I think it's a great place.

You received a copy of our introduction about cutting edge economics. What was your reaction to it?

I have three comments. The first is that I don't feel cutting edge. Whenever there's new research, that's cutting edge. What else is new? Maybe it sells to call something cutting edge, but I get very offended when people say this is cutting edge, especially when they say it about something that I disagree with. New research that overturns some of the old stuff is true in any field that is in flux. Second, I liked that it stressed that economics has moved from being an ideological closed field to being much more open to links in and out of other fields. I think that's a real step forward. Third, I don't like to be thought of as heterodox. I know other people think of me that way, but that's just my personality. It's not really true at all. I do take strong stands as a way to shake things up, but I'm just a traditional scientist.

One final question. We had to choose a limited number of people to interview. Do you think we have all the fields represented?

The only thing I could add are young economists who collect a lot of data, and that would be people like Sendhil Mullainathan, Steve Levitt, Michael Kremer, and Abhijit Banerjee. These people are young, they are very smart, and they do lots of theory. Levitt did work explaining declining crime associated with abortion. A lot of people think that he's fascist, but he's just doing his work. Michael Kremer went into Africa, collected data to answer questions, or he does experiments where they just lay money on people and see whether they build schools or not. Banerjee collected data on small-scale farming in parts of India where they passed laws favoring it. You just can't work from the big data sets that come from the federal government. You have to go out there and collect data. I believe that the NSF should pay people to go and collect data. Collecting data is something no one did in my generation, but the new guys are saying, "Okay—we've got to collect the data, so let's go and collect the data."

Herbert Gintis

External faculty, Santa Fe Institute
Emeritus Professor, University of Massachusetts

INFORMATION ON THE WEB ABOUT HERBERT GINTIS
http://www-unix.oit.umass.edu/~gintis/

EDUCATION
B.A. Mathematics, University of Pennsylvania, 1961
M.A. Mathematics, Harvard University, 1962
Ph.D. Economics, Harvard University, 1969

SELECTED PUBLICATIONS
Schooling in Capitalist America: Educational Reform and the Contradictions of Economic Life, with Samuel Bowles. New York: Basic Books, 1976.
Democracy and Capitalism: Property, Community, and the Contradictions of Modern Social Thought, with Samuel Bowles. New York: Basic Books, 1986.
Game Theory Evolving. Princeton: Princeton University Press, 2000.
Moral Sentiments and Material Interests: On the Foundations of Cooperation in Economic Life, with Samuel Bowles, Robert Boyd, and Ernst Fehr. Cambridge: MIT Press, 2004.

SPECIAL HONORS AND EXPERIENCE
Also taught at Harvard University, University of Paris, New York University, Columbia University, and the University of Siena
Professor of Economics, University of Massachusetts, 1976–2002
Visiting Scholar, Institute for Advanced Study, Princeton, New Jersey, 1977–78
Museum of Education's *Books of the Century* award for *Schooling in Capitalist America*, 2000
Cochair of the MacArthur Foundation Network on the Nature and Evolution of Norms and Preferences
Currently Emeritus Professor of Economics at the University of Massachussetts and External Faculty, Santa Fe Institute, Santa Fe

CHAPTER 4

Robert H. Frank

Henrietta Johnson Louis Professor of Management and Economics,
Johnson Graduate School of Management, Cornell University

∾

The interview was conducted at the home of Robert H. Frank in
Ithaca, New York, on March 14, 2002.

How did you get interested in economics?

As a student at Georgia Tech I majored in mathematics. They
didn't have an economics major, but they did have some elective
courses in economics. I took two of those, introductory micro and
macro, and I liked them both. Then in my senior year, they were
shorthanded in the math department. I and one other student were
given an opportunity to teach a freshman math course. We each
had a class to ourselves. I was responsible for picking the book, for
making up my lecture notes, making up the tests, doing the whole
thing, and I absolutely loved it. So I thought, "Wow, here is a career
I hadn't considered before." I thought being a teacher would be just
fabulous. It seemed like such fun. So the issue for me then was to be
a teacher of what. I didn't really think I wanted to be a mathematician. I was doing fine in math, but I didn't see it as an area I wanted
to pursue a career in.

∾

After graduating in 1966, I joined the Peace Corps for two years for a variety of reasons, partly because I didn't know what else to do. Those were the waning years of graduate deferments; you could still receive a graduate deferment, but I didn't know what I wanted to do in graduate school. So going into the Peace Corps made sense. It gave me the practical advantage of allowing me to gather my thoughts about what I wanted to do next in my life, without worrying about the draft. So for two years I taught math and science in rural Nepal. When I was there, I got interested in economic development, which probably 95 percent of the volunteers did once they got overseas. I thought studying economic development might be what I wanted to do. I read a bunch of economics books, took the GRE, and applied to a number of graduate programs in economics. Berkeley gave me the best fellowship, so I went there. I went to Berkeley with the expectation of being a development economist, but they didn't have much to offer in development. I also considered Wisconsin and Michigan for graduate work, and I was turned down at Harvard and Stanford.

You have received your M.A. in statistics from Berkeley. Is that standard?

It wasn't standard, but it wasn't that hard to do either. Berkeley probably had the best statistics department in the world. They would give you credit for your econometrics courses, and if you took the background probability courses, all you needed was three more courses, and you got a master's degree. It was an extra credential for not much cost, and that's why I did it. When I think back, it probably was a pivotal decision, by accident, because I don't think I would have been on the Cornell recruiting list except for that. I came close to not getting the Cornell job, and as far as I know, it's the best job by a good margin that I would have gotten at that time. I remember having an interview scheduled at Wisconsin, but Cornell called and said I had a week to decide whether to accept their job offer. The Wisconsin interview was two weeks later, so I accepted the job at Cornell. I have no way of knowing if I would have gotten the job at Wisconsin. The only other job offer I received was at a small school in the Midwest. I went there to give a talk a couple of years ago and was thinking how differently things would have unfolded if I had taken that job.

So you initially went into economics because of an interest in economic development, and you go to Berkeley and it wasn't there. How did you decide what areas to study?

You needed two fields at that time. Econometrics seemed like an obvious one. I had a math background and was going to do the probability sequence anyway, so I did econometrics as one field. And macroeconomics was my other field.

What was your dissertation on, and were you happy with it?

It looked at the effect on private labor supply of public service employment programs. I wouldn't urge somebody to read it, no. I never published anything out of it. But it was a good experience. I wasn't sure what I was doing back then or the direction I was going. I didn't see a lot of people on the Berkeley faculty whom I could point to and say, "That's where I want to be twenty years from now." I thought about dropping out of the program in my third year and maybe even in the early part of my fourth year. I was making loudspeakers and selling them and sort of liked doing that and thinking maybe I would pursue something else.

How was Berkeley at that time—did you like the department? Did you think it was a good department for you?

It was a good department for me; it was the luck of the draw. I received a Ford Special Career Fellowship. It essentially gave me a free ride for four years, which meant that I didn't have to take out student loans. They wanted you to be a TA for two terms during the four years. So I got to be a TA for graduate micro, which was a good learning experience. If you did well in the graduate micro course in the first term—it was a two-term course—it pigeonholed you as someone they wanted to treat well. And I did well and received good support all the way through.

Were there professors you liked at Berkeley?

I could tell George Akerlof was a really interesting guy; I liked him a lot. Tom Rothenburg, the econometrician, was a good mentor for several graduate students, including me. I liked Dan McFadden a lot too. I was also impressed with Bob Hall, but he didn't stay very long; he was only there the first year or two when I was there.

You came to Cornell, and your publications at that time seem fairly traditional—family location constraints and geographic distribution of female professionals. Would it be fair to describe your early writings as traditional?

In some sense they were certainly more traditional than what I am doing now. But the writing I was doing then is similar to what I'm doing now in that it's based on my own observations and attempts to resolve puzzles I see in the world. It wasn't an attempt to extend some issue in the literature so much as something that I saw in the world and puzzled over. An exception would be my "Spell of Unemployment" paper (1978), which was a technical extension of something Steve Salant wrote.

So what holds all your work together is the observational phenomenon of trying to explain what one sees or observes?

Yes. If I do have a trait that's different from more traditional economists, it is that I'm more disquieted when I see something that I think should be one way and it's a different way. I feel more troubled by that than many other people seem to be.

Would you say this is very similar to the approach that Thaler takes?

He's also observation and example driven. So we certainly have that in common. Yes, it certainly sounds similar; I never asked him how he would describe himself on that dimension. But it's certainly consistent if you look at what he has done.

You mentioned one of your fields was macroeconomics, but you are known for your microeconomics.

I taught graduate macro for a few years when I first arrived at Cornell, but I am loath to let anyone know that at this point.

Your work in behavioral economics: is this something that gradually happened, or was there something that just hit you that opened your eyes?

To the extent that the work I do is observation based, that's been a common theme from the beginning. The stuff I do that would probably be considered less traditional began after I came back from Washington, D.C. I was the chief economist at the Civil Aeronautics Board from 1978 to 1980.

How did that come about?

I think of my career as a sequence of unplanned accidents. I went down there in the summer of 1978. My first wife and I had separated in 1975, and she had a city-planning degree and couldn't really find a way to use it in Ithaca. We were committed to being in the same town with our kids. But she took a job in Washington, and our two sons stayed with me in Ithaca for two years. This arrangement proved difficult for both of us, so I started looking for some way to be in Washington. The department had a connection there at the Civil Aeronautics Board because of Fred Kahn, who was then the board's chairman. He also had been our dean in the Arts College when I first came to Cornell. Kahn is a man I admire enormously, somebody whose work I thought was interesting, and it seemed like it would be good to do work similar to what he was doing. I had just gotten tenure, and my first year in Washington was my sabbatical leave, and then I took a year's extension. I thought I wasn't going to be able to go back to Cornell because my first wife and I were both committed to being in the same town with our kids and I didn't think there would be any way to work it out at Cornell. And then, right in the middle of my second year, she got a really good job in Ithaca. The man she had been seeing bought the house right next door to mine, thinking we weren't coming back there. So she moved back, took the boys back to Ithaca, and I followed a few months later, and so we lived right next door to each other for three years. And then they got a house about a block from there, and then we bought a house a block and a half the other way. Throughout that whole time the boys could just walk back and forth between the two houses without any big planning or disruption. So that was our main goal, to preserve that type of arrangement.

At the Civil Aeronautics Board did you do any work that you feel was important, and did you learn something about the nature of work in Washington?

I learned from that experience that I didn't want to be an administrator. I didn't enjoy doing that. There was just so much stuff to read and do and little fires to fight; I didn't like doing that. I liked being a policy adviser. I liked writing memos. I wrote a long memo to the board predicting that we would see over time a huge shakeout and at the end there would be only a handful of airline carriers. At that time everybody's model of the industry was that it was a con-

ROBERT H. FRANK

111

stant-cost industry and that you could launch a start up and compete successfully.

When did the big change happen?

I got there in August of 1978, and the deregulation bill was passed in October, and that set a five-year timetable for a transition from full regulation to no regulation. So we were in that transition during the time I was there.

At the time you were in Washington, D.C., was this the time where you started getting more interested in policy issues, micro issues, more unorthodox views?

At the time I was at the CAB, the prevailing view behind the deregulation movement was that the airline industry was an atomistically competitive industry—that it was a perfect free-entry market. You can start with just one plane, and so on. And they had cost studies showing that the average costs of large and small carriers didn't seem all that different. I wrote a long memo to the board saying that these cost studies were misleading; in an environment in flux you'll see small firms with an advantage because they can adapt quickly. So Southwest was doing very well then, and PSA—those were sort of the poster cases for small is effective. But I said that at some point the environment is going to stabilize and then there will be enormous scale advantages once the formula is worked out and you don't have to be nimble and able to shift on a dime. Maintenance, crew scheduling, use of counter space—all these lumpy things you need to work out—reservation systems, and the preference of passengers to be on the same airline when making a connection—all that and more you can do so much better with one carrier than with many. So I felt good about being out front of where the industry was going. At that time, they were all worried about the fare differentials, the huge supersaver discounts, because they didn't think they were cost justified. And I did a memo that I later published as a paper, arguing that there were very substantial economies of scale at the individual flight level: the bigger the plane is, the lower the cost per seat. So the discounts were really just a simple Ramsey pricing device, and they were absolutely consistent with healthy competition and not a symptom of monopoly, and we shouldn't be doing anything about them.

When you were in the Peace Corps, did that have an impact on your values and the way you look at how to do economics?

The Peace Corps was a transforming experience. We had a really good language program in the Peace Corps. I took Spanish in high school for four years, and then I took a year of German in college, but I couldn't really speak either of those languages proficiently. The Peace Corps language training was totally different. They didn't do any grammar: they'd give you a simple sentence, and you would repeat it back, and they would vary it and ask you questions, and you would just talk and build on what you'd been doing for six hours a day, and at the end of thirteen weeks we could talk. I got to Nepal, and a few weeks later I was teaching math and science in Nepali. So the whole idea of trying to give people a complicated theoretical framework as a way of teaching something dawned on me as being totally absurd, and that had a lasting impact on me. I didn't recognize it then, not explicitly. I've only written about this recently. I think in my teaching I've always tried to have a stripped-down, simple approach with a lot of repetition, and that's what I think that language program gave me. I don't do anything complicated; I certainly don't do anything complicated at first and make sure people are drilled and facile with the easy stuff before I move on. The easy material is the most important because once you master it you can make progress on your own.

The other way the Peace Corps experience had a profound effect on me is having lived the idea that context matters for your assessment on how well you are doing. The house I lived in there would be rated as totally unacceptable in any town in the United States. It had a thatched roof that leaked when it rained hard. There was no electricity or plumbing, none of the basics that even the poorest family would take for granted here. If you lived in a house like that here, you'd just be embarrassed about it; you wouldn't be normal if you didn't feel embarrassed about it. There was never any sense of being embarrassed about it over there; it was a perfectly good house in that context. To experience something like that firsthand affects you in a way that's different from just hearing about it.

Did that affect your interest in distribution issues?

Not right away. If you are isolated enough, things don't seem that bad. I now know that things were bad in some ways that cried out for something to be done. You didn't see babies dying often, but if you had five kids, you'd lose a couple of them, and that's horrible. I've never lost a child, but I can't imagine anything more horrible than that. But that wasn't part of my salient experience there; it was sort of a pleasant village life, and there weren't a lot of tensions. People seemed to be in contact with lots of people. I think I came away with the idea that being poor is less important than in fact it might be.

The issue of community and the importance of its values then?

Yes, although I don't think I ever thought about it in those terms. Where I think I got into the positional stuff was in Washington when I was remodeling a townhouse I bought. About eight months after I got there, I bought a townhouse that had a unit upstairs and one downstairs. We first gutted the top unit. I hired people on my own, and these guys would come and stack up sheetrock joint compound buckets as their scaffolding and then put a two-by-ten across and climb up on that, and once in a while it would collapse, and they'd end up on the floor. I asked why they didn't get scaffolding, and their answer was that it took too much time to set it up and it was expensive. They couldn't afford the ten or fifteen minutes in the morning to set it up or the actual purchase price of it. And these same guys would come to work in brand-new vans everyday—not two-year-old vans but new ones with stereos, bars, carpets. Very lavish vehicles. And they took a great interest in them; they were very cognizant of them. It struck me that if they all had a three-year-old van, that would have seemed almost as good, and they could have paid for the scaffolds with no trouble and have money left over. That was the example my early work on positional goods built on.

In 1980, you are back at Cornell, and you seem to start doing quite different work. Was it because now you have tenure and you can work on what you really want? Did Washington change you? Or did you observe some things and decide that this is what I'll write on now? What caused the change?

I don't think there was a change basically; I didn't get much done the first three years I was on the faculty at Cornell. I published one paper during that time, and it was one I had written in graduate school. So I was casting about for what to do those first few years, and only late in the game did I get on to some interesting things to pursue, and to my good fortune that work got accepted quickly. The papers I published for tenure were published right at the end. They all got accepted on the first try; there were a lot of things you wouldn't expect to work out nearly so neatly. I was working against the odds. The fact that I got the job at Cornell and that I got to keep it was based on a very contingent set of facts in my career. It was the same when I came back. I didn't have an ongoing research program; I was just sort of seeing things and reacting and writing about them. So I came back and tried to figure out what to write about, and one of the early things I wrote about was positional externalities, which I cast as a safety regulation idea. I was teaching a course where I was doing a lot on Coase then, and being immersed in that discussion and teaching it so much made me think about the implications of consumption externalities for wage distribution, and that produced a string of things, which led to *Choosing the Right Pond.* That's basically my post-CAB trajectory.

Do you think that if you had worked on this before, it would have been acceptable for getting tenure?

Well, those papers got published in good places, so yes, if I had gotten them published in good places, probably that would have overcome people's prejudices. People don't rely on their own judgment on these issues. My very favorite junior colleague just got denied tenure, who's going to end up better than any of the people who voted against him, just because he's doing some oddball stuff that gets published in nontraditional journals. One of our external reviewers condemned him for that, even though he himself did very similar stuff published in similar journals at the same career stage. My junior colleague is someone doing work across four disciplines, which almost guarantees that it's not going to appeal to a frontline disciplinary journal; it would be an anomaly if it got published in a journal like that. So I tracked down the vita of this reviewer and his first six years' post-Ph.D. papers. Four of them were in one of the journals where two of my junior colleague's papers were, and the rest were in journals that I've scarcely heard of even now. People see good journals, and they think it's okay; if they see journals that they don't think are front ranked, then they just assume it's not any good.

In 1991, you did your behavioral intermediate micro book. You seemed to be moving in a trajectory to writing more for the general public and less for the profession. Is that a fair description of your movement?

Yes. I think back on my career, and I probably made some strategically unwise choices about which mode to write in at a few junctures. But the Cornell department always seemed to me like a few other departments, where the question is how can I make this more complicated, not how we can simplify this and make the essence clearer. A lot of what I did was a reaction to what I perceived as excessive formalism on the part of the people around me, which I think is a problem in the profession generally. People are too quick to say, "Isn't there some way to make this more complicated?"

Who are some of the economists in the past, or perhaps today, that you respect and influenced you?

First would be Coase and Schelling by a broad margin because what they have engaged in the most has been externalities. You don't need to explain why Coase is an important source there. He's just a profoundly original thinker and insightful writer on the issue. Schelling's work is in the same mode; he sees interesting examples and puzzles, doesn't get too technical when he tries to explain them, and is unbelievably good at it.

It was in the 1970s when the profession started to look at externalities seriously and the development of environmental economics. This is also the time that a lot of your work was starting to be developed and took off. Do you think you were just hitting it at the right time?

Oh, that's interesting. I never thought about it that way, that externalities were in the air. But I think my positional externalities work just came about by chance at that time. Maybe I was affected by the fact that I was teaching some material that stimulated me to think about that issue in ways that tie into the externalities literature.

Your comment that in your teaching or in your writing you try to avoid being complicated and look at commonsense ideas that everyday people notice—and that maybe our formalistic models are missing some things and you are trying to bring those things into our models— this is an interesting comment—the idea of just observing things and then trying to incorporate them. Do you think that the traditional neoclassical micro model is able to do that?

Yes, I think that I am much closer to the neoclassical approach than most people in the new economics and psychology movement. Danny Kahneman is a deep pessimist about rational choice framework models; he doesn't think they can survive scrutiny at all, and indeed there are some interesting, deep anomalies. I was teaching a course called "Departures from Rational Choice," and I organized it into two parts, departures from rational choice with regret and without regret. The with-regret examples were the kind of Kahneman-Tversky-Thaler examples where there is some cognitive illusion or judgmental heuristic that people employ and they get the wrong answer in some contexts. And if you explain to them why they got the wrong answer, their typical reaction is to accept the fact that they screwed up and seem motivated to try to do things differently.

The other class of examples that I did in the course were ones where, once you explain why the observed behavior was inconsistent with the traditional model, people didn't seem at all to regret their behavior. Take tipping on the road, for example. When you explain to people that eating a meal at a restaurant along an interstate highway means that you can leave without leaving a tip and not suffer any consequences in the future, they don't say, "Well, thanks for the insight, and I'm going to do that from now on." They seem puzzled by the fact that the model would predict that behavior, and they don't seem to think that they'd want to do that. They think that the waiter did his part and they would feel bad if they stiffed him, and whether or not one would be affected in the future just isn't the issue. So those things are not cognitive errors at all; they're just a reflection of the fact that people are pursuing something different from what the narrow version of the rational choice model says.

Do you see your work as trying to incorporate as much as you possibly can within the rational choice model?

Yes, that's the way I see it. I think many Chicago economists don't like doing this sort of thing because the Becker/Stigler article makes a good point: if you are free to dream up any old taste you want, then you don't really have a predictive model. An important part of my work is to try to broaden the list of concerns that enter the utility function, but in a principled way. You don't just stick a taste in. I've tried to offer a reasoned account of how different tastes, like a concern for the well-being of another, might help agents make their way in competitive environments.

What would you say are your guiding principles for what to allow in there?

The one I just stated, if a taste can be shown to either promote your effectiveness or at least be consistent with survival in a competitive environment, then you can put it in.

Is that on a broader social level or just any individual level?

On the individual level is the criterion I use. So the fact that my gift to the United Way may help the town prosper counts only if it helps me prosper in a way that compares favorably to what I gave up. So it's not a group-selection argument; it's what people see as the warm glow that they get from giving to a charity, from helping other people, from leaving tips when they are on the road, from not shirking when they can get away with it. My task has been to explain how people who get warm glows from doing such things might nonetheless prosper in competitive environments.

Looking at the two-way interaction between economics and preferences in your work of trying to include issues like social status and fairness, do you believe that the traditional constrained maximization model is able to take those things into consideration? Do you find conflicts? Do you need to expand the model?

Once you put in a taste for these things, then it's just like a taste for pushpins. It's the same model as before; it's constrained maximization. You want to be clear about what the purpose of the model is. If you want to say that someone has a taste for doing the right thing, alright, you put a taste in for that, and there's a taste for own income and consumption. But you don't want to say to your kid, "Well alright, you care about doing the right thing, you care about getting more consumption. Weigh the trade-offs, and when you get enough more consumption, then do the wrong thing." That's clearly not the way we think about the taste for doing the right thing. It's meant to be a moral principle that trumps other things, but in descriptive terms, it does seem that people are more likely to stray when the temptation rises. So it is not a way to teach morality or think about morality, but it seems okay as a descriptive model.

Our taste for fairness, would that be the same?

Yes, that's the same idea. The challenge is to show how somebody with a taste for fairness competes effectively in a competitive market, despite the avoidable costs that he incurs by pursuing that taste.

Three of the other people whom we've interviewed are Ken Binmore, Herb Gintis, and Matt Rabin. Would you say your approach is similar or different from their work?

Binmore sometimes seems to take a narrower view than mine. The idea that somebody might care about fairness for its own sake, I suspect that's not something that he warms up to. I think he would view that as soft minded and sort of assuming the answer. Yet I think you can't avoid the conclusion that people care about fairness for its own sake.

Would you say, then, looking at empirical evidence, looking at experimental evidence, is important in making judgments of what to include and what not?

Sure, yes. If you said there ought to be a taste for *x* and all of the evidence said nobody seems to care about *x*, that'd be a strike against you certainly.

But if the experimental evidence shows you there is, would you then accept that as a testable outcome?

You mean if my model says there shouldn't be a taste for that but the experimental evidence says there is? Well that was the precise position of the neoclassical model *ex ante*. The model said that there shouldn't be a taste for fairness. If you look at the Darwinian framework as the intellectual underpinning of that model, it would seem that you should care only about the things that promote your narrow goals. But the evidence was fairly clear that people did seem to care about more than that. What would I say? Partly I got to thinking about the challenges posed by these broader goals. You see the concern about status, or the concern about fairness, and then you ask, "Well this seems to motivate people to incur costs that they could avoid. How is that consistent with our belief that people had to struggle to acquire scarce resources all through the eons?" The explanation for why that taste could be in there is obviously ad hoc—you see the taste first, and then you cook up the explanation. The trick is does your explanation predict other things outside the data that led you to construct it?

Matt Rabin, I think of as having brought the idea that people care about fairness further into the mainstream by showing how you can model the idea formally. He has begun by positing a taste for fairness and then showing how you can run with that by embedding it in the kinds of sophisticated deductive models that economists are accustomed to using, and I think by doing that he's probably done more than anybody to drag these ideas into the real mainstream.

What do you mean by the real mainstream?

Well, where ordinary economists would say, "Hey there's something for me there too." If they think it's going to be just two-by-two tables and experiments, most economists have a lot of human capital that isn't well utilized if it switches to that mode. But if you can actually do the kinds of optimization exercises that economists have gotten good at, that suddenly creates something that is worth working on. Something that is not that costly, in an opportunity cost sense, to turn your attention to.

And Herb Gintis?

I don't have as clear a sense of how his career has evolved. I remember thinking of him and Sam Bowles and David Gordon early on as articulate people on the Left, and I've taken issue with all of them at various junctures. My work on positional externalities offers an alternative to the Marxian view of why we regulate workplace safety and other things, why competition doesn't give us good outcomes. The Marxian view is that it's because greedy capitalists have market power and they exploit people, and that's hard to square with all the evidence that things are pretty competitive out there in both the labor market and the product markets. The positional externalities approach suggests that you get a lot of the same social ills as in the Marxist litany, but it also explains these as equilibrium outcomes in which no individual actor confronts further profit opportunities. The Marxist explanation, in contrast, leaves a lot of cash on the table. That group was one of my targets in that work. I think of Bowles, Gintis, David Gordon, Tom Weisskopf as being really smart people but operating within that explanatory framework where there are billions of dollars of cash on the table.

There has been quite a change in Gintis's thinking.

Oh yes, I was responding to my first contact with him. I have since then run into him at MacArthur Foundation conferences, and I recognize that he's totally become a behavioral scientist in the years since. He knows the literature I used to know better than I know it now. He's doing experiments in other countries; he could describe for you the full range of ultimatum experiments; he could tell you which culture it is where you'll turn down an offer where you get 70 and they get 30.

What year was it that you did this work responding to Gintis and to Bowles?

That was really the work that went into *Choosing the Right Pond*, which was published in 1985. That was the work I was doing when I came back from Washington.

Gintis has been drawing a lot of his work from game theory, experimental economics, and evolutionary economics. Do you find that any of your work draws from that?

Sure, nothing complicated. But you get a lot of progress from some simple game theory models. Experiments have been incredibly important.

You are both in the management school and the economics department, correct?

That's still barely true. I was full-time in economics until 1990, and from then until this fall I was half-time in each. Starting this fall I am quasi-full-time in the management school, which means I teach my introductory course once every other year in the Arts College. That's now my only teaching in the Arts College.

Has that influenced your research at all?

I think I am more interdisciplinary than most economists. The business school is more interdisciplinary than economics departments typically are.

How would you judge business schools versus economics schools?

You didn't see a lot of good economists in business schools in the past, but that of course has changed. I think research coming out of business schools is more problem driven now than the research coming out of economics departments, and to my taste that tends to be on the average more interesting, although there is still a lot of interesting research coming out of economics departments.

You have given a lot of public talks. It seems like you are writing more for the general public. To get your ideas listened to and accepted, do you believe that it is better to go public or work internally within the profession, like Matt Rabin? Are they complementary, and if so how do you see them fitting together?

Usually I publish papers on the idea first in professional journals. But I had a paper on the winner-take-all issue with Phil Cook that I consider the best paper I have ever written, and five or six journals turned it down. We never did end up publishing it. But until then all my books had grown out of papers I had published in journals. *Luxury Fever* grew out of a paper that I published in an economics journal too.

Do you believe that your work has received resistance from the profession?

I was just telling you about the paper I got in the mail today critiquing the paper Cass Sunstein and I did on cost-benefit analysis in the *Chicago Law Review* last year, and yes, there is a lot of resistance to the positional issues. There's not so much with the winner-take-all, and the emotion stuff doesn't attract resistance, maybe because a lot of people just don't take any interest in it. But there is something about the positional issue that seems to kindle a fierce resistance. It's an interesting thing because there's the long history in the profession that we take no judgmental stance on what people care about—that's their business—and yet if people care about relative position, that's somehow not their business.

You have written some popular books, and some of them have taken off. Has your department, the profession, accepted that you have been doing more of this popular writing?

These are not books you take to the beach; they are not selling hundreds of thousands of copies; they're difficult books, and they are aimed at serious readers. I'm writing across several disciplines, so I can't write these books aimed at an economics audience or else they won't reach the rest of the people who are interested in these issues.

I attempt to be rigorous in the construction of my arguments. I'm uncomfortable when people say these are pop books because I don't think of them as that at all. Peter Salovey, a psychologist who did the foundational work on emotional intelligence at Yale—then along comes Daniel Goleman, a *New York Times* reporter, and essentially takes Peter's ideas and writes a pop book about them. He doesn't get them right in many cases, but that's what I think popularization is.

If you go to most economics departments and say, "What do we want your professors to be doing?" they will say publishing in the top five journals and not books.
It's clear that articles published in the leading journals are the gold standard in economics.

Yet Cornell has gotten lots of publicity. You're probably one of the best-known people here. So from the administration you'd think that they would be very pleased with your published books.
The interests of the university and the interests of an individual economist aren't necessarily the same. I think it is useful for Cornell to have someone write about issues that are publicly discussed, but it is not particularly useful as an economist to publish a book. As a professional economist, I don't think that enhances your standing by much. Somebody did a regression once trying to explain the variations in wages among academic economists, and number of books published was a variable having a negative coefficient, which they interpreted to mean that you actually earn less when you published a book, or because you published a book. I don't think that's true. The kind of people who publish books are the kind of people who tend to earn less—they would be historians or history of thought specialists mostly or writing in other areas of economics where the wage is lower anyway.

Sherwin Rosen wrote a review of your Winner-Take-All Society *that was reasonably positive and good, but there were attacks on a fair number of things. How would you respond?*
I debated Sherwin Rosen on a panel at the University of Chicago Law School a couple of years ago. His position essentially was that this was his idea and it wasn't such a great idea anyway. It was actually Marshall's idea, and you can also find it in Smith. Sherwin had an interesting formalization that leads him in a completely different direction than from the formalization that Cook and I worked out. Our claim was that you got inefficient investment patterns on the strength of this reward system, and that wasn't at all Sherwin's claim. Our claim was that the winner-take-all reward structure was widespread. I don't have any second thoughts about that claim. You

might want to go to the *University of Chicago Law Review* and read the transcript of that discussion.

Do you look at your work at all investigating the formation of values and norms, or do you just accept them?

If I see a norm, I want to know why there is one. What's the problem this norm is trying to solve?

Do you see these values and norms as being endogenous in an economic system?

Sure, yes. Different societies have different norms, different problems are more salient in different environments, and you only have so much capital to use to construct norms, and you would invest it in the norms that would do the most good. So yes, they're surely endogenous to a large extent. There are some norms you see everywhere. Norms in general are endogenous in the sense that there is some structural problem in all likelihood that created the need for the norm. Would you call it exogenous or endogenous? It didn't rise out of thin air; it's driven by some inconsistency between individual interest and collective interest generally.

Your Luxury Fever *seems to be more policy oriented to me than your previous books. Is that a direction you see yourself going?*

You could think of that book as a brief on behalf of the progressive consumption tax. I'm very interested in inequality now, what the real costs of inequality are for people in the middle.

So you are interested in developing policy that will change something. Does that go back to your feeling about the Peace Corps, wanting to go in and make some difference and change something?

Probably. I have always gotten involved in political campaigns, and if I were in an organization, I was usually an officer in it, taking an active part in some way. My interest is definitely in the policy vein now.

We sent you the draft introduction. Any reactions to it?

It reads very nicely. I hadn't anticipated the organizing principle of it. I was surprised by that, the complex systems organizing principle, just because I had never thought of myself as having anything directly to do with that. I now see some oblique connections. I've been to the Santa Fe Institute a couple of times and think that this is all linked together in complicated ways and there is a lot of interesting dynamics in it. I still think my intellectual capital is more with the old static maximization model. I have an instinct about when something is not at equilibrium and an ability to spot the tension in a picture—there's cash on the table here, and something seems wrong.

You say "cash on the table" quite a bit; that's a very Chicago and Coase term.

The world is incredibly competitive. People who offer these non-competitive models for why things are the way they are I don't think grasp the essence of how it is out there. It's way more competitive than when we started. When we first started, it wasn't that hard to get tenure. You needed six papers, and some of them had to be in good places. Now, people have ten, twelve, and thirteen, and maybe they get it and maybe they don't. We weren't in the office all weekend, at least as assistant professors, and those kids are in there all the time now. Baseball players used to go fishing and drink beer in the off-season, and now they lift weights and run and take instruction, get counselors, get sports psychologists to get their mental attitude honed. In every niche there is more competition.

You say we live in a competitive world, and you see the competition increasing. What is causing that increase?

The kinds of things that you need to make markets work faster and better we have more of now, information mainly. We know if there's a good supplier somewhere, we can find him. We can get whatever he makes to us in a hurry; it's cheaper to ship it. There are more dependable, reliable sources of evaluations of the things we might buy; *Consumer Reports* keeps telling us, "Here are the top twelve refrigerators, and three are consistently on the top of that list." You wonder after awhile, "Why is anyone buying items four through twelve on that list?" And after a while those items go away in fact. The increased concentration isn't a symptom of less competition; it's a consequence of more competition.

In your book The Winner-Take-All Society, *you talk about the undesirable aspects. What do you consider some of the undesirable things about competition?*

I asked myself, "Why this resistance to the positional idea?" And I think it's because the invisible hand theorems go out the window when rank is one of the important sources of rewards.

ROBERT H. FRANK

It changes all the welfare?

Yes. You just can't say that the best system will be one in which you turn individuals loose to do as they will. There are considerable distortions if context matters more for some goods than it does for others. In that situation you get an excess of spending on the context-sensitive goods and too little resources devoted to the ones that don't depend very much on context. When I say "context," the evaluation of your house depends a lot more on the context where you are than your evaluation of your vacation time during the year. That's context-sensitive too but to a lesser degree, according to the best evidence we have about that. So you get too much money spent on houses and not enough time spent on vacations as a result. That seems to be for some people an invitation for government involvement and meddling and regulation that will mess up the economy. That's not the way I see the policy implications emerging from that whole argument.

How do you see them?

I think it's just an externality. It's like smoking, and probably tax policy is the best instrument we have to deal with the issue. It's not a perfect instrument, but the whole idea that you would have detailed government prescription of what you should consume seems like a formula for a bad outcome.

One of the arguments that we are making in the introduction is that there's a mainstream that is very broad and then there is an orthodoxy that we talk about. Do you feel there is a current orthodoxy that you are violating, or do you see yourself as part of mainstream? Does that fit your vision?

I haven't seen that division before. To the extent that I'm comfortable with the idea of talking about a utility function and constraints and maximization, I'm certainly in a long tradition in economics; there is nothing at all oddball about that. I find that on cost-benefit analysis I take positions that put me to the right of people at Chicago, often to my surprise and theirs. I'm more of a militant willingness-to-pay advocate than many of them are. I think you can't do any of that unless you are willing to tackle the distributional issues along with it. I used to call my work in this mode "radical pragmatism." This was twenty years back I was using that term. There've been some books published in the last year or so called the radical middle, or something like that. I don't know if they're talking about anything that I am talking about. The methods are more like the methods of the right, but some of the policy implications come out resembling those of the left more than those of the right.

How do you see your work fitting into the broader economic research program? Do you see a broader mainstream research program out there, and if you do, how do you see your work relating to that?

Slowly there's increasing interest in positional issues. I receive more and more papers to review all the time from people trying to work out what are some of the implications in different contexts. There are now some people trying to gather evidence on which goods are context-sensitive, which ones aren't, and where the imbalances are likely to be. So that's coming into the ordinary. The fact that what people call behavioral economics has now become okay certainly puts a whole new spin on a lot of stuff.

You see behavioral economics as part of mainstream?

More and more. It's hard to really call it way out of the mainstream. Sendhil Mullainathan, who was an undergraduate here, was the most extraordinary student I ever had. He would take 32 credit hours (the standard load is 15 or 16); he would take several graduate courses each term; he was taking graduate price theory as a freshman in the department. He got a triple major in math, econ, and computer science. He went on to Harvard to do a Ph.D. in economics, and he was easily the hottest student in the market when he came out four or five years ago. Only a few years before, the best departments wouldn't have been bidding against each other to hire a behavioral economist like Sendhil.

You think the change occurs at the better departments first, and then the rest follow?

Yes, I think so. Which is kind of interesting in the context of your study. For example, I think a better group than my colleagues in the business school would have promoted this assistant professor that just got fired. They would have been confident enough to say, "All right, he's doing some interesting work," and look at what he's saying instead of where it appears. It occurred to me right after I got to Cornell that Frank Levy probably wouldn't get tenure at Cornell, but Berkeley felt perfectly comfortable giving him tenure, and MIT too. He was not doing anything fancy; he was just a smart guy doing some interesting stuff.

In your forthcoming book, What Price the Moral High-Ground? *(Princeton, 2004) what's the argument there?*

That's the title essay in a collection. That essay was published in the *Southern Economic Journal* in 1996, and it's an empirical labor market study trying to measure how much less you have to accept in order to land a job that you regard as morally satisfying. There are nine papers in the book, and most of them are published somewhere else, and I've sort of just rewritten them to make them into a whole.

What do you feel about coevolution? How is it important?

That's where you get the runaway arms races in evolution, as when you've got a parasite and a host evolving in tandem. For me, I think the interesting application of that is sincerity and mimicry. There's enormous value if you can send a signal that proves you are sincere, but of course that creates a golden opportunity for somebody to pretend to be sincere and get the same payoff and not incur any of the costs of sincerity. If you look at the signal sending and signal detection mechanisms that are triggered when we try to size people up, there's evidence that they're very complicated. A lot of brain capacity is devoted to that, and that's usually an identifying feature of an arms race.

Traditionally, neoclassical economics has been focusing primarily on issues of efficiency, and some criticize that it is not focusing enough on distribution. Dick Norgaard said that in the 1930s when he started to see the need of economists going into government using cost-benefit analysis, the profession had to respond to that, so they started developing economic policy that made a conscious decision to focus on efficient questions instead of issues of distribution. What is your view on this? In your work you really want to bring in distribution besides efficiency.

I think efficiency is the first goal and not because distribution doesn't matter but because, unless you are efficient, you're not doing what you could be doing for everybody. There's a diagram I use in my principles course. I show it to them thirty times during the semester just to hammer it home, and it's two pies, a small one and a big one; the caption is when the pie gets bigger, everyone can get a bigger slice. If you are not doing it efficiently, if you are working with a smaller pie than you could be working with, then you are compromising the interests of everybody, rich and poor. So I think you've got to be efficient, but my "Willingness-to-Pay without Apology" paper is one where I argue that you can't be efficient unless you can transfer. Solving the distributional issue, up to a point, is a precondition for efficiency. Here's the example that drives the paper: You have a public decision about whether to switch the public radio station from all music to all talk. It's free to do it, there's no extra cost, and nobody cares except three people, one rich guy who wants you to do it and two poor guys who don't. The two poor guys feel just as strongly as the rich guy, but they are opposed and he's for it. The rich guy, just because he has more money, is willing to pay $1,000 to see it happen, and the two poor guys will pay only $100 each. Should you do it? Cost-benefit analysis says of course: it's an $800 gain in economic surplus if you do it. But people object, saying it's not fair to let this guy's preferences trump theirs. Citizens are supposed to be equal in the eyes of the law. Well, that sounds good, so you don't make the switch, but then you are flushing $800 down the toilet. So you should make the switch. But if you are a democracy and two opponents can block the switch, they have two votes to the one.

The solution is just to make the tax system more progressive. Tax the rich guy $500 extra, cut the taxes of the two poor guys $250 each, make the switch, and everybody wins. A general criticism of cost-benefit analysis is that the willingness to pay is biased in favor of the rich. Well it is, but we should still use it. But we can't use it in a democracy unless we attend to the distributional consequences of using it. The problem is that we don't use willingness to pay; we just use all these inefficient distributional schemes. The most vivid example is the exemption for older vehicles from the pollution control laws in California. If you look at the sources of smog in L.A., the majority of the NOx and the unburnt hydrocarbons come from cars fifteen years and older—they are just massive generators of pollution compared to new cars. The reason that they are exempt is because poor people drive those cars and it would be too big a burden on poor people not to exempt them. Well, it costs you about $900 a pound to get NOx out of the air if you tighten the standards on new cars, but you could get that same pound of NOx out for something like $15 if you get rid of an older vehicle.

There would be an argument where redistribution adds to or increases efficiency?

If you could attend to the distribution, if you could give the poor some more money and let them buy a three- or four-year-old used car, then the rich would be better off, they wouldn't need such expensive equipment on their cars, and the poor would also be better off.

So why don't we think in these terms?

You have to read the paper. This is the grand riddle. This is an obvious thing we ought to be doing, and we are not doing it. So my project is to try and account for that.

We had to choose people to interview. Is there anyone you feel we left out, any type of research left out?

Lists like this are horrible because most people aren't on them, and there are a million choices. Uncovered territory didn't leap off the list at me.

What do you see as the most important changes in the profession in the last twenty years? Or has it changed?

Yes, of course, things are moving faster now. As concerns the area I am closest to, the intersection between biology and psychology and economics, the profession is more open to ideas than it was fifteen years ago. It was hard to get papers published in good journals then. I felt like a big weight was taken off me by getting some of my earlier work published in visible outlets. I felt free to explore issues in a broader way because it at least had the imprimatur of being certified up to the profession's standings. I think that is a big difference. Complex adaptive systems, of course, didn't even exist as a topic in the discourse fifteen or twenty years ago. I don't remember reading anything much about that.

Can you name some individuals in the last twenty years who have helped with these changes?

You'd have to include Thaler on the psychology and economics list. He was probably the first economist to really bring the Kahneman/Tversky stuff into the picture. Rabin's been an important second generation player in this effort.

Let's talk about third and fourth generations now. Where do you see the profession going?

This will be a self-serving comment. But when I described how I partitioned my "departures from rational choice" course early on, if you look at welfare economics, the efficiency losses from the fact that we use judgmental heuristics and sometimes take sunk costs into account when we shouldn't, are probably going to end up being not very important in the grand scheme. The attempts to make money off these things in the stock market are interesting and statistically significant, but the margins are tiny. I think when the stakes are high people get pretty close to what the prescriptive decision is from the rational choice mode—not always, but most of the time. When you look at the efficiency losses arising from collective action problems on the motivational side, they're in the trillions of dollars. So inefficiencies stemming from the motivational side haven't received the attention they deserve in the policy realm yet. We are not in a position now to talk about major changes in tax policy, unless it's a tax cut for the rich. That's an anomaly in my view; I'm puzzled by that since the tax cut for the rich doesn't seem to be anywhere near the top of the voters' agenda according to surveys. It also seems inconsistent with the movements in income distribution that have occurred in the last thirty years. The literature that suggests that there will be output gains from making taxes less progressive has been thoroughly debunked. I like to think that a bad idea like that won't survive indefinitely, but it's still in the driver's seat now.

You just can't get time to talk about a lot of things. The Democrats can't talk about the death penalty; they all have to support it. The moment you hint you might have ambivalent feelings about the death penalty, the moment you let it slip that it's costing us $4 million to prosecute each case, that we could put a killer in jail forever for $200,000 and maybe spend the difference to save more lives somewhere else, you are immediately branded as being soft on crime. If you talk about a tax increase, you're immediately branded as unmindful of how wasteful government is. There's this "it's your money" argument. If you don't want to have a government, that's fine—then it's your money. But then you also won't have an army, and you won't have a country for long, and then you'll have somebody else's government, and you'll pay taxes to them. So if you are going to have a government, you've got to have taxes, and you have to talk about what you should tax and how much you should tax and what goods the government should provide. Starving the government doesn't seem to be a very efficient way to eliminate government waste. They've had the Proposition 13 movement in California, where they tried to curb government waste by starving the government of tax revenue, and they ended up knocking the schools from first down to forty-eighth in the nation when they did that. It is the same people who are against waste in government who seem to be the most reluctant to vote for campaign finance laws that would give them less of an incentive to vote subsidies for their contributors, or special favors for them, which are some of the really egregious examples of government waste.

I think that's all an anomaly. I think that when things start to change on an issue like this, they often change explosively. Timur Kuran wrote a nice book a few years ago, *Private Truths, Public Lies*, noting that 90 percent of the people can be against something privately and yet 80 percent will publicly be in favor of it, but the moment a few key people begin to speak out, it can ignite a prairie fire. I think at some point this issue will be squarely on the agenda and we'll have the conversation. There is a lot of progress we can make; the optimistic aspect of there being incredible waste in a situation is that this means there is huge opportunity for gain. I think at some point we are actually going to collect some of that.

One thing that doesn't fit into the general model that you use is multiple equilibria in an equilibrium selection mechanism, so it makes it much more difficult to define externality and talk about these things in a way that you would normally talk about. Where do you see those issues fitting?

One of the contributions of the psychology and economics movement has been to suggest principled ways of selecting equilibria from lists of potential ones. The fairness literature has had a particularly salient influence there, and there have been others.

What questions are economists trying to answer now, the answer of which will change the economics profession?

I think of it in terms of the things I am interested in and not so much the questions that other people are trying to answer. My interest lies in the motivational aspects because I think that's where the real money is, that's where the real cash to recover still lies. I don't think it's possible to engage in fine-tuning with taxes according to context dependence, but there's some interesting research being done now trying to measure the extent to which the demands for different goods are context dependent. I think we are going to need a better-developed literature before we can confidently describe important differences in context dependence among goods and identify specific distortions arising out of individual decisions. So if you want to know which numbers I am keenest to see, those would be the ones because they are attached to such a big-ticket ultimate payoff. Do I think you'd find a whole lot of other people in the profession who'd say that those are the questions they'd most want to see addressed now? I think you'd go all next week without finding anybody to say that.

One of the themes that we have found in these interviews, when talking about the changes in the profession and where it should be going, is a belief that the profession should move away from very formalistic scientific models to a more interdisciplinary/transdisciplinary approach. Do you agree with that?

Yes. I think there have been real advances made in that second mode compared to the kinds of increments we were seeing at the margins in the first mode. In general, it's not that formal modeling doesn't yield incredibly useful insights; it obviously does. We have a collective action problem: the individual assistant professor's interest in choosing a level of formalism is different from the profession's collective interests. If you were one of two assistant professor candidates vying for a tenure slot, and you could choose whether to be slightly more formal or slightly less formal in your modeling approach than the other candidate, it's been a hands-down winner to be slightly more formal, at least during the last thirty years. Because that's true, you've seen an escalation in the level of formalism, and that creates one of these arms races that we see in so many other areas. So the equilibrium level of formalism has been like the antlers on the elk: they're the right width for the individual animal, but they're maladapted from the point of view of the group as a whole.

I think the profession has to take some stance if it wants to encourage the right level of formalism. A paper I published in the *AER* in 1987 came back with a reviewer's report that said get rid of the first part of the paper and make the appendix the paper. I did it and felt it was a worse paper for it; fewer people probably got the idea straight. I think it would be better if editors would say, "Try and persuade the reader that you've got something worth caring about here and then use the appendix to persuade those people who care that what you are doing is consistent with the formal model."

But we are not doing that well. I can't say that we aren't doing it at all; you could say that the *Journal of Economic Perspectives* was an attempt to introduce more of that in the profession.

Are you optimistic about the economics profession?

Yes. I'd say it's poised for a seismic shift. I think that you are right that change does come gradually, internally, but there are key moments in history when things move real fast. And I think we are getting close to one of those.

Robert H. Frank

Henrietta Johnson Louis Professor of Management and Economics,
Johnson Graduate School of Management, Cornell University

INFORMATION ON THE WEB ABOUT ROBERT H. FRANK
http://www.johnson.cornell.edu/faculty/profiles/frank/

EDUCATION
B.S. Mathematics, Georgia Tech, 1966
M.A. Statistics, University of California at Berkeley, 1971
Ph.D. Economics, University of California at Berkeley, 1972

SELECTED PUBLICATIONS
Choosing the Right Pond: Human Behavior and the Quest for Status. New
York: Oxford University Press, 1985.
Passions within Reason: The Strategic Role of the Emotions. New York:
W. W. Norton, 1988.
The Winner-Take-All Society, with Philip J. Cook. New York: Martin
Kessler Books at the Free Press, 1995.
Luxury Fever. New York: Free Press, 1999.
Microeconomics and Behavior. 1st ed. New York: McGraw-Hill, 1991; 5th
ed., 2003.

SPECIAL HONORS AND EXPERIENCE
FAF Professor of American Civilization, Ecole des Hautes, Etudes en Sci-
ences Sociales, Paris, 2000–2001
Chief Economist, Civil Aeronautics Board (CAB), 1978–80
Fellow, Center for Advanced Study in the Behavioral Sciences, Stanford
University, 1992–93
Georgescu-Roegen Prize for best article published in the 1996 *Southern
Economic Journal:* "What Price the Moral High Ground?" November
1997
President, Eastern Economic Association, 1999–2000
Leontief Prize for Advancing the Frontiers of Economic Thought, 2004

CHAPTER 5

Matthew Rabin

Professor of Economics, University of California at Berkeley

❦

The interview was conducted November 9, 2001, on the University of California campus at Berkeley.

How did you get interested in economics?

I became interested in economics back in tenth grade. Before then I was interested in science. I have a memory of reading *Free to Choose* by Milton Friedman and some of Galbraith's books in high school and being more convinced and fascinated by Milton Friedman and his arguments. I found Galbraith's ideas paternalistic compared with Friedman's, although I have come to be more sympathetic with his views about automobiles and other cultural matters as I have gotten older.

Where did you go for your undergraduate studies, and what was your reaction to your early classes in economics?

I did my undergraduate work at the University of Wisconsin at Madison. In regard to my first economic courses, I didn't have a strong reaction. I was mathematically advanced and found the introductory classes interesting but easy. I got a job doing some research at the Poverty Institute at Wisconsin. My uncle, Eugene

❦

Smolensky, was there, and he provided advice as well as family to visit. I don't specifically remember a lot about the courses that I took. My undergraduate honors thesis was an application of game theory. Even though I didn't have any background in it, I did a simple model of an oligopoly with lags in consumer response. I was trying to see how those lags would affect the simple dynamics of oligopoly pricing models. Unfortunately, I solved it incorrectly.

So even as an undergraduate you were interested in expanding traditional economics?

I didn't have in mind rejecting or expanding traditional economics. But the material in my honors thesis didn't come from my courses. The work I did at the Poverty Institute at Madison was applied. But it was during this time that I decided to be a theorist. I had a double major in math and economics. My Ph.D. was pure theory.

Where did you go after graduating from the University of Wisconsin?

I went to the London School of Economics and from there to MIT for graduate work. I applied to what I was told were the best graduate programs in economics. The list did not include Chicago or Berkeley because I was told they were not particularly good places for graduate students at that time. Other than that I just applied to the best places and was told MIT was the place to go. I had no specific knowledge of MIT beyond knowing it was the best of graduate schools. So I just decided to go there based on that. I don't remember thinking much about it. I went to LSE because I finished a semester early at Wisconsin, and spent a half a year there. There I sat in on Ken Binmore's game theory course and worked with Julian Le Grand. I have been back to LSE several times since then.

Did you enjoy your experience at MIT?

Yes, in general, it was a positive influence. MIT taught me how to think critically, and it also turned me into a decent economic game theorist. Oliver Hart was one of my early advisers. Bob Gibbons taught me game theory. Drew Fudenberg, who joined the department after I got there, became my main adviser. He definitely had a positive intellectual influence on me. But I think it's fair to say that I had my own interests, and I was doing my own thing with a lot of support. I was intellectually engaged at MIT, but no one steered me.

What was your dissertation topic?

My dissertation topic was in pure game theory. It was about cheap talk, a formal model of credible communication in abstract terms. It focused on what statements that I say, given my private information and incentives, you should believe are credible. It was the basis of my job market paper that appeared in the *Journal of Economic Theory.* Joe Farrell was the first person in economics that looked at cheap talk. I read some of his stuff and became a big fan of his work, but it was Bob Gibbons who introduced me to cheap talk. Drew was not a fan of the topic initially but was very supportive of my research.

What was the reaction of your professors to your dissertation?

Overall they were supportive. When I first started talking about cheap talk to Drew Fudenberg, he aggressively told me he didn't believe in the stuff. It wasn't a topic that he would have chosen. But he said he would read whatever I wrote. When I gave him something, he read it within twelve hours, and from that moment on he was very encouraging. Within game theory, cheap talk, in its own minor way, might be considered subversive.

How is cheap talk subversive to game theory?

Let me rephrase that. It is not that it is so subversive, but was seen as something of a violation of the paradigm. You can't derive predictions about cheap talk from first principles of rationality alone. The fundamental theorem of cheap talk is that with rationality alone, and virtually any standard game theoretic solution concept such as Nash equilibrium, you can never guarantee that people will communicate their private information, so there is always a babbling equilibrium.

For example, even if it is common knowledge between us that we both want to meet for lunch, and I call you up and say, "Let's go to restaurant A rather than restaurant B," there is always an equilibrium consistent with rationality for you not to believe what I am saying. Given that I know that you are not going to believe what I say, I might as well randomize what I say. But when there is no reason to disbelieve what someone says, we believe him or her. To maintain the rationality assumption, you want to do a reality check on making sure that the incentives are to actually tell the truth. So what was subversive about this is that, unlike most game theory, we weren't deriving the prediction out of the incentives and rationality assumptions alone; we were making additional assumptions.

Were you accused of being ad hoc?

Yes, but not by Drew and the people at MIT, who were mostly supportive. Bob Gibbons was one of the few game theorists at the time that was already on board with cheap talk. But to this day, theorists do not make these additional behavioral assumptions.

Are there game theory journals that will not publish papers on cheap talk?

No. That's making it too organized or too ideological. But my taste as a theorist is sort of nonstandard. Fun for me is developing new assumptions. This is contrary to the sensibility of most economic theorists, for whom fun is deriving surprising results from known assumptions. I'm interested in how people communicate and how they react to that communication. This might require different assumptions than the traditional ones that are made. In my *JEP* paper with Joe Farrell, part of the argument we make is that if you back up and look at what fascinates game theorists, there is something slightly amiss. Take the famous example of coordination problems, how you meet someone in New York when you don't coordinate and make a plan.

Schelling, and many people since, have all this interesting stuff on focal points, lots of learning inclination models, lots of experimental game theory, how people focus on a focal point, and so forth. Most of the experimental work is done by artificially preventing people from communicating. Now from Joe's and my point of view of the billions of meetings that take place in New York each year, how do 99.99999 percent of them happen? Do they happen through clever focal points, through signaling, through all the things game theorists talk about, or do they happen because people talk to each other and plan where they are going to meet?

Game theorists are just inherently not as fascinated about people coordinating through simple communication even though as an empirical reality this swamps all other forms of signaling as ways people convey information. My comments here may partly be my retroactively reconstructing what some of the resistance is to my current work.

In reference to Schelling's work that cheap talk may at times be superior to conventions based on focal points, when would this be and when would this not be and why?

It's not so much a matter of being superior but more the way coordination happens. There are lots of experiments about coordination games that artificially prevent people from talking to each other. I have gotten in several arguments with game theorists and experimentalists about this. I'm being quite unfair because I have had this argument enough with friends and I could give you the counterarguments for why we still want to study these coordination issues.

Now there's a new genre of smaller numbers of experiments that give people message space but just don't give them English. An experiment or a coordination game may, for instance, let people convey ten messages, M1 through M10, but the experiment doesn't tell us ahead of time what these words mean, and we watch language evolve in the laboratory. Fine. I can think of other situations such as walking around in the middle of Paris where this is relevant because I don't speak French, and so we don't speak a common language. But for the most part, the way people use language is that they don't have to invent the vocabulary they need to converge on the focal meaning of the vocabulary in real time or for each new economic situation. It seems a legitimate assumption that most economic exchanges take place between people who speak the same language.

Were you studying psychology in graduate school, or did this come later?

I've never had a psychology course in my life. I don't think MIT had many psychology courses; they had instead cognitive and brain sciences. It is my impression, though I can't say I carefully looked into it, that if you try to do psychology at MIT, you study computers, not humans. This, by the way, is also an argument I have with fellow theorists. Many theorists are more interested in computer science than about psychology. I happen to be the opposite in terms of my interest. I was interested a little bit in graduate school in artificial intelligence and cognitive science. I would go and hear Marvin Minsky speak, for instance, so I did have some interest in it. But I didn't sit in any of these courses at MIT. When I arrived at Berkeley, I sat in on two graduate courses in psychology. I looked at my first year here as a makeshift postdoc. I immediately sat in on psychology courses and tried sitting in anthropology courses. So I clearly came to Berkeley with interdisciplinary interests. My recollection was that I had no serious interest in incorporating psychology into economics until I came to Berkeley, although a friend from graduate school later told me I talked about psychology all the time.

After you graduated from MIT, what were your plans?
I mostly applied for postdocs. Berkeley was the only place I applied for an assistant professor position. I think I could have gotten offers from most of the places I wanted to apply to.

What year was this?
This was 1989. The fall of 1988 is the year I was on the job market. I think a lot of the reasons I wanted to come here were personal; I wanted to be in this area. Also, Berkeley is a very laissez-faire department in terms of research styles, and it's a very friendly department.

Was George Akerlof a key person in bringing you here? Were you interested in his work at the time?
I was sort of fascinated by his work. Up to that time I had only done economics and game theory, and he was part of the general package that made Berkeley attractive. George has sat in on lots of anthropology and sociology courses, and I wanted to do the same.

What is the best name for the work you do? Your Journal of Economic Literature *article was titled "Psychology and Economics," which is the working title of your book in progress. On the other hand you have the Institute for Psychological Economics here. Finally, there is the* Journal of Economic Psychology. *Do these terms mean the same thing, and if not what are the differences?*
The more popular term, which I actually dislike, is *behavioral economics,* popularized by Richard Thaler, although he may have gotten it from Simon and March. I don't really know. I have no interest in disowning the movement. I merely dislike the term *behavioral* for two related reasons. One is that it reeks to me of Skinnerian psychology; it's not the type of psychology where consciousness is important. And then the second related reason is normative rather than positive. A lot of my real interest isn't in showing that the demand curve for cigarettes doesn't look like what economists think it looks like but rather in showing that it doesn't reflect utility

maximization that is assumed that it does. For my money, so much of what is eventually going to really matter about this research isn't in its better predictions about behavior but better understanding of welfare.

Do you have any feelings about the difference between multidisciplinary or interdisciplinary or transdisciplinary?

I never really thought about it. I like to read in a lot of disciplines. I'm in many ways an archconservative in terms of economic methodology and advocate doing things like economists do it, and not like sociologists or political scientists. What I do is import psychology into economics to develop what will be a more sensible empirical economics. So then in that sense it is not interdisciplinary; it's not feeding across from each other.

I have a fantasy that some day psychology will actually be improved by economics. For the time being, that's not going to happen. Psychologists are just not as equipped to incorporate economics as we are to incorporate psychology because their math training and their mode of thinking is just not always the best. As a game theorist reading social psychology texts, I think, "Wouldn't it be wonderful if social psychologists understood game theory better?" I was also shocked to read experiments in equity theory discussing why people divide things certain ways, without even a hint of economics in some of this work. There's no recognition that maybe one of the reasons a little girl took both apples rather than sharing isn't because she thought it was the equitable thing but she just wanted both apples. Old-fashioned self-interest might be something psychologists don't have a sufficient appreciation for. So for a variety of reasons, what I am all about is bringing psychology into economics. In that sense, it's not about making one big, universal social science.

What is your general feeling about the methodological approach that is used in traditional neoclassical economics? Do you think it restricts new ideas coming into economics? Are you comfortable with it?

Is it restrictive? Yes. Are there costs to the mathematical methodology? Yes. Do I feel comfortable that those costs are for the most part worth it? Yes. I can tell you the one real restriction of methodology of economics that I'd probably like to do away with, and this I attribute partly to reading McCloskey in graduate school and sort of thinking about it over the years. When all is said and done, researchers should say what they actually think is true. Methodology should not be used as a reason to not talk about what you really believe. I believe in statistical testing, I believe in formal modeling, and so forth. But I am frustrated by people claiming they have a methodological right not to even think about an obvious assertion, or declaring for some methodological reason that they're not supposed to think about something that seems to be important. So whenever it feels like our formal language or our methods don't let us think about some issue, at least I want openness that says, "Yes, this seems important to me. Yes, we are missing something."

I sometimes call it "you-can't-stop-me empirical work." In it somebody reports some econometric results based on a formal model and reports that they can reject this hypothesis but can't reject that hypothesis. I want the right to raise my hand and say, "Look, do you really think this is what's going on? Your formal model claims that people are doing this. But here's the thought experiment and here's the real experiment of a different situation that I doubt your formal model will fit."

I want people to feel they have an obligation to say either "Well yes, I think the model is probably flawed that way," or "Yes, okay, now I see. I'm going to abandon this model because I don't think it's going to fit," or "I disagree with you: I really do think this interpretation is what's going on, and I do think it will apply to that." I don't want to hear the statement "We don't have that data, so I don't want to answer the question about whether I think this is going on."

Within that confine, I very much appreciate the methodology of economics and the power of precise statements and statistical tests relative to other social sciences that don't have these standards. I just want to see formal models and statistical tests as tools to learn what is true about the world, not as pretexts for avoiding that task.

Let's return to the economics of psychology and experimental economics. Vernon Smith has claimed that one difference between experiments in economics and experiments in psychology is that psychological researchers are willing to lie to their subjects. Do you think that the economists will get to that stage as they pursue experimental economics further?

The role of experimental economics has been overwhelmingly positive. While there are many instances where the ideologies of experimental economics have been taken too far, it has been over-whelmingly positive to do certain classes of experiments for "real stakes." The experimental economists make a fetish of money, which is not even in our formal theory, as the only thing that moti-vates people. In that sense I don't think experimental economists quite understand how radical a rejection of traditional economics some of their methodological work really is.

Who said that the only thing people want to do is to walk out of the laboratory with more dollars from their games? It's an empirical proposition whether undergraduates are much more motivated by an extra fifty cents or by getting a gold star or the respect of the experimenter or their peers. But generally monetary stakes help, and sometimes they are crucial. I'm interested in fairness. If I ask you hypothetically if you get a million dollars whether or not you would be willing to share some of this with me, from an econo-mist's point of view, that's a different proposition than what you would actually do if you had a million dollars. To understand things like the difference in the trade-off between self-interest and emo-tions, you need a monetary component.

There are also other ways in which experimental economics has been an improvement over psychology. One is sharing the data; experimental economists share data. Perhaps it would have been different if experimental economics had fallen into different hands, but in the hands of such leaders as Vernon Smith and Charlie Plott, the ideology has been that all data have to be available. That's not true of psychology. I believe that many economics journals have an official policy—they will not publish experimental work unless the authors promise access to the data by others. Partly this is techno-logical. It is feasible these days because of computers, while it wasn't in the 1950s.

The lack of deception is overwhelmingly positive. But I think there is an element of cynicism in this being used retroactively as a license to ignore an entire other field. I think it is silly to argue that we learn nothing from experiments that use deception.

Assume that there are thirty experiments in psychology that all say the following thing. If an economist tells me that we don't want to consider those results because we don't consider experiments with deception in them, I disagree. It's simply a position to avoid engaging the evidence. I find that frustrating. But the rules that economists have developed have partly influenced psychologists.

MATTHEW RABIN

145

Do you think that the power of the existing methodology in economics allows it to pick up and incorporate and appreciate the work that you are doing?

Yes, and not just what I am doing. I want to talk about the incredibly rapid, and incredibly positive, spreading of David Laibson's formulation of hyperbolic discounting and the self-control problem into economics. It has everything to do with its precision. He offered a precisely stated alternative model that we can test implications of. It's profoundly important for lots of economic questions. For example, the net effect is going to be to make the model simpler and more practical because of the mini-industry we have going in trying to reconcile actual savings behavior and other behavior. Ten years from now we'll have simpler models of lifetime savings behavior that are going to have more explanatory power. For some other topics it's going to take longer.

I am interested in types of Bayesian reasoning. There are a variety of ways in which that's a little bit harder conceptually, mechanically, and technically to incorporate. But here too, I wouldn't be surprised if the net effect of introducing certain types of bounded rationality and heuristic mistakes enters into our studies of stock market behavior and similar issues. Eventually, it might even simplify our models.

In the solution to the hyperbolic discounting issue, is it really just a matter of getting the proper mathematical formula, or is there something more fundamental? It appears that Robert Strotz back in 1956 was really the first person to discuss this. Would this be an example of the cutting edge of economics of that day? Why was it ignored then, and how did it come to attract more attention recently?

Let me deal with the second question first. I think part of the answer is that game theory wasn't invented until after Strotz. He did a shockingly good job. Game theory would likely have progressed faster than it did if people had thought about how Strotz and others had engaged some of these issues. But basically why the Strotz stuff didn't catch on is technical at its core.

Some in ecological economics argue that something like hyperbolic discounting can be used to resolve normative problems in discounting intergenerationally, resolving the tension between needing positive discount rates for capital markets to work and the argument of Frank Ramsey that, morally, discount rates should be zero, a compromise some call the "green golden rule." What do you think of this?

I think that normatively discount rates should be zero.

You have been quoted as saying that you are participating in the second wave of behavioral economics. How does this second wave differ from the first wave?

I used to describe it, but worry that this would offend Dick Thaler more, as "postanomalies behavioral economics." What I mean by the second wave is moving beyond critiquing the standard assumptions and providing verbal alternatives. In the second wave we start formalizing the alternative economic models. Sometimes I describe it as third-wave behavioral economics in which now we are starting to see the empirical testing.

Does this come from experimental economics?

I'm not as big a fan as I think many people are of trying to replicate economic institutions, such as markets, in the lab and claiming that you've tested something about the economy. I am much more a fan of uncovering insights about individual motives and thought processes and decision-making in the laboratory. I think real markets are a lot more complicated than anything experimentalists have ever tested. By empirical testing I really mean the third wave is field empirics. I use a lot more experimental evidence than field empiric evidence. I am a huge fan of experiments. But the eventual hoped-for goal is to do field empirics to really test the usefulness of our stuff.

Now, I don't say this as a criticism of what the earlier-generation behavioral economists have done. I see this as the natural and inherent order of research. It has to happen this way. The fact that I like to argue for the present existence and usefulness of second-wave behavioral economics is not a critique of the earlier stage where the main task was to start convincing economists that the current set of assumptions and certain domains were sufficiently bad and misleading that they needed to be improved.

A more or less orthodox presentation of consumer theory can be found in Varian's graduate micro textbook. In there he presents four axioms of preference that must hold in order for a utility function to exist: reflexivity, continuity, transitivity, and completeness. You have reported many studies that would seem to undercut these. Would you agree that the endowment effect of loss aversion undercuts continuity, that transitivity is undercut by time inconsistency, and that complete-ness is undercut by projection and lies?

No.

No? Let's start with the first one. Why doesn't the endowment effect undercut continuity?

Maybe it undercuts differentiability.

Continuity is a necessary condition for differentiability.

Yeah, but logically you can have a continuous function that isn't differentiable.

Okay, so you're saying it's got a kink?

Yeah, as a first approximation you can think about the endow-ment effect as introducing a kink. You want to use the kink because you want to talk about a sharp change in preferences in the gain versus loss domain. But literally, differentiability isn't the main interest. The precise mathematics of it aren't that important. But it's more important to understand how much preferences and tastes and behavior are driven by changes and contrast rather than absolute variables. So merely understanding reference dependence and the central role of loss aversion is more important than cram-ming the endowment effect and loss aversion into the rational choice framework.

We have seen that the argument for loss aversion is coming from many sources—empirical evidence, psychological evidence, field evidence, and, in environmental economics, the difference in how much people are willing to pay for something versus what they demand to be com-pensated for losing something. Doesn't this evidence fundamentally undercut continuity?

I refuse to think that this is the important focus. People have started to write down completely rational choice versions of loss aversion. All you have to do is to introduce a reference to do that. Now there are particular ways in which endowment effect and loss aversion are, in fact, not rational. But, in fact, what we're seeing is largely seeded by a real aspect of preferences, a mistake of various sorts. Part of that mistake is projections that people overreact to losses and gains because they anticipate that the sensation of loss or gain will last longer than it will.

Another chunk of it is what I call mental accounting or choice bracketing. Here you may get into some transitivity issues and so forth. It doesn't end up being coherent preferences once you realize that when people are given a series of separate problems, instead of integrating them, they make a choice in each separate problem such that the global outcomes from all of these problems don't add up to a global decision they themselves would even approve of.

I try to play off the standard model. Part of what we are trying to do is to quickly improve economics in its own terms. To do that, we make incremental, hopefully at times rapid incremental, progress in modifying the standard approach. An important distinction in a lot of these situations depends on understanding which behaviors are really essentially consistent with rationality. To some extent the endowment effect and loss aversion are like that. To a very large extent, departures from self-interest are just about people caring about a different set of things than people are usually modeled to care about. You certainly have things that violate some of the axioms of real preference theory such as transitivity and coherent, rational utility maximization framework. But you always want to try to find some tractable model.

Why do you continue to use utility functions so much in your analysis?

All models are false, but they can still be useful. I do the same thing all economists do. One of the deleted footnotes from my original psychology and economics paper, now in the *JEL*, sent economists to the dictionary to look up the phrase *ad hoc* and the word *parsimonious.* The purpose of the footnote was to show them that the connotations of these words are exactly opposite of what we've come to adopt them as in economics. *Parsimonious* is "stingy," not the ultimate compliment that economists think it is. And *ad hoc* is also not the ultimate insult: what a lot of economists do, even when they don't acknowledge it, is ad hoc in the best sense of the word.

People are complicated, life is complicated, economic institutions are complicated, and to address particular questions, you highlight particular aspects of things. In order to address certain questions about people having different preferences, using utility maximization is useful. There are a lot of ad hoc decisions in modeling. It's a very interesting cognitive feature of economists that we don't recognize our own ad hoc-ness but we notice it in others.

Economists think they had this wonderful model of risk preferences in part because they would write down one utility of wealth function when people are dealing with small-stakes risks and write down another one when they are looking at large-stakes risks. They weren't admitting to themselves, or to the editors of journals they were publishing in, that these are just wildly inconsistent claims about where things were coming from. So we were just changing the utility function, just to fit a particular behavior, and thinking we had all this evidence that people were behaving rationally.

Sometimes that's the right approach, but we ought to recognize that that's an inconsistency. I don't think economists recognized that they were doing it. And so the new approach is going to have hopefully more self-aware ad hoc.

Where do you see your work on fairness going?

There's a lot of experimental work these days. The term that I like is *social preferences.* How do people take into consideration other people's material payoffs? I think there are important caveats having to do with choice bracketing and separation, but for many purposes one can usefully look at these as a model of preferences. I used to get into huge fights about this. Many economists wanted to see turning down money in the ultimatum game as irrational behavior. The level of energy economists have spent, either for methodological reasons or interpretational reasons, in believing that people turning down money needs experiments, that this isn't rational behavior or that it indicated that people didn't understand the experiment, just seems to me bizarre.

A rhetorical technique that I use is just telling the audience to take off their economist hat. It actually works. I tell them to stop thinking of all the creative ways you can interpret this behavior that you see in the laboratory as self-interest and to start asking if there is really anything strange about the interpretation we are giving. You have $10 to split; you offered to keep $9 for yourself and give me $1. And I turn that down because you are an ass, and I'm willing to spend that dollar to punish you. That seems to me a perfectly plausible interpretation of people's behavior. I would ask the audience, "What planet are you from?" if this strikes you as some weird behavior. And it's a case where I think economists, and especially experimentalists, had it so much in their mind to start fetishizing money and self-interest that they were just losing sight of a very simple interpretation.

Why are you so against ultimatum games?

Because it has led to a lot of confusion.

Is there something beyond the ultimatum game to deal with the fairness issue?

There is. Lots of games. One of the contributions of my paper with Gary Charness is to prove that there exist games that aren't the ultimatum game. It's proof by construction. The ultimatum game is not very good for discerning social preferences, and it's not particularly economically interesting.

Is it reciprocity that lies behind fairness?

It's one of the things.

Before the interview, we sent you a draft introduction about the cutting edge of economics. Any reactions to it?

I thought it was interesting; I liked it. The stuff about complex dynamic systems didn't work for me, especially as an opening gambit. I thought the breakdown of the orthodox and the heterodox and the mainstream and the distinctions between them was quite interesting and helpful. But in terms of many critiques of the mainstream, I actually feel like a conservative.

In fact, I have various fears in teaching psychological economics. One is of attracting graduate students who are just hostile to economics. Another is all the people who want to use evolution and other approaches to explain departures from classical models rather than using evidence of departures to do better economics. It is still a source of constant frustration to me the number of people who contact me and tell me that they are really interested in behavioral economics and that they're going to do some neat work providing an explanation for why people experience the endowment effect, or that they are going to come up with essentially computer science models to explain psychological biases. A lot of this just makes me cringe because it's just not what I feel that I'm doing. It misses the point. I don't want to use good old-fashioned economics, abstract economics, first principles to explain the psychology. I think a lot of that is either wrong or beside the point. I want to create better models of people and plug those better models into economics. I have a real fear, because I am a believer in mainstream thinking, that behavioral economics is going to attract graduate students who don't like the math, who don't like the precision of economics, and who don't like economics but would prefer to do philosophy or computer science. I don't want that; I see myself as doing normal science.

MATTHEW RABIN

151

What do you see as the most important changes in the economics profession in the last twenty years?

I think it's informational economics and game theory and, in the last five or ten years, psychological economics. (This is making me feel a bit old.) There's been a movement from game theory being an exotic new field twenty-five years ago to being a field course when I entered graduate school in 1985 to now being required graduate study. Game theory is now part of economics education at virtually all top Ph.D. programs.

I always considered game theory as gradually evolving into the mainstream. It is manifestly a natural continuation of mainstream methodology and thinking. There was resistance when I entered graduate school. But most of that resistance has faded. But in many ways, the direction that psychological economics is going is really replicating the way informational economics and game theory developed.

Where do you see the economics profession going in twenty-five or fifty years?

In the *Journal of Economic Perspectives* they asked various people to make these predictions. Dick Thaler framed it in terms of replacing *Homo economicus* with *Homo sapiens*. That's perfect. We are certainly not going to be abandoning most of our classical theory any time soon. In broad terms, we're going to see things moving towards incorporation of more realistic models of people in economic situations.

Now, I can also give you more specific thoughts about what I see in the future for psychology and economics. In ten years' time, hyperbolic discounting is going to be part of core macro. It's going to be there because it matters. I can see the social preferences and fairness stuff becoming pretty mainstream in labor economics a few years from now because it matters. All it will take is for economists to start getting more comfortable with fairness. Money illusion is no longer going to be a verboten topic; it's not going to be the dirty secret that everyone outside of Chicago knows is real but also knows is illegal to talk about. It's going to become above ground.

I also anticipate a major change in welfare economics. For Western developed economies, I think, there will be improvements in understanding what preferences are important to people, the relative preference work that Richard Easterlin and Robert Frank and others have been talking about for several years. I think relative preferences will start to be understood as a really major fact about what Western economies should care about economically. We will better understand the wedge between behavior and welfare because of mistakes people make in pursuing their own satisfaction. I think a lot of people are a lot less happy than they could be because of their credit card debt.

In America we're a fat society in every sense of the word. Similarly, and more so outside of the United States, smoking, and in the United States drug choices, unsafe sex behavior, all these sorts of things bring nontrivial amounts of misery to lots of people in this affluent society. I think a lot of this is that for people maximizing lifetime utilities is really a hard thing for people to do, both because of misprediction and because of self-control problems, especially for young people. I think, if you go back sort of to the roots of economics, the whole reason we care about consumer theory, the whole reason we preach to economic students about rent control being good or bad, is because we think that markets and free choice are what make people happy. Where people lack self-control, that isn't so clear. People making mistakes like becoming drug addicts are relatively big-ticket items in terms of consumer satisfaction compared to some of the other issues we've discussed.

I really think about a more sophisticated, better grounded, revealed preference theory of using tools and insights of economics. I'm looking for a recognition of the types of errors we make and ways to study these types of errors to help design policy. We want to let people pursue the preferences that are really their preferences and to help incentivize people correctly.

One could design policies for those people who are already sufficiently addicted or enjoy certain types of vice goods enough that makes it the right thing for them to do, to consume these products, to let them pursue those, while designing different policies for others. There is some great practical stuff by Laibson and Thaler and others on designing policies for improving savings behavior that doesn't involve just the government coming in and saying, "You gotta save more; you are saving too little," and forcing everybody to save more. Instead it focuses on getting the incentives and policies right so that people who really should be saving more will choose to save more and to reinforce for those who are doing things correctly already.

In some ways my vision sounds really radical because it seems to involve interfering with people's incentives in such a way as to change their behavior to improve their outcomes. I actually believe that it's not such a terribly radical proposition in a world where we come to better understand people.

Matthew Rabin

Professor of Economics, University of California at Berkeley

INFORMATION ON THE WEB ABOUT MATTHEW RABIN
http://elsa.berkeley.edu/users/rabin/

EDUCATION
B.A. Economics, University of Wisconsin at Madison, 1984
Ph.D. Economics, Massachusetts Institute of Technology, 1989

SELECTED PUBLICATIONS
"Incorporating Fairness into Game Theory and Economics." *American Economic Review* 83 (1993).
"Cheap Talk," with Joseph Farrell. *Journal of Economic Perspectives* 10, no. 3 (1996).
"Psychology and Economics." *Journal of Economic Literature* 36 (1998).
"Risk-Aversion and Expected Utility: A Calibration Theorem." *Econometrica* 68 (2000).
"Choice and Procrastination," with Ted O'Donoghue. *Quarterly Journal of Economics* 116 (2001).

SPECIAL HONORS AND EXPERIENCE
Also taught at London School of Economics
National Science Foundation Research Grants, 1992–94, 1997–2001
Fellow, Center for Advanced Study in the Behavioral Sciences, Stanford University, 1997–98; Econometric Society, 2000; and MacArthur Foundation, 2001–5
John Bates Clark Medal, American Economic Association, 2001
Marshall Lecture, European Economic Association, Lausanne, 2001

CHAPTER 6

William A. ("Buz") Brock

Vilas Research Professor of Economics, University of Wisconsin
at Madison

∾

*The interview was conducted in the John R. Commons Room at the
University of Wisconsin in Madison in June 2002.*

Could you briefly recount your path to becoming an economist?

I grew up on a farm in Missouri, so I got to see economics working on a firsthand basis. It was an accident that I went to college; no
one in my family had. I was sent up to Grand Rapids, Michigan, to
live with my aunt so I could afford to go to a junior college. I wasn't
prepared. The first day I was sitting in class and saw the professor
scribbling something on the board, and I asked the person next to
me: "What's that?" He said, "Math induction—you don't know
what math induction is, you're in a lot of trouble." So it was rough
at first.

I remember having trouble with calculus, so I went in to see my
teacher. I noticed that he had a problem written on the blackboard.
It had lots of sines, cosines, and transcendental equations. I asked
what he was trying to do, and he told me that it was a proof about
some polygons being extendable to n-gons. I was an engineering
student, and I had a T square and a compass, so I took some big

∾

paper and drew the polygons to see if the principle he was looking for held true or not. At around 20 or 21-sided polygons, I started noticing an increasing divergence. So it was obvious that the principle did not hold for *n*-gons.

I drew up a bunch of these diagrams and took them in to him, telling him that the principle did not hold. (Back then I didn't know how to say that the conjecture is false.) I showed him the drawings and the divergence. He asked me how accurate the drawings were, and I said they were pretty good. He asked to see them. I came back a week or so later, and the blackboard was empty [laughter]. . . . Ever since then I have been hooked. Science is just a hoot—trying to figure out what's true and what's not using any tool that I can come up with.

But you didn't graduate from a Michigan school. You graduated from the University of Missouri.

Some of the professors at my college suggested that I should go to a real university, so naturally I thought about going to the University of Missouri at Columbia since in the state of Missouri that was the big time. So, starting my sophomore year, I went there. Soon after I arrived, I met Russell Thompson, who was a young economist from the University of Minnesota and had just come down to teach agricultural economics. He posted a job for a graduate research assistant on the bulletin board. Despite my being a sophomore, I talked him into hiring me. We got along just great and ended up writing some papers together (Brock and Thompson 1965, 1966). The process got me hooked on economics.

In my senior year I asked Russell whether I should go to graduate school in economics or mathematics. He said math, and when I asked him why, he said that economists tend to have a hang-up about math and it is much easier to learn math when you are young. So if you get a Ph.D. in mathematics from a first-rate department, math will be second nature, and then you can concentrate on the economics. So I went to Berkeley to study mathematics. I think that was great advice.

Is it great advice for everybody who goes into economics?

Well, it does take a long time. You end up getting a degree in a subject that is not your direct interest. A lot of natural scientists think that you can get right into economics. But economics is a different way of thinking that takes a long time to grasp. Most people never grasp it.

How did you grasp it?

I don't know; maybe it might have been because I've been thinking about it since I was seven or eight years old because of living on farms and seeing the ups and downs of agriculture. So I think it was just living with it. I've heard people say that Canadians make great trade economists because it's a small country and they see all the distortions that result from trade restrictions.

I learned quite a lot about economics and how the economy worked from my experiences on the farm. I remember one story that I have used in my classes. It was about the chicken farming we did. We had a lot of chickens, and they were called cage layers because they were confined to cages where there is barely enough room for the chickens to turn around in the cage. We arranged the chickens in three stories, placing a board of Masonite between the various stories to catch the excrement.

Later on some agricultural scientists figured out that if you removed the Masonite, the cost in production and dirtiness of the egg was very marginal. So soon the chickens were there on top of each other with nothing between them, and I would use this as an example for my students of how the competitive system pushed margins to the limit. If you can save even the smallest amount, farmers would be induced to do it. One time I went a bit too far for some students in the discussion of this. I was teaching freshmen at Cornell, and I was using this example as a parable of the social structure of the lower classes. It didn't go over too well with one of the students who was rather right wing. I recall that he reported me to the dean, but I remember that the dean just thought it was funny.

Did you actually see corn-hog cycles?

Yes, but most farmers were rather sophisticated about their lack of knowledge, although not necessarily about what they did about that lack of knowledge. I remember my dad saying, "It must be time to get out of the hog business because I want in, so all the smart money must be getting out." I remember the chicken business. There was a company that would guarantee that they'd pay you, say, thirty-four cents for a dozen eggs. Since the costs were below that, we got into the cage-laying business; we had 3,000 or so chickens.

WILLIAM A. ("BUZ") BROCK

For a couple of years we were making good money. But then lots more people got into the business, and the store market price fell to something like twenty-five cents a dozen. So the company that had given the guarantee went bankrupt. So I learned at an early age that sure things were not necessarily sure.

How did you hook up with David Gale?

That was a stroke of luck. He came to Berkeley from Brown University at the same time I went there. I remember I was sitting in George Dantzig's class in linear programming next to another student, Richard Sutherland. He was scratching away on a tablet, and I asked him what he was doing. He said that he was a student of David Gale and that he was working on this economic growth problem, which was basically a convex infinite horizon mathematical programming problem. I had read a lot of Gale's work, and so I went to see him. I ended up becoming his Ph.D. student and writing a joint paper with him (Brock and Gale 1969).

You went to Berkeley around the time of the Vietnam War. Did that affect you at all?

It made me very skeptical of government, but anyone growing up in agriculture was already very skeptical of government.

As a math Ph.D. how did you end up getting a job as an economist?

David Gale played an important role, I believe. Then, the job market was not as formalized as it is now. David made phone calls, and I was offered a job. Lionel Mackenzie was interested in my work, so I ended up at Rochester. Rochester was a perfect place to nurture a young person. I'm very fond of them to this day. There were many interesting people there including Hugh Rose, Sherwin Rosen, Stan Engerman, Bob Fogel, Ron Jones, and Rudy Penner.

Your antigovernment views would fit nicely with the views at Rochester, but your more leftist views about politics don't fit so well.

I guess I'm a leftist libertarian who recognizes that the standard economic doctrine has to be amended a lot because of externalities. But I like to go after big externalities, not the exotic ones that get you published in the journals. The big externalities are Ec. 101 externalities like environmental externalities (Brock 1977).

How do you differentiate the big externalities from the little ones?

Big externalities are ones where there are large costs being offloaded. A canonical example would be trucking costs. Newberry's study on trucking showed that damages that trucks cause may increase with the fourth power of the size of the truck. If that externality were not internalized, there would be serious social costs. My favorite slogan is that all cost causers should be forced to bear their own costs.

From Rochester you went to the University of Chicago. How did you get there?

I got a job offer from Chicago, and it seemed like a really exciting place to be. So many economists from Rochester had Chicago connections.

Did you have political differences with the Chicago economists?

No. They seemed to have the same views as I did in many ways (Brock and Evans 1986). My views became a lot more nuanced because Chicago economists are very sophisticated in thinking of market-oriented ways of correcting externalities rather than using government. There's also a lot of Coasian thinking around Chicago and Rochester, emphasizing private solutions between differing parties rather than government solutions.

You represented a major shift for Chicago—moving away from the Stigler, Friedman, Becker heuristic approach to a very formal mathematical approach. Now the formal mathematical approach pretty much dominates Chicago. Did you feel an odd man out?

You should probably ask them, but I can guess. I remember at Berkeley there was a social psychologist type who was interested in mathematicians, so he gave us a test of tolerance of ambiguity and fuzzy stuff. I remember all the mathematicians scored way over here; they had no tolerance for that, and I'm way on the other side, with lots of tolerance for it. So I thrived on the literary Chicago approach that I joined. I love that kind of debate and argument. I remember talking to Milton Friedman a lot. Milton just likes people who will let logic take them where it leads them.

So you don't see yourself as a typical mathematician?

I guess not; if I did, I wouldn't be in economics. But I love the beauty of mathematics. I am closer to being an applied rather than a

WILLIAM A. ("BUZ") BROCK

theoretical mathematician. But the distinction becomes somewhat blurry at times. When we were working on the BDS (Brock, Dechert, Scheinkman) statistic, there was a tricky move in proving that the first-order asymptotic distribution of the statistic was invariant to estimation error. If it was, we could use it on estimated residuals. It turned out that there was a beautiful symmetry in the expression for the statistic that allowed us to eliminate the terms that you usually have to correct the first-order asymptotics for, and that kind of thing is just pretty. That's a real high when you get one of those. But I like it when the mathematical work I do has some application to reality too.

You seem to have less faith in the core model than do most Chicago-type economists. For example, you advocate Bayesian model averaging.

When I was at Chicago, I hadn't gotten into a Bayesian type of thinking as much as now. Arnold Zellner was there, and he was very influential, but in those days you were hamstrung in doing Bayesian analysis by lack of computational power. So you had to restrain yourself to specialized distributions. That made a lot of more classical statisticians uneasy. But Bayesian analysis integrates much more naturally into decision theory of the type that economists like.

You have commented that in the early days when you found multiple equilibria, that to get published you had to hide them, but that now you search for multiple equilibria.

In the earlier times the profession was trying to focus on empirical discipline. They felt that if you didn't have so many equilibria, you would have more discipline with your analysis. So I had to hide any multiple equilibria in footnotes where future researchers could find them but where referees were less likely to see them. This view about multiple equilibria certainly wasn't unique to Chicago. For example, in growth theory we were searching for sufficient conditions for a unique steady state, not for examples of multiple steady states. Finding sufficient conditions for a unique steady state was considered the much more challenging mathematical problem, and it was felt that it might have some relevance for how the real economy worked, if there were enough markets around and enough opportunity for price discovery (Brock and Burmeister 1976).

You are heterodox in some of your views and orthodox in others. Have you found much negative reaction to your work because you weren't following the standard path?

I certainly don't have anything to complain about. The profession has treated me very well. I remember talking to Chicago colleagues about my paper emphasizing multiple equilibria (Brock 1974). They were quite intrigued: "Why do you have so many equilibria here since this is the Friedman-Sidrauski model?" It's true that I did have to do an innovation—a version of plain vanilla rational expectations (Brock 1975). That generated a lot of interesting technical questions as well as intellectual ones. I had attributed the multiplicity of equilibria to the price level being in the utility function.

As the cost of computation has gone down, what is standard changes. Because of Moore's Law we are getting more and more tools available at our disposal. Techniques like Bayesian econometrics, bootstrapping, Monte Carlo methods, and agent-based modeling and evolutionary dynamics that previously were analytically intractable are now becoming computationally tractable. That expands the horizon of tools that people have, which expands the standard view.

When did theorists become more open to multiple equilibria?

I don't know. To me this shift in methodology is puzzling. I just like to look at evidence and what your tools can handle. It's actually much easier to find examples of multiple equilibria than to find sufficient conditions to get rid of them. In ecology there is a very natural reason for looking at multiple equilibria because there is a fair amount of evidence that points to alternative stable states.

There are a lot of shifts in economics that I find rather puzzling. People argue all the time in economics about fads and so on. That's why I think it is really good to be anchored in solid, empirically based economic methodology. I wouldn't necessarily call it Chicago methodology. I would just call it economics driven by the facts.

Had your politics been Left, not libertarian left, do you think Chicago would have hired you? Say you were Herb Gintis before the change.

That's one thing I liked about Chicago. I recall signing a letter for George McGovern in the *Times* when I was at Chicago. The attitude at Chicago seemed to be that free speech was something that was precious. So I never felt any pressure at all. You had to endure a bit of ribbing, of course.

WILLIAM A. ("BUZ") BROCK

163

You seem to have evolved with the changes in economics much more than most in the profession. Any reason for that?

I have never been absolutely sure of anything. I'm not a scientific dogmatist, so I like to try to keep an open mind. But on the other hand, there's a tradeoff. You want to keep an open mind, but you don't want to open it so far that your brain falls out. At times you've got to settle down and do some specific work.

What brought you to Wisconsin?

That had to do with my roots. Both my wife and I are country people. I love the University of Chicago. I've never been at such a place that has such a commitment to pure science. I love the joke about Chicago that has a bunch of students examining a football and trying to figure out what to do with it and eventually ending up performing trivariate integration to compute the volume of it. I love that kind of atmosphere. All I think about is science. But we are country people, and dealing with Chicago was difficult. My wife picked a set of acceptable places, and Wisconsin was one of them. Wisconsin has been a very good place to be.

Why did it take ten years for your famous paper that computes the BDS statistic to get published?

That's a good story. We sent it to a certain high-prestige journal initially in 1987, and it was rejected. Now all of us have been rejected by such journals. I remember one economist telling me he was never rejected, which made me think of my dad's story of a deer hunter who told him that he never missed when he shot at a deer. To that my dad said, "You ain't hunted no deer."

Anytime you're doing work that seems somewhat unconventional, you face this. Although from today's perspective, seeing the BDS statistic as unconventional seems a bit strange. The BDS statistic has become about as conventional as you can get.

While it was rejected, I think it is fair to say that we were partly responsible. The paper went through a number of passes, each of which took a long time. The reality is that I don't like to revise; it's boring work, and life is short. As the revise and resubmit process was going on, the ideas in the paper were being used. A number of papers began extending it, and three of us wrote a book, which included a lot on it (Brock et al. 1991). Finally, they ended up rejecting it.

When that happened, the person who edited the *Econometric*

Reviews heard about the paper and asked if he could publish it. We said yes, provided you don't make us revise it any more. We had lives to lead, and the users already had it. A fourth author, Blake LeBaron, did a lot of key work in the revision, writing software to make it useable (Brock et al. 1996).

I don't especially worry about where something is published. I remember George Stigler once saying that every article in a first-rate journal gets read by three people—two referees and the author, and sometimes I'm not so sure about the author. Getting papers published in top journals requires spending time formatting and worrying about expositional matters that I'm not interested in. I recognize that there are tradeoffs. You can have more fun and reserve your energy for initial research, or you can format papers for prestige journals. I made my choices, and I'm willing to pay the price. Nothing's free.

What I hate is this modern tendency to evaluate economics departments by how many pages they publish in journals, which are ranked based on impact factors. To me, this is just tree cutting; it has nothing to do with science. To me the use of such methods by a department to rank prospective hires is a sign that the department is not able to read.

It is often said by those who know your work that you have done so much but are not widely known because you do so many different things. Any comment? Is there a connecting thread that holds your work together?

I think there is a connecting thread to my work. My initial work concerned analyzing forces for stability. I found sufficient conditions for various intertemporally recursive models of the economy that showed that the system was stable. Later work looked at situations where the system was unstable and looked at empirical methods to study whether there is any evidence for stability or instability (Brock 1986, 1993). These are really tough problems. To a mathematician many of the causes of instability are obvious, so I got interested in less obvious causes, such as homoclinic bifurcations in the context of information paradoxes (Brock and Hommes 1997, 1998). To me, it was a surprise that homoclinic bifurcations play a role in that type of instability, which dates back to Grossman and Stiglitz, although information paradoxes were around in the discussion long before that. So, in my view, my later work is directly tied to my earlier work.

WILLIAM A. ("BUZ") BROCK

Some have said that my most recent work is undermining rational expectations. I don't see it that way. My view is that it is rather a type of superrational expectations. In the real world, fully structural rational expectations are not free. You have to pay a Chicago tuition, which, since it is a private university, is quite expensive. In our framework there is a fee to get the information. The issue is when will it be worthwhile to get that.

In analyzing this problem we discovered that there was a tuning parameter of the intensity of choice—how fast people would move from one strategy to another. If that tuning parameter passed a critical value, you got a homoclinic bifurcation.

How did you get involved with the Santa Fe Institute?

I got involved because Ken Arrow invited me to the first meeting. There was a big cauldron of ideas there, but they have spread widely now. I try to keep up in a lot of areas. I spend a lot of time reading; I probably read too much because nothing seems new to me under the sun, and I scan the Internet, clicking through websites; I'm fast with a mouse. The Santa Fe Institute is a fun place to be.

You and Brian Arthur are the only two who are in both of the Santa Fe volumes (Anderson et al. 1988; Arthur et al. 1997a). How do you see the Santa Fe Institute having changed over the ten-year period between the two volumes?

I think initially it was much more interested in time series work. Then, the interest shifted more toward evolutionary agent-based work. It is possible that much of the time series work went proprietary—like the Prediction Company. (I can imagine comedians saying that any of the stuff that had commercial value went commercial.)

I think that there were a lot of statistical mechanics type of physicists at the first meeting—Phil Anderson and Richard Palmer, for example. But economists were interested in that too. I suspect that I was more influenced in my work on intensity of choice approach to social interactions by the McFadden and Manski tradition in the discrete choice literature (Manski and McFadden 1981), plus the statistical mechanics literature in mathematics, than by the physicists. Putting those two together and conceptualizing the set of problems that you can attack with those two sets of tools is what underlies my paper on social interaction with Durlauf.

When did you start working with Steven Durlauf on these types of questions?

We hired him for a job at Wisconsin, and we started working together as he was in the process of moving. He was working on similar ideas and models that I was working on. There were a number of such models floating around in the 1990s. The problem was getting them into a framework where you could do econometric analysis, and confront, head-on, issues of correlated unobservables, and distinguish spurious from true social interactions that have a social multiplier that is policy relevant. Making that jump hadn't been done (except for Manski's work); the physicists weren't equipped to do that; those are econometric problems. It's a hard problem, but we're trying to make a dent in it. I really lucked out when I came to Wisconsin because here at the Institute for Research on Poverty the sociology department is really good and there are excellent interactions among researchers.

One of my favorite teaching examples of the type of problem we were getting at is the problem of identifying the importance of social interactions among high schoolers. If you look at the best friends that your kid hangs out with, their GPA will be correlated with your kid's GPA, even after you condition on everything else that you can possibly find to condition on. But yet that could be due to peer selection bias, or an unobserved variable. Durlauf and I developed techniques to try to answer that question by looking at these things from different time scales (Brock and Durlauf 2001a, c).

How does the econophysics movement tie in with your work with Durlauf on social interactions?

Econophysics has really grown, and there are a lot of different strands. There's one strand that focuses on minority games. There's another strand that works with a lot of statistical physics models. Another strand involves scaling laws. Yet another strand is agent-based simulations. I'm sure I'm leaving out some elements, but that gives you a sense of the range. The type of work Durlauf and I are doing has more to do with the statistical mechanics models because they are interacting agents systems. But the issues are a lot different. We are interested in separating spurious from true social interactions that have a policy multiplier and determining how the data should direct policy consideration.

There was one study by Evans and some others cited in Durlauf's and my *Handbook* chapter (2001c) that found that when you did something like a Heckman neighborhood selection correction then the social interactions parameter would disappear. Typically what happens when you do a correction of this type is that the social interactions parameter will often disappear or the estimate of it will get a lot smaller. Now that's a concern that just doesn't come up in the problems that econophysics typically studies. They're interested in other issues, whereas in social science, issues such as correction for selection bias and econometric identification are key.

You've been very careful about not pushing complexity too far, arguing that complexity is just a natural growth in issues that economists always have been interested in.

Complexity is very hard to define. I think Seth Lloyd, who was cataloging definitions of complexity, is up to over forty the last time I looked. He might be over fifty now. It's a real tough problem. Without a definition it is hard to figure out what you are pushing when you push complexity. Economists tend to yawn when you tell them that the system is highly interconnected with lots of interacting agents. Adam Smith knew that. There's more to modern complexity theory than that. If you tried to characterize complexity, it's probably characterized by computational/analytical methods of dealing with large highly interconnected systems and using tools like large-system limits to say something concrete about those systems and divide them into universality classes that have common properties independent of the mathematical details of each subsystem.

Do you see a problem with the work that goes under the name econophysics *that pushes technical solutions based on scaling laws but not really having any knowledge of economics underlying it?*

I think what happens is that a lot of the scaling laws are being done by people who are not trained statisticians. A statistician is trained to look at something like the conditional predictive distribution, and there are many processes that reflect many different conditional distributions. After all, what we're really interested in is economics—policy-relevant prediction and control. So there are lots of stochastic processes with very different conditional distributions that will generate the same scaling law. I tried to make this argument clear in my own piece on scaling laws, which some people interpret as critical (Brock 1999). But I didn't see it as critical; I don't want to shut off work on scaling laws. I think scaling laws generate valuable evidence that we want our class of stochastic processes that we are working with to be consistent with. They should generate unconditional objects that look like the scaling laws that people find. I should point out that economists were working with scaling laws before econophysics came about—look at Pareto distributions.

I think many of the people doing econophysics are very good at handling large masses of data, and we want to learn from this. It is true that the way some of them write their articles will put most economists off because it will have some ignorant, ill-informed remarks about economics that are essentially at a principles text level, and often not a very good principles text level. Then the economists will get furious and won't read further. When I read this stuff, I screen out all the nonsense, and I take what's of use, and I encourage other people to do the same.

The second Santa Fe volume had two competing approaches: one focused on statistical mechanics; the other was the self-organized criticality approach of Per Bak (1996) and others that leads in the direction of scaling laws. How do you see those two approaches relating to each other?

In the sandpile models the argument was made that there is no exogenous tuning. This is one of Per Bak's favorite arguments. In interacting-particle-system-type models, which are the type used in statistical mechanics, there is a tuning parameter. For example, in Ising models of a ferromagnet the inverse temperature is the tuning parameter. That tuning parameter has to hit a critical level before you would get the scaling law that people like Per Bak were looking for. A parable for thinking about this is a two-dimensional lattice of lightbulbs which can be on or off. If the lightbulb is on, the lightbulb next to it is likely to be on. As you increase the tuning parameter from zero, where you just see a random lighting effect, you start seeing islands of on and off lights developing. If you were at criticality, when you measure the size of those islands, you would see islands of all sizes. A histogram of those islands would look like a power law. You see these kinds of power laws all over the place. In an article I wrote, I made a joke that if you whisper $1/f$ noise at a physics conference, that you will draw an agglomeration immediately. There is just so much interest in this among physicists.

The idea of these sandpile models is that sandslides from drip-ping sand on a table will follow a power law in size and length when the sandpile is at a critical size. Some people saw this as a grand uni-fying principle to explain anything. They argued that you didn't need any tuning parameter; that's why it was called self-organized criticality. Of course you had to feed it, so it is a little too quick to say that there isn't a tuning parameter. Actually, it is pretty easy to endogenize the tuning parameter in an economic context. All you do is have a person making choices and you maximize entropy. If you do that subject to side constraints, you get probabilities that look like Gibbs probabilities. Then the tuning parameter is related to the LaGrange multiplier of the constraint.

In an article of mine in the Arthur, Durlauf, and Lane book (Brock 1997), I set up a problem like this: Maximize entropy subject to sum of the probabilities equals 1 and average utility of the choos-ing equal to a target, call it U^*. Rank the utilities of the choices from the lowest to the highest, with U^* somewhere in between. For each fixed U^* you will get an intensity of choice parameter in the Gibbs probabilities that will solve the maximum entropy problem subject to these two constraints. The LaGrange multiplier on the U^* con-straint measures how hard it is to achieve. The higher the intensity of choice, the closer you get to the maximum when you are choos-ing.

So you can think of choosing essentially randomly like I do when I go the grocery store. (When I do the choosing, my wife really bawls me out—she's saying put more effort in pushing up your U^* in our language. When my wife chooses, she really puts a lot of effort into it. So her intensity of choice is much higher than mine.) Now, I have a tradeoff, so I set up a little side model of this tradeoff that captures my cost of time. I can either spend time doing a good job of choosing, or I can spend time thinking about modeling doing a good job of choosing.

So then I make U^* a function of effort, and I maximize U^* of effort minus the cost of my time times effort. By doing that I endog-enize my beta. My point is that any external tuning parameter can be endogenized depending on how you look at the problem.

My view is that the people who were making the argument that the tuning parameter was exogenous were doing the intellectual equivalent of a dog marking his territory. This kind of a thing in sci-ence annoys me, so basically when I see it, I try to do my part to stamp it out. That's why I wrote this paper—to show people how easily one can endogenize beta in a way that Gary Becker made famous in his treatise on the family (Becker 1981). These simple little micro models really prompt your mind in asking interesting questions. So when you write it out this way, you start asking questions such as "What about people who have a high opportunity cost of time?" They probably won't spend a lot of time pricing a candy bar at the local PDQ; they will just pick up their favorite brand. You can start thinking about habit formation; for these type people, if a choice worked well for them in the past, they will likely continue it. It unleashes creative economic thinking rather than just saying a parameter is exogenous or it is not.

So I guess my feeling is that the approaches are complementary. The sandpile model is very useful for thinking about chain reactions—where pressure builds up and then relaxes in a series of cascades. But to do any inference on the presence of a scaling law requires enormous amounts of data. I think that people who try to argue that stock market returns are generated by a sandpile-type phenomenon simply because you notice that volatility, or unconditional returns, scales like a power law are pushing the evidence further than it can be pushed. When you look more carefully at those scalings, you see that they don't scale like a power law, or at least not very well. If you look at them in different frequencies, then the power laws have self-similarities embedded in them. So if you look at monthly, weekly, daily, or hourly data, the tails get thinner. Monthly returns have much longer tails than hourly returns, which is inconsistent with a self-similar process. I think one has to be very careful handling this stuff.

Didn't you and Durlauf model the issue of turf protection in your paper on economic theory and the evolution of science (Brock and Durlauf 1999)?

We were looking at philosophy of science issues. Durlauf had a lunchtime seminar going here on the topic, and I've always been interested in it. So we got to thinking about how to model the evolution of different schools of thought in any science. Of course we chose our own since we know that one best. So we used our social interactions model to model this issue. One of our graduate students extended it by looking at citation clubs. It's fun. It's something that we all like to gossip about, so we thought that a model of it with which you could ask econometric questions of would be great. You could even estimate the half-life of a school.

WILLIAM A. ("BUZ") BROCK

Can you summarize the main results for us?

The basic idea is the following tradeoff. On the one hand scientists are rewarded if their models predict out of sample better than rivals. On the other hand, they are associated with a reference group, the graduate school tradition they grew up in or whatever, and there is a cost to deviate from the reference group because they need letters of reference from advisers or chances of getting sympathetic referees. We modeled that cost as a function of deviating from the mean of your reference group.

Researchers would choose models based on the costs and benefits. If you come from an open or eclectic reference group, you have a lot more freedom than if you come from a homogeneous reference group. We had a quadratic cost, and we set it up in an interactions system model.

The tuning parameters in the model were the intensity of choice and the social interactions parameter—how much you got penalized for deviating from the mean. If the product of the intensity of choice times the cost of deviating was greater than one, there would typically be three equilibria. You could get stuck in an undesirable equilibrium where the models weren't predicting as well as a rival model. Since prediction in economics is hard to tie down, we presented this as a real possibility.

Where would you fit in that model in terms of your costs?

I suppose I pay a price because I don't belong to any particular school. I have a very high intensity of choice. I'm not sure how expensive that is. I think the safest thing to do is always look at the evidence. How well does the theory predict out of sample? I'd be open to any view that predicted out of sample better.

Where would you put Chicago economists in your model?

I say they come out pretty darn good. Suppose you see some pattern that looks analogous in view of theory. Of course, the instinct of Chicago is to look for some government rule as the ultimate source of the problem. I tried that algorithm when I worked for government, and that's a pretty good algorithm.

A lot of your recent research has been involved in ecological economics. How did you get interested in this area, and what type of work have you been doing?

I've always had a latent interest in that area, but you can only fry so many fish in twenty-four hours a day. My recent interest stems from Karl-Göran Maler, the director of the Beijer Institute in Sweden, inviting me to a conference in Zimbabwe that was run by the Resilience Alliance. An ecologist named Buzz Holling ran the ecological wing of it, and that piqued my interest. They are a great bunch of people to work with. A lot of our recent work can be seen in a recent book edited by Gunderson and Holling called *Panarchy* (2002).

A key model of yours in ecology is the lake game model in which there are fast- and slow-moving variables and sudden shifts from one state to another (Brock and Starrett forthcoming; Carpenter, et al. 1999a; Carpenter et al. 1999b). How does this model differ from the old catastrophe theory models?

I suppose there is a relationship. In the Thom version of catastrophe theory (Thom 1975) you assume a gradient flow, and then you classify the elementary catastrophes. Basically, the lake game model is an example of bifurcation theory that has a classification theory with it, but those classifications are not constrained to gradient flows. The equations you look at don't have to satisfy the symmetry conditions that they have to in catastrophe theory. So even though landscapes are often used as a metaphor in ecology, there really isn't a landscape function in many of these systems. But there is a classification theory for bifurcations.

The primary bifurcations in ecology are codimension 1 bifurcations; you have a one-dimensional parameter in a continuous time system. There are generically only two of those in continuous time. To find them, you linearize the system at a steady state and compute the eigenvalues. If they are all negative, they will be locally stable. You then ask which largest real part eigenvalue reaches a positive real value first. If it is real that reaches the positive real part, that's one kind of bifurcation. If it's a pair of complex eigenvalues that reaches the positive real part, that's another kind. Those are the only two kinds you can have with continuous time.

In the discrete time system you linearize it and look at the unit circle in the complex plane, and you can have three bifurcations. The additional one is when the first eigenvalue that reaches the boundary of the unit circle is real and passes through –1.

When I teach this, I use what I call the Samuelson's boat metaphor because I think I first heard it in one of Paul Samuelson's lectures. You have a real long boat, and people are watching whales.

WILLIAM A. ("BUZ") BROCK

Someone on the right side yells, "Whales!" and then all thousand people go to the right side. So the boat starts to sink. So everyone runs to the other end of the boat, and it sinks even more. That's when the intensity of choice is really high. When the intensity of choice is low, and someone yells, "Whale!" only a few people move, and there is no stability problem. That's a way of looking at the minus 1 bifurcation.

In some of these models it seems that you have introduced your social interactions parameter. Do the models tie together?

There's quite a bit of conflict going on in deep lake ecology, and nobody knows for sure whether it has alternative stable states or not, whereas experiments have been done in shallow lakes that prove they have alternative stable states. So we had this quasievolutionary model where we allowed different management styles to compete in an evolutionary framework. The earlier work that we did looked more like an economic management model, but it was of a coupled economic ecosystem where you had the possibility of alternative stable states in the ecosystem. When you managed the economic system, if you did not discount the future, you might manage the whole system in such a way as to eliminate the alternative stable state.

In the evolutionary model, to what degree were the dynamics due to a Bayesian decision making process rather than an intensity of choice process?

It was primarily an intensity of choice process, although there wasn't an intensity of choice parameter in it; it was more like an agent-based system.

Much of your concern about ecological economics is about whether there are critical thresholds at which point you move to an undesirable equilibrium. How do we learn what those critical thresholds are without moving to them?

That's a tough question that is heavily discussed in the ecology literature. Some of the ecologists call it Holling's Frustration. Humans just keep pushing the system until it goes over the threshold. It generally happens when there is a slow-moving variable that reduces the resiliance of the system that is expressed by large shocks. In the Resilience Alliance view of human-dominated ecosystem management, the humans will keep pushing the margins as long as they don't see visible evidence of damage. For little shocks they won't see any visible damage, but then a big shock will hit, and you're pushed over the threshold.

In the lake case farmers will typically try to get ahead of the planting season, so they will put manure on the ground when it is still frozen. If you get a big, rare rainfall in early spring before the soil thaws, the manure will wash into the lake, and you've got problems.

To try to detect how close you are to a threshold, ecologists look at species that move on fast time scales, which are very sensitive to the pollutants that are causing the problem. What's happening to them gives you a leading indicator that something is going to happen. It's a bit like the mine canary. Of course the problem is trying to get the forces that manage the system to respond to these early warning signs, but that gets into political economy, and we don't want to get into that. We know why a lot of science does not get applied.

Can you talk about how you see Bayesian analysis can be used in policy-making?

We are working on a program here at Wisconsin that gives you a sense of it. Imagine that there are two competing views of global climate change that are held by equally eminent scientists. Say you have a class of models of each view. In traditional econometrics, if you held one of the views, you would estimate a model in that class, and you would conduct statistical inference tests. You would set up no climate change as a null hypothesis and see if you accepted or failed to reject the null. A Bayesian would do the same. But they would set up a prior and look at the data, and within that class of models they would report the posterior, which you would send to the policymaker. It would be up to the policymaker to make use of it and choose policy accordingly.

The kind of approach we are taking in our work is when you have two competing core theories and the evidence isn't strong enough to resolve disputes between the holders of the different views. In this case we argue for Bayesian model averaging. In this approach you start out with a prior with each core class of models. So you do a Bayesian analysis within each core class. Then you do another Bayesian estimation across the two core classes. You start out with a prior, and you let the data speak, giving you a posterior across the two classes of models, as well as posteriors within each class. Then you can do decision theory where you would take this generalized posterior. This procedure seems to push you towards a more cautious and less certain reporting of your views. So one might look at it as an honest way of reporting the true level of uncertainty because it includes theory/model uncertainty, as well as the usual uncertainty that you report in a conventional statistical analysis, be it Bayesian or classical.

There seems to be considered conflict between evolutionary theory and ecological theory. This conflict may carry over to economic theory as well. On the one hand classical ecologists might be like equilibrium theorists in economics; much of the mathematics is very similar to what's in economics. On the other hand evolutionists would argue that there really isn't an equilibrium but everything is just constantly changing and evolving. Any comments?

That's a tough question. Even in equilibrium theory if you change it to where you are chasing a moving target, it can look evolutionary. One project that we are working on in the Resilience Alliance gets pretty close to talking about that. In that we build a unified ecological, genetic, and economic model where we actually write down the dynamics of the gene pool and try to manage that along with the rest of the ecology (Brock and Xepapadeas 2003 and Brock and Xepapadeas 2002). So the species were in a Tilman-type model, which is more of an equilibrium-type model, where they were all using a common limiting resource, say like nitrogen. Then the species that can get by with the least amount of the limiting resource will end up driving everyone else out of the system. So that is a type of equilibrium. But if the limiting factor itself is moving on a slow-moving dynamics, then you would have the whole system chasing a moving target. Genetic dynamics have to do with dynamics of the genotypes.

We got into this because we were interested in the economic valuation of biodiversity. Much of the ecological literature uses a phenotypic approach where you look at things like Shannon indices, or just count the number of species, or use DNA-related measures of biodiversity. But that doesn't really get at the functional role of biodiversity. What economic value does biodiversity have? So we made up an example where the standard biodiversity difference measures would be zero but the functional biodiversity of the system would end up generating an arbitrarily large value (Brock and Xepapadeas 2003). The parable is to think about Bt *(Bacillus thuringiensis)* corn versus non-Bt corn. This is a genetically altered corn. All you did was to alter a very small piece of a very large genome. So from a genotypic biodiversity point of view the difference would be almost zero because it is such a large genome.

The heart of this problem has to do with resistance buildup because you are genetically engineering the corn to destroy a pest called the European corn borer. So Monsanto and other companies that are involved in Bt corn urged the farmers to plant a reserve of non-Bt corn. The genetics of the pest can be modeled as a one-locus two-allele genetics (which actually is too simple, but it is good enough for a parable). What happens is that each farmer has an incentive to plant all Bt corn. But if they do, resistance builds up, and the economic value of Bt corn is destroyed. But if each farmer maintains biodiversity—some Bt corn and some non-Bt corn—it is possible to maintain the resistance.

Unfortunately, if the genetics isn't just right, the bugs will win. So that is an example of a mixed evolutionary/equilibrium model where you model the force of the evolution precisely. The model got very hairy, so we used a combination of MatLab and analysis to consider the issue. The main point that we made is that much of the work on biodiversity measurement really needs supplementation to be economically relevant. Here is an example where the biodiversity on phenotypic measures and standard diversity measures is essentially zero. But if you are eating corn, and the pest kills corn entirely, you can see that the economic effect would be large.

Do you consider yourself working on the edge?

I consider myself a normal economist in the sense that I'm always driven by evidence.

Do you consider normal economists as being primarily driven by evidence?

Well, I'd like to think so. . . . I agree there are schools of thought, but I'd rather see less ideology and more careful reporting of the true level of uncertainty. That's what we really need. I think it is less ideology in economics than it is finding a paradigm that appears to have done a pretty good job for its users in the past so they don't want to give it up. As my dad always used to say, "If it ain't broke, don't fix it." So on the one hand I can understand when people remain tied to their model in the face of somewhat contradictory evidence. But on the other hand people who make policy statements when the data might equally well support two paradigms are not following good practice. I think we need a more honest reporting of uncertainty. When there's theory uncertainty and model uncertainty, I think we ought to report it. Durlauf and I made this argument in an article we wrote for the World Bank on growth regressions (Brock and Durlauf 2001b).

A lot of scientists in other sciences ask me about how we in economics report uncertainty. Do you report something besides error bars, conditional on a model? And I say we do a lot of that. Other sciences are moving in a direction that takes into account model uncertainty. That is what prompted a lot of the activity that has been going on in Bayesian model averaging. It gives you a quantitative language that you can use to report model uncertainty. I believe that as the profession gets more into using cheap computing time that we'll see more of this.

So you think that what is seen as ideological bias has really been just a limit of the technology and not a reflection of individuals placing a barrier to protect their models?
I think the limitation of the technology made it really cheap to maintain a protective barrier. But now computers are everywhere, and with continual technological change it will be much harder to do.

What are the new tools that you see that will really change economics?
Bootstrapping and methods of statistical inference that are related to it. Then there are newer techniques like bagging and arcing. These are all computationally intensive inference techniques.

Will that reduce the value of theory?
I don't think so. I think what will happen is that the theory will adapt to the new environment. For example, some of the theory that I've been doing with Cars Hommes and a young math guy at CeNDEF (Center for Nonlinear Dynamics in Economics and Finance), Florian Wagner (Brock et al. forthcoming), is essentially doing analytical mathematics for agent-based simulations. Agent-based simulations is a huge industry that has exploded. You can see it on Leigh Tesfatsions's and Blake LeBaron's websites. Most of that work is computational, not analytic. So what we've been doing is using mathematical ensemble–based methods to write down mathematical models of their agent-based models and get analytical

results for them by taking large-system limits, doing bifurcations analysis, and so on. So I see pure theory as remaining.

While it is a different type theory than was done before, there are precursors, such as the large-economy limit work of Aumann, Debreu, Hildenbrand, Kirman, and others. As I said before, there is nothing new. That work looks very much like this ensemble stuff. The difference is that they weren't focused on dynamical systems, whereas we are because agent-based models are dynamical systems. Then we use some of my past experience in econometrics to recognize that temporary equilibrium equations of these agent-based systems of LeBaron resemble functions of sample moments (Brock and LeBaron 1996). When you recognize that, you are prompted to take a limit over types. At that point you are looking at population moments.

If you do the above procedures with any framework that yields Gibbs-like probabilities, you will recognize in these equations functions that look like moment-generating functions of probability and statistics. You can get tables of moment-generating functions for all types of distributions, and these give you closed form expressions for the dynamical systems that you get in large-system ensemble limits. With that you can do bifurcation analysis and classify the bifurcations and isolate the forces that lead to stability and instability. Sometimes you find that more heterogeneity hurts when it is coupled with a very fast rate of evolutionary change.

Some recent work of LeBaron suggests that when you slow things down in a financial market that you might get a better performance. That's the idea behind the Tobin tax instituted on an international level. The point is that you can analyze policy questions like that and actually get analytical results. Of course you have to trade off. Most of the agent-based literature doesn't have the price discovery function of markets that the noisy rational expectational literature has. So the price discovery function has to be traded off for the added insights of this model. If you put in a Tobin tax, the price mechanism wouldn't discover information as rapidly as it did otherwise.

We obviously missed many people who are working to expand economics along the lines we discussed. But do you think we missed representatives of the various approaches that are changing economics?

I thought you covered just about everything, recognizing the size limitation of the book and the need to keep some focus.

WILLIAM A. ("BUZ") BROCK

In your model with Durlauf, an economist at the edge would have a high intensity of choice. Is there any other factor that would identify someone as being an economist at the edge?

Someone told me in the middle of my career that you've only got so much time and there is a frontier. You can do two things on this frontier. You can work an area and establish your claim. If you do, you'll be identified with that area, and if the area really takes off, you will be the leading representative of that area. That's a conventional career path, but it's kind of boring in my view.

Alternatively, you could live more dangerously and let your mind wander, working more than one area and hoping that there is synergy between the areas and that you can dig deep enough into each area and make a contribution. My approach has been a little bit different. What I like to do is to scan the intellectual landscape in economics, see where there are gaps that need to be filled. Then I jump in and try to fill them. I like to stay and try to work on a gap for whatever time it takes to see that the gap is fixed—then I decide I'm not needed anymore, so I go on.

Where do you see economics going in the next twenty-five to fifty years?

That's a bit like the efficient markets hypothesis—if I could predict it, I would be rich. But I can throw out some wild guesses. I think ultimately economics is policy driven—it is driven by the great policy issues of the day. So I think we will see economists working on things like functional biodiversity because environmental pressures are getting stronger. I could even see economists joining up with ecologists working on issues like optimal habitat design, which considers the tradeoff between the costs to taking land out of production and keeping economically valuable biodiversity. I also think we'll see more work on alternative stable state systems where the evidence isn't clear. There will be a consideration of the alternative approaches to policy—maybe some mixture of the precautionary principle followed in Europe, in which the burden of proof showing that a new product will not harm you lies with those who want to introduce it, and the full speed ahead principle in the U.S., in which the burden of proof lies with those who suspect that the new product will harm society.

We'll see an expansion in the usefulness of the models. As more and more quantitative tools become available with cheap computation and as people get skilled in moving between analytics and computer-assisted proofs, computational simulation techniques in general will expand enormously. I try to use a mix of that in my own work, as the price of computer time continues to fall.

As I argued in my contribution to Colander's book on *Complexity Vision and the Teaching of Economics* (Brock 2000), I think pedagogy will change and students will be simulating models in their work rather than just doing analytics. The decrease in cost of computation will increase the use of simulation in teaching more and more. Agent-based models wouldn't have existed without computers. I just hope that people don't forget how to do the mathematics since one needs mathematics to understand what's going on inside the models in the computer.

WILLIAM A. ("BUZ") BROCK

William A. ("Buz") Brock

Vilas Research Professor of Economics, University of Wisconsin at Madison

INFORMATION ON THE WEB ABOUT WILLIAM A. ("BUZ") BROCK
http://www.ssc.wisc.edu/~wbrock/

EDUCATION
B.A. Mathematics, University of Missouri at Columbia with Honors, 1965
Ph.D. Mathematics, University of California at Berkeley, 1969

SELECTED PUBLICATIONS
"Optimal Growth under Factor Augmenting Progress," with David Gale. *Journal of Economic Theory* 1 (1969).
"Distinguishing Random and Deterministic Systems." *Journal of Economic Theory* 40 (1986).
"Nonlinearity and Complex Dynamics in Economics and Finance." In *The Economy as an Evolving Complex System,* edited by Philip W. Anderson, Kenneth J. Arrow, and David Pines, Santa Fe Institute Studies in the Sciences of Complexity, vol. 3. Reading, MA: Addison-Wesley, 1988.
"A Formal Model of Theory Choice in Science," with Steven N. Durlauf. *Economic Theory* 14 (1999).
Growth Theory, Nonlinear Dynamics and Economic Modeling: Scientific Essays of William Allen Brock. Edited by W. Dechert. Cheltenham: Edward Elgar, 2001.

SPECIAL HONORS AND EXPERIENCE
Also taught at University of Chicago, Cornell University, and University of Rochester
Bernard Friedman Memorial Prize (for excellence of Ph.D. thesis in applied mathematics); Fellow of Econometric Society, 1974; Sherman Fairchild Distinguished Scholar, California Institute of Technology, 1978; Guggenheim Fellow, 1987; Fellow of the American Academy of Arts and Sciences; and member of the National Academy of Sciences
External faculty member, Santa Fe Institute, 1987–2002
Distinguised Fellow, American Economic Association

CHAPTER 7

Duncan K. Foley

Leo Model Professor of Economics, New School for Social Research

∾

The interview was conducted on November 30, 2001, in Duncan K. Foley's apartment on West 106th Street in New York City.

How did you get into economics?

When I was at Swarthmore College, I took Principles of Macroeconomics from Bill Brown, and I was totally blown away by the Keynesian Cross. (I'm still a big fan of the Keynesian Cross.) I majored in mathematics with minors in economics and philosophy. I didn't take many courses in economics, but I did learn basic economic theory. In Swarthmore's honors program at that time, a minor consisted of two intensive seminars. One I took was Economic Theory with Joe Conard, which was the equivalent of a year of graduate macro/micro theory; the other was Macroeconomics with Bill Brown, which explored what were then frontier issues in econometrics and modeling. The level was high—I remember we did a good deal of R. D. G. Allen's *Mathematical Analysis for Economists* (1938).

Two specific events from that period stick in my mind. One was arguing with Conard about choice theory. I didn't think that it was a very good theory for explaining most actual economic decisions,

∾

like buying a candy bar from a vending machine. Conard suggested that it would be a good idea for me to learn the theory thoroughly before criticizing it. Somehow that touched my heart, and I did study a lot of neoclassical theory.

The other incident was in Macroeconomics with Bill Brown. Partly as a result of my nagging, we tried to make an econometric model of the U.S. economy. It started as a very ambitious project but ended up very primitive and minimal as we realized just how difficult it would be to estimate a full model. I think in the end it boiled down to a lot of accounting identities and maybe something like a production function. We ran the program as a simulation at Haverford College's computer center. The model (as I realize now) was unstable and produced growing two-period oscillations. I had really expected it would track U.S. GDP and was very disappointed. I think this was the beginning of a lifetime process of disillusionment with econometrics.

How did you decide where to go to graduate school?

When I graduated from Swarthmore in 1964, I wasn't intending to pursue an academic career. I wanted to go into the Foreign Service or politics. I interviewed successfully through the first stage for the Foreign Service in the spring of my senior year, but at that time I had a romantic entanglement with a noncitizen. The Foreign Service rules require the spouses of officers to be citizens, and it would take a minimum of a year for someone to become a citizen. So I had a year ahead of me, and one of the options was to spend it studying economics. I applied to a couple of graduate schools in economics, and perhaps because both Conard and Brown had gone to Yale, I wound up going there. I didn't give too much thought to this decision because I thought it would be only for a year. Then during the summer of my senior year the romance fizzled, so I arrived in New Haven with no real reason for being there. I'm afraid I was a rather rebellious graduate student.

What do you remember about your courses?

The course I remember with the most pleasure was Herbert Scarf's Mathematical Economics. I thought, and still think, it was fabulous. The other courses were not so fabulous. Part of the problem was the style of teaching. I was coming from Swarthmore's honors program, which gave me a lot of freedom and time to explore and figure things out for myself. I was used to reading a broad reading list and then synthesizing the material in seminar papers. At Yale, I was back to the much more passive learning mode of sitting in classes and listening to lecturers who were in some cases not particularly brilliant.

As a result of my honors economics seminars at Swarthmore (Yale's John Fei had been one of the outside examiners my senior year), I was exempted from the first-year core theory courses at Yale, but I was still bored. In January, before the second term started, I decided to leave. My adviser, Jim Tobin, told me not to be so hasty. Since I had been exempt from the first-year courses, he said I could take my qualifying exams at the end of the summer of my first year and then start a thesis. The prospect of finishing a Ph.D. in no more than three years induced me to stay. It was while working with Scarf and writing my thesis under him that I started to get interested in economics.

What did you like most about Scarf's course?

In many ways the course forecast the next twenty years of economic theory. It started with linear programming and went on to nonlinear programming, the Kuhn-Tucker-type theorems, and turnpike growth theory. Then we did the proof of the existence of general equilibrium, in which the standard Arrow-Debreu arguments were presented from Scarf's point of view. In the second part of the course, he taught the algorithmic approach to the computation of general equilibrium prices (Scarf 1973), and integer programming, which remains a largely untamed frontier of research. Scarf's presentation of integer programming gave me some insight into how intractable the problem of increasing returns and indivisibility were going to be for the general equilibrium research program.

These problems, in fact, lead straight to one of the key elements of the current complex systems approach to economic modeling. At the core of the complexity vision is the recognition of a fundamental nonlinearity and instability associated with local increasing returns; this is what brings about multiple equilibria and the failure of the system to settle into equilibrium. Economists, of course, had encountered these issues before Scarf (1960), going at least back to Adam Smith and the widening division of labor. For example, Allyn Young (1928) worked on a lot of these problems.

Arrow (1962) dealt with this in his learning-by-doing model, which can lead to multiple equilibria and complexity. How did you view this at the time?

I read his paper at the time and thought it was empirically reasonable with regard to Swedish steel mills, but it was not a turning point in my own thinking, and it did not lead me to work on that problem. I already knew that costs typically fell over time in real-world technological sectors from my three summers as a computer programmer in the instrumentation and control company where my father worked as an industrial physicist. This experience imprinted me with an engineering approach to many economic problems. I had the idea, for example, that it might make sense to measure the impact of monetary policy by finding the relevant transfer functions through Fourier analysis (which was a method we were using to study control problems in industrial plants). This engineering perspective easily led to the idea of continually falling costs and such corollaries as Moore's Law, which has had remarkable success in predicting the path of technological change in the chip industry.

Tell us about your thesis.

My thesis adapted the methods of general equilibrium theory to the problem of public goods (Foley 1967). In method it's closely related to Koopmans's (1957) work. It has some results that I still think are neat. I proposed an analog of competitive equilibrium for public goods, which I called public competitive equilibrium based on a weak unanimity requirement for changing public goods allocations, and proved that it was Pareto efficient, which a lot of people found hard to accept at the time. But the method was exactly the same as Koopmans's proof of the Pareto efficiency of price equilibria. I also showed the existence of a public competitive equilibrium with a proportional lump sum tax schedule. In proving this existence theorem I independently discovered Negishi's method for proving the existence of Walrasian competitive equilibrium, which is based on moving along the Pareto efficient surface by changing household weights in a social welfare function rather than using a tatonnement argument on prices.

In the thesis I also discussed the politics of setting average tax rates and tax schedules through majority voting, which recapitulates and extends some basic results of social choice theory. I also developed a critique of the notion that interpersonal welfare comparisons are inherently impossible, which other scholars later developed in the literature on fairness. The idea is to ask two agents at equilibrium to rank each other's bundles according to their own preferences. There are only three possibilities: if each prefers the other's bundle, they could make a mutually improving trade and hence aren't at equilibrium; if each prefers his or her own bundle, the allocation is envy-free or fair; and if they both prefer one bundle, it seems safe to conclude that the one with the commonly preferred bundle is objectively better off than the other.

You use a highly mathematical modeling approach to economics issues, which seems to be only indirectly related to policy. How do you see your work fitting in with policy?

I tend to work on rather fundamental methodological and theoretical issues that form the foundation of policy-type analyses, and as a result the implications of my work for policy are often not immediately apparent. I have a strong interest in history and institutions. I studied Greek and Latin as an undergraduate. Thucydides and Plato tend to be buzzing around in my mind when I work on abstract problems in economic theory. Philosophy offers a much wider range of ways to think about society and politics than neoclassical economics recognizes. This gap became increasingly acute for me as time went on. During the Vietnam War I became concerned about how relevant the abstract theories of general equilibrium economics were to the critical historical problems of our age.

I remember almost fainting at times in micro theory courses when I started to teach indifference curves and Pareto efficiency theory. I kept asking myself: "Is this an honest way to represent society and its contradictions to students?"

As I mentioned earlier, I didn't accept consumer choice theory as an undergraduate; I never liked it. One of the things that increasingly struck me was how peculiar the technical language of economic theory is when you parse it out in ordinary language. You talk about "marginal utility" or "rational expectations" or "efficiency"; these are very potent (normatively laden) and powerful phrases that cannot be quarantined as purely technical expressions in economics.

You once wrote (Foley 1999) that you "did not learn enough about the sociology and attitudes of the economics profession to navigate its world comfortably." Can you explain what you meant by that statement?

I wrote that, I believe, about my time at Yale, partly because I didn't stay there very long and partly because I was somewhat an outsider among the other graduate students. I was more interested in mathematical economics, and I was more alienated from the professional aspirations of many of the students. I believe what I meant is that I didn't understand how hierarchically organized the discipline was and how much power key figures in the profession have over journal acceptances, promotions, and so forth. I didn't really have an idea of how ideologically attuned the system was. I also made things worse for myself by alienating some people through a sort of immature insolence.

When you were finishing up at Yale, did you have a vision of what your life would be like and what your research agenda would be?

Even when I was writing my thesis, I was still planning to get out of economics. This was before the major escalation of the Vietnam War, which ended the possibility of someone with a pacifist background like myself from going into the Foreign Service. I was already a pacifist prior to the war as a result of attending Quaker meetings from when I was nine years old and becoming a member of the Society of Friends when I was fifteen. So at that time I was still viewing economics as something of a detour and thinking that after two years of graduate work I would go back to Philadelphia and get into politics or theater. That shows a stunning lack of self-knowledge on my part. I had similar blind spots when it came to the economics profession.

But you were on the inside; clearly the Yale faculty had picked you as somebody whom they could place at the highest level.

But they were wrong, too. They didn't know me much better than I knew them. From their point of view, I was a bright student with the right math skills and the ability to do interesting work in economics. I didn't have any ideology to speak of at that time, except maybe my pacifism. It was the Vietnam crisis that made my views come out. It directed my thinking to issues of the U.S. national role in the world, which remain just as problematic thirty-five years later: what is capitalism, and how does it work on a world scale?

The Vietnam War influenced my career choices, as it did for almost all of my male contemporaries. I planned to do alternative service as a conscientious objector if I was drafted. But it turned out that the Selective Service system viewed university teaching as working in the national interest, and worth a deferment, and this made continuing for a while as an economist all the more tempting. This was a period of high demand for qualified Ph.D.s, and several schools expressed interest in hiring me. I chose MIT partly because my wife, Helene, had moved from her original MAT program at Yale (leading to a career in high school teaching) to an M.A. in classics, and Boston was a better place for her to pursue a classics Ph.D.

How did you find MIT?

MIT was a powerfully wrenching emotional experience in a lot of ways. I was there from 1966 to 1973, and a lot of things happened. At a professional as well as personal level two important events were my cordial friendship and collaboration with Miguel Sidrauski and Sidrauski's unexpected death in 1969 just as we finished work on a book (Foley and Sidrauski 1971).

This was the also the height of the Vietnam crisis, with riots in Harvard Square and the Sanctuary Movement at MIT. I remember sitting fire watch at the MIT libraries and mediating the case of an MIT professor very sympathetic to the radical students whom the school wanted to fire. It was a period of violent polarization in which many young scholars with radical sympathies were subjected to disciplinary sanctions essentially for the expression of their political views. I remember in the fall of 1969, which we spent on leave in London, I went to academic hearings at the London School of Economics, which was trying to fire Lawrence Harris for chairing a meeting that led to a sit-in.

MIT itself is just a very tough place, Vietnam or no Vietnam. MIT exists to be right on the top of everything. The pressure to get grants, to publish, to be the leader in the field, to guide the field forward was intimidating. I found the pressure to institutionalize and even monopolize cutting edge work counterproductive and upsetting. You would sit and say, "Well, am I going to be able to improve on or even equal the careers of people like Samuelson and Solow?" It seemed hopeless. Another problem was that I felt increasingly uneasy about following the career path of the generations ahead of me, in part because of their entanglement with political power. I had a negative personal reaction to that type of intellectual style and the kind of success it represented, despite having a lot of respect,

and indeed awe, for the extraordinary personalities of that generation. I did not find it a very nurturing environment, especially for
doing anything fundamentally new.

*Miguel Sidrauski came to MIT with a Chicago Ph.D. What were his
politics, and did you have problems with him coming out of Chicago?
How did all that work out?*

Miguel was an Argentine Jew, and his wife, Martha Sidrauski,
had strong left-wing sympathies. She had close connections to people who later were *desparecidos* ("disappeared," that is to say, mur-
dered by right-wing vigilantes). Sidrauski was less left-wing than
Martha, but much of his sympathy lay in that direction. He was also
a committed Zionist. He was grateful to Chicago for the scholarship
that brought him there, and was one of their best students, but he
had a certain amount of ambivalence about buying the whole of the
Chicago line. For example, leaving aside the book we wrote
together, his reputation rests largely on two brilliant articles that he
wrote on macroeconomics and money. In one, based on his thesis
research, he puts money in the utility function and works out how a
representative agent intertemporally optimizes to arrive at a
demand for money (Sidrauski 1969), and studies the conditions for
the neutrality and superneutrality of money. In the other, published
in the *Journal of Political Economy* (1967) ("Inflation and Economic
Growth"), he studies a model similar to Tobin's "Money and
Growth," in which money is not neutral because when the rate of
inflation rises it reduces the real rate of return to money and makes
capital more attractive as an asset, thus increasing the investment
rate. So he was not what I would call a pure Chicago economist.

Who else was at MIT at the time, younger people?

There was a wonderful group. The immediate group contempo-
rary with me included Michael Piore, John Harris, Matthew Edel,
Joe Stiglitz, Sidrauski, Duncan MacRae, and Pranab Bardhan. Marty
Weitzman came in 1968, I believe. Karl Shell, with whom I have had
a close and warm friendship, was just leaving MIT to move to Penn
and found the *Journal of Economic Theory.*

*When you were at MIT, did you consider yourself part of the econom-
ics profession, or did you see yourself as being co-opted into the profession?*

There were things about it I liked. I always loved teaching; I love working with students. So it was natural for me to get involved and interested in curricular issues at MIT. I became interested in how we should organize the first-year graduate courses and make them more effective. I felt that I was doing a lot of good work in that area. I was also writing books and some articles—a lot less than people would have liked, but they were published in good places. I think I survived there because I was not committed to staying. I saw it as a temporary episode and never invested much psychologically in the issue of getting promoted and staying there for the long term.

What were some of the curricular changes you wanted to make in the core courses at MIT?

When I first came there, the core microeconomics was a semester with Bob Bishop, who did Marshall's Principles and then a spring semester with, I think, Samuelson. The macro core was a semester with Solow and one, I think, with Albert Ando. My idea was to divide each theory sequence into four minicourses. There were now four modules in each of macro and micro; in micro two were effectively the previous material, which Bishop and Samuelson taught. I taught a new one on general equilibrium theory. I believe the other micro module was game theory. Macro was structured in a similar fashion.

So you were responsible for MIT moving more toward Walrasian orthodoxy?

Yes, in a sense, or at least for bringing the general equilibrium perspective there. This was also the period of the Cambridge Capital Controversy (Harcourt 1972). Nobody, curiously enough, talked to me about the Cambridge controversy at the time. Later, I became interested in the topic and wanted to know what people at MIT had been thinking. I asked Karl Shell about it, and he said, as far as he remembered, Solow and Samuelson viewed the Cambridge, England, position in the capital controversy as a lesser threat to their ambitions for neoclassical theory than the work of Gerard Debreu. I think that is interesting, and the more I think about it, the more I think it has a core of truth.

So it might be said that you made Gerard Debreu safe for neoclassical orthodoxy at MIT?

They felt they had to have it. One great thing about MIT was that they were so student oriented and interested in making sure that people would come through the department with what they needed to play leading roles in the discipline. The faculty was in touch with what was interesting and what was going on. They were very eclectic, pragmatic, and willing to tolerate the teaching of ideas they didn't personally favor.

So with your research you felt out of touch with MIT. Your research agenda on general equilibrium theory didn't really fit MIT's problem-solving approach.

I think that's right. I had a series of discussions with Joe Stiglitz, who had the office next to me the first year I taught at MIT, about methodology, whether one needed a unifying vision for economics. He took what I think was a much more Bob Solow view of the way to work: you pick a problem, you build a nice model, and then you go to the next problem and the next model. If the two models are not very consistent with one another, you don't spend a lot of time worrying about it. I, on the other hand, believed you needed a unifying vision, and if you could not put the models together into a coherent whole, then they were suspect. Curiously enough I think Stiglitz and I may have changed positions to some degree on this with the passage of time.

Let's see if we have this right: You're at MIT and doing fairly well. You are still ambivalent about staying in economics, and your teaching and research would be considered a little out of the norm for MIT but still within the mainstream of the profession. Are you caring about economics at this time? You are worried about the Vietnam War and your publishing, but are you generally comfortable?

There were three crises affecting me at that time. The first was a result of the Vietnam War. I wanted to know more about the roots of social theory and in particular to read Marx. I knew there had to be some economics that addressed the fundamental issues in world politics more deeply than neoclassical theory. The second crisis was brewing in my research. I had a research program centered on trying to introduce money into the general equilibrium system, and I was becoming increasingly convinced that this was never going to happen. I didn't quite understand completely why it wouldn't work, but the more I tried to follow that line of thinking over another the more I got stuck, and this made me suspect I had formulated an impossible problem. The third crisis was that I, like many people of my generation through the Vietnam period, was becoming more radicalized. I expressed a radical sensibility that certain members of the department had a hard time with. I was asking questions like "How come we have a department where middle-aged men sit in large offices with windows, while young women working with them sit in small offices without windows?" In response I got a lecture about comparative advantage. That was the stage of the conversation at that time. These issues were causing more and more tension between some faculty members and me. At a certain point, I felt that I was getting a strong signal that it might be more comfortable if I went somewhere else.

At MIT the freest people seemed to be those junior faculty who had decided to leave and a few senior faculty who had internally emigrated away from the dominant MIT view. Among the latter I was closest to the econometrician Harold Freeman for political reasons. But most of the senior faculty were not very supportive. I remember telling one senior professor that I doubted the relevance of the concept of Pareto efficiency to actual policy and his responding that if I felt that way I should get out of economics altogether.

You moved to Stanford in 1973. How would you describe the intellectual atmosphere at both MIT and Stanford?

When I left MIT for Stanford, I moved to a completely different milieu, in which the level of discussion of curricular development and research methodology seemed to me much lower. At MIT, the subtext of the discussion was, How serious is this work? How important is this work? What's important about it? They were not dogmatic about it. When I say MIT wasn't a place to do new stuff, it wasn't that they weren't interested in new stuff. They were. But the level at which new stuff had to be presented had to be very mature, ready for prime time, and they were not very patient about nurturing new approaches over the long term.

Let me give you an example, which came up later. I was trying to think about this whole problem of microeconomic equilibrium. So I said, "Let's look at anthills, let's look at yeast, and how do they organize themselves?" This type of question later turned out to be a major theme in the complex systems literature, but at that time it was quite unfamiliar to economists. I started to try to write some papers exploring these issues, trying to make some models along these lines. There were some MIT faculty members who found this abstractly interesting, but they would look at the models in terms of their immediate prospects for publication and were troubled by the large amount of work that evidently still had to be done.

Another example was my first flirtation with statistical mechanics, which occurred while I was still at MIT. At that time I was interested in the notion that price should not be scalar, that it should be represented by a probability distribution. I only knew a little bit of physics, but I had the feeling that statistical mechanics could provide a framework to model price formation. But I ran into a problem, which was that the physics literature I read presented statistical mechanics as applying only to ergodic systems and I couldn't see how one could argue markets were ergodic systems.

At Stanford, on the other hand, I experienced the intellectual atmosphere as much more polarized, politicized, and dogmatic. I had the feeling that some people (not by any means all) in the Stanford department had real trouble in approaching ideas that were new or different from their own in an open-minded and curious spirit. At MIT I also felt that people were much more confident about expressing their doubts so that you knew more clearly where you stood. With some Stanford colleagues I experienced serious and troubling lack of communication, even of frankness. It was not an easy environment for me to operate in.

There may be some lessons from my experience about the difficulties of "cutting edge" research. I had a lot of ideas, but I was not really encouraged to explore them. I often got the feeling that people regarded the work that I was doing as so far out, requiring so long to develop and publish, that it was not something I should be doing. There are strong pressures for you to think about tenure and publish a lot of papers, which is at odds with the pursuit of new ideas that require a lot of slow development. So I guess it is fair to say that most of my colleagues at both MIT and Stanford didn't understand very well how I looked at the world and the discipline of economics. I felt there was almost nobody who was anywhere near the same wavelength that I was to talk about these issues and problems.

Who brought you to Stanford?

My wife, Helene, got a job at Stanford in the classics department. So I started asking around about jobs in the San Francisco area. I think it was Peter Diamond who called up Paul David and asked if there were any chance of Foley coming out because his wife had gotten a job there. He responded positively, and negotiations began. So I was a faculty spouse. I recognize now that I should not have gone to Stanford without tenure. I probably could have gotten a tenure offer if I had been willing to be more patient, but at the time I still wasn't seeing myself as a professional economist. In fact, I was pretty sure I was going to go off and do something else such as work in the theater. I wasn't especially worried about tenure at the time. Stanford came up with a three-year position and said that they would definitely decide whether to promote me or not in the second year. I later understood that by not insisting on receiving tenure I probably signaled that I did not take myself seriously.

We arrived at Stanford in the fall of 1973, thrilled to be there. It was a new life; it was relaxing, and it gave me a chance to do a lot of work. I had five papers come out in 1975.

You mentioned earlier your concern with your research agenda, particularly with trying to get money into general equilibrium theory. Where did the five papers come from?

They were to some degree cleaning up loose ends, although, some of them could have been longer research projects. One was a paper with Rob Engle (Engle and Foley 1975) on band spectrum regression, which was a new econometric approach at the time. Another paper with Martin Hellwig addressed the money and general equilibrium issues by looking at market equilibrium with liquidity constraints and price uncertainty (Foley and Hellwig 1975). This paper used some of the dynamic programming methods that later became central to recursive approaches to macroeconomics. There was also a paper on two specifications of asset equilibrium where I tried to deal with some of the stock-flow issues that were raised by the Foley/Sidrauski model (Foley 1975a). Finally, there was my *American Economic Review* paper on ideology (Foley 1975b). Some people really didn't like that paper.

One of the big unifying themes throughout your entire career has been your concern about theoretically dealing with money. Is that a core issue for you?

I think it's like Odysseus's journey of return to Ithaca. Constantine Cavafy's poem "Ithaca" addresses Odysseus's feelings when he finally reaches Ithaca after ten years. Cavafy says, you know Ithaca is not a very grand place, you've been to more amazing places, you've seen the bizarre and the glittering jewels; Ithaca is just a small island. The last lines of the poem says, don't ask too much from Ithaca; it has given you a beautiful journey. I learned a lot about money. I learned a lot about theories of money. I don't think I am anywhere near to the synthetic view of money that I was looking for. That's one of the big lacunae in economic theory.

So you haven't reached Ithaca yet?
No, and I probably never will.

At Stanford, you had quite an interest in Marxian economics. Did your interest start there, or does that interest have earlier origins?
When I was at MIT, I had tried to read Marx. I had some conversations with Steve Marglin, who was at Harvard and going through a major transformation of his interests in a radical direction. Sam Bowles and Herb Gintis were in Cambridge, fighting unsuccessfully for tenure at Harvard. But at that time I had the typical reaction of neoclassically trained economists to reading Marx, which was to understand Marx's theory as a general equilibrium model with a single labor input and to wonder why the wage would not be competitively bid up to eliminate profit.

It was really at Stanford that I managed to understand something of Marx. I wanted to learn more about it, like many other people. American imperialism was fighting Communism in Vietnam, and I wanted to know what this was all about. At Stanford there were a number of people interested in Marxist and classical approaches to political economy. Jack Gurley was in the economics department, and Don Harris was a visiting professor. There was also a group in the anthropology department around Bridget O'Laughlin, who was a particularly important intellectual resource for me, along with a group of very able graduate students in economics interested in political economy, including Tracy Mott, Michael Carter, Susan Carter, Jens Christiansen, Sandy Thompson, Gita Sen, and Chiranjib Sen. They were a group of bright and energetic students.

Don Harris was a key figure in insisting that political economy be approached as a serious intellectual issue. Remember, I went to Stanford in 1973, and in 1970 was Kent State, 1971 was Cambodia, and we were heading toward the withdrawal of American troops from Vietnam. These were very emotional political issues. Harris reminded us that political economy addresses very serious intellectual questions and requires rigor and formal analysis. He said that you should look carefully at Sraffa, you should look carefully at Marx, you should understand what they really have to say—let's get rid of the slogans, let's get rid of the politics, let's look at this as economics (Harris 1978). At Stanford there were some very good intellectuals who wanted to build an analytical framework and solve problems from a Marxian perspective. The great advantage of reading Marx there was the feedback you received in interpreting what you were reading. That was tremendously helpful to me. There's no doubt that Marx's ideas are powerful. Like the Ancient Mariner, it grabs you and pulls you off in an interesting way; I was pulled pretty strongly in that direction. I was also quite taken, like many people, with reading French Marxist philosophy, which struck me as brilliant and fresh. (I've since learned to be a bit more cautious about some of its claims.)

Did you play a major role in getting Don Harris tenure at Stanford?

Yes I did, and that was a big strategic success for me. The department had decided, under tremendous pressure from students, that they needed someone to teach classical and Marxian economics (they called it Alternative Approaches to Economics). Despite not having tenure, I served on the search committee that ensued, which had to choose, for example, between the people like Thomas Sowell and Don Harris for that role. The committee persuaded the department to make an offer to Harris. Unfortunately, I don't think Don has enjoyed his time at Stanford, partly because his health deteriorated.

How did you find the intellectual climate among those who were doing Marxian economics? What changes did you see in the way Marxian economics was being viewed?

The notion of a formally elaborated Marxian economics, an attempt to do for Marx what Arrow and Debreu (1954) did for Walras, to try to understand what the paradigm was and what Marx had to say about it, was at that time just barely emerging from a hugely confused and politicized sloganeering kind of radicalism and revolutionary politics. At the time there was a lot of sectarianism; there were different communist parties, each of whom thought they knew what Marx was about. Students were at sea about even the most fundamental questions. In retrospect a lot of progress was made in clarifying issues and making clear expositions of fundamental ideas available during this period.

Two of your key papers on Marxian economics, both coming out in 1982, were in the Journal of Economic Theory *(Foley 1982a) and the* Review of Radical Political Economy *(Foley 1982b). What was the genesis of those papers?*

The work I did on Marx had a lot of continuity with my earlier research in public goods, macroeconomic dynamics, and money. The first paper I wrote about Marxian economics was about public goods, a paper rarely read (Foley 1978). I wrote it for a conference in Belgium, to which Richard Musgrave invited me. The *JET* paper addresses Marx's circuit of capital conception from volume 2 of *Capital,* which links closely with the stock-flow issues that I had been interested in and integrates money with production. The circuit of capital was also a natural topic for the kind of mathematics (integral equation representations of dynamical systems) I was interested in.

In the *RRPE* paper I approached the "transformation problem" from the point of view of Marx's theory of money. Its main interest in my view is not so much as a solution to a transformation problem; it's mainly to understand that Marx's theory of value is really a theory of money. When I first wrote it, I thought it was a pretty good idea, so I sent it to the *American Economic Review.* I got a letter back from Bob Clower, who was then the editor of the *AER.* I still have the letter, which roughly said, "Dear Duncan, I usually thank people for sending papers to the *AER,* but in this case I really cannot do that. I think this paper is absolutely useless; it contains no insights or information about money or value, and I am not going to send this out to referees." I finally published the paper in the *Radical Review of Political Economy,* which had, and still has, a collective editorial policy. I think I received twelve referee reports about the paper, and they were all over the place. Some loved it; some hated it. *RRPE* did a special issue where they put together a whole range of papers on approaches to the transformation problem. I suspect this paper is the most cited paper I ever wrote. Probably very few people in mainstream economics know about it, but it is widely read internationally. This was cutting edge work in my view.

I still think the basic point of the paper is sound, despite some valid criticisms of specific formulations in it. Marxian economics had curiously drifted into treating value theory without any discussion of money. If you read Marx, that's not right, the first three chapters of the first part of *Das Kapital* (Marx 1867) are all about money. Everybody seemed to have dropped that out of the big picture of what Marx was trying to say, with a disastrous effect on the influence of Marxian economics in economics. Everybody thought that they had to translate everything into labor values with Marx. For example, Ed Wolff (1975) wrote a path-breaking paper called "The Rate of Surplus Value in Puerto Rico," published in the *Journal of Political Economy,* where he used input/output tables to calculate embodied labor coefficients and then converted the Puerto Rican national income accounts into embodied labor terms. The process of converting to labor values is very cumbersome and difficult, but the numerical results of those transformations are not very different than the ones you get if you use wage and profit shares in untransformed data. The other person who was on to the monetary approach to the transformation problem was Gérard Duménil.

My submitting the transformation paper to the *AER* brought out my lack of understanding of the sociology and norms of American economics; I really didn't expect that kind of reaction from a responsible editor. I wish I could tell you that this episode was a special case and that kind of editorial ignorance and arrogance is now unacceptable, but I'm afraid it still persists. In fact, I just went through this recently at mainstream journals with a paper I wrote with Tom Michl, a model of social security from a classical perspective.

What led you to leave Stanford?

The first indication I had a problem at Stanford was when I tried to get the department to live up to the commitment they had made to bring me up in the second year of my contract. I marched into the chairman's office and said I should be coming up for tenure in the fall of 1974, "because this was the deal when you hired me." They said, "Oh there's just one problem. There's a freeze on promotions, so we can't consider you now. Only necessary promotions will proceed." I said, "Okay, what's a necessary promotion?" "Well, if you had an outside offer, that would be a necessary promotion." I said I didn't want to get an outside offer because I didn't want to move away from Stanford. "Well that's just too bad," I was told. This happened twice. In the fall of 1975, after the Harris appointment stuff, they convened a tenure committee. The signals I was getting were generally positive. The senior faculty who were talking to me said I had all the right papers and they loved my teaching, etc.

There were, in retrospect, some more sobering signs. A student came to my office privately and warned me to be careful. Before the Harris offer had been made, one senior faculty member in the powerful group that was really running the department had called me into his office to say, "Duncan, if you want to stay, you have to go for this slot in alternative approaches." But I said, "I'm not the right person for that; it's not what I want to do."

Nonetheless, it looked like everything was in gear. They had the tenure committee meet early, and I received a very positive report, which was signed by the majority of the members. However, there was a large minority opposed to my promotion, with some people not present. So no decision was made. From the formal point of the review, what they did was to table the tenure application and reappointed me as an associate professor without tenure. At that time I had been an untenured professor for ten years. I was a fairly prominent person of my age group and discipline, so this reappointment was a difficult thing to read. I talked to almost all of the senior people. I asked them, "What does this mean?" I wasn't able to get a straight answer from anyone, except from one person, who said, "What this means Duncan is that you need to get another job."

There was a lot of controversy about the department's handling of my case. The students were up in arms and arguing that the decision had to be appealed. They went to the dean and explained that this was a bad decision. The dean told them that Foley has to appeal because he is the injured party; he has to allege that there was some impropriety or procedural flaw in the department's handling of the case. I went to see him and said, "I don't know if any impropriety took place because the procedures were confidential, so how would I know?" He told me that under the rules I was supposed to figure out if any impropriety took place. The students were very disappointed that I would not make a big campaign about the job, and that was partly because I wasn't interested in staying at Stanford.

Other issues came up. I remember being asked: "Are you a Marxist economist?" I always had trouble finding an honest answer to this question that would satisfy the person asking. I tended to reply something like: "I think of myself as an economist trying to work on the problems that interest me from whatever point of view strikes me as helpful. Marx's theories of the circuit of capital of money provide some important insights in macroeconomic problems. I find some of Marx very convincing. Historical materialism, for example, seems to me to be a helpful philosophical framework in which to situate social science. Does this mean I accept all of Marx's ideas? No. His theory of proletarian revolution looks internally inconsistent and historically wrong." But many people, both sympathetic and hostile to Marx, find that kind of answer unsatisfactory.

The difficulty I faced was that the controversy at Stanford threatened to spill out into the larger world of economics. People started to wonder: Is there something really wrong with Foley? Why would the Stanford department do something like that if Foley hadn't done something bad? It was becoming clear the decision would make it harder for me to find another job. I rather hurriedly (probably, in retrospect, too hurriedly) tried to generate some job offers and received three: from UC-Davis, from NYU, and from Barnard. By that time, I didn't particularly want to spend more time in executive committee meetings of a mainstream economics department arguing about personnel issues. The Barnard job seemed like a good compromise because it put me in intellectual contact with some excellent economists at Columbia without involving me directly in their departmental politics.

Did you go to Barnard with tenure?

Oh, yes. I didn't make that mistake a second time. The irony is that I had come to Stanford thinking I would get out of economics, but by the time I left Stanford, I was once again interested in economics. Barnard turned out to be a good environment for me to teach and work in.

While you were at Barnard you became interested in complexity: how did that interest come about?

My interest in complexity developed out of my work on the circuit of capital. The circuit of capital is basically an accounting framework, which can be turned into a dynamic model through the addition of some behavioral assumptions such as an investment policy. Thinking along those lines, I rediscovered something that Richard Goodwin (1951) had discovered before, which was the possibility of a limit cycle when you have a nonlinear accelerator effect. One version of that is in my *Journal of Economic Behavior and Organization* paper (Foley 1986a). I liked that result, and it got me interested in studying nonlinear dynamics, although not really complexity, or even chaos. I was mostly interested in bifurcations, in limit cycles as models of fluctuations.

What is interesting about these models is that they generate

fluctuations endogenously. How do you view the economy?
Do you see it as a stable equilibrium process that fluctuates because of being hit by external stocks? Or do you view it as a dynamical system that has endogenous instability, which is always moving around?

The latter struck me as being the more intellectually interesting hypothesis about industrial capitalism.

Let me digress for a moment. One of the criticisms of my work at Stanford was that I didn't contribute anything to the debate about rational expectations. Actually that's not quite true. Sidrauski and I wrote a chapter (1971) where we dealt with rational expectations in the perfect foresight version. But from my point of view, I didn't see anything that new in rational expectations; it looked to me like a restatement of the complete contingency markets version of general equilibrium in the Arrow-Debreu model (1954). Some of the rational expectations theorists were slow to realize that, because they formulated expectations in terms of probability distributions rather than contingency prices, but the relation to complete markets equilibrium is generally accepted now; Sargent and Hansen have clarified the point in their book on linear-quadratic recursive macroeconomic models.

Lucas (1972) first came on my horizon with his islands paper, which I, like most people, found very clever. But I didn't think it was world-shaking. I didn't see it as anything that would change my way of approaching macroeconomics. The big problem with rational expectations is that it is not operational except in one case, the case Sargent and Hansen worked through using quadratic utility functions and a linear production system. That's the only case where you can actually compute rational expectations equilibria, even with a representative agent. In more general economies, you can show that rational expectations equilibria exist, but the way you show it is essentially using Arrow-Debreu (1954) existence theorems. If you look at other work in the rational expectations tradition, what they do is effectively to use linear-quadratic models as approximations.

What about your work with Peter Albin? How did you come to work with him?

I met Peter, I believe, at a conference at the New School in 1987–88. He was giving a paper that used a cellular automaton to model monetary policy (reprinted in Albin 1998, as chap. 4).

Like everyone else who sees a cellular automaton model, I was fascinated by the graphical representation. However, I thought it should be possible to put more economic content into it. It seemed like one of these cases of importing a model from another discipline and forcing an economic interpretation onto it. Now that I know Peter, and have thought more about it, I think my first reaction was unfair. I also knew Peter's son, John, who took my course at Barnard in Marxist economics. Peter and I started to chat and have lunch, and I kept pushing him to do something with more economics in it. That led to the paper on trading two commodities around a circle, which was published in *JEBO* [*Journal of Economic Behavior and Organization*] (Albin and Foley 1992; Albin 1998, chap. 5). I discovered that as a result I had become part of the complexity revolution when Josh Epstein nominated me as the economist to be on the board of Princeton University Press's Complexity series.

In your recent work with Peter Albin you worked on a coevolutionary model (Foley and Albin 2001). How do you see the new emphasis on coevolution relating to other concepts such as the Veblenian institutionalist approach to evolutionary economics and the game theoretic approach to studying evolutionarily stable strategies?

Evolutionary stability strikes me as a kind of structural robustness of behavior. If you can show that a particular type of behavior survives robustly in a wide class of models, it is certainly one reason to be interested in that behavior. For example, Axelrod's (1984) result that cooperation survives as a strategy in competitive tournaments with a high probability is quite suggestive. Rationality isn't the only possible source of behavioral regularity. For another example, go back to the two-person zero-sum game, where the minimax mixed strategy is imposed by the structure of the situation. It really doesn't matter if a rational human being or a computer or a servomechanism is playing the game: the only way to succeed is to choose that randomized behavior.

The things that interest me, that convince me at some level, tend to have that character of robustness to them. How far can you get with the two-person zero-sum game? Well, the finance literature shows that you can get some mileage from it. A lot of the finance literature is based on arbitrage rather than utility maximization, which is in the minimax tradition.

There does seem to be an evolution in your work. All of it seems to be concerned with explanations of how the aggregate system stays together. You have gone from general equilibrium to Marxian analysis to understanding matters of complexity. Each of these offers quite different explanations, but all of which deal with the same question. Is this consistent with your view?

After I published *Understanding Capital* (Foley 1986b), several things happened. One was the developing collapse of Communism. I was interested in the dynamics issues that I saw coming out of the framework of Marxian economics. But at the same time, I made a conscious decision that it was time to try and bring some insights of Marxian economics back to some of the issues that had originally intrigued me about economic stability. I understood that somehow I was drifting back, at least methodologically, and in terms of the questions I was addressing, toward the mainstream. At the same time, the mainstream, I'm thinking here of the work such as Benhabib and Day's (1981), was drifting toward me. I think you're right that the problem of the articulation of microbehavior and macrophenomena has been a recurring preoccupation for me.

Is that issue the bridge between general equilibrium theory, Marxian/classical economics, statistical equilibrium, and complex systems theory?

It wasn't obvious to me at the time, but I think in retrospect that's correct. My interest in Marxian economics led to work in macrodynamics, following Goodwin's path. And I became aware that if you took a disaggregated circuit of capital model with many firms, but didn't force them onto the same trajectory, you would have a complex system. (The circuit of capital models I published did assume that all of the firms were going to move on the same trajectory, for the sake of analytical tractability.) This leads back to my old interest in statistical mechanics as well.

You worked with Albin for years to get your book out (Albin 1998).

Pete suffered a disabling stroke in the early 1990s. At that time he was working on a manuscript to summarize his thinking on complexity for Oxford University Press. It became clear that he wasn't going to be able to finish it himself. The next best thing I could think of was to collect his key papers on complexity, most of which had appeared in *Mathematical Social Sciences,* in a book. I was able to interest Princeton University Press in the project and undertook the editing myself.

Your introduction to the book is almost a book in itself.

I felt that people would need an introduction to appreciate Albin's work. The introduction synthesizes material that I had been teaching in my seminar at Columbia on complex systems and economics with Pete's key ideas. Albin is not always easy to understand. His papers are brilliant and original, but he can be a rather digressive writer; when he raises an issue, he doesn't always push the argument to its end.

Your statistical mechanics interest and entropy approaches appeared in 1994 with your article in the Journal of Economic Theory. *How would you respond to Paul Samuelson's (1972, 254) charge in his Nobel address that, "There is really nothing more pathetic than to have an economist or a retired engineer try to force analogies between the concepts of physics and the concepts of economics. How many dreary papers have I had to referee in which the author is looking for something that corresponds to entropy or to one or another form of energy?"*

The first thing to point out is that a major offender in this respect is Paul A. Samuelson. A lot of his best work is derived from physics, and it is hard not to see the whole utility-based neoclassical theory in any other light. Phil Mirowski makes this case in two books (1989 and 2002), and I think he's basically right. A few weeks ago I met Eric Smith, a young (not retired) physicist who is working now at the Santa Fe Institute, whose work, in my view, puts the question of the formal identity of classical thermodynamics and utility theory economics beyond dispute.

My first reaction to his statement is that this is vintage Samuelson protesting too much. But my second reaction is that in many ways he is right. I see a lot of the same work he refers to in which physicists trying to do economics don't do it very well. However, I don't think that we can just dismiss this literature. There is a widening group of physicists who are successful in their physical research and powerfully interested in economic issues. The most acute of them know that they don't know enough economics and they are going to start linking up with economists. This is the one thing that's going on right now in Santa Fe. They are going to get better at economics.

Much of the work coming out of this research involves generating power-law distributions for economic variables.

Yes. I think that's a very important line of work: skewed, self-similar, and fat-tailed distributions are extremely common in economic data. I got interested in the empirical regularities in the distribution of wealth and price movements from reading Pareto, Champernowne, and Mandelbrot. The history of the study of the distribution of wealth is fascinating; the resilience of the evidence for power-law regularities in the distribution of wealth is exactly matched by the complete neglect of this empirical regularity in mainstream discussions of distribution based on factor price theory. It doesn't take much thought to see that you are never going to get power-law distributions out of neoclassical distribution theory. Suppose you start off, as a classical economist might, with a population whose only difference is their native intelligence, or temperament, or something that affects economic productivity. What's a likely hypothesis about how intelligence, talent, or economic effectiveness is distributed? Probably according to a Normal Probability Law. The economic distribution you get from that assumption is not going to look anything like a power law. So how do you go from the standard economic approach to the empirical reality? Real-world labor and asset markets somehow magnify these inherent differences, although exactly how is not yet clear.

You recently moved to the New School. What led to that move?

It was not because of dissatisfaction with Barnard, where I liked my students and colleagues. I would say I had three motivations: to do more graduate teaching, particularly more thesis advising; to have some room to innovate in the graduate economics curriculum; and to have a more open institutional situation that would allow for some entrepreneurship in department-building.

I'd been hanging around the New School ever since I came to New York, and since I'd been going to meetings and seminars there, I almost always had one or two graduate students from the New School working with me during my time at Barnard. The New School also appealed to me because of my interest in Marxist and Keynesian economics since it is one of the few American departments committed to studying those traditions seriously and in depth. From a personal point of view, I was fifty-seven years old, and this looked like the last chance I would have to make a change.

How did modern economics get to where it is today?

The stage was set, I think, in the decades before the Second World War. There was already the development of a mathematically oriented theoretical economics, both growing out of the classical/Marxian tradition in the work of people like von Neumann, Sraffa, and Leontief and out of the marginalist tradition through figures like Marshall, Fisher, Edgeworth, and Hotelling. There was the creation of the classical school of statistical analysis, which opened up new methods of approaching quantitative data. The idea of synthesizing these methods into a mathematically grounded theoretical/empirical science on the model of twentieth-century physics was already in the air.

As it turned out, this project was greatly accelerated and shaped by the crucible of the Second World War and the Cold War that followed. Modern economics still reflects the shape it received in those years, to my way of thinking.

I think Mirowski's (2001) book *Machine Dreams* provides the best analysis of that process I've seen. Reading Mirowski's book opened my eyes both from an intellectual and sociological point of view. It goes through the story of American economics and related disciplines starting with the Second World War and through the Cold War. Just as you wrote in your introduction, he argues that the starting point is John von Neumann's work on economic problems.

One of the book's main intellectual themes is that institutions and funding are very important. Mirowski asks, "Where were all of the big players in the 1950s and 1960s, and what did they do later?" He traces it all back to operations research from the Second World War. That's when interest in linear programming intensified. The RAND Corporation was the big conduit for the movement of operations research ideas into economics. Samuelson, Solow, Arrow, and Dorfman were all associated with the RAND Corporation early in their careers.

So where did modern orthodoxy come from? Mirowski says it has three centers. The most important was the Cowles Foundation, and the most important person there was Koopmans. There was a shift from what he calls Cowles Mark 1 with Jacob Marschak at the center to Cowles Mark 2 under Koopmans's leadership. Cowles Mark 2 was the cradle of general equilibrium. The focus on general equilibrium occurred at the same time as the move of Cowles from Chicago to Yale. The Office of Naval Research largely financed the

Cowles Foundation at Yale. The other two important sources of economic orthodoxy are the Chicago and MIT schools, but he thinks that they were less important in shaping the fundamental theoretical structure. Personally, I agree. What Mirowski makes clear is how intricately involved modern economics was with the Cold War and the federal national security state.

This helps to explain what I earlier called my naivete. When I walked into the Cowles Foundation at Yale in the fall of 1964, I knew nothing about the Office of Naval Research or who Tjalling Koopmans was in relation to the national security establishment. But it affected me. These influences shaped the stories I just told you about my experiences at MIT and Stanford. What was the big fuss at MIT in 1969? It was about defense research (not so much in the economics department but in the political science department).

Research during the Second World War on optimal antiaircraft targeting led to game theory, for example the minimax mixed strategy solution for two-person zero-sum games, which randomizes behavior and in fact maximizes entropy. Where do we see randomness of this kind in economics afterward? We see it in finance: shooting down an airplane is very much like trying to beat the market. Where does the orderliness in the market that we see come from? In my view, it does not come very much from regularities in individual behavior, except those that are imposed structurally by the situation. It comes from something like a statistical mechanics of the situation. Statistical mechanics in turn is the seedbed of complex systems theory.

When von Neumann turned to the question of generalizing the two-person zero-sum game to the non-zero-sum game, his original solution was that you would introduce a third player who would absorb the surplus, or supply the surplus, and try to apply the zero-sum reasoning. He was not going toward a Nash equilibrium, which envisions psyching out the opponent, because he did not think the Nash program would lead to determinate results. Von Neumann decided that to solve this problem he needed a better understanding of automata, of algorithmic entities, which would interact in these kinds of situations. So he started his work on self-reproducing automata (von Neumann 1966), which is an important source of complexity theory.

Do you have any comments about our introduction about the cutting edge?

I liked the general idea. I had questions about a couple of points. One has to do with your orthodox/heterodox, mainstream/cutting edge distinction. I think you are getting at something that is quite real. But there's a problem of the nonparallelism of these different categories. *Orthodoxy* and *heterodoxy* refer to the consistency of theoretical/ideological systems, while *mainstream* is a sociological/political category. There is cutting edge work in both orthodox and heterodox economics and in both mainstream and nonmainstream economics.

I think there is a big difference between the sociological nature and structure of the economics profession in the nineteenth century as compared to the economics profession after the Second World War. In the nineteenth century there wasn't this structure of tenure or journals or what I would call the monopolization of power that we find after World War II. I think that the centralization of power in the American economics profession during the Cold War period was something new.

The second point is your discussion of how work moves from the cutting edge into the mainstream and becomes part of it. Your discussion has a lot of truth in it, but it's not the only way that it happens. You almost make it sound like a rational process. In your account cutting edge work becomes working papers, and then journal articles, and eventually changes the textbooks. That's true in some cases but not in others. I'm thinking, for example, of *JEBO,* where it wasn't so much a case of academic papers moving from being less visible working papers to more visible journal articles but a case of *JEBO* moving from being a nonmainstream journal to a mainstream one without losing its quirkiness and its position as a flagship for some of the cutting edge work in economics. I think it is also important to distinguish different cases. Take, for another example, experimental economics. It was mostly created by massive NSF funding. That's in contrast with Marxian or Post Keynesian heterodoxy, which have to survive hand to mouth.

Do you think there is a current orthodoxy? Does your work violate it?

I would say if there is orthodoxy, it's much weaker and less monolithic now than it was twenty years ago in American economics. Economics today is a group of different subfields. In each of these subfields you can find a kind of orthodoxy.

Actually, as one comes closer to our own time, it becomes harder to make judgments. I think what's interesting in recent history is the paradigm shift that didn't occur. Because of the infusion of new technology and new mathematical methods, the stage was set for a paradigm shift after the Second World War. There wasn't one. It always struck me that it was very strange that the main project of post–Second World War economics turned out to be a recapitulation of neoclassical economics focusing on cleaning up technical issues rather than taking off in another direction.

You have stated that "the unity that has been imposed on the American economics profession through the journal refereeing process, tenure reviews, and the homogenization of graduate programs has compromised the ability of the profession to give substantive answers to the questions society wants to resolve." Would you elaborate?

Perhaps things are getting better in some ways. The high point of dogmatic orthodoxy in economics was the 1970s and 1980s, when all of these struggles we've talked about occurred.

I prefer to think about the future in terms of whether there is going to be a recognizable discipline of economics at all. Economics was invented as a professional discipline not so long ago, and it has had to struggle to establish itself as a coherent theoretical discipline based on a unity of subject matter and method because economic phenomena can be studied from many points of view. For example, a lot of the papers getting published in the big journals now are really just generic social science applied to a economic data. There's no strong connection to a unified theoretical perspective in economics.

Were rational expectations a key part of the orthodoxy in the 1970s and 1980s?

They tried to establish rational expectations as an orthodoxy. There were cheerleaders for it, but as you pointed out in your introduction, it never quite made it. In a sense, it collapsed from its own weight and its own empirical implausibility. When you characterize macroeconomics as being in chaos, I think that's closer to the mark.

So you think that it's not just macroeconomics that's in chaos, it's all of economics, including principles?

What do people get out of Principles of Economics courses? Often I walk into a principles course and ask myself, "Do I really have something to teach these students?" It's sometimes hard for me to teach the received doctrine because I spend so much of my time questioning mainstream economics. But when I talk with students, I realize there's a huge amount that economists know that they need to know. But what is it? Well, it's a little bit theory, but it's much more stuff like national income accounting, institutions, and some economic history, all organized to understand what is happening in the real world.

Obviously we had to choose a limited number of people to interview. In making that choice we tried to get representatives who are doing different cutting edge research. Do you think we left out any research areas?

Yes, I think you've left out one important area, the evolution of a new orthodoxy in macroeconomics that emphasizes efficiency wages and structural unemployment. The Phelps conference at Columbia University is an interesting example. They are trying to form a new center for mainstream macroeconomics, maybe a little left of center, to replace rational expectations. Stiglitz, Woodford, Aghion, and Frydman organized the conference. They are trying to promote Phelps (1994) as the patron saint of the new approach. In many ways that makes sense; Phelps was working parallel with the Chicago economists right along. He led the way with microfoundations and the natural rate of unemployment. Then the Chicago economists got control of those ideas. The argument of the conference organizers is that Phelps was really on the right track and we need to come back to it.

As a final question, what do you see as the future for economics?

When I see economics, I see a besieged city, torn by internal dissension. But the pressures outside the profession pose the most serious threats. The physicists are really on the economist's case. Doyne Farmer claims that 30 percent of all physics dissertations have chapters on economic or financial topics. The psychologists are also on the economist's case. The sociologists are also out there claiming their piece of the economic turf.

Economics is a large part of social life, and it generates a huge amount of data and a huge number of interesting questions. There are always going to be people working on these issues. The question is how are they going to be working on them? A physicist trying to explain fluctuations of financial prices with a stochastic process model doesn't fit Robbins's definition of economics as the allocation of scarce resources among competing ends. Or when a sociologist comes along and looks at migration in labor markets by doing

DUNCAN K. FOLEY

211

some regressions of immigration on wage levels and employment opportunities, without specifying preferences, or the supply and demand of labor, is that economics? It's certainly work on an economic phenomenon. I suspect, on the other hand, that there is always going to be a market for economic policy advice and analysis, which is a stronghold of traditional economics, despite a growing sense among politicians and the public that you can get an economist, using economic tools and models, to defend any policy position.

The study of economic data surely has a future, but the question is whether it will be recognizable as economics in today's terms and whether it will exhibit any real unity of subject matter and method.

Duncan K. Foley

Leo Model Professor of Economics, New School for Social Research

INFORMATION ON THE WEB ABOUT DUNCAN K. FOLEY
http://homepage.newschool.edu/~foleyd/

EDUCATION
B.A. Mathematics, Swarthmore College, 1964
Ph.D. Economics, Yale University, 1966

SELECTED PUBLICATIONS
"Portfolio Choice, Investment and Growth," with Miguel Sidrauski. *American Economic Review* 60 (1970).
Monetary and Fiscal Policy in a Growing Economy, with Miguel Sidrauski. New York: Macmillan, 1971.
"A Statistical Equilibrium Theory of Markets." *Journal of Economic Theory* 62 (1994).
Barriers and Bounds to Rationality: Essays on Economic Complexity and Dynamics in Interactive Systems, by Peter Albin, edited with an introduction by Duncan K. Foley. Princeton: Princeton University Press, 1998.
Growth and Distribution, with Thomas R. Michl. Cambridge: Harvard University Press, 1999.

SPECIAL HONORS AND EXPERIENCE
Also taught at MIT, Stanford University, and Barnard College (Columbia)
National Science Foundation Grant Fellowship, 1964–66
Member, editorial boards of *Journal of Economic Theory, Journal of Economic Literature, Journal of Economic Behavior and Organization* (Coeditor), *Metroeconomica* (Associate Editor)

CHAPTER 8

Richard B. Norgaard

Professor of Energy and Resources and of Agricultural and Resource Economics, University of California at Berkeley

ᖇ

The interview was conducted November 10, 2001, at a variety of locations on the University of California campus at Berkeley

How did you get into economics?

I don't think anybody grows up wanting to become an economist. In my case, I didn't know what I wanted to be. I did well in high school; I got into Berkeley and started out as a math major. I quickly discovered that mathematics was too abstract at a time when I needed grounding in reality, to figure out how I was going to connect to the world around me. What I really enjoyed doing was being a river guide. I was taking members of the Sierra Club down many of the rivers of the West. The most important part of this experience was being a guide in the Glen Canyon on the Colorado River before it was flooded by Lake Powell. I took David Brower, the executive director of the Sierra Club, through the Glen Canyon six or seven times, so I was able to spend seven weeks with him back in the early 1960s. It was an empowering experience, and a very frustrating experience, to see a place that was incredibly beautiful going under water. I thought about being a biologist, so I could

ᖇ

study these places before they got destroyed, or a hydrologist. There are many areas in the natural sciences that I enjoyed studying, but I also started taking economics courses. I took these classes largely on the basis that economics is driving the changes in the environment; it's economics that's got to be changed to save places like Glen Canyon. Even then, the decision wasn't that clear whether I would major in economics. In my final semester at Berkeley, I had the choice of taking five courses in economics or five courses in geography. And though I knew the five courses of economics would be painful, that's where the power is, so I did the economics.

What was your reaction to your first classes in economics?

My early experience with economics at Berkeley was somewhat mixed. I wasn't a great student. I got a B in microeconomics, I believe. In macroeconomics I was constantly arguing with my professors about models that had no resources in them, no land, no petroleum, nothing that was driving the system. So my concerns were really predating Herman Daly's (1973) macroeconomic view of environmental economics. I had read Harrison Brown's *The Challenge of Man's Future* (1954), but my economics professors were saying resources and population were not an issue. If we grow fast enough, everything will work out fine. It constantly bothered me, so I argued with them about it. There were other courses where my arguing was appreciated. I took a course with Michael Brewer in resource economics in the agricultural economics department. I also took a course with Peter Diamond, who was in econ at Berkeley at the time, and though he was very mathematically oriented, we still could argue about basic principles and models. He appreciated that these arguments were coming from an undergraduate student. Brewer and Diamond basically got me into graduate school because they appreciated my arguments. There were people who accepted me, and then people who had trouble with me. I had trouble with them too. From Berkeley I went to Oregon State for graduate work. But even then, I was weighing things: should I go for what's really fun and enjoyable, or should I go into economics?

Was your degree at Oregon State in economics?

It was in agricultural economics. It was basically in natural resources economics, but there I also learned hydrology. I did a minor in water resources engineering. My master's thesis was on how the dams on the Columbia River affected navigation on the lower Columbia River. I thought I was going to be doing cost-benefit analysis, but I ended up doing fluvial geomorphology and actually got two publications in fluvial geomorphology from my master's work (Norgaard 1968, 1971). For every dam proposed for the Columbia River, the Army Corps of Engineers came up with numbers for the transportation benefits on the lower Columbia River. In fact they had no idea what the relationship was. I found twenty-seven years of data in the depth and dredging surveys in the basement of the Corps's offices and at least came up with some interesting findings.

From Oregon you went to the University of Chicago. Can you tell us about your experience at the University of Chicago? Did you enjoy it?

Chicago was a full immersion cultural experience for me. All through my undergraduate years, and even through my master's program, I was busy being a river runner, a photographer, and an environmentalist. It was very difficult to do any of those things in Chicago; I went 100 percent into studying. There were cultural shocks, but Chicago was very much in the oral tradition. You could argue your point. People were expected to listen to your argument and go back and forth; it was extremely intellectually stimulating. By then I had pretty much abandoned my mathematics, but that was fine because you didn't have to take mathematical economics courses and the core theory courses were not that mathematical. It was really about whether you could understand the basic logic and be able to use it. Basic logic is fun, so I enjoyed it, but it did get a little heavy; I'd go to parties and people would be drinking and still talking about economics. They talked about economics day and night. Harry Johnson was amazing. He was totally plastered most of the time I saw him at Chicago, but he could still argue economics. That part was a little depressing, but I did well at Chicago because I wasn't distracted by all the other things I would rather be doing. Even Milton Friedman appreciated my finding a solution to a problem on a final that he hadn't thought of. There was a lot of openness to novelty, though I didn't bring out my environmental side because there was no one to talk to about my environmental interests. So I hid that and played their game.

How did you choose your dissertation topic?

I picked my dissertation topic before going to Chicago. When I was a senior at Berkeley, I read a book by Barnett and Morse (1963) titled *Scarcity and Growth: The Economics of Natural Resource Availability,* published by Resources for the Future, a think tank in Washington that was funded by the Ford Foundation. The book suggested that we don't have any resource problems; maybe there were some environmental problems, but there were no resource problems. It looked at cost trends for natural resource commodities from the late nineteenth century to 1957 and found that resources got cheaper, and anything that gets cheaper could not possibly be scarce. They did admit that certain sectors, like lumber and fisheries, had some problems. But since logging had shifted from the east to the west coast of the United States, even forest product prices had fallen. Overall, costs and prices of natural resources dropped because of the development of technology, and we shouldn't be overly concerned about natural resource scarcity, particularly in the United States.

Something felt wrong to me about their broad conclusions, and for my Ph.D. dissertation I picked a specific sector, the petroleum well–drilling sector in the United States, and really sorted out the differences between resources and technology and their relationship. Barnett and Morse just looked at the net effect and said clearly we don't have a problem because technology is overriding resource scarcity. I felt that you might want to know how important resources really are, and what drives the development and use of technology, and what kind of technology we might need for the future. I was able to show that resource scarcity was a very important issue in petroleum development in the United States and the effects of new technologies on costs were also extremely important (Norgaard 1975). I should have pursued the issues in my dissertation more thoroughly during the next decade because it was an important topic then.

Did you receive support from the people at Chicago for your dissertation?
I received financial support from T. W. Shultz at Chicago, who had Ford Foundation funds. But he was not interested in the resource angle at all. Back in the 1930s, he pushed the agricultural profession out of the nineteenth century by telling them to stop thinking in Ricardian terms about land scarcity and to focus on technology, which is more important than extensive and intensive margins. It's all in the technology, he said. So he wasn't interested in the resource side of my dissertation, but he was interested in the

technology side. Eventually, I shifted to Arnold Harberger and George Tolley as primary advisers for my dissertation, but Shultz continued to fund me. I was only at Chicago physically for 18 months. Since I came to Chicago with a dissertation topic, and I passed my courses smoothly, I was able to take three of the four written exams back at Berkeley during the summer, which were proctored in the agricultural economics department where I eventually became a professor. I didn't spend a lot of time in Chicago. If I had been there three or four years, I'm sure I would have had difficulty doing what I was doing.

After graduation, what did you do, and how did you choose your particular area of research?

I was at Chicago in 1969–70, when the environmental movement was breaking out. Being anxious to get out of Chicago, I went on the job market well before I had taken my fourth written exam and still hadn't been advanced to candidacy. The Chicago faculty was nice enough to write letters. I was the only environmental economist from a name brand university. There were water resource economists from the agricultural schools, but nobody from Harvard, MIT, Yale, Princeton, Stanford, or Berkeley economics programs that did resource or environmental economics.

Did you look at yourself as being an environmental economist at that time?

I looked at myself as being an environmentalist and an economist, asking questions that an environmentalist would ask. Those were different questions than a water resource economist would ask, though I had done a master's paper that was basically water resource economics. What we now think of as environmental economics was about to define itself over the next five years, but I was an environmentalist and an economist.

Did environmental economics exist then? Were there programs and courses?

Well, there was a beginning. There were some courses. But it wasn't widespread by any means, just a few authors and some material in textbooks. It's really from the 1970s on that it booms and environmental economics becomes a standard course in regular economics programs.

What do you think led to the popularity and development of environmental economics?

The ideas were really quite powerful. It was a way of taking basic market economics and saying you have environmental problems because markets don't work everywhere and, for that matter, cannot work everywhere. That was certainly where we were in the beginning; it was a critique of the market system. There are many types of goods that can't be consumed by individuals. It follows that you don't see a demand curve for them as individuals and that therefore the market won't work. It was a justification for collective action and government intervention. The emphasis shifted dramatically during the 1980s towards making markets work, on setting up tradable permit systems, for example, on the premise that the less government the better. Of course, we are still stuck with the collective decision on what the environmental goal should be and how permits should be distributed between parties. These ideas were being developed in the 1970s and seemed to make sense. There were also cases already in existence where cities had set height limits, six stories on average. If you want to go twelve stories, you had to buy up somebody else's six stories; if you want to go nine stories, you could buy somebody else's three. So environmental economists didn't invent the idea of tradable permits. There were already markets out there to reach environmental goals.

When did cities start using markets on height levels?

It started up in the late 1950s or early 1960s, way before economists thought it up. The South Coastal Air Quality Board regulating air quality in Los Angeles was also doing pollution trading before economists were theorizing on this. They said that they were putting a cap on the pollution in the south coast air basin, and if you want to pollute somewhere new, or just pollute more by expanding your refinery, for example, you're going to have to reduce the pollution someplace else—buy some business out or buy pollution control equipment for them. So companies were saying, "How can we go in and get the cheapest way of reducing pollution?" It became a practical thing simultaneously as it became theoretically acknowledged. It wasn't discovered by economists theorizing on paper; it was discovered out there in practice.

Did you support this type of research? Were you part of it?

Yeah, I wrote papers on that. I wrote a paper in the early 1970s on how we should be charging by the cubic yard for vehicles going into our national parks. Winnebagos were on the rise, and I hated them. I figured if someone owned a Volkswagen, they should pay $3 a day to go to a national park, and if you want to take a Winnebago through the same gate, you ought to pay whatever it is in proportion to the cubic yards you are bringing in—the eyesore you are bringing in. I wasn't terribly fond of the idea of charging for the wilderness; there were a lot of economists writing about the willingness to pay for going into the back country and then charge people for going into the back country. I said no, but it's good to do studies to find out what people are willing to pay.

How was your research received at that time? Did you get a lot of resistance? Did you get a lot of complaints when you presented at seminars?

No. In the early '70s environmental economics was very much appreciated. I moved rather quickly into the economics of pesticide use, the economics of biological control (Norgaard 1976). Half of my appointment at Berkeley was, and still is, in agriculture research, so I am obligated to do some. The work I was doing on insecticide use mostly fitted within an environmental economics framework. But I was getting flak, not because the environmental side wasn't appreciated but because the chemical industry was in bed with the agricultural industry and the university, at least the agricultural side of the university. So I got into hot water politically, and it wasn't the farmers that were upset with me. The farmers were interested in reducing their insecticide use.

Eventually graduates of MIT and Harvard moved into environmental economics, elaborating it in ever-more-sophisticated mathematical economics. I was not a part of that then. So I was replaced with the microeconomic mathematical approach to environmental economics.

Was that because of your work being more applied?

My work was applied, but I had good graduate students building good mathematical models and doing the best econometrics of the time. But increasingly, I was not doing the sorts of things that the economic profession rewards people for doing. I was thinking about problems across the differentiated context of real agroecosystems and real agricultural social and political systems. Market failure per se is not a difficult concept, so it was clear that if I wasn't going to become a mathematical environmental economist, or a highly technical econometrician, I was obsolete. I was on the scene in environmental economics very early, but I was quickly made obsolete within the mainstream of environmental economics, though I continued to go to the environmental economics meetings. We informally founded the Association of Environmental and Resource Economists in 1974, though I think it wasn't officially founded until several years later.

Which of the environmentalists of that time influenced you, not necessarily economists but environmentalists that had an impact on your thinking?

I was very much influenced by David Brower while he was executive director at the Sierra Club. He became too radical for the Sierra Club and founded Friends of the Earth, and when he got kicked out of Friends of the Earth, he formed Earth Island Institute. David was one of those rare people who became more radical as he got older, and that continued until his death last year. So he continued to influence me. Because he became more radical, he was always a new man. David felt you just needed a backbone and should do what you believe in. You should speak out, do what's right. Through him and other ties with the environmental movement, I met many people who influenced me.

Recently you stepped down as the president of the International Society for Ecological Economics (ISEE). When and how did the new field of ecological economics appear, and who invented the term?

Well, I didn't step down; the society now has a constitution and an election system that says the president's term is for two years. To my knowledge, the adjective *ecological* first modified the noun *economics* in a presentation made by Robert Costanza (1997) at a conference in Stockholm in 1982 that was organized by the ecologist Ann-Mari Jansson (1984). In 1987 Juan Martinez-Allier had written a book with Klaus Schlüpmann titled *Ecological Economics: Energy, Environment and Society.* He seems to have come up with the term independently of Bob Costanza, who used it four or five years earlier. At a meeting in Barcelona in September 1987 a group of us decided to start a journal titled *Ecological Economics,* with Costanza as the editor, and a society to support the journal. So the ISEE was effectively organized in Barcelona, with thirty to thirty-five people there.

How would you define ecological economics? What is it, and what makes it different from environmental economics?

Environmental economics says there are environmental problems and then there's economic thinking and maybe if we just applied our economic thinking to environmental problems we can gain some insights. The insights were extremely powerful. It led to the ideas of green taxes, which are being pushed again, and using tradable permits, which are reasonably successful, and carrying out environmental evaluations as a basis for determining levels of pollution regulation. It's been extremely effective in the United States and has become institutionalized within the Environmental Protection Agency and some of the other federal agencies.

Ecological economics doesn't reject environmental economics, but we reject some of the ways it is used. We also raise questions that might not be found in traditional microeconomic environmental economic courses: What's the role of resources? What's the role of environmental services? Where do market failures come from? Can you really have unlimited growth? And then we're eclectic: we have Marxist economists (Barkin 1995; Foster 2000), we have institutional economists (Hodgson 1993), and we have Austrian economists (Faber and Proops 1990). We also collectively admit we need all these different approaches to economic thinking. Economies are extremely complex; why try to understand them in just one way? We also have ecologists though not as many as we'd like to have. We want ecologists and economists to have a discourse with one another. Ecologists have seven or eight different models that don't all fit together under a metamodel. Some of their ways work very well with microeconomics: the population-biology models of ecology work smoothly with market models; food-web models and input-output analysis are pretty much the same stuff; optimal foraging theory mimics profit maximization. So we have all of these crossings and parallels.

Is ecological economics really the new way to do natural resource economics? Is it a redefinition?

Natural resource economics predated environmental economics and was more eclectic, applied, and institutionalist. But it lacked the macroeconomic concerns of ecological economics. The old natural resource economists from the 1930s through the 1960s knew things about hydrology and range management and were very practically

RICHARD B. NORGAARD

223

oriented and grounded in their approaches (Ely and Wehrwein 1940; Clawson 1950; Scott 1955).

Can someone doing ecological economics do it within the neoclassical paradigm?

You can, but there are tensions. We accept the market model among many models, but this does not mean we accept the assumptions reinforced by the neoclassical culture of environmental economics. I see the tensions at ecological economics meetings when you have a straight environmental economics presentation and they don't question their results or bring any other way of thinking into their arguments. Yet we want those people to come to our meetings so they can listen to us. In Montreal, at the Canadian Society of Ecological Economics meetings, we had some very straight environmental economists present a paper, and ecological economists jumped all over them. I stood up and said, "Hold it, we want them to be here to listen to us and you're telling them what they are doing is no good. How do you think they are going to learn about what we're doing and expand their frames of analyses?"

Is ecological economics terribly heterodox?

Yes, I hope so.

Are you saying that what ecological economics can provide traditional economics is to be more pluralistic in approach and not be so narrow with just one methodological approach, even when one approach might have much merit?

Yes. The argument is that we live in an extremely complex world, and any particular way of thinking is a simplification, and it's not going to be right. No matter how you simplify the world, you're going to leave out something important. Maybe you have the right simplification for critical aspects of a current crisis, but it's not going to be the right simplification for the next crisis, or even for the next phase of the current crisis. The idea that one simple way is good for all crises is just stupid.

How would you respond to the comment that this approach leads to ad hoc solutions?

You have to pay very close attention to the logic you are actually using, be specific that you are following a particular logic, be consistent within that logic, and when you shift to another logic, say so and shift, but shift all the way. Being ad hoc means that you borrow a little bit here and a little bit there, and you can find papers that kind of move along from one line of reasoning to another without identifying when they are shifting. In some of my own papers, I say let's look at it one way and then let's look at it another way. When different frameworks lead to complementary insights and policy suggestions, you feel a little more confident, and when your insights are discordant, then you keep thinking. You have to be careful to keep your separate patterns of thinking separate and not just blend them altogether (Norgaard 1985, 1989). This does raise an interesting question. If all we have is multiple models with multiple insights, then how do we make decisions? That's why I come down strongly for democracy, for taking expert and disciplinary knowledge to the people for them to sort out rather than pretending that experts and scientists will reach the right conclusion. There have been too many examples, from chemical agriculture to nuclear power, where that has not worked well.

What's your perception of the relationship between ecology and economics, and more broadly between biology and economics?
The main difficulty with incorporating ecology with economics is that economists have been mimicking physicists since day one. There's no doubt about physics still being the king of the sciences for economists as they try to cozy up close and sound like physicists. There are numerous economists who have said that biology is much richer and more interesting and that social systems are more like ecological systems than physical systems; Alfred Marshall is an example (preface, 1890). But the perceived clarity and unity of physics is something that all of the sciences admire and try to strive for. That gets in the way of good thinking; we have to take advantage of multiple ways of thinking. It hurts biology less because biologists seem to be more comfortable with multiple ways of thinking. But even in ecology some say we just have to get all these different patterns of reasoning about ecosystems together into the one overarching right model. I don't think this is the right approach.

In ecological economics, some researchers have attempted to develop an alternative approach inspired by Nicholas Georgescu-Roegen (1971), which emphasizes analysis of energy flows and a focus on the law of entropy. Do you think this has been successful, and where is this going? Is this the future for ecological economics?

This is a branch of ecological economics, and for some ecological economists it's almost all of ecological economics. I find following energy and material flows yields interesting insights. This is the first law of thermodynamics. The second law has certainly been a driving force in raising questions for a long time. There are ecological economists who are still pursuing how to make the connection between the second law and economics. I do not know enough about it to have a strong position, though I do have some critiques that I do bring out in the appendix of my book *Development Betrayed* (1994), in the bibliographic essays. What Georgescu-Roegen argued has considerable intuitive appeal, as long as you are thinking of the earth as a closed system. The fact that we have gone from being entirely dependent on the sun to having aspects of our lives, such as industry and commerce, being dependent on fossil-hydrocarbons makes us more of a closed system than we used to be. The fact remains, however, that if we didn't have the sun heating the earth, we'd be dead in three days. Unfortunately, engineers initiated most of our energy accounting, and they are blind to our obvious dependence on the sun for heat and to drive the photosynthesis on which our agriculture and forestry depend. But still the way we do our energy accounting suggests that our economy is driven by fossil-hydrocarbons, and we are going to run out of them.

Renewable energy is really dominant in our lives still, yet we talk about it as if it were exotic, as if getting a little more would be a big leap rather than some adjustments on the margins. Georgescu-Roegen kept trying to bring the sun in, but in chapter 8 of his book he said that the Great Plains of the United States would inevitably be degraded because of the second law. You have to ask, where did the Great Plains of the United States come from? It was built up through biological processes, and those processes were driven by the sun, and change will go on. Entropic degradation, however, doesn't describe the kind of changes that will go on in the Great Plains. So he didn't understand biology, and so it is pretty devastating to have to include him among the founding fathers of an academic society that calls itself ecological economics. If we can find ways to bring in the second law, fine. But it has serious limits for saying something important about an earth open to the sun.

What is your major critique of orthodox or neoclassical economics?
My major problem is with the culture of economists and their use of the neoclassical model, not the model itself, because the

model is no better or worse than a lot of other models. So my major concern is with economists' unthinking use of the neoclassical model to the exclusion of other models. But I am also concerned about the assumptions they begin with when they apply the model, and their willingness to use the model only halfway. For example, they forget that distribution is just as important as allocation, and they pretend that the welfare economics that rose in the 1940s and 1950s solved all those questions. It is apologia. The rich are getting richer, and nobody is saying anything. So it is the culture of economists and the abuse of their model that I find frustrating and irritating.

It seems that you always had some tensions with traditional neoclassical economics but that there came a point where you became very clear and very focused on wanting to go into a coevolutionary approach. How and when did this transition occur?

The transition occurred when I was in Brazil. I was spending a lot of time in the Amazon jungle in 1978 and 1979 dealing with the problem of sustainable development there. I was invited by the Ford Foundation to join their team in Brazil to work on resources and environmental issues. It was a point in my life when I needed a change. I had gotten divorced as well as a bit tired of my colleagues in the agricultural economics department at Berkeley. I needed more money to pay for my former wife's half of what was now my house and was open to a new adventure in life. I had spent a lot of time in Alaska during the 1970s, and I liked the idea of big frontiers, and the Amazon was a big frontier with native people, change was driven by beliefs in manifest destiny, and there were other parallels with Alaska. So I was in Brazil, struggling with what sustainable development—environmentally compatible development—in the Amazon would look like. It was after the Brazilians had built their highways, and the cattle had come in, and the agricultural colonization projects were not going well. A lot of stuff was going wrong. Neither the Marxist nor neoclassical market models seemed to address what I witnessed in the Amazon and why Western-style economic development had failed there for over four hundred years.

I was reading a lot of biology, ecological theory, and trying to understand tropical ecosystems at that time. I was reading Paul Ehrlich. I had already met him through John Holdren at Berkeley in the Energy and Resources Program (Ehrlich et al. 1977). He was an important source for my understanding and use of coevolutionary theory, but he is a source for everybody in coevolution. Ehrlich and Peter Raven wrote the key article in 1964 that provided strong documentation of plants and insects coevolving, and a nice story and enough empirical evidence to make it look convincing. There was also literature on diversity and complexity, including a critical review by Robert May (1973). There was the belief that complexity led to stability. All of these questions were being asked in the context of tropical ecosystems, which were certainly the most complex, the most diverse of terrestrial ecosystems. This was a blooming era for new ecological and theoretical thinking, and a lot of it was centered on the Amazon. I had access to that. I was also reading cultural ecology, looking at how the anthropologists were explaining change and development and cultural adaptation to environmental systems and the influence of environmental systems on myths and belief systems. I was really seeing the relationship between culture and ecological systems, and the importance of diversity at many different levels—both ecological and social and how they interact. In this setting, I began to develop my own coevolutionary perspective about change and development (Norgaard 1981).

What brought it all home for me was when I served on an Amazon planning team in Brasilia. There were nineteen people on this planning team. It was a diverse group with different backgrounds. I had only been in Brazil for thirteen to fourteen months, but I had spent more time tromping around the Amazon than any of the Brazilians on the planning team. I kept saying that we really needed to get the planning team out in the field and see the cattle ranches and the colonization project, to check out how things are working—to see stuff on the ground. But there was no interest whatsoever. Their response was to just bring in the scientists, use reports and maps; we've got everything we possibly need. Why would you actually want to talk to people? Why would you want to see it on the ground? When I was involved in planning controversies in Alaska, we used scientific information and maps, but we also went out and looked around and talked to people, to get some ground truth through the experiential knowledge of the people. So it appalled me that these planners could think that they could plan without going out there.

It raised other issues like, How did development come about in Europe? How did it come about in the United States? Well, not by planners but by a lot of experimentation, a lot of failures, and few successes. The successes seemed to fit in with existing features at the beginning and then change the whole system over time. I said, "Oh, that's coevolution." That's what I was reading in the biological literature, and it seemed to apply to development.

So you started to think about development in Europe and North America after your experience in Brazil?

Yeah, the experience in Brasilia told me that development didn't occur by planning but by experimentation. As much as we think about history, there are no key things that bring development about. For example, it wasn't like the railroads settled the West in the United States—it was by horseback, canals, prairie schooners, stagecoaches, and railroads. The railroads became dominant at a particular, later stage of the development of the West, but they are not the whole story. Yet afterwards, it seems like we knew exactly what we were doing when we built the railroads. So coevolution hit me over the head. It was a way of bringing in the biological pattern of understanding change that I acquired in the Amazon as well as the role of experiential and indigenous knowledge working along with science. It allowed me to see a new paradigm for analysis and think more deeply about sustainable development (Norgaard 1984a, b, c).

If the economics profession bought into your coevolutionary theory, what would economic theory look like? How would it change how economists approach issues?

First, I would only want coevolutionary thinking to be only a part of economics. Coevolutionary thinking moves you away from the arrogance of prediction, planning, and optimal policy design. It moves you towards experimentation; it moves you towards recognizing contextual differences across a country or across different countries. It basically says that it is probably better to run a lot of small experiments and watch them. Get those who are running the experiments to be part of the learning process and then assemble every eighteen months, or thirty-six months, and talk about how things are going and what should be changed. It is not the extreme of putting all of your eggs in one basket such as a massive nuclear power program to solve the energy crisis. It's much more experimental and dynamic and focuses on learning as you go. It's more contextually oriented and acknowledges that in different ecosystems you ought to be running different experiments. Understanding change as coevolution would help us be more humble.

Can you give us examples of experiments that could be done?

One example is the promotion and use of renewable energy. The technical experiment you would use in North Dakota would be different from the experiment you would use in Florida or California. There would also probably be different types of policies that would fit the resources of the different states. Instead we tend to say we'll subsidize output from particular types of renewable energy and that will be federal policy. Maybe we need something more experimental coming from the communities involved.

How does your view of coevolution relate to the views of evolution of old institutionalists like Veblen (1898), Hodgson (1993), and Boulding (1981) or even Nelson and Winter (1982)?

Institutionalists have drawn on evolutionary ideas and have critiqued economics for ignoring evolution. Boulding drew on biology more than others, but you have to remember he also was president of the American Economics Association. Kenneth Boulding was a remarkable man, but even his evolutionary thinking was of a particular construct. He had a lot of human progress going on in his models; he had lots of things evolving in a very hierarchical way. There was a physical level of evolution, a biological-level evolution, a social institutional evolution, and a knowledge evolution, but he didn't really have everything coevolving. He had hierarchical systems evolving, in parallel but not coevolving between levels.

Veblen invoked evolution in multiple ways. His writing sparks a lot of thoughts, but I have little sense of his overall argument. Hodgson, like me, is very interested in the methodological implications of thinking in evolutionary terms. Nelson and Winter have been better at writing for economists, but even they complain of being ignored.

You argue in your writings that Darwin (1859) had the concept of coevolution without using the term. Why did it take so long for this idea to reappear?

The easiest way to explain evolution is to think of fixed physical niches in the environment to which species adapt in a progressive manner over time. With a fixed physical niche, the species gets better and better over time. Thus many conflated evolution with progress. However, Darwin understood that species adapt to each other, that niches consist partly of other species, and that they then coevolve over time. Beyond the added complexity, I don't know why it took so long for coevolution to surface or why Ehrlich and Raven's (1964) article woke biologists up so wham-o.

What do you think about the developments in evolutionary game theory coming from the work of the biologist Maynard Smith? (1982)

I don't read the game theory literature much. I had a student in mathematics who used repeated, multiparty game theory to demonstrate the evolution of chaotic systems. So it can illustrate different developments. I read *The Evolution of Cooperation* (Axelrod 1984), but I don't know Maynard Smith's work well enough to comment on it.

What are your thoughts about the relationship between coevolutionary theory and complexity theory, chaos theory, game theory, and the work done at the Santa Fe Institute? Are they connected or related?

Coevolution is evolution within a system. How do you describe that system? Is it fairly steady with occasional introductions from outside the system? Is it steady with occasional mutations on the inside around which things then coevolve? Or does it have complex dynamics such that species have to have certain traits to survive conditions that you don't observe ninety-nine years out of one hundred? Much of the Santa Fe and complexity literature is really about how such systems might arise and their response to disturbances, and that is important. How does coevolution work? Is it rapid change, species evolving quickly, or species evolving slowly? If you get jumps in evolution, then that's going to affect the system itself. But I haven't seen Santa Fe models of ecosystems changing that then have evolutionary change on top of that. I have an NSF biocomplexity grant that will get me into this literature again.

One of the criticisms that those who do chaos theory or complexity theory have of neoclassical economics is that it relies on predictability and rationality. Does coevolutionary theory question this reliance on predictability and rationality?

There's certainly a connection between chaos theory and coevolutionary theory, and maybe this gets us back to institutional economics. The assumptions that neoclassical economists make about preferences to complete their theory are so rigid and so uncharacteristic of people that it's been critiqued from several different levels. Preferences aren't smooth, and preferences aren't set; people's preferences do evolve. Also we act differently in our family than we act as individuals; we act differently in our churches than in our bowling clubs. We act differently in different settings. The institutional economists bring that out, the sociologists bring it out, but the core theory of economics can't handle it. The complex systems people are saying that systems can have multiple equilibria and they can bounce between them. That seems so much more descriptive of my understanding of social dynamics.

How has your major book on coevolutionary approaches, Development Betrayed *(1994), been received by economists and noneconomists?*

The book was extremely difficult for me to write. I wasn't writing it for economists; the ideas were too wild and exciting and far reaching for me to translate their significance to economists. I was writing it for an interdisciplinary audience, a very philosophical audience. I certainly received a better reception from anthropologists, cultural ecologists, and in particular, ethnobiologists than from economists. Other readers have included environmental sociologists and environmental historians. But not many economists, though John Gowdy (1994) wrote a similar book at the same time, although less philosophical. The institutional economists have picked it up a bit. They are including me in one of their sessions at the AEA [American Economics Association] meetings in January. Geoffrey Hodgson (1993) includes my ideas in his history of evolutionary economics thought. But I have never heard a mainstream economist refer to my book even in casual conversation.

In your book, the section on environmental epistemology seems to critique the epistemological method used in economics and in the social sciences generally. What is environmental epistemology, and does it critique neoclassical economics?

It critiques almost everything in Western thinking. To explain how my thoughts developed with respect to evolutionary epistemology, I need to say what's in my coevolutionary model. In the model I have knowledge systems, value systems, social organizational systems, technology systems, and environmental systems, all working on each other. The traditional scientific approach assumes a fact-value dichotomy; there are no values in your model. Values are applied after you've collected all the facts and sort out the possible outcomes. Yet how can you explain the past without having values inside your model? The insight of environmental epistemology is seeing how values have to be inside our pattern of thinking. The fact-value dichotomy just has to go away. I also began to see that how we have historically thought we understood environmental and social systems coevolved with the systems themselves. Agricultural soils now reflect our historic beliefs in the use of chemicals. So science itself has to be reflexive. Our economic systems reflect our past understandings of economic systems. Nothing is simply "out there" to be studied by itself; everything is connected to past values, ways of knowing, earlier technologies, etc.

How do you assess the current status of the postmodern critique of economics?

The postmodern critique of everything is heavily driven by "we are inside our model." A lot of postmodernism acknowledges how we think is patterning where we are and will pattern where we go. Thus, my coevolutionary model is very postmodern because I have knowledge inside the model. They have knowledge inside their pattern of thinking. It's not just that there is a reality out there, it's that the reality that we know has been created by how we have thought about it. This is really scary to modernists. Of course, a lot of postmodern critique is of dubious quality, but then I would argue that all of the modern neoclassical economics that ignores history is also of dubious quality, just in a style we are comfortable with.

Is it possible to actually obtain answers to scientific questions, or are we stuck with an open-ended irresolution?

Well, we are certainly stuck with being inside our own treadmill, but the treadmill keeps changing, and you can identify the treadmill. There are still scientific laws we must recognize and live with, such as the first and second laws of thermodynamics. Coevolution will still occur. The Newtonian dream of prediction and control is fading, but many civilizations have made decisions and succeeded for as long as modernity without this dream. Still, I worry about the transition when we fully awake from the dream.

RICHARD B. NORGAARD

You have used the coevolutionary perspective as a way of exploring the relationships between values, social organizations, technology, and the environment. How does this approach provide insight into economic thinking?

I really need to write something about coevolution of economics with social organization. Mathematical economics has coevolved with its mathematical tools and is certainly coevolving around computer technology now. But I am mostly interested in how economics has coevolved with social organization. I'm interested in how, especially in America, economics has coevolved with bringing economics into public decision making—the government. Economics had a very small role to play until the Great Depression, and then it began to play a significant role. For example, The Flood Control Act of 1936 stipulates that cost-benefit analysis shall be done.

Is there a coevolution between policy-making and economic theory over time? If so, how does this operate?

As economics was drawn into government, it began to need to have single answers. When we are asked to do cost-benefit analysis, we are told to provide answers based on efficiency and to ignore the distributional side. Almost every government decision is about who is going to have the right to do something, and that's a redistribution of rights issue. Yet we try to answer these distributional issues as efficiency questions. It's kind of known, but it isn't known. In many ways, it's been formalized in public policy economics, maybe the worst kind of economics. Questions about environmental justice become moot if you follow environmental economics logically, as Larry Summers did when he wrote his famous memo inside the World Bank about putting polluting industries in poor countries. The logic says it makes sense to put the polluting factories where the poorest people live because they die early anyway before they get cancer and their lives are only worth seventy-five cents an hour. This is the logic of environmental economics as it's done now. But it's not morally right, and it is not even good economics.

Also, there has been a coevolution in that the use of partial equilibrium analysis in policy has fed the triumph of Chicago neoliberalism where academic economists have captured political discourse, which in turn has fed back into academia and the evolution of economic thought. Many of these policies have been admirable, such as tradable permits in environmental policy. But the dominance of partial equilibrium analysis has limited the evolution of economics because alternatives could have filled up some of those spaces. As budgets for education tighten in Europe, they too are narrowing what constitutes good economics, even as new ideas are being explored at the best universities in the U.S. Misuse of partial equilibrium analysis weakens governments and collective decision making, which in turn encourages the rise of individualism and the spread of individualistic market theory. This is certainly coevolution.

You have published several papers with Richard Howarth on problems regarding discount rates and intergenerational equity (Howarth and Norgaard 1990, 1992, 1993). Can hyperbolic discounting resolve these problems, or are they more fundamental?

I've always been concerned with the long-term questions. Back in the '70s, there was this revival of Harold Hotelling's (1931) model that had sat around for forty years, when the energy crisis came and people started asking, "How do you allocate resources over the long term?" His model assumes an infinitely lived rational agent making a good investment, and that's how you allocate resources over time. In the '70s I said, "What if you transfer rights to future generations? What if future generations have rights? How does the Hotelling model handle this?" My colleagues weren't interested in pursuing that with me. They knew optimal control provided the right way to frame the problem, but I knew their theory was at least incomplete.

In the late '80s, Richard Howarth joined our energy and resources program at Berkeley as a graduate student. He had actually been a joint biology-anthropology major at Cornell and did a master's at Wisconsin in their energy program but hadn't taken calculus. We said, "Take calculus before you come to our program," and he did. He came to work on issues of resource scarcity, along the lines of my own Ph.D. work, but then began to think about questions of distribution and allocation over time. He learned how to work with overlapping generations models to address the questions about the distribution of rights that had been on my mind for so long. He did it first with two generations, three periods, one overlap period, and started going on out and showed that when you give future generations rights then the rate of interest goes down. The rate of interest just changes with time; it's just a price, just like every other price, not something deified.

RICHARD B. NORGAARD

235

When you worked on this, did you encounter this paper by Robert Strotz, from 1956, which was apparently the first to suggest that there should be different discount rates for different time periods?

We did not at that time. But our work doesn't say there "should" be different rates; it just lets the discount rate be determined inside the model, just like all the other prices are determined inside a general equilibrium model in which the interest rates are determined. The normative question is not the rate of interest but rather that we need to ask whether rights should be transferred to future generations. And if we should, then our model simply describes what happens.

What is generating this lower interest rate?

I think the dominant effect is that there are fewer investment opportunities in the early time periods when rights are transferred to the future. The supply of investment opportunities or the demand for capital has shifted backwards.

What should the discount rate be? Does this model tell us?

You are still putting the emphasis on the discount rate. When I think about future generations, do I have to go into a discount rate mode at all? I don't. I just think about future generations. The discount rate is just another price—why should I say what the price of corn should be or the price of land should be? It's just an equilibrating mechanism. All my "shoulds" are outside of economics: they're moral shoulds; they're shoulds in another realm of reasoning. Economics doesn't have any shoulds.

When we asked Matt Rabin, he answered that morally it should be zero.

That acknowledges that at a moral level of reasoning we don't use a discount rate; we just think about future generations. I think what you implicitly say is, "Oh, it must be zero." And I'll say, "Okay, for some realm of questions like the right to an environment with no carcinogens or limited accessibility to carcinogen exposure, let it be zero." But what I think Rabin is really saying is that we should do unto future generations as we would have them do unto us, though of course they never get the chance to make such choices. It was for this reason that John Rawls developed the idea of the "veil of ignorance" (1971). It is important to keep in mind, however, that all prices change when we give rights to future generations, not just the discount rate. So, setting the discount rate to zero is a second-best solution.

In terms of policy-making, would you rather that those doing cost-benefit analysis used some kind of hyperbolic discounting?

I would rather have the democratic process talk about the rights of future generations. Then, after you've done the rights discussion, you can do some cost-benefit analysis. There need to be some prior discussions that set the stage. Thus, if we decide upon the goal of income equality in twenty-five years, cost-benefit analysis can be done using that assumption. That would be putting the moral decision up front. We certainly have to be moving away from the inequality we have now.

Both you and Matt Rabin question standard welfare economics that came up in the 1940s and 1950s. What is your primary concern?

Welfare economics arose as economists were drawn into government and asked to do cost-benefit analysis to pick what was best in economic terms. This could only be done by ignoring questions of the distribution of initial rights driving the broad nature of our market economy as well as ignoring who got what from government projects. The task of welfare economics was to rationalize a very limited approach to economic reasoning. Welfare economics clearly identified the problem as the need for some sort of social welfare function, something imbued with values outside of market reasoning that indicates preferences for who gets what, for more or less equality, etc. (see, for example, Bator 1957). Economists then reasoned that, though they had no basis themselves for determining a social welfare function, surely any project that moves all parties to a higher level of well-being, a Pareto superior move, is preferred to a project that helps some and hurts others. In fact, depending on the nature of the social welfare function and distribution of income in a society, even Pareto superior moves may decrease welfare. Then, they reasoned that so long as the winners compensated the losers so that all were better off, the project should go ahead. And then economists continued down the slippery slope and argued that the winners do not need to compensate the losers, in fact, because with sufficient projects with random distributional effects, being a winner or loser would net out. Thus by 1971 one of my thesis advisers, Arnold Harberger, published in a preeminent journal that the third premise of applied welfare economics is that it makes no difference to whom the benefits and costs accrue (Harberger 1971). I remember arguing with him as a graduate student that completely ignoring questions of distribution was tantamount to saying that whatever the market is doing is right, . . . and he seemed to agree!

The work I have done with Rich Howarth using overlapping generations models demonstrates that sustainability is a matter of intergenerational equity, not a matter of efficiency. An efficient economy is always better, but it is not necessarily sustainable. A perfectly efficient economy could deplete resources and leave future generations worse off. To obtain sustainability, we need to delve into how we care about future generations, and this question must be addressed as an ethical question at a deeper level than the day-to-day value choices we make in the context of prices generated by what looks to be an unsustainable economy. So all of the rationalizations we made as economists to avoid having economics be interactive with moral reasoning and politics are now preventing us from addressing long-term sustainability, preventing us from addressing North-South equity issues that need to be resolved before we can have global agreements on climate change and biodiversity loss, and preventing us from addressing questions of environmental justice here at home. Quite frankly economists are like highway engineers who know how to make perfect roads but are afraid to work with society on the obvious question of to where we should build roads.

What about the issue of the respective roles of heterodox, orthodox, and mainstream views in policy-making?

I have been on the edges of policy-making, some in the state of California as an environmental economist, and am currently serving on the Environmental Economics Advisory Committee of the Science Advisory Board of the U.S. Environmental Protection Agency (EPA). I am the token ecological economist. I have served on lots of National Academy of Science committees advising the federal government on scientific policies as an interdisciplinary scholar who can bridge between the heterodox and the orthodox and the biological sciences and other natural sciences. The environmental community pressured the U.S. EPA to have more heterodoxy on their Science Advisory Board: "How come you have so many mainstream environmental economists?" "How come you don't have any ecological economists?" Herman Daly served for a year, felt he wasn't being listened to, and left. That's when they asked me.

I have only been to one meeting so far, which was pretty amusing. The Clinton administration mandated that trade agreements have environmental assessments. So the U.S. trade representatives sent their chief economist over to the economics part of the EPA and said, "How are we going to do this?" They hired an economic consulting firm that proposed a model of trade that says trade is about countries moving towards their comparative advantages. The model estimates which sectors of the economy will expand, which will contract, and how this will change air pollution, resource use, soil erosion, and so on. The discussion went on for thirty-five or forty minutes before I raised my hand and said that that's the wrong model. "Trade agreements are about liberalizing capital flows, and this model is about comparative advantage. And in fact, liberalizing capital flows reduces comparative advantage. So you have a model that's orthogonal to what we are actually doing." This stopped everybody cold for fifteen seconds, and then one economist said, "We don't have a good model for the liberalization of capital." Then they said, "Well if we don't have a model, then this is the best we can do, so go ahead and do it." I said, "Well, the EPA sponsors a lot of environmental economics research. Would this fall under the realm of environmental economics research, getting the right model to do our job?" There wasn't any interest in pursuing this: I think it was just a political hot potato. Why would the EPA want to promote research on the real economic impacts of trade?

So policymakers are often locked into very standard models but are under some pressure to open the doors a bit to some heterodox views. But those heterodox views are in trouble if they dent the inertia of the orthodoxy?

But in this case, it's just orthodoxy. I wasn't trying to introduce a coevolutionary or institutionalist interpretation of what was going on. I was playing the role of a straight neoclassical economist, only an honest one. The problem is that straight neoclassical economics often doesn't have a model for what's actually happening in the economy. What was irritating was that my fellow economists, as neoclassical economists, as members of the Science Advisory Board, agreed but said we should still go ahead and do this inappropriately. This happens quite frequently in applied economics. But for the Science Advisory Board to bless it, I don't think that would happen in biology or physics, though I'm sure it happens in agriculture.

RICHARD B. NORGAARD

What do you think should happen? What types of process should go on?

I think we should be truer to our models. Neoclassical economics is a powerful way of thinking, but it's not as powerful as it is being made out to be. I think economists have gained additional power inside the political process by abusing their own theory. That abuse is swept under the rug, and I think it hurts policy, scholarship, and how we teach, and a lot of economists are totally unaware of it.

Why do you prefer the term "constructive dissent" to "heterodox"?

I read your opening chapter with heterodox and orthodox and thought that your wording was not as constructive as it could be. The diversity of economic thinking broadens the mainstream. Some strong economists in the mainstream get frustrated and disturbed by what is going on, but deal very constructively, yet in a dissenting way. I try to be a constructive dissenter. I would say that my over-lapping generations work is a dissenting position from the culture of standard economics. It is a dissenting position from our gut reaction, thinking about time as a discount rate. But I want to be constructive. I dissent from the mainstream while trying to make it richer and deeper. There are a lot of people who are just critical, critical, and critical. Criticism is valuable, and a lot of my work is seen as critical. But I try to construct other patterns of thinking. I criticize the mainstream for not being more open, but I am not inherently against the use of market models.

Who is a "strong economist" in the mainstream who has changed its thinking?

Clearly, a lot of Chicago economists have changed the profession from a fairly pragmatic, progressive, synthetic vision to a much more narrow, neoliberal one. Among my heroes, however, Kenneth Arrow is somebody who is strong, able to listen to quite a few views, and isn't disturbed by contradictions that don't seem to be easily resolvable. He's also been constructively participating in some of the environmental debates over three decades and still involved in climate change issues.

It appears that many heterodox economists are constantly criticizing the market system or the neoclassical model but aren't replacing it with anything. Do you look at your work on coevolutionary theory as being critical but also as providing alternative ways of dealing with important economic issues?

Yes, that's certainly the way I would hope to be seen. We tend to want to have the right answers; economists are very monotheistic. So monotheists see any alternative thinking as criticism. The search for one right way of thinking is not limited to the orthodox.

So this could be Marxists or heterodox economists as well as mainstream ones?

Yes, Marxists frequently read my stuff and say, "But you don't have power in your coevolutionary model, so it must be wrong." Well, in some ways there is power all through my model. Dominance affects selection but also gets overthrown over time and sometimes quickly. So there is power in my book but not in the way that the Marxists think about it or use it. On the other hand, you have neoclassical economists who say that efficiency is the most important issue and can't understand why I would write a book without talking about efficiency. And I have institutional change but pay little attention to the institutional economic literature. Addressing all of these constituencies would have complicated my message so much that I am not sure anyone would find the core message.

In neoclassical models they deal with power by assuming competition. The Marxists use class struggle. Would you say that you deal with power using a biological coevolutionary methodology?

Yes, it is a more general way to look at power and dominance. The Marxists say power is under capitalists' control who dominate institutions and the technologies we live with. The coevolutionary model says that there are lots of different capitalists putting their money in all kinds of different things and then we see who is selected. Of course, there is power as the Marxists know it, but the coevolutionary perspective helps us think about power in other ways.

Do you believe that coevolutionary theory can provide economists with better insights into welfare economics?

I would be pleased if in the future economists would just honestly say that the social welfare function is an evolving function as we learn and as our society changes. The political process is the best way we have of representing that social welfare function. It's highly distorted by corporate power now. I would really like a democratic process that was truly democratic, and then I would really love to have an economics that worked with democracies, instead of an economics that was called into the democratic process and then used in a very authoritarian way. Most economists think politics is corrupt, crazy, undependable, a waste of time, and that we can come up with better answers faster for the public interest than the politicians. But I would really like to have economics be in discourse with democracy, rather than trying to replace it. I have reached this position through my coevolutionary thinking and my understanding of economics together.

How do you view relations between economics in the United States and the rest of the world, both generally and with respect to ecological economics?

I only know Europe through my European colleagues, so I can only say what they say. It's been my understanding from working with European colleagues for twenty to twenty-five years that there was far more diversity in economic thinking and less institutionalization of economics in governmental processes before the 1980s. So things that were happening earlier in the United States began to happen more strongly in Europe in the 1980s. By the 1990s the diversity that I knew in Europe in the 1980s was under great threat.

Is this from U.S. influence?

The influence from the U.S. side is there, clearly. American economists take the lead in the development of economics because we're a very big country with great wealth. But we also have the biggest effect on the World Bank and on international policy more broadly. Being the dominant country, our economists have a bigger play. With the vast majority of Nobel laureates being identified with the United States, the American way of thinking about economics is pressed onto Europe. There has been quite a bit of influence in the late 1990s, partly because the neoliberal worldview has been constraining budgets. By the late 1990s, European universities were under extreme financial pressure, so they developed tighter selection criteria for new professors and for the promotion of existing professors. The criteria became, "Well, if you are like an American economist, you must be good; if you're a German Institutionalist, we can probably squeeze you out." Thus, diversity in European departments has been under pressure. It's a combination of how economics has been affected by university budgets and philosophies of government and the dominance of American economics in global systems.

Is there less institutionalization or less connection to policy in the U.S., where high theorists have little to do with policy, or in Europe, where economists seem more likely to play policy roles?

Economists in small countries have better access to their government. The best thinking of economists can be applied to economic issues without institutionalizing economics as much. When you are a really big country, things get institutionalized more. Smaller countries can get a lot of diversity with scholars from different countries so close by. They still get together and meet and learn from each other. So the diversity between them gets reflected in how they think collectively, how they teach. Then you don't get as big a bureaucracy of economists because each government is smaller than ours. The high-level scholars have better access to the government, but they are not as institutionalized as in the U.S.

One odd source of the diversity, which a lot of people have criticized and that may be breaking down, may be the tendency in Europe, compared to the U.S., to be much more inbred in the universities. Do you see the European universities having more of their own schools of thought, their own distinctiveness?

The London School of Economics is certainly more conventional now, but it was less conventional historically. With British economics you tend to get these homegrown scholars in their own home universities. In Germany you get to sit by the Herr Doctor Professor's knee for twenty-five years until you get to be Herr Doctor Professor yourself. So you can't possibly be sitting and listening to the bigger conversation that might be out there. You have to pay obedience to the authority. That part of the heterodoxy of Europe is not a good model.

You have mentioned that progress toward dealing with environmental challenges we face today is in limbo. What are the environmental challenges we face today? Is there anything we can do to get out of that limbo?

The big environmental challenges are global. I think we have done reasonably well on the regional and national issues, though the Bush Administration is trying to reduce our commitment. We still need to work harder on issues of environmental justice. A lot of the challenges now are issues of equity: North-South equity, intergenerational equity, and more along the lines of my coevolutionary book, issues of cultural tolerance. The value of cultural diversity is something we still need to bring in. We are not well equipped to deal with many of these global issues. Neoclassical economics can deal with the distributional issues if we get serious about them. But we've had fifty years of legislators asking us to give one right answer and not deal with this question. We also had fifty years of the Marxists unsuccessfully dealing with these issues. Our environmental future really depends on how we address distribution.

In your Review of Social Economy *paper (Norgaard 1995a), you argue that materialism lies behind the environmental crisis. Why and how is it materialism?*

I think that paper was another effort to try to open us up to a bigger worldview. Why are our lives so structured around the material stuff that we own? Why does our sense of identity constantly need to be bolstered by going out and buying stuff? Why isn't our sense of identity the understanding of important things in life, structured around our ability to think, our ability to be social? I argue that people as individuals have coevolved around the market institutions economists have rationalized, making it easier to put more emphasis on our material lives, less on our lives as one of the most social of social species. If we could increase that portion of our lives, dramatically, which is the same thing as saying materialism would be pushed back dramatically, our environmental problems would pretty much go away.

How do you see McCloskey's (1985) views on rhetoric in economics?

I think McCloskey's arguments about economics being far more powerful than many other social sciences because of its rhetoric than its mathematics are correct. Regarding metaphors in biodiversity literature and science, we are having more success speaking to the public about biodiversity, rather than climate change, because there are so many more metaphors being used in the biodiversity, such as biodiversity being a great library of knowledge. It is just full of rhetoric that is good for communicating to the public. Whereas the greenhouse effect is really an analogy for climate change, it's not an appealing metaphor. So we are not communicating about climate change with good metaphors. I have argued that we use "limits" as metaphor in ecological economics, and that perhaps it is the most functional we have, but I still am disturbed by its casual use (Norgaard 1995b). I am trying to think if there are ways of explaining the coevolution of ideas and knowledge, words and ideas, in economics. Certainly, the invisible hand was so powerful that it became a belief about how markets work rather than a good description of how markets work—it so bolstered the belief in markets, and unrealistically so.

How would you describe your current research agenda? How has that research agenda changed recently?

For the past couple of years, my research has been toned down because I have been the president of an international society and I am also the father of now three-year-old twins. The research I am currently doing is on trade, environmental pollution, and governance. For the last ten or twelve years, these are the three big issues in international trade, yet economists have not built a model that puts them all together. I have managed, with a series of graduate students, to come up with a fairly interesting mathematical model. We start with a Salop model that was developed to explain the relationship between monopolistic competition and the location of firms, the role of distance in being able to collect a monopolistic rent. I have applied that model, building in pollution, building in governance, and letting the circumference of a circle used in the Salop model be a metaphor for the globe. I haven't been able to publish it successfully in a journal, although it's appeared in the proceedings of a conference at the University of Tokyo meeting on Asia-Pacific relations that just came out (Norgaard and Kojima 2001). It works out somehow that when I write economics even using formal models, people pick up the idea that I'm critical, that I'm writing this stuff to corrupt economics. The *Journal of Political Economy* rejected it as political, despite its formal mathematics. All economics, of course, is political, as implied in the title of Chicago's journal.

I am also initiating a project funded by the NSF on how we think we understand complexity. I argue that there are at least four ways and that to a large extent they are complementary. Our agency structure and policy processes, however, are largely set up around the first and historical understanding that our separate disciplines will surely merge into coherent understanding, for we are all studying one reality. This project falls in the realm of environmental epistemology, but I hope to shape some papers from it for the economics community too.

RICHARD B. NORGAARD

What questions are economists trying to answer now that the answer would change the economics profession? Are economists now asking interesting questions?

Which level of economics are you talking about? There are interesting ideas coming out of game theory and complex systems, chaos, and evolutionary thinking. Whether they will change economics, I don't know. I think it will change economics in the top twelve or twenty graduate programs. A lot of limited economics today is institutionalized in public policy programs as applied economics, where it will affect practice for decades to come. I don't see a lot of changes in how we write textbooks and teach economics for the masses for a while. I think we'd have to have a really major shake-up, another Great Depression before we see the innovative thinking at our best universities affecting how economics is practiced. Of course, one does not hope for disaster in order to see things really moving or substantially changing economics.

What is your reaction to the chapter we sent you on the cutting edge?

I don't like the term *cutting edge* because that metaphor assumes that economics advances at its front, at its cutting edge, and even if you argue that ideas are coming in from the side, they are coming in from constructive dissenters, from the heterodox. Much of my work is outside of economics, and yet even that which is outside gives me new perspectives on what is happening inside. It's not the case that mainstream economists, let alone the orthodox, have a cutting edge that leads the way. The mainstream gets wider or narrower as it lets other ideas in and as older ideas get squished out. Of course, the problem is that most newer ideas get squished out. The cutting edge to me is an incorrect concept. Certainly there are people chipping away at the cutting edge of orthodoxy, but what they do is not terribly interesting. So I'd dispense with that term.

Do you feel that there is a current orthodoxy in economics that you are violating with your work?

I think the best way to answer this is to go back to my frustration with economics: it is not with its particular theories but with the attitudes of economists that I have problems. Somehow, even when I am trying to write to economists with their own models, they pick up that I must have some other agenda. I do, but my other agenda is just to open up the profession to natural science, the other social sciences, and moral philosophy.

Do you find by working outside of economics in biology, anthropology, and sociology that you are provided with the insight to really understand the connection of economic systems to other types of systems and how to deal with environmental, globalization, or trade problems?

Yes, that's a correct summary. Occasionally I team teach courses with ecologists, and in that teaching I relearn ecological thinking, which helps me think about systems in different ways. Some of my work is straight market models, but I am trying to push them further. My selection of what I want to push is certainly directed by the bigger picture to which I am exposed by working outside of economics.

Is one of your objections to the term "cutting edge" that it implies merely incremental change?

Yes, cutting edge strikes me as small, mostly technical changes on the margin. I had the good fortune of taking a course with Robert Mundell, who at several points in the course said, "All of my original ideas aren't original; I just read Alfred Marshall and it turns into Robert Mundell." I'm sure that wasn't entirely true, but when you go back and read the classics, you find that they were reading moral philosophy, they were reading natural science. They were much more in tune with the big world around them than the modern academic who, in order to stay ahead, has to be a specialist and interact only with economists. I think if we pay more attention to each other across the disciplines and to big world problems, we'll spend less time doing small cutting edge work.

When you have acted in multidisciplinary settings, in some cases with the National Academy of Science or other groups or just teaching with ecologists, how open are the people in these other disciplines to ideas that you might bring from economics?

Biologists are very open. They certainly have their own schools of thought, with people pushing particular positions. But they tend, at least the ecologists I work with, to go out in the field and talk with one another. Do economists go out and look at the south side of Chicago or what's happening in the bay area of San Francisco and actually talk about the economy? A lot of our barriers to communication, between Marxists and institutionalists and neoclassicists, might go away if we put ourselves in the field and talked about what is happening. So the biologists communicate better with each other and are also better listeners to economists. But we say things that trip them up because our words mean different things, so it takes a while to communicate economic concepts to biologists.

What is an example of a word we use that would trip them up?

Their concepts of *efficiency* are much more material, biological, food and stuff oriented. Our concepts of *efficiency* are in some ways more systemic than theirs. It's the whole economic system that we think of as efficient or inefficient.

What do you think about the debate over multidisciplinary versus interdisciplinary versus transdisciplinary? Is ecological economics the latter, and are these meaningful distinctions?

We put *transdisciplinary* on the front of our journal, *Ecological Economics*. With transdisciplinary one needs to know the core models and cultures of the disciplines and work across them and ask questions across them. This does not mean they fit together because there may be no metamodel and you may not be able to work in their intersection. But you deal with multiple patterns of thinking. Sometimes they fit, and sometimes they don't, which is pretty exciting in itself. In the 1960s and '70s, interdisciplinary came in when we were supposed to seek out the unexplored intersections between disciplines. Someone studied enough economics and enough hydrology to work in their intersection and become a water economist, if not a very good economist or a very good hydrologist. There are lots of multidisciplinary programs where students see an economist, an ecologist, a soil scientist, and others from different disciplines. The student is supposed to learn something from each of them and put it all together somehow.

What do you see as the most important changes in the economics profession in the last twenty years?

The opening up of the top dozen economic departments in the United States during the last decade has been pretty exciting to watch. In the decade before there was a lot of shutting down around the market model in these departments. But now I see, at least at the top universities, an opening up. As I indicated, I don't know how this new openness will get translated into the profession. It might mean more exciting and open textbooks that go beyond just presenting the one right way of thinking about economics. If this openness could be translated in policy classes, and institutionalized within the economics profession, that would really be exciting.

Maybe it will take a major global crisis before the profession really gets out of its current rut.

Where do you see the economics profession going in the next twenty-five years?

You are asking a coevolutionist to predict! I just expect to be a part of the process. Personally, I am interested in setting up some sort of a responsible economists' group—a group of economists who would be watchdogs of policy debates based on economics. The group would not be the same as Physicians for Social Responsibility because they're not really arguing for the responsibility of physicians as physicians. Economists ought to be concerned about social responsibility too, but I'm more worried about economists not having quality control over their own profession. Whether there is such a group or not, I would hope that we would see a greater honesty in applying the breadth of economic understanding to policy debates in the coming years.

Richard B. Norgaard

Professor of Energy and Resources and of Agricultural and Resource
Economics, University of California at Berkeley

INFORMATION ON THE WEB ABOUT RICHARD B. NORGAARD
http://socrates.berkeley.edu/erg

EDUCATION
A.B. Economics, University of California at Berkeley, 1965
M.S. Agricultural Economics, Oregon State University, 1967
Ph.D. Economics, University of Chicago, 1971

SELECTED PUBLICATIONS
"Economic Indicators of Resource Scarcity: A Critical Essay." *Journal of
Environmental Economics and Management* 19 (1990).
"Environmental Valuation under Sustainable Development," with Richard
B. Howarth. *American Economic Review* 82 (1992).
"Intergenerational Transfers and the Social Discount Rate," with Richard
B. Howarth. *Journal of Environmental and Resource Economics* 3 (1993).
*Development Betrayed: The End of Progress and a Coevolutoinary Revision-
ing of the Future.* London and New York: Routledge, 1994.
"Ecological Economics." In *Encyclopedia of Global Environmental Change,*
edited by Ted S. Munn. London: John Wiley and Sons, 2001.

SPECIAL HONORS AND EXPERIENCE
Founding Member, Association of Environmental and Resource Econo-
mists, 1974
Policy Analyst, World Bank Team to Negotiate and Implement Policies to
Protect the Environment and Indigenous Peoples, Northwest Consoli-
dation Project, Polonoreste, Rondonia, Brazil, 1988
Member, Economics Advisory Committee, United Nations Environment
Program, 1992–95; Founding Chair, 1994–97; Board of Directors,
Redefining Progress, San Francisco, California, 1994–; Science Advisory
Board, Environmental Economics Advisory Committee, U.S. Environ-
mental Protection Agency, 2001–3; Board of Directors, American Insti-
tute of Biological Sciences, 2001–President, International Society for
Ecological Economics, 1998–2002

CHAPTER 9

Robert Axtell

Fellow, Center on Social and Economic Dynamics (CSED),
Economic Studies Program, the Brookings Institution, and Visiting
Associate Professor of Economics, Johns Hopkins University

H. Peyton Young

Scott and Barbara Black Professor of Economics, Johns Hopkins
University, Professorial Fellow, Nuffield College, Oxford, and
Codirector and Founder, CSED, the Brookings Institution

The interview was conducted on May 6, 2002, at the Brookings
Institution in Washington, D.C. During the middle of the interview
H. Peyton Young joined us. The speaker is Robert Axtell unless
specified.

How did you get into economics?

In high school, I had very little interest in economics. My father ran a road construction company, so I was familiar with day-to-day issues of economics, and from him I learned about unions and other things, but that was about it. He was an engineer, and my math and science interests led me to engineering school at the University of Detroit (now University of Detroit Mercy), a small Jesuit institution. I got a degree in chemical engineering, with a minor in economics. I spent summers working at Exxon when I was in undergraduate school, and I quickly learned that economics, not engineering, drove the world. At Exxon, I worked on computational design of chemical plants and refineries, which accelerated my interest in computation.

While I liked doing the math and the technical parts of engineering, it was clear to me that in the corporate world it was business people who were making the decisions, the MBAs, etc. After graduating I briefly considered getting an MBA, but eventually I applied to a spectrum of Ph.D. economics and policy programs. I chose Carnegie Mellon because it had strong programs in everything computational.

Your degree was in public policy?

Yes. So I am not an economist in the same sense as Herbert Simon is not an economist. My degree is actually from Carnegie Tech, the engineering school. The best thing about Carnegie Mellon was that they were very loose about course requirements, so I had flexibility in the courses I could take. There is no economics department there as such; there's the Graduate School of Industrial Administration—that's the business school—and something called the Department of Social and Decision Sciences. There are people in the Public Policy School, like Linda Babcock and Richard Florida, who are doing mostly economics. Bennett Harrison was there when I was, and I took courses from him. The Department of Social and Decision Sciences also has behavioral economists. But most of the economists actually sit in the business school, so most of my Ph.D. coursework—microeconomics, game theory, operations research and a little bit of macro—I took from the business school.

For microeconomics I had an excellent teacher named Bart Lipman, now at Wisconsin. He taught a very nice course that was not Varian, not Kreps, but a mixture of the two plus his own economics of information component. There are many great teachers at

Carnegie Mellon University (CMU): Lester Lave was great on the relation between economics and policy, and taking operations research (OR) courses from Gerry Thompson was tremendous. I remember courses by Sanjay Srivastava on mechanism design and Steve Spear on aggregate dynamics that led right to the research frontier. I could go on and on.

I also did a lot of computing coursework. I worked with Greg McRae, now at MIT, who at the time was using supercomputers for policy purposes, simulating tropospheric ozone formation in the Los Angeles basin in order to figure out how to better regulate vehicle emissions. CMU is an amazing place for anyone into computing. It seems like almost everyone there is doing something computational.

What was Herbert Simon's role at Carnegie Mellon?

Simon was a professor of psychology, although his e-mail account always carried the School of Computer Science extension on it. He didn't have much to do with the Graduate School of Industrial Administration when I was there. Occasionally he would make dismissive remarks, saying that it was being taken over by the economists. He sometimes said that he probably had had some success in economics because he never learned to think like an economist.

At the Eastern Economic Association meetings in 1991 he said that in the 1950s in journals such as *Econometrica* economists wrote papers about how businesses should run their operations—normative statements about how they could improve their operations through linear programming, through inventory control, and so on. By the 1980s the same journals still published papers about the optimal way that firms should behave, but they were no longer normative statements. They were claims that firms actually did this! For Simon, this was the way economists thought: that if there's a better way to do it, then firms must be doing it. He was very critical of crude evolutionary arguments, of the type Friedman made, for instance. There is a great set of papers in the *AER* in the late '50s or early '60s by Simon, the philosopher Ernest Nagel, and others on these "as if" arguments.

The only course Simon taught while I was there was his graduate-level introduction to cognitive science. I remember that this was a large class for CMU, with perhaps fifty or sixty students, drawn from many departments. That course mainly gave the

Simon/Newell conception of cognition as complex information processing. He recapitulated the many experimental results that led to his view of the necessity of treating cognition as a process. This is the basis of his notion of procedural versus substantive rationality in the bounded rationality literature.

How far back was Simon doing experimental economics?

He started back in the '50s, I believe. The foundations of cognitive science are partly due to A. Newell and other people back in the '50s and early '60s. One canonical statement of this is "Human Problem Solving" by Newell and Simon (1971). It's full of experiments. These are largely not economic experiments, but there are interesting social components in some of them.

What was the topic of your dissertation, and how did you choose it?

Simon's course in cognitive science that I mentioned was very important in picking my topic. Its focus was on how people think and make decisions. It's impossible for someone to take that course and maintain a rational economic actor framework for how economic agents decide.

This course was not [so] much about economic behavior; it was about how people solve problems in laboratory settings. Simon would situate subjects in the laboratory and watch how they would solve problems. Having done that, he would build mathematical models of how these people were actually solving them. The models had a learning component in them, but also there was never a meaningful way that you could say people were acting optimally in a minimum amount of time according to some theory of rationality. Cognitive science was about observing how people solved problems and trying to figure out the underlying model of information processing.

In that course I did a project on how people make decisions in the aggregate, you know, groups and so on. Simon had worked on this in the '60s, and he got me interested in it. In my dissertation I just extended that general idea. Its title was "Aggregation Theory for Dynamical Systems."

Carnegie Mellon is not a place with a vast endowment, so for many students their research work is highly correlated with projects funded by NSF or some other outside agency. I was working on a project associated with climate change at the time. The people that funded my dissertation had bought into the idea that it's a heterogeneous world out there, with lots of different emission sources and economic factors, and that it was reasonable to ask the question: how can you build and aggregate representative agent models that will be of some use for them?

A key point of my dissertation was that macroequilibrium does not imply microequilibrium. In philosophy this is known as the fallacy of division, to attribute properties to a different level than where the property is observed. I believe that the Nash program of game theory suffers exactly this problem. The Nash program rests on the empirically false claim that all social regularities result from microscopic, agent-level equilibria, and those are the Nash equilibria or some refinement.

The problem is what to do about it. You suggest that agent-based modeling allows us to see something about this problem that we haven't seen before?

Agent-based modeling, which I first heard about in Santa Fe, is useful because one has some very complicated math at the microscopic level. Every interaction and adjustment involves dynamics and is not a fixed point; it involves constant flux and very high-dimensional dynamics. But at the social level you have stationarity and something like aggregate fixed points. But fixed points can't be used at the microscopic level where everyone is adapting and adjusting to one another, where everything is constantly fluctuating; that's the hard part mathematically, and that's where computation helps us. Macroscopic regularities emerge from the interactions of the agents. Basically what I'm saying is that equilibrium among agents is sufficient for macroequilibrium, but it is not necessary.

The assumption of agent-level equilibrium today is so ingrained in the mainstream that some people will just not admit that it is only sufficient. One time I was giving an agent-based model paper in which the agents were constantly adapting to one another but stationary statistics were coming out at the macro level, and a Rochester economist expressed a standard sentiment. He said to me, "Look, this paper is crazy because the only kind of agent behavior you can have is either pure strategy Nash equilibria or, if you want to be dynamic, mixed strategy Nash."

Another concrete example concerns when I was considering where to send that paper. I was at a university where a leading journal editor was in the audience. He made some positive comments about the paper, and I made an offhand remark that maybe I should send the paper to his journal. He said that if I sent him the paper, it would start with two strikes against it because it uses nonrational actors and it derives its results computationally versus analytically.

Couldn't that be a reasonable response to new methods? One doesn't know exactly what is going on in them, so you pass on papers using them?

Unfortunately, reacting that way is probably a dominant strategy.

Have you calculated how to break into that dominant strategy? Have you analyzed it with your model?

I think there is a way to trump that response. If you can make the model generate empirically relevant results, then you change the burden of proof. If a game theory model is internally consistent and it has everything worked out, and everybody is doing the right thing at the right time, and the results seem plausible, that's one thing. But if you can say, "Look I have this other model which is not quite the way you want it to be, because of its rationality assumptions and so on, but it actually explains these otherwise unexplained data that are out there," such empirical arguments change the burden of proof from me to them. I have often tried to follow that approach.

What is the reaction to that approach?

It's been reasonably successful. When Joshua Epstein and I first started working on agent-based modeling, we thought that economic theorists would be our main audience because it is a way around the hurdles that are impeding progress for theorists: it allows us to put in heterogeneous actors; it allows us to put agents in a social network and doesn't require that we only consider equilibria. As Richard Freeman pointed out to us, our natural audience is not theoretical economists but applied economists. They are most in contact with the data and know the most about computing.

Once you finished your dissertation, what did you do?

Coming from Carnegie Mellon, there is a signaling problem for some Ph.D. students. If you get a degree from social and decision sciences, people don't know if you are an economist or a psychologist. In my case, coming from the engineering school with a public policy degree but with training in computer science and economics, people wanted to know what I was. So I did not participate in the economics job market.

As I was finishing my dissertation in the winter of 1991–92, I went to the Santa Fe Institute (SFI) winter school on complexity and scaling, largely at the behest of John Miller at CMU, and I was quite taken by the work going on at SFI. Murray Gell-Mann, Phil Anderson, and Geoff West were all there giving lectures on things such as power laws and scaling in physics, biology, and related fields.

So I thought I would do a postdoc at SFI. But then I met Joshua Epstein from Brookings, who was working on mathematical models of violence, wars, drug epidemics, and related things on the fringes of political science and economics. He studied political science at MIT but is trained in economics too. At that time he was involved in organizing a joint project with Santa Fe, Brookings, and the World Resources Institute, and I decided to join him. He and I worked closely together for several years, culminating in our 1996 book *Growing Artificial Societies.* This gave rise to the birth of our research center at Brookings, the Center on Social and Economic Dynamics; I think that, early on, the work we were doing was considered too far from the mainstream to receive funding from conventional sources. The funding for the center came originally from the MacArthur Foundation.

Once the center was formed, Peyton Young agreed to join as codirector, and his role has been crucial. Peyton saw that what we were doing had quite a lot of affinity with what Tom Schelling had done, and with his own work on evolutionary dynamics. In our book we credit Schelling for this method. Tom had moved in the early '90s to the School of Public Affairs at Maryland, where Peyton was teaching. In 1994, Peyton brought Schelling down, and we had a great day showing him the early version of Sugarscape with the Schelling model (1971) also running full speed. Whereas Tom had moved pennies and nickels around on an 8 x 8 checkerboard, we were doing things on a 100 x 100 lattice on a fast computer, but it was the same idea. Tom would ask what the effect of some change would be, and we could click a button and show him a graph instantly.

Somewhere you quote Schelling as arguing that as agent-based models become more complicated, it becomes harder to discern cause and effect.

I think Schelling articulates a KISS principle (keep it simple, stupid). When our book came out, we had a media event; we invited science journalists and other people to come and Tom was in the audience. There were several questions asking, what if you give the agents some additional capabilities, some additional rules, some additional interests or whatever? After about the fifth question of this type, Tom stood up and said that he thought that this modeling approach benefits from having as parsimonious a representation as possible. This reflects the perspective in his great *Micromotives and Macrobehavior* book. In economics we don't build in the things like the blood pressure of an agent or its hair color. We are keeping this as parsimonious as possible. I remember that this ruffled the sensibilities of the *Scientific American* journalist in the audience, who took issue in print.

Doesn't that leave you open to sensitivity questions?

Yes it does. But as long as the models can be adjusted to fit the real world I think such questions are secondary. It would be a happy situation if someday we have two or three or ten distinct models, all simple, purporting to explain the same social phenomenon. Then we could look at the microstructure of such models and use experiments to determine which alternative theory is most credible. But today there is a paucity of theories for many important social processes; I would probably even say most social phenomena. Today, we do not have coherent models that "grow" fundamental human social organizations, like the family, private property, or the state, although people have been theorizing about these things for hundreds of years. The conventional theory of the firm is an example. Where are the models that show firms coalescing in large populations of self-interested agents? Today we have either the simplistic unitary actor model of the firm or else the principal-agent-type models in which there are only a few interacting agents.

Someday we will have detailed cognitive models—no doubt computational—for how people really behave in certain contexts. These will certainly not be simple. Then we can insert these into the heads of our agents. Today there are some early versions of such things, programs that report on how people will behave when they go to restaurants, for example. One of them is a program at Carnegie Mellon called SOAR (state, operator, and result theory).

But if you're drawing from a sample that has an infinite number of possibilities, what does your model tell you?

I think Schelling's basic answer, and what our answer has come to be, is that if you can give a simple model that explains the data, then you demonstrate that you don't need to add the blood pressure of the agent to get the data to come out right. You want to have the model be as simple as possible but, as Einstein said, no simpler.

You have argued for an existence theorem and suggest that agent-based modeling can be used as a test of theoretical results. If one can show that, given the assumptions that you've made, you cannot derive something consistent with the pattern in the data, then the theoretical results are meaningless.

That's right; sometime agents can be used as theorem buster. One thing that might eventually be done is to take every conventional economic proposition and subject it to the following test. Simply situate a bunch of self-interested actors in a plausibly empirical environment, and let them interact according to some plausible behavioral rules, and see whether they get that proposition coming out, yes or no. Of course what you would generally find is that on some conditions you would, and on some other conditions you would not, get it. So the agent model can show the boundaries of relevance of the proposition.

That would be a great thing to do from first principles. You situate the agents and give them plausible rules and ask: do they produce the predicted results? I think the answers would be mixed. Some things would be easy to reproduce, and others hard to reproduce; rational expectations equilibrium would be very hard to reproduce. I think many of the theorems of macroeconomics would seem brittle according to this program, attainable only under highly unrealistic conditions, like full-blown agent rationality, for instance.

One of the things you look at in Sugarscape is evolving preferences. When you have evolving preferences, you often don't get convergence. How much do the preferences have to evolve for things not to converge?

I think about it in mathematical terms; there are two manifolds coevolving. One would be the price adjustment process, and the other would be the preference dynamics. Basically, if the preference evolution is slow compared to the price evolution, the system converges. If preferences evolve rapidly and the price mechanism is slow, you would have very erratic pricing. It's an empirical question, but I think you can imagine both kinds of situations.

Is the Sugarscape model the one that was used in the study of the Anasazi culture?

ROBERT AXTELL AND H. PEYTON YOUNG

The Anasazi culture model (Dean et al. 1999) was motivated by the Sugarscape model. Anthropologists saw the Sugarscape model as similar to the closed communities that they dealt with empirically. It turns out that the code base for the Anasazi is in our Ascape framework, so we actually morphed it—all of our work today is in this Ascape framework. We (Axtell et al. 2002) have a new National Academy of Sciences paper that quite closely reproduces the historical patterns of settlement in the actual Long House Valley of the Anasazi. What it does not reproduce is this en masse departure at the end of the period, but it comes close. We don't get people moving en masse out of the valley, but we do get a rapid decline in response to some microclimatic event that made living there very difficult. I think that model is a modest success because it gets the population numbers about right in the aggregate. It also reproduces the settlement patterns over space. Spatial modeling is something that's hard to do with economic data today.

Going back to the basis of your book, where did object-oriented programming, which combines data with algorithms, come from, and how do they make your systems special? How does this program compare to others you have worked on, such as Ascape, the codes for Schelling's model and the Young model, etc., all with similar methodologies?
I think the importance of tool development in economics is not always appreciated, As Robert Lucas wrote somewhere, new tools allow you to see things you couldn't see before. Of course, he was thinking about mathematical tools. Object-oriented programming was a paradigm that emerged in the '80s in computer science. It makes it possible to have a coherent representation of an agent, although that was not the initial motivation. The initial motivation in computer science was to make a closer connection between data and the functions that operate on the data. The idea of objects as a way to encapsulate data and methods evolved over time and has led further to the notion of patterns. For example, a traffic intersection involves a certain pattern of interacting objects: vehicles come into an intersection; they interact with a traffic light object that has its own behavior and which leads to certain kinds of behavior by the vehicles. Agent-based computational economics is simply the study of a certain class of patterns within object-oriented programming, involving self-interested agents interacting directly with one another through social networks.
It's not necessary to do agent-based modeling with object-ori-

ented programming. Early attempts, like Brian Arthur's El Ferol model (1994), which he demonstrated to me in 1992 when I was at Santa Fe, had only a simple representation of how the agents were working. What object technology gives you is a coherent methodology for building arbitrarily complicated complex systems with interacting agents. The original Sugarscape model used objects in a traditional, but not a sophisticated, way. That's why we have moved to Ascape. Ascape is a Java-based framework for the creation of agent models that we have invested several years in developing. It's freely available to academic users on our website (www.brookings.edu/dynamics/models/ascape /main.htm). It takes the object idea to its logical extreme. It allows anybody to gin-up a model relatively easily. Instead of twenty thousand lines of code, like the original Sugarscape model, the Ascape version of Sugarscape lives in maybe a thousand lines of code. Most of the grunt work associated with object initialization and graphics programming is handled in the background for you. It's basically a tool for the elaboration of agent modeling as a new methodology for economists and other social scientists. It's a technological backbone for articulating agent-based modeling into the research and educational communities.

In a paper with Axelrod, Epstein, and Cohen (1996), you aligned the Sugarscape model with the Axelrod (1995) culture model. How did that whole exercise work out?

The issues we were looking at in that comparison were how robust a simulation model is and how reproducible the results are. It was primarily the idea of Bob Axelrod and Michael Cohen. Bob had articulated a model of cultural dynamics in which there were agents situated on a lattice—immobile agents like a cellular automaton—but they were exchanging cultural "tags." We asked: "Can we constrain the Sugarscape model in such a way that we actually would cover this model as a special case?" These kinds of replication activities are not often done for computational models because of the time and expense.

Axelrod's agents were fixed in space, and ours in Sugarscape were mobile, so we had to turn the motion off. We found that to reproduce his results we had to get involved in some nitty-gritty details in order to get the model right. One of the things that turned out to matter a lot was how we let agents be active every period. It turned out that there was a difference between permitting every agent to be active exactly once each period, albeit in a random order as in Sugarscape, versus activating the agents at random so that they were active on average once during a particular period. That subtle detail in the microstructure of interaction mattered to reproduce the result. This kind of information is oftentimes underreported in journal articles.

If it took that much tweaking to make them similar, what have you shown?

We showed that it is useful to look at many different kinds of interaction regimes. We built that capacity into Ascape, and there are two or three other program systems around for doing these systems models, Swarm from Santa Fe and RePast from University of Chicago–Argonne. Because we have these things canned, a researcher can now have agents interact once per period or have them interact with a uniform probability of interaction or a variety of other ways. In the abstract, where it would have taken Bob a lot of time to reprogram his whole model, because all his agent interaction code was tied into the details of his Pascal code, in Ascape you can just change one line of code and determine whether the results are robust or not.

Could one say that one has a public goods problem, that it's clear that what we need is this gigantic super modeling system that one can use, and researchers can use, that would essentially push sensitivity analysis back but it's not in anyone's interest to provide it?

That's fair to say. Some people in the agent-based modeling community, which is a couple hundred strong, believe that we should have a type of Manhattan Project for developing a large-scale software tool which would have every possible variation embedded in it. Everyone could then use that tool, learn how it works, and study in general how things like sensitivity work and so on.

I hold a slightly different view—one that allows competition at this early stage of the paradigm. The best model platform will be arrived at through what Darwin called "requisite variance." Currently, there are a lot of variations in platforms out there, and we'll see which innovations are the most useful: Leigh Tesfatsion has a nice platform, SymBioSys, Santa Fe, has one, Chicago Argonne has one, and we have one. There are a variety of other ones too. I think they are all quite different in form and function. Eventually a very general-purpose software tool will probably make sense, but at this point I am more in favor of having heterogeneity.

How do these models relate to SimCity and the new popular game the Sims?

There is a symbiotic relationship between certain agent-based modeling researchers and some of the game people. For example, John Holland has invited Will Wright of Maxis Entertainment to Santa Fe conferences. The difference is SimCity, and those other very beautiful, fun games, don't have any deep social science content. There's no truly purposive activity, no utility functions used to rank alternative actions. They aren't really agent based on the microscopic level. On the other hand, the Sims invest a lot of personality details into the agents that do in fact matter for decision making but which economic researchers in general don't consider. So I believe that the gaming community is outstripping researchers along some dimensions.

One of the themes that has been running throughout our book and several of our interviews is the issue of introducing psychology into economics. Might the Sim games actually be a sign of where we are going with economic modeling?

It's complicated and unclear. There are some computer science researchers who are working in distributed artificial intelligence, in which instead of having one intelligent entity, as in traditional artificial intelligence (AI), you have several that interact socially. As people learn to use object technology to give utility functions to objects, or agents, then you move into multiagent systems, which refers to models where there is purposeful behavior on the part of actors. Many of the developments in games, entertainment systems, and on-line Internet worlds feature multiagents systems. Increasingly these researchers adopt game theoretic motivations for their agents. Essentially, they adopt what they find in Mas-Colell, Whinston and Green. Those of us in economics point out the many caveats to this approach. Most agent-based people in economics are trying to put in behaviorally more realistic assumptions, whether it is hyperbolic discounting or whatever. It's a primary motivation for using the computational agents. So there is a tension today between agent researchers in computer science and economics. It's an open question as to how the future will unfold.

It sounds as if the computer scientists believe more in orthodox economics theory than economists do.

As I stated earlier, it was impossible for someone to take Herbert Simon's Introduction to Cognitive Science course at the graduate level and then have a rational economic actor view of the world. I believe we should build in empirically observed behavior. For example, in a retirement model that Josh and I did (Axtell and Epstein 1999), we had people not simply computing their best possible behavior relative to their asset base but also using the behavior of other people in their social network to condition their own behavior. Our discussant of that paper at a Brookings conference, Robert Hall, was quite happy with the framing of that problem that way, although curiously he sympathized with our computational approach but thought it odd that we needed to defend it.

In that paper you stated, "The model behaves as if all agents are rational and that none are," and that there must be at least some agents who act rationally in order for the aggregate rational outcome. Could you comment on these statements?

In that paper, it's the obverse side of the usual coin. The usual coin, in Simonese, is that in a plausible economic environment it's very hard to imagine that economic actors could really figure out what the globally optimal behavior is—the world is just too complex. The obverse side is that with sufficient social learning you can have only a few people doing the right thing yet still approach a globally optimal decision.

In other general environments, can you still get a rational outcome without anybody being individually rational?

I think you can. This is the idea of swarm intelligence and is quite different in character from the first welfare theorem, which some people like Stokey and Lucas call the invisible hand theorem. To me Adam Smith's conception of the invisible hand is much closer to a swarm of myopic agents than to an omnipotent auctioneer.

I think it's also the case that in a more complex environment you can also get behavior that is demonstrably not right. There's a nice paper by Todd Allen and Chris Carroll (2001) about macroeconomic dynamics. They looked at the same kind of model for consumption behavior with stochastically varying income. Instead of assuming that all people solve very complicated stochastic dynamic programming problems and get the right answer, they assume that some get the right answer and others imitate them. This can lead to inferior outcomes by people imitating someone who just had a lucky draw from the income process. The point is that in complex environments the imitation process can lead to suboptimal outcomes.

Learning processes can do quite odd things. Blake LeBaron's agent-based models are quite useful in demonstrating this (Arthur et al. 1997b). He shows that there are regimes of rational expectations but there are also realistic regimes where people are constantly looking at each other trying to figure out what's best to do and that there can be big departures from fundamentals.

In 1996–97 there were lots of articles about Sugarscape that described you as a god, at least for Sugarscape. Since then there has been far less popular press. Why?

One reason is that we haven't done much with Sugarscape since writing the book. A second reason is at that time the science journalist John Horgan (1997) went on this attack against Santa Fe in general but also against agent-based modeling specifically. Various people jumped on the attack bandwagon. I remember one of the most important critiques by Maynard Smith, which asserted that anything could be gotten out of computational modeling so it is unclear whether it is a useful scientific paradigm. An important part of my work since then has been to try and make the models empirically credible, by bringing data to the models, although not necessarily empirically savvy enough so that an econometrician would buy into it.

The Sugarscape book was not about that. The Sugarscape book was a primitive statement of what could be accomplished with this new technology, so Sugarscape never had any empirical ambition. I think that there remains a fertile stepping-off platform for experiments, so there is in fact a large body of work in that domain. I can show you several hundred papers by economists, sociologists, and computer scientists that have taken departures from the Sugarscape model. Some added a tax to the Sugarscape world, some made the resource background much richer, and some changed the interaction structure. There are a bunch of papers that do those departures, but they are not about the empirical content of the model.

One of Horgan's criticisms of Santa Fe and complexity concerned the idea of complexity depending on the edge of chaos. What is your view about that? Is the edge of chaos a reasonable idea?

It depends on whether the models are of physical and natural systems or social science systems. It seems to me, and to many of my colleagues, that nonlinear dynamical systems have little to say to social science. Fixed coefficient models in social systems just do not seem very plausible, primarily because the coefficients are not likely to stay fixed over any long period of time. The nonlinear systems that we think about are actually low-dimensional nonlinear systems and in the real world interactions that are relevant to social science involve high-dimensional nonlinearities that we still can't capture. It's not easy to compress the large-scale heterogeneous world of a million actors into three equations. This is aggregation theory all over again and why I think "edge of chaos" ideas are only notionally relevant for social science.

Let's talk about your work extending Zipf's Law for firms. Is there a similarity between Zipf's Law, Gibrat's Law, Pareto-Levy distributions, power laws, scaling laws, and self-organized criticality? Are these all just different names for the same thing?

My work has been largely on Zipf's Law as applied to firms (2001) and on cities as a secondary study (Axtell and Florida 2000). It, too, relates to my background with Herbert Simon. In the '50s Simon and some other people built on what Gibrat knew, that firms were quite skewed in their size distribution (Ijiri and Simon 1964, 1977). Simon pointed out a variety of stochastic processes that generated such skewness. It turns out that the data were only known for the largest of firms—the publicly traded firms and other large firms that Gibrat could go around and collect data on. So my modest contribution has been to take all firms that filed income taxes in 1997— the first year for which data were readily available electronically— and show that the distribution that applied to the upper tail, the largest firms, also applied down to the smallest ones.

Scaling laws and power laws are terms in physics for what is conventionally known by statisticians and economists as Pareto laws. Essentially they're statistical laws where one of the parameters is the exponent in a power relation. One of the most interesting technical aspects of the Pareto-Levy distributions is that there exists a generalized central-limit-type theorem for them, so-called "stable" processes. This seems to be not often taught in graduate econometrics courses. But if the variance of a random variable does not converge, so it is not finite asymptotically, then the conventional central limit theorem goes out the window, and these astable distributions must be looked at. For example, take the two hundred largest cities, or one thousand largest firms, say, and compute a moving variance for city size or firm size. Plots of these statistics clearly diverge, so any attempt to use the normal or even lognormal distributions in these contexts is misguided.

Of what relevance are these laws to economics?

In my view these laws pose very strong technical limitations on the kinds of theories that make sense. It's very hard to get a neoclassical model to reproduce these skewed distributions, which makes them suspect. Let me be as concrete as possible, going back to Simon in the '50s. He argued that according to the U-shaped cost curve picture of the world if all firms in an industry have more or less the same cost curve over some stochastic variation and parameters, then you should expect a normal distribution of firm sizes. That is of course completely falsified by the data; you get something that is very nonnormal. Now, you have others who say that the neoclassical model says nothing about the size distribution, in which case it's not an empirically meaningful theory.

The late Per Bak (1996) argued very convincingly, although maybe only notionally with no theorem to substantiate his intuition, that any static equilibrium model can never produce a power law. If you take a model in static equilibrium and now start shuffling the parameters around, it's going to essentially produce normally distributed fluctuations. In order to get highly nonnormal distributions you need instead to be out of static equilibrium, perhaps in some dynamic steady state configuration such that fluctuations can possibly take you far away from where you were. Stock market price fluctuations have this power law character, as Mandelbrot (1963) noted long ago, but only today does there seem to be systematic work trying to come to terms with such data. Here I am thinking of Thomas Lux (1998) and some of the econophysicists (Mantegna and Stanley 2000). The distribution of firm size is similarly skewed. For example, even though the modal firm size in the U.S. is one employee, and the median is around seven to eight employees, the average is closer to twenty. Yet when we think about domestic policy, we almost inevitably have large firms in mind.

In my view these laws suggest that instead of seeing the economy in a static equilibrium we should think of it more in a dynamic steady state with individual agents not necessarily in equilibrium. To capture this dynamic notion, the agents have to be in flux, con-

ROBERT AXTELL AND H. PEYTON YOUNG

stantly adapting to one another. With a dynamic configuration, which can be captured by agent-based modeling, you can get these skewed distributions to come out. You don't get that when you have static equilibrium, when everything has gone to a fixed point at the agent level.

What has been the reaction from the regular economists to your 1999 paper and more generally to your work on the Zipf's Law (Axtell 2001)?
I'd like to start out by telling you what Herbert Simon told me when he saw the modeling paper about skewed distributions. In essence he said that it was crucial that we figured out a way to bring a large amount of data to bear on an agent-based model that had previously not been done. Here we compare the model output not only on firm size distribution but also the firm growth rate distribution and things like firm lifetimes and other empirical data. So he was heartened by that kind of thing.

As a footnote, the Nash equilibria in that paper are unstable, so there is no meaningful way in which the game theoretic solution is anything like a fixed point at the agent level. It is startling to read Simon's book reviews of von Neumann and Morgenstern or Luce and Raiffa that he wrote back in the 1940s and 1950s (Simon 1945). He notes that even though a game theory approach is very interesting as an attempt to mathematize human behavior, and even though there seem to be interesting equilibrium concepts emerging, he was very skeptical about the ultimate utility of game theory if the focus was just going to be on how people outguess one another. I think the fact that my firms model could reproduce certain empirical data using agents that could not be reproduced with analytic game theory was somewhat heartening to him.

The final irony of this is that I requested this firm data from the census bureau for a long time, but it only arrived the day Herbert Simon passed away. So he didn't see that paper. Many economists are uncomfortable with the idea of the agent level being out of equilibrium and constantly adapting. But they are interested by the empirical data. Boyan Jovanovic was very surprised that there could be such skewness down to the small-firm level, that there were so many small firms, and that so many large firms are privately held. I was told before sending my paper to *Science* (Axtell 2001) that few economists read *Nature* or *Science,* but I have been surprised by how many people have seen that paper.

The econophysicists are coming in and saying, "See? You economists don't know what's going on. We are cranking out all these scaling laws and power laws. Why don't you guys get with the program?"

Part of the problem economists have with econophysics is that many of the econophysics models don't have purposeful behavior underlying them. It's just some stochastic process that gives the right answer. If econophysics makes a contribution to economics, it will be by merging purposeful behavior models into their processes that gives the right answer. It could be by taking existing economic models and making them sufficiently stochastic or sufficiently like one of their known physical processes that gives the right answer. I think this would be a contribution because a trouble with most market models today is that in equilibrium there is no trade. Sargent says that the no-trade theorem works the rational expectations assumption hard. It seems to me it falsifies the rational expectations hypothesis.

I understand that you are currently not entirely happy about how Mirowski (2002) has treated your work in the new book Machine Dreams. *Do you care to comment on this matter?*

I am actually very sympathetic to what Phil has written. He takes umbrage with some of the history we have written about agent-based modeling. We give lots of credit to Schelling as the progenitor of this area, while he seems to think that we need to go back to von Neumann for historical relevance. But von Neumann's work is pure cellular automata, and Schelling's work is somewhat different, with fully mobile, self-interested agents. Still, I think Phil's book is useful and interesting.

I disagree with his conclusion where he describes four or five different futures for computational economics. He is sharply critical of several, and he goes on to describe an automata theoretical view of the future of computational economics. I think it would be difficult to see how that could play out in large scale. So I think that the version of the future he calls Simulatin' Simon, in some kind of a tongue-in-cheek but slightly pejorative way, is in fact the way the future will unfold, but he dismisses it, essentially for being too neoclassical.

Since your training is interdisciplinary, do you consider yourself an economist?

I sit in an economics program at Brookings, and so I consider

ROBERT AXTELL AND H. PEYTON YOUNG

myself an economic scientist, a researcher in economics. The luxury I have here is that I get to work on agent-based computing full-time, and I don't have to teach out of the textbook, so I have a broader view of what economics is than some people. The environment here at Brookings is very hospitable to the work that we are doing. Brookings has always been quick on its feet when it comes to computation, as you may know. Larry Klein did lots of the early large-scale econometrics here. And even when I came here, there was still a vestigial social science computer center doing large-scale economic policy models.

All of us in the Center on Social and Economic Dynamics are on the edge of economics in some sense. Most of us are members of AEA and other economics societies. Although Peyton Young's degree is in math, he's a professor of economics at Johns Hopkins. Josh Epstein has taken lots of economics at MIT, but his degree is in political science. The other director of our center, Carol Graham, has a background in political economy from Oxford. So we are all on the fringes of what would be considered card-carrying mainstream economics. But here at Brookings we never have to defend our approach to one another since we are all on the same page. And Bob Litan, the director of economic studies, who is a J.D./Ph.D., has been extremely supportive.

Do you see being separate as contributing to keeping you outside of the mainstream?

I'm not sure. I teach at Johns Hopkins on a regular basis, I teach agent-based modeling there, and when it comes to graduate students deciding what work to do, many of them are leery about having a portion of their dissertation in this area. So I think there is a common perception that this work is sufficiently outside the mainstream, that it is risky for graduate students.

Is it difficult to publish your work in agent-based modeling?

Yes, as one editor said to me, any paper using agent-based modeling starts with a couple of strikes against it. *JEBO* publishes papers in the area, but the mainstream journals are still resistant. The *AER* has only one paper that would qualify as an agent-based model so far; *Econometrica* has none. The *JPE* has not had a single paper. And the *QJE* had one paper, which was a baby step away from a conventional model. The baby step was to let the agents be very heterogeneous, but they still retain equilibrium at the end of the simulation, and rationality is still well defined. But it's a first step. I believe that as agent-based models become more empirically relevant, it will be increasing difficult for them to be turned away. Time will tell.

You have had considerable success using complexity models for advising policymakers. What have been the greatest limits and frustrations you have encountered while doing so?

Actually, we have tried to use agent-based models in a sparing way with policymakers. These models have only been around for a short time. They are like the new kid on the block. They're very useful for presenting results; they're visually attractive and appealing. For example, if you show a congressman a spreadsheet, he falls asleep, but if you show him a model with dancing colors on it, he gets excited. However, I believe at this time applying agent-based models directly to policy is premature. The modeling methodology is still under development, and the conclusions have to be taken with a grain of salt. They should be used primarily as a decision aid, not as a decision maker.

Having said that, I might mention that there have been several corporations and government agencies that are trying to use agent-based modeling in the operation of their business or their agency. And I think it is fair to say that there is reasonable success in doing so. For example, Josh Epstein and I did a project where we created an individual agent model of a large theme park to try to help them predict where the queues would be and what they could do about them. This involved as many as fifty thousand agents, each with idiosyncratic preferences for the attractions and tolerances for standing in lines. The project was recently described in a *Harvard Business Review* article (Bonabeau 2002) on commercial applications of agent modeling. There are also several government agencies that are doing similar things.

❧

At this point in the interview, Peyton Young, the codirector of the Center, whom we had invited earlier, stops in and joins the conversation.

❧

Why don't you tell us a little bit about how you got into agent-based modeling?

Young: I was increasingly dissatisfied with standard game theory. It seemed to me that the usual assumptions about agents' level of rationality and common knowledge of the game structure are not credible descriptions of what real people face in most strategic situations. It also seemed to me that too much emphasis was being placed on repeated interactions by a fixed set of players—usually just two players. In reality, games are often played by a changing cast of characters drawn from a large population. I wanted to see whether one could rebuild game theory from the ground up when there is a large population of individuals who interact from time to time but they are not fully aware of the process in which they are embedded.

Were the other people you were talking with pushing the edges and boundaries of game theory?

Young: Of course there were others—though in the mid-1980s when I first started to think about these things, there weren't many. Analogous ideas were, however, being actively discussed by theoretical biologists—notably John Maynard Smith and William Hamilton. Another source of inspiration was the work of Robert Axelrod, who showed how the Prisoners' Dilemma game could be reanalyzed using the idea of natural selection. In a population of players with different strategies, pairwise interactions lead to a dynamic in which strategies with high payoffs tend to displace strategies with lower payoffs. These models generally assume *no* rationality on the part of the players—that is, players did not *choose* strategies; they simply *have* strategies. I decided to study a different version of this setup in which players choose based on information about how strategies have done in the past; that is, they are purposeful but not omniscient.

How do you see Ken Binmore's work fitting into all this?

Young: Ken Binmore has been one of the pioneers in developing this approach. Among other things he showed how evolutionary game theory can be used to think about the evolution of norms and preferences. He argues in particular that our ideas about fairness can be understood as the product of evolutionary forces operating over very long periods of time (Binmore 1994, 1998). Similarly I have shown that norms in bargaining and fair division can be analyzed in an evolutionary framework and that some of the most common norms—such as equal division—have a powerful evolutionary underpinning (Young 1993b).

While it is fascinating to think about how conceptions of fairness may have evolved, it is also worth asking how people actually divide different kinds of benefits (and burdens) in society today. Do norms of fair division that we see in practice bear any resemblance to philosophical theories of justice, such as the greatest good for the greatest number (Bentham) or maximizing the position of the least well-off (Rawls 1971)? Do such norms differ substantially among societies? In my book *Equity in Theory and Practice* (1994) I investigated these questions not within an evolutionary framework but within a framework that considered the problem of revealed preference for fairness itself, using case studies as the jumping-off point. I found that while real-world norms of fair division often contain echoes of philosophical principles, typically they represent a balancing or tradeoff among different principles and cannot be neatly pigeonholed. They also vary substantially from one type of distributive problem to another so that notions of how to fairly divide the tax burden are not the same as norms for dividing scarce medical resources, for example. There is quite good evidence for the proposition that different norms evolve to solve different kinds of distributive problems and that these norms reflect broad cultural differences among societies.

In our interviews with them, it was clear that Matt Rabin and Ken Binmore have quite different views of how fairness, for example, should be analyzed as a preference.

Young: These theories are still in the making, and there's credibility to different points of view. Time scales are always an issue when one is talking about evolution. Preferences may take much longer to evolve than cultural norms for example. The longer the time scale, the sketchier the evidence we have for early conditions. This is not to say that there is no evidence: one can probably learn quite a lot about the nature of early human societies by observing behaviors and norms in primitive tribes today (Boyd and Richerson 1985). Nevertheless, the longer the time scale, the more speculative the theorizing tends to become and the more uncertainty there is as to whether a given evolutionary process correctly represents actual historical development.

When you went into this, did you know it was going to be difficult to publish, or did you expect there to be this reaction in terms of publishing?

ROBERT AXTELL AND H. PEYTON YOUNG

Young: To be honest I didn't worry much about where the work might ultimately be published. In fact I could not have predicted that the results were going to be worth publishing. I believe this is often the case with research—it leads in unforeseen directions and is influenced by many chance events, including whom one happens to talk with. When I first started to think about these questions back in the 1980s I was at the University of Maryland. It happened that some of the leading researchers in dynamical systems theory were in the mathematics department. At the time I was teaching a graduate course in game theory that attracted students from mathematics, statistics, computer science, and many other fields in addition to economics. Dean Foster was among the students in the course, and he introduced me to the theory of perturbed dynamical systems being taught elsewhere in the department by Mark Freidlin and Alexander Wentzell.

I had already begun working on the evolution of strategic choice in populations, but instead of adopting the replicator dynamics of Axelrod and the biologists, I wanted to incorporate more purposefulness into the choice of the agents. So I assumed that they chose best responses to the history of play as they understood it. In other words, they operated with a low level of rationality on fragmentary information gleaned from their own (and others') experiences, sometimes making blunders and unexplained choices. The difficult question was, what notion of equilibrium is appropriate to characterize such a system? At the time the standard concept of equilibrium was a version of asymptotic stability introduced by Maynard Smith and known as evolutionarily stable strategies.

I was dissatisfied with this concept because it could not cope with situations where persistent random influences are present, such as mutations or errors; it makes little sense to talk about one-time deviations from equilibrium if the system is in fact constantly deviating from its present position. Inspired by the framework of Freidlin and Wentzell, Dean Foster and I devised the idea of stochastic stability to describe systems that are constantly being bombarded by stochastic influences, and we showed that it leads to quite different predictions than the standard concept of asymptotic stability (Foster and Young 1990).

Only at this point did we start to think about where to publish the results. Unfortunately the economists we talked to were not very receptive to the idea. Since we were critiquing a standard notion of evolutionary equilibrium in biology, however, we decided to send it to a biology journal, *Theoretical Population Biology*. Frankly I didn't think it stood much of a chance there either, especially since we lacked any credentials as theoretical biologists. Luckily the editor, Marcus Feldman, took an interest in the paper and decided to publish it.

Was the reaction what you expected? And does the reaction say something about the economics profession?

Young: There is such a thing as being a little too early with an idea. When we submitted the paper, in 1988, economists were not thinking in these terms. Yet within just five years, a wave of articles began appearing in *Econometrica* and other leading journals (Young 1993a, b). It is remarkable how quickly the climate of opinion shifted.

When did the idea of evolution become acceptable to economists, even a hot topic?

Young: Ideas like these migrate. Evolution has obviously been around for a long time in biology. In fact one can argue that it originally migrated from social science into biology, and after developing there, it migrated back. I do believe that ideas from biology are going to have a major impact on economics in the twenty-first century, just as physics did in the nineteenth century.

How about agent-based modeling? Is this still ahead of the wave?

Young: There continues to be a fair amount of resistance to agent-based modeling among economists, or perhaps it is just a lack of appreciation for its possibilities. For me it fits quite naturally into economics because it deals head-on with the issue of heterogeneity among economic agents. Why then has the approach not yet been widely accepted? One frequent criticism is that the dynamic behavior of such models cannot be rigorously analyzed. Hence one is reduced to making inferences based on simulations, which is not good enough for publication in most journals.

Actually it isn't true that we cannot analyze such systems rigorously. Using methods originally developed in stochastic dynamical systems theory, one can in fact rigorously characterize the long-run behavior of extremely large (but finite) Markov chains with small perturbations (Young 1993a). So it is not correct that we need to rely on simulations when dealing with agent-based models.

Furthermore, simulations play a very important role in understanding the dynamic behavior of such systems, and they supplement theoretical results in a useful way. For one thing, even if a system can be proved to behave in a particular way in the long run, this says little or nothing about its behavior over the short and intermediate run. Simulations under a range of parameter settings can uncover important transient features of the process. (If one were in an argumentative frame of mind, one could insist that the mere proof of a system's long-run behavior is not acceptable for journal publication either; one must also *exhibit* how it behaves.)

A second important role for simulations is to communicate results to nonspecialists. In the Center on Social and Economic Dynamics at Brookings, agent-based models are routinely applied to issues of public policy. It will not come as a surprise that most policymakers are not interested in the equations, models, and proofs that underlie a model. They want to see how it works. Most importantly, they want to see how changes in parameter settings and modeling assumptions change the nature of the conclusions. Furthermore, it is my experience that theorists who have no trouble understanding the formal properties of a model will nevertheless not really understand it intuitively until they see a demonstration.

Are there any other places where simulation is being integrated into the curriculum?

Young: At Johns Hopkins there's a course regularly offered both by Rob and a couple of others in the computer science department.

Axtell: I think the cross-discipline people are doing it; in economics a small group of people are doing it; in political science a small group. Michigan has a group that cuts across different departments and includes Axelrod.

Does that mean the disciplines are going to be redefined?

Young: It takes somebody on the faculty to champion a new approach in order for students to become exposed to it and to spread the idea in a serious way. It is starting to happen at some institutions but has by no means penetrated most of them.

Axtell: Let me give you an example that I think is useful. Back in January 1998, we had a workshop at our center that one could reasonably say included most of the people doing computational and evolutionary work. It was held in a room that held a few dozen people. Next week in UCLA there is going to be a conference called

Agent-Based Modeling in the Social Sciences, and there's a couple hundred papers. So the field is growing.

Young: There is another thing I feel that agent-based modeling can help us understand, and that is the effect of different levels of rationality on the behavior of an economic system. Ultimately, of course, the degree of rationality and level of sophistication in decision making is an empirical question. It is reasonable to suppose, however, that there is quite a range of behaviors in practice. How does this heterogeneity play out when economic agents compete? For a long time economists have speculated that in some settings, such as financial markets, evolutionary forces would tend to drive out the less rational individuals because the latter will tend to lose money.

It is only in the last few years, however, that conjectures like these have been subjected to careful analysis. Larry Blume and David Easley have done pioneering theoretical work on this problem (1992). Blake LeBaron (Arthur et al. 1997b) has examined this issue using agent-based models of trading in financial markets. He assumes a population of traders who vary in the number of periods of past information that they can use to forecast future prices and make trading decisions. Simulations suggest that the dynamics of such a model are surprisingly complex: there are periods in which long-memory traders do well and other periods where short-memory traders do well. The bottom line, however, is that the long-memory traders do not necessarily drive the others from the market.

A question that came up early in at least one of your papers was whether you had to have some rational agents for an aggregate rational outcome to emerge. Do you think some individual rationality is absolutely necessary to have emerging aggregate rationality?

Young: My book *Individual Strategy and Social Structure* (1998) examines a variety of situations in which agents choose best responses to fragmentary or partial information, such as information gleaned from their neighbors. Occasionally, however, they may make idiosyncratic choices that are not best responses, due, for example, to errors of perception, experimentation, and other stochastic influences. In this framework agents have a low level of rationality: although they optimize myopically, they do not think ahead or really understand the process in which they are embedded. It can be shown that systems like these often gravitate toward equi-

ROBERT AXTELL AND H. PEYTON YOUNG

librium solutions that are normally justified by high-rationality game theory, such as subgame-perfect equilibrium, the Nash bargaining solution, and so forth. It can also be shown that when agents have different levels of sophistication (i.e., they try to outsmart the other agents by anticipating their behavior several steps ahead), many of the equilibrium selection results remain intact (Hurkens 1995; Saez-Marti and Weibull 1999). In this sense the precise mixture of rationality levels may not matter so much as the presence of some rationality. To come back to your question, however, I doubt that one can get rid of rationality altogether and obtain the same results.

Is there a current orthodoxy in economics that you feel you are violating?

Young: I probably violate orthodoxy a good deal of the time. Indeed I don't find it very interesting to take received theory and merely push it a couple of small steps ahead. At the same time I don't think it is appropriate to abandon some of the foundational assumptions in economics, such as the notion that economic agents are basically purposeful. However, I do not accept the proposition that agents are ultrarational and always use information optimally. By the way, even if agents were perfectly rational, that does not mean that they maximize self-interest in the narrow sense. Other factors enter into economic decisions that, for want of a better word, might be called social factors. I am particularly interested, for example, in the ways that norms and customs shape economic decisions (Young and Burke 2000). Indeed, I believe that customs play a much bigger role in determining economic outcomes than is commonly acknowledged.

Actually there is a sense in which agent-based modeling conforms to orthodoxy rather than challenging it. A touchstone of economic thinking is methodological individualism—the idea that aggregate economic phenomena should ultimately be explained by or derived from the behaviors and choices of individuals. One can question whether this program has been fully successful. It seems clear, however, that an agent-based modeling and evolutionary game theory fit within this general tradition. The whole idea of this program is to construct systems of interacting, heterogeneous agents and to examine their aggregate dynamical behavior. In contrast to representative agent models, for example, this represents a return to earlier ways of thinking in economics.

To come back to your original question, though, the major sense in which my work departs from conventional analysis is that I do not assume that an economy is in equilibrium. The fundamental idea of evolutionary game theory is to explore how (and whether) equilibria come about from out-of-equilibrium conditions.

Axtell: Epstein and I wrote in our book that there are four basic tenets of the orthodoxy that we are relaxing. They are (1) rationality: we use a type of bounded rationality or no rationality; (2) heterogeneity: we use heterogeneous agents; the conventional approach is to use homogeneous agents; (3) social networks: we consider interactions not just in some soup but also in a social network; and (4) equilibrium: we do not require agent equilibrium as a condition for aggregate steady state.

Which of those four do you think the established mainstream has been the most open to in the last six years?

Axtell: There is a big trend toward bounded rationality in the best applied dynamics and games and various other things. And I also think social networks is one that Durlauf has pioneered with other people (Brock and Durlauf 2001a). We also find an increasing acceptance of heterogeneity. Of course, it is very hard mathematically to relax all these things at once.

Young: Heterogeneity doesn't violate economic orthodoxy. Nobody denies that people differ. It's also not that controversial to say that people make decisions using information from social networks. Up until recently, however, it has been extremely difficult to construct models with heterogeneous agents and social links that are computationally tractable. Recent advances in computing power allow us to simulate these kinds of models with much greater ease. We have also made substantial progress in understanding their theoretical properties using ideas from statistical mechanics and stochastic dynamical systems theory.

Axtell: Here's the subtlety: People would say, "I'm not sure how to deal with it, so I am going to go back to my own assumptions." Then the agent-based model will come along which will relax their assumptions, and they say, well, it may depend on one thing or the other thing, or you guys didn't frame it exactly right, and instead of using lattices why didn't you use *random* graphs, instead of using *random* graphs why didn't you use small worlds. Of course people are not going to deny that social networks exist, but people are going to say that there is too much arbitrariness.

ROBERT AXTELL AND H. PEYTON YOUNG

Young: I agree that people sometimes resort to that type of refuge.

Is it a reasonable refuge? Can't one argue that a field has its own approach, and faced with something new, it is reasonable to be hesitant?

Young: One can always say that new theory is mere speculation until the data are in hand and then hope that the theory will quietly go away due to a lack of data. A more constructive response would be that new theories suggest new hypotheses to test and new kinds of data that need to be gathered. My hope is that models that incorporate social networks will stimulate more empirical research on the structure of such networks. This line of study has traditionally been the domain of sociologists; perhaps the new work in economics will reinvigorate it. It is also worth pointing out that theory can identify situations where the precise nature of the network actually doesn't matter very much. For example, in my book *Individual Strategy and Social Structure* (1988, chap. 6), I show that while the topology of a network may have a major impact on the speed of transition to an equilibrium, the nature of the equilibrium itself may be quite insensitive to network structure.

It seems that the big assumption that you found the most resistance to is the equilibrium assumption.

Young: This is the big question for me. It's a peculiar feature of economics that notions of equilibrium have tended to precede a rigorous specification of the learning process that is supposed to lead to that equilibrium. In physics one generally begins with the specification of the dynamics, and the identification of the equilibria or steady states comes afterwards.

Axtell: One tension that exists is the equilibrium at the agent level versus the equilibrium at the macro level. Much of the focus of today's work in economics is largely about Nash equilibrium, which is at the agent-level equilibrium. Yet there can be social regularities that do not require Nash equilibrium. If every few years a white-collar worker changes jobs, this has much more to do with the idiosyncratic opportunities encountered by a self-interested agent in a complex system than it does with Nash equilibrium.

You seem to be critical of the Nash equilibrium model.

Axtell: In your first chapter you give von Neumann a leading role as the dominant intellectual figure in twentieth-century economics. Just to refresh your memory about what von Neumann's reaction to Nash was, when Nash came to his office to describe his result on the existence of mixed strategy equilibria in finite games, von Neumann, who had introduced fixed points into economics with his *RES* paper of the '40s, thought it was a triviality.

What have been the most important changes in economics over the past twenty years?

Axtell: The quantity of mathematical theories is increasing roughly in proportion to the number of researchers involved, linearly over time maybe, yet the computational power available to us on our desktops in the last twenty years has grown by a factor of a million; there's going to be continued relative growth in those two proportions.

Twenty years ago the PC was a new kid on the block. Just think how much you use your PC today when twenty years ago it didn't exist. That's a radical innovation whether you are doing regressions or anything econometric. We've only just begun to understand how to utilize the computational powers that have been made available in this period. There are the Ken Judds and John Rusts of the world using these machines to do significant numerical economics, but you just can't fill up a gigabyte of RAM with equations; you can't write down a billion equations.

Numerical economics fails to utilize the vast increases in memory and storage density that the information revolution has brought us, and so it seems like a dead end. More generally, there is no way to fill up a gigabyte of RAM with computer code that you've programmed. The agent computing paradigm relies on a small compile-time, large run-time model, where we specify agent behavior and interaction in a few thousand lines of code and then simply replicate the agents stochastically to fill up all available memory resources.

In your work on price discovery you propose lateral exchanges and parallel processing as models for the emergence of market equilibrium in contrast to the Arrow and Debreu approaches. How does that fit with the John Rust (1996) and Ken Judd (1998) approach?

Axtell: It may be that the only thing that numerical computational economists have in common with agent-based computational economists is that we both use computers. Rust and Judd basically find numerical solutions to the equations that are written down in conventional economics. The agent-based approach involves a new use of the computer. It is a much more decentralized, distributed approach to economic modeling, in which we instantiate these purposefully behaving objects inside the computer and let them interact. We have no equations governing the macro level. The macro level emerges from the interaction of the agents. So there are no fixed-point algorithms clearing the markets at all times.

Parallel processing is characteristic of any large-scale distributed process, with decentralized, local information. Everybody has his or her own idea of how the world will unfold. That seems to be a natural way to think about how markets really work, as opposed to the centralized view of the auctioneer where there is one entity that clears all the markets and knows all the prices and knows exactly what utility functions everybody has. It's very close to an Austrian view, but the Austrian view says that there's heterogeneous knowledge and decision making out there and from these there emerges the right price, the socially right price, thus their "price discovery" terminology. I think what the LeBaron (Arthur et al. 1997b) and Lux (1998) agent models of financial markets tell us though is that what emerges is something very different—what emerges is something that is based on an interacting ecology of decision rules. It may be the socially right price, it may not; it may depart from the fundamentals, it may not. I think the mechanism is very Austrian in its description, but what emerges is clearly not Austrian.

What have been the most important changes in economics over the past twenty years?
  Young: If you had said thirty years instead of twenty, then I would say the development of noncooperative game theory and its incorporation into economic analysis. This was quite belated and really didn't occur with any seriousness until the 1970s.

Why did it take so long, and what brought it about?
  Young: There was, of course, a great flurry of activity in the late 1940s and early 1950s. Some saw game theory as the next revolution in economics, but for various reasons it did not take off for quite some time. Beginning in the 1970s, there was an explosion of activity, and game theory revolutionized such fields as industrial organization, mechanism design, and the theory of voting. In a more fundamental sense, game theory challenged a basic tenet of classical

economics because it called attention to situations in which individuals acting in their own self-interest do not necessarily arrive at a social optimum. Previously these situations had been viewed as exceptional or peripheral; game theory showed that they are ubiquitous.

It's very interesting, by the way, that game theory eventually came to roost in economics rather than in mathematics, where it originated. In the 1940s and '50s, indeed up until the 1970s, game theory was considered to be mainly a field of applied mathematics and operations research, not a subject within economics. Eventually it migrated, and as with many other migrations, it was the result of two forces: a push and pull. Many mathematics departments began to view game theory as too applied, while in economics it responded to a demand for greater formalization and rigor.

After a period of great success, however, the relevance of game theory, at least in its traditional form, is once again being called into question. The chief doubts revolve around game theory's heavy reliance on rational decision making, Bayesian updating, and common knowledge of the strategic situation. Over the last ten years or so there has been a noticeable shift toward behavioral models that are built on rules of thumb and simple adaptive mechanisms, rather than Bayesian rationality in its purest form. This shift has been buttressed by the results of laboratory experiments by economists and a greater appreciation of similar findings in psychology. There has also been a renewed interest in the ways in which culture and social context affect decision making and in the possibility that culture, institutions, and economic outcomes must be viewed as coevolving systems. I believe, in fact, that the study of institutions, and the ways in which different institutional forms (including markets) evolve, is one the most exciting areas of economic research today.

Looking forward now to the next twenty-five to fifty years, where do you see economics going?

Axtell: Most computer scientists believe that Moore's Law will stay in effect for the next twenty to twenty-five years, which means doubling computer power every twelve to eighteen months. So essentially over twenty years you'll have another vast, almost incomprehensible growth of computing power and the kinds of new economic models that can be built. The increase in computer power is this big elephant in the room, and if you don't jump on it, it's going to trample you.

ROBERT AXTELL AND H. PEYTON YOUNG

So does that mean that agent-based modeling will become central to economic methodology?

Axtell: It depends. Hardware is not the only issue; software matters a lot. Agent-based modeling must be grounded in theory. Peyton's work on perturbed games is in fact an example of a theoretical foundation that could be provided for agent-based systems. We need to have a mathematical foundation in order to build robust software systems that then can be used as simulation tools and simulation engines. That software challenge is a significant one.

How different will these distributive processes be, or will we just be getting fancier ways of getting more standard results?

Axtell: Maybe what would be possible fifteen or twenty years from now is that you would be able to have richer cognitive models of actual human decision makers. Could psychologists supply them? Maybe. Could cognitive scientists supply them? Even better. Could neuroscientists supply them? Well, presumably that would be even superior. If you had accurate models at the neuro-level, you could stuff about one hundred thousand of those into a computer, and presumably you would have very fine-grained predictions generated about the financial markets or used car markets or whatever.

Neural networks are something we can actually handle today, using available computer power. I'm talking about a model where there are 10^6 neurons to represent one individual, and now you have a thousand instantiations of that. Whether this is economics now or just cognitive science depends on whether you have an economic problem under study. Why isn't that economics?

Now a different issue occurs in real financial markets. All the big Wall Street houses are also using computers, very powerful computers, to do their forecasting. So maybe academics will always be one step behind, and you never can have your computer fully represent what their computer is doing and so on. The reason why presumably that is not necessary is that the power law data, for example, on price fluctuations is largely invariant across London, New York, and Tokyo. There are some regularities and universal processes going on in these markets; presumably they have not changed in the last twenty, thirty, forty years, and they are still effective over markets. So my first answer is that we will have this vast increase in computer power and hopefully we can harness it. I don't see any way to harness it with numerical economics. The only way to harness it is with an agent-based approach where you can stuff the memory full of agents.

A footnote on this is, when you are doing agent-based modeling, if you only write the rules for one agent, and you replicate everybody else, you get heterogeneity stochastically. So you won't face the software constraint that if you want to use a billion bytes of memory, you need a billion lines of code. A different thing to say is the Sid Winter critique of the theory of the firm. The theory of the firm is not a mythological individualist one today; it's about multiple rational actors in some kind of a principal-agent model. In general, the theory of organizations has largely been relegated to sociologists, even though Simon worked on this forever—he did his dissertation work grounded in sociology. Organizational science is part of OR. But it seems that only today, and only in the future, are we going to have the capability to do very high-fidelity, multiagent models of organizations. We will, in a sense, change the view in economics of organizations from being a unitary actor or a few actors to being the model of General Motors with three hundred thousand employees. Having that fully functional, we can write down the incentives for every individual. It's possible that the computer makes possible a full-blown computational version of institutional economics.

I'm not sure how it's all going to play out, how the research will be, but I guess my claim is that the ability to build an entire macroeconomy out of agent specification is going to radically change the way we look at economics. And I think that the main casualty of this is going to be low-dimensional equation-based structure. So macroeconomics according to a few low-dimensional sets of nonlinear dynamics is going to be the main casualty as we can stuff the machine full of agents who are behaving in some boundedly rational way, behaviorally richer way. With that machine full of agents you can find out what processes give the empirical data on the distribution of real income and wealth. Then you can move them out for three years and see what happens. I think it's a new way to do macroeconomics; it's a new way to do policy. When these tools will come on-line depends crucially on funding for this line of research. As I said before just briefly, most of the NSF money we have gotten to date is from the computer science directorate, not the economics directorate.

Looking forward now to the next twenty-five to fifty years, where do you see economics going?

Young: As I said earlier, one of the most important areas of research is the study of institutions. There are two different avenues that are being pursued here. One is to study the emergence and robustness of different institutional forms. Ultimately this will blend historical analysis with elements of game theory and dynamical systems theory. A second arena in which institutions are receiving greater attention is in response to the policy demand for decentralization and a greater reliance on markets. Take the recent move toward deregulating the utility industry. The recent experience in California turned out to be a bit of a fiasco, but it highlights a problem that isn't going to go away. Economists are increasingly being called upon to design or redesign various kinds of markets. Prominent examples include the design of auction mechanisms for selling oil, minerals, spectrum rights, and other publicly held resources. In designing such institutions one must get the details right—the information structure, the nature and number of players, the constraints they operate under, and so on. Game theory is one of the key tools for solving such design problems, but it must be integrated with experiments, simulations, and institutional knowledge.

You are talking about something that goes far beyond what we now see as institutional economics?

Young: Yes. This is a pragmatic, almost an engineering, version of institutional economics, like building bridges. Actually one of the worries I have is that economics could eventually split into two subjects, one theoretical and the other applied—like the difference between physics and engineering. I hope that this will not happen and that pragmatic design will stay within the mainstream of the profession.

Of course, there are many functioning markets that aren't up for redesign but that we don't really understand very well. In fact it is rather extraordinary how few markets we do understand. How do particular markets work and why do they have the form that they do? There has been some progress on answering these questions in particular cases. For example, Al Roth and Marilda Sotomayor (1990) have provided a convincing picture of how matching markets work, using a blend of theory and empirical observation. In the same spirit, Weisbuch, Kirman, and Herreiner (2000) have analyzed the dynamics of the Marseilles fish market using a combination of theory, data, and simulations. In my view this is one of the most promising areas of economic research.

I think it is very interesting that the fish market has become this revived model. If you go back to Marshall, that was his original model of distinguishing time horizons in markets.

Young: There are a great many institutional forms that qualify as economic markets. One could think of alternative market forms as species that compete for acceptance as a way to solve a specific kind of allocation problem.

Axtell: Say it's 1990 and your job is to design a new NYSE, new SEC rules, and all you had to go on was the efficient market hypothesis and maybe some early experimental results. You would naturally have thought of equilibrium, rational expectations, and so on. Now along come artificial stock markets and the richer set of experimental results we have today. The agent-based model teaches us that there's a very different picture of the market than we had even a decade ago, involving a continually coevolving set of market predictors that coexist in transient, steady states, but never agent-level fixed-point equilibria.

So my question would be—and I think about high-rationality game theory in this context—"If the NYSE rules owe little to Walras-Arrow-Debreu general equilibrium, why should the spectrum auctions rely on game theoretic auction theory?" In reality, the NYSE and SEC rules have evolved and coevolved over time. So why shouldn't newly designed markets also have a more evolutionary and less deductive character? It may just be that modeling institutions will be the "killer app" for agents in economics.

Young: Many institutions are so complex that one mistake, one omitted variable in the design phase, can spell disaster. Designing institutions is a hazardous process. This is no doubt one of the reasons that institutions get copied. If you have a working model, it's better to copy it than try to design one from scratch. Institutional forms spread because they work, even though nobody quite understands why they work.

We're just about at the end of our time, but we have one final question. We interviewed a variety of people here, and we obviously had to make some choices. Did we leave out anybody?

Young: You left out Tom Schelling, one of the great pioneers in a number of the topics we are talking about. He's been operating at the edge for years.

Axtell: No, but I would like to comment on your paradigm of the twenty-first–century economics and where it is going. I am biased, but I think that the twenty-first century will vindicate Simon as a progenitor of computation playing a crucial role, and recognizing that agency matters. I think what is called "low-rationality game theory" will come to the fore. Simon's (1945) review of von Neumann and Morgenstern made exactly this point.

Robert Axtell

Fellow, Center on Social and Economic Dynamics (CSED), Economic Studies Program, the Brookings Institution, and Visiting Associate Professor of Economics, Johns Hopkins University

INFORMATION ON THE WEB ABOUT ROBERT AXTELL
http://www.brookingsinstitution.org/dybdocroot/scholars/raxtell.atm

EDUCATION
B.S. Chemical Engineering, University of Detroit, 1983
Ph.D. Decision Sciences, Carnegie Mellon University, 1992

SELECTED PUBLICATIONS
"Aligning Simulation Models: A Case Study and Results," with Robert Axelrod, Joshua M. Epstein, and Michael B. Cohen. *Computational and Mathematical Organization Theory* 1 (1996).
"Foresight as a Survival Characteristic: When (If Ever) Does the Long View Pay?" with Robert Ayres. *Technological Forecasting and Social Change* 51 (1996).
Growing Artificial Societies: Social Science from the Bottom Up, with Joshua M. Epstein. Washington, DC, and Cambridge: Brookings Institution and MIT Press, 1996.
"Coordination in Transient Social Networks: An Agent-Based Model of the Timing of Retirement," in *Behavioral Dimensions of Retirement Economics,* with Joshua M. Epstein, edited by Henry Aaron. New York and Washington, DC: Russell Sage and Brookings Institution, 1999.
"Zipf Distribution of U.S. Firm Sizes." *Science* 293 (2001).

SPECIAL HONORS AND EXPERIENCE
Also taught at George Mason University and Johns Hopkins University
Fellow, Brookings Institution, 1992–97
Member, Santa Fe Institute, 1993–
Best Paper Award, Technological Forecasting and Social Change, 1996
Simulation Software of the Year Award, Chaos Manor, Byte, 1998

H. Peyton Young

Scott and Barbara Black Professor of Economics, Johns Hopkins University, Professorial Fellow, Nuffield College, Oxford, and Codirector, CSED, Brookings Institution

INFORMATION ON THE WEB ABOUT H. PEYTON YOUNG
http://www.econ.jhu.edu/People/Young

EDUCATION
B.A. Mathematics, Harvard University, 1966
Ph.D. Mathematics, University of Michigan, 1970

SELECTED PUBLICATIONS
"Stochastic Evolutionary Game Dynamics," with Dean Foster. *Theoretical Population Biology* 38 (1990).
"The Evolution of Conventions." *Econometrica* 61 (1993).
Individual Strategy and Social Structure: An Evolutionary Theory of Institutions. Princeton: Princeton University Press, 1998.
"Competition and Custom in Economic Contracts: A Case Study of Illinois Agriculture," with Mary A. Burke. *American Economic Review* 91 (2000).
Strategic Learning and Its Limits. Arne Ryde Memorial Lectures. Oxford: Oxford University Press, 2004.

SPECIAL HONORS AND EXPERIENCE
Also taught at Oxford and University of Chicago
Sumner B. Myers Thesis Prize, University of Michigan, 1970
Lester R. Ford Award, Mathematical Association of America, 1976
Deputy Chairman, Systems and Decision Sciences, the International Institute for Applied Systems Analysis, 1979–82
Erskine Fellow in Economics, New Zealand, 1990
Fellow, Econometric Society, 1995
Member, Science Steering Committee, Santa Fe Institute, 2001–
Executive Vice President of the Game Theory Society, 2004–
Fulbright Distinguished Chair in Economics, University of Siena, 2004

CHAPTER 10

Kenneth Arrow

Professor (Emeritus) of Economics, Stanford University

∾

The interview was conducted at Kenneth Arrow's home in Stanford on August 10, 2003.

Could you comment briefly on your overall reaction to our project?

Economics as practiced is enormously different in orientation and detail today than it was when I was a graduate student. I got into economics because I was interested in statistics, not because I was interested in economics. At the time Columbia was one of the few places you could study statistics. When I went to graduate school at Columbia University, the dominant views in economics there were totally antitheoretical and critical of received wisdom; the direction was highly empirical. The dominant figure at Columbia was Wesley Mitchell, although few economists today would know of him. At Columbia in 1942 there was no course in price theory at all. Hotelling had a course in mathematical economics, but that was for an extremely small number of students. Instead the department had a course in the history of theory. Columbia wasn't unusual; at the time institutionalists of one kind or another dominated a number of economics departments. My point in raising this history is that there is nothing new in the idea that theory is controversial.

∾

The absence of a theory course led to one funny aspect. The faculty felt the need to examine the Ph.D. students in theory, but since there was no course in theory, doing so was difficult. They had an ingenious solution: you went to a professor and negotiated a topic, and then you were examined on that topic. John Maurice Clark, the nearest thing to a theorist that Columbia had, examined me in theory.

The hot topic of the day was imperfect competition. So something like game theory was already around back in the 1940s. It's funny how things come around. Mitchell was on leave when I was there, and Arthur Burns replaced him. Burns was one of the smartest men I have ever known. Keynes wasn't mentioned in Burns's course, and this was 1942. At Harvard and Chicago students would have gotten more theory, but it wouldn't have been a dogmatic competitive theory; for example, Chamberlin was teaching at Harvard, and he even had some experiments in his class. I had to learn neoclassical economics by my own reading. As far as my formal education in economics, I learned exactly zero about neoclassical economics in my courses.

One of the arguments we make in the introduction is that it isn't helpful to call the economics done today neoclassical. Would you agree with that?

The ideas that people behave somewhat rationally and somewhat foresightedly are central to economics. But there are major differences in the knowledge attributed to agents. I think one of the biggest differences between 1950 and 2000 is the much greater role given now to the role of knowledge and information, and the theorizing about knowledge and information. Nobody would have denied the importance of these in 1950, but the tools to handle them formally did not exist then. Probability thinking was pretty much unknown to the average economists in 1950.

The idea of some type of rational action is still at the core of economics. It can be expanded in many ways. Similarly, the idea of competition remains important. The difference is that the kind of person who would have been a rigid competitive equilibrium person now writes game theory papers. I think there is still a lot on the agenda of applying game theory to economics. The big issue that needs to be cleared up in game theory is summed up in the word *general.* The question is how to generalize all the noncompetitive elements in the world into a theory.

Game theory tends to be partial equilibrium, and somehow it must be generalized since the effects in the general model may be quite different than in the partial model. A game in one part of the economy—say a patent race—likely influences the rest of the economy. In general equilibrium you can trace out the links, and we aren't close to being able to do that in game theory yet. These links are important because sometimes the main effect of a change can be quite separate from the particular area you are looking at. I was at a meeting recently where a paper was discussing the effects of education. It showed that education affects land values, which in turn affects residential patterns. The paper argued that these effects are not second-order effects but are large. The implication is that something like educational vouchers may have surprising implications.

One of the ideas in our introduction was that you have to view the economy as a complex system. You cannot get at the entire model from microfoundations, and thus you have to approach it in alternative ways. What's your view on that?

My view of that is that it is true and unfortunate. The problem with much of the complexity work is that it doesn't seem to lead anywhere. It does tell you that what you are doing is probably not going to work out very well, but turning that into a positive theory is much more difficult. The idea that people have difficulty computing the system has a long history; you can see it in Veblen, for example. But nothing followed from his insight. Herb Simon is the great apostle of this view. He's a great figure, and his work did lead to a research program, but in my view, it fizzled out. But not everyone sees it that way, and I think everyone should work on what they think is productive. Methodologically, I have always been a believer in pluralism. I do what I can do best, and other people should do what they have a comparative advantage in. You need a variety of talents in a field. I have no problem with the view that someone should do experiments and someone else should do agent-based modeling. You get insights from each of them.

Let me give you a bit of personal history that sheds some light on complexity. As you know, I had a stint as a meteorologist when I was in the military service. There was pretty good theory underlying meteorology such as thermodynamics and hydrodynamics. In fact, the theory struck me as much better founded than our theory of microeconomics. In meteorology there was a micro theory and a macro theory, although those terms did not exist then. The issue was not so much whether the theory is true; it was whether it was effective. Can you do anything with the theory? Unfortunately you could not do much formally with it because turbulence caused problems in applying theory. In principle turbulence could be taken into account, but in practice it was impossible to take it into account because of computing problems. So what you did instead was to draw maps and find patterns. And you could find patterns. The theory did sort of inform you about those patterns, but it did not predict them, other than very generally.

There were a few qualitative principles that come from the physics that helped you in analyzing the maps. But it was really just some simple rules—in the U.S., weather patterns typically moved from west to east; fronts tended to deepen and then dissipate. Combine the theoretical knowledge with these extrapolations from where the system had been moving, and you made a prediction. My understanding is that that approach is still used.

But with the new computer simulation and the better data, they are improving the rules of thumb every year. Today the computer finds the patterns and can give much more accurate forecasts—it's still the same process; it's just much more refined. The complexity approach says that that's the way you do it. You have the law of one price in economics, and then you search for patterns—you fit the data to the generalized theory.

That does not lead to any mechanical statement, but it probably is descriptive of much that is done. In the search for patterns there are patterns that persist and patterns that change, and a key question is what separates them. For example, in the literature on growth there is an emphasis on the question of whether latitude matters. If there is one variable that cannot matter in and of itself, it is latitude. There is also the literature arguing that natural resources are bad for you. That's based on finding a pattern.

You've been very much involved with the Santa Fe Institute. Are you now frustrated that it hasn't gone where you would like it to go?

I don't get frustrated easily; I'm a person with relatively low expectations. The Santa Fe Institute has not developed a consistent economics program. There are a variety of people associated with it with varying degrees of individual interest. Who is active at a particular moment determines which way it goes. The very broad ideas that come out of chaos theory such as the edge of chaos are dubious and do not seem to be the things that will provide any real insight.

One idea I think is especially promising is the idea of analyzing the stock market through learning algorithms, with each individual specified by a genetic algorithm and each learning in a coevolutionary way. If you tune the parameters correctly, you can generate patterns that look like the stock market data. The patterns you get with Brownian motion models are much too smooth. Now Brownian motion has no economic significance whatsoever; it is simply a useful analytic tool. So in financial economics you have an analysis based on pattern recognition—Arch and Garch. It is a sophisticated generalization, which nonetheless gives you some insight into what is occurring and why constant volatility models don't work.

What do you think of the econophysics movement?
Econophysics is very productive of data analysis. It is dominated by power laws, but the question is where do you go from there? For example, it is possible, by taking several normal distributions with one process depending on another process, to reproduce data that gets heavy tails. That doesn't prove that that's the right model, but it is an interesting avenue to follow. I think the movement by Per Bak (1966) pushing universal laws is a very courageous movement. However, I am dubious about it; it doesn't precisely fit any specific area. I think what the power law approach really gives you is a mathematical method—when you see something similar happening in different fields, it's likely a mathematical identity that's behind it.

Buz Brock argues that some of the nonlinear models that show sudden transitions can be very useful in fitting the theory to the data. He argues that we can actually get measurements when we are close to a transition point and that those measurements can be useful for policy. That seems a quite different view from a general equilibrium view.
It is general equilibrium; there's nothing in general equilibrium that precludes multiplicity of equilibria. I haven't worked much on uniqueness, but I have worked on stability, which is closely related, and what you get are some stringent conditions to guarantee stability. So you know multiple equilibria are possible. Certainly if you have local effects, those local effects can affect the global equilibrium you arrive at. An example is peer effects. Peer effects seem important in a wide variety of cases. If most people in an area go to

college, or alternatively if most people in an area are criminal, then individuals introduced into that area are likely to follow that path. The one thing that bothers me about that is that if you observe a number of societies, you should be seeing more of a multimodal distribution than you do get. It's an empirical question, not a theoretical question.

One of the suggestions we make in the introduction is that changes occur from within and that the heterodox community is often just not aware of the enormous diversity within the profession. Any comments on that?

I have a hard time separating heterodox and orthodox. Reading something like the *NBER Reporter,* I find that the number of papers that would now be considered economics are much broader and diverse than they were thirty or forty years ago. (However, even earlier, institutionalists would have considered these papers economics.) Economists are now writing on topics that previously would have been considered sociological or even legal topics. We see this in all types of papers, such as work on crime. Another example is work on foreign exchange markets. Today, economists will focus on how the rumors spread, what news is relevant, or how susceptible people are to herd effects. Whether you call this economics or not, economists are doing this analysis, and it is recognized as perfectly legitimate research. But these changes are changes in subject matter, not doctrine.

Another development is the influence of psychology on economics, which is now obvious. It started in the 1950s with the studying of learning. While there were some good papers, somehow the approach didn't develop, and those papers were neglected. Now, psychological economics is developing in a variety of ways.

How does this development relate to Simon's program?

Much of it is a concrete version of it. I'm not sure what something like hyperbolic discounting and the criticism of expected utility theory, which goes back to the beginning of the subject—Allais's questionnaire—has to do with bounded rationality, but most of the work in psychology and economics is connected to it.

In deciding what topics are allowed to be considered in economics, we argue that there is an elite and that this elite plays an important role in the evolution of the field, quite separate from their work. Is that consistent with your views?

It is certainly true that at any moment in time there are gatekeepers and that there are elements of a closed system in economics. I've known papers that I thought were original that had a hard time getting published. But whether these gatekeepers are the most famous people is questionable. Given the number of journals, even if the elite spent all their time refereeing, they could not keep up. Gatekeepers are a broad spectrum of the profession.

But you're right, there is a type of filter that a group of top economists play. It is difficult to characterize however. Who is precisely the elite, and how do you become a member? That's unclear. You have to see the elite as a highly malleable group. You publish a paper that is recognized as important, and you enter the elite. But in my view, the elite, if there is one, is not a group that protects the status quo. Instead it values innovation; they are looking for new ways of looking at issues. If you just repeat what everybody knows, you are not going to get a great deal of credit. More specifically, the simple-minded idea that the elite in economics is all conservative, or neoliberal, is simply wrong.

I think the elite is slightly more conservative (methodologically) today than they were thirty or forty years ago, and I think an important reason for this is that the degree of technical competence is infinitely higher. Because of this higher technical competence, it is easy to fill journals with highly competent papers, which means that there is less search for innovative papers. Earlier, an original paper that was somewhat messy had a somewhat better chance to get published. I think that few would deny that referees are often short-sighted and narrow and that money is left on the table in the refereeing process. But that is more attributable to the system generally, and less to the elite.

In our introduction we distinguished an intellectual aspect and a sociological aspect of characterizing economics. We said that orthodoxy was an intellectual category, mainstream was more of a sociological category, and the heterodox category combines the two. Two of the people we interviewed were Herb Gintis and Duncan Foley, both of whom were on the edge of heterodoxy. Do you have any comments on their interviews?

I don't have much to say about Duncan's because I wasn't at

Stanford when he left. There was one aspect of his interview that concerns me however—the part that quotes Mirowski as almost seeing Koopmans as a CIA agent. I think that is a total misrepresentation.

I can say a bit more about Herb because I was at Harvard when Herb was there. There was never a question about tenure for Herb because he and Sam Bowles left for U. Mass. after Sam did not get tenure, before the question of tenure for Herb was on the table. In Sam's case I was heavily involved in the losing side. I think that incident is insightful for this concept of an elite. There were at least three former presidents of the AEA at Harvard at the time, and all of us were for Bowles, and of course he lost. In some sense there is a body of opinion that is out there that is not represented by the elite, and it is often less open to innovation than is the elite. Arguing with Gintis was a great pleasure. We had a long debate once about whether and how society forms the norms that govern our actions.

Many of the interviewees saw you as helpful and open to new ideas.

I don't have the strongest convictions in the world about either politics or economics. I've always had the idea that there is a vast amount that is unknown. Therefore, any theory we have should be treated not as the truth but simply as a useful reference. Early in my career I felt that it was very important to get the competitive equilibrium theory right. As I told you before, that was not the theory I was taught, and when I was examined, I was examined in imperfect competition. I came into my work, as indeed most theorists in the early 1940s did, with the idea that competitive equilibrium was not a good description of the economy. Therefore, I wanted to clear up what the theory was, but that doesn't mean I found it a useful description of the economy.

As I think more about complexity theory, I become more convinced that there is some sense in which we will never know how the economy operates. From complexity theory one can see that even simple systems can generate outputs that are extremely complex and that one cannot pull out the original system from our observations of reality. But there is no guarantee that there is a simple system underlying our reality; it may very well be a complex system that underlies our complex system.

In trying to sort this out, stationarity is an important concept. Theoretically, if you can encompass everything, you should have a stationary system. So lack of stationarity means that you are not looking at the whole system. But for practical purposes, we are not going to be looking at the whole system, so the Markovian idea that the world will be stationary if you are inclusive enough is not especially helpful. So, in answer to your question, I may be open because I am always looking to learn something.

You are seen both as an exemplar of orthodoxy and a purveyor of the new. Do you see this as an evolution of your position or as simply a consistent approach that adapted to where economics was?

I like to see myself as consistent in the sense of sticking to the same policy of learning from experience. I was recently criticized in an article in the *Journal of Economic Methodology*. O'Brien (1998) said my work on innovation was all wrong. He argued that the trouble with my work was that when I was a graduate student, I had studied a lot of mathematics and statistics and I didn't have time to study industrial organization. I found this argument pretty weak; it struck me that if by 1960 I hadn't learned anything since 1940 when I studied, I'd be pretty embarrassed.

I came into economics with the idea that the world is full of imperfect competition. I looked for problems—things that I felt needed to be done, and introducing uncertainty into the general equilibrium system seemed one of them. I was helped in having a statistics background, which allowed me to have the insight into how to do it; the mathematics was trivial. It's an example of the advantage of transdisciplinary work.

At the time I was very interested in economic planning, granted that there were all sorts of externalities and all sorts of imperfect competition; I was very much taken with the Lange Lerner view, and I really believed in some type of socialism. How does the state plan, taking into account incentive problems? By introducing the future and uncertainty, I was attempting to make the model better fit the real world. It seemed to me that you had to get that right before you went any further.

Now, I was vaguely aware through all this time that information was a valuable commodity that was worth buying. Practical problems, such as how big a sample size should you have, were second nature in statistics, and such questions seemed very relevant to economics. So the question of information was very much on my mind, although I didn't focus on it for a while. But that came to a head when I was asked to study the economics of medical insurance. Then the whole idea of asymmetric information came out. I gave it a sociological explanation—that societies need to have trust—but that was not the direction that the literature actually went.

Are you the one who developed the concept of moral hazard?
I'm the person who imported it from insurance literature. The term *adverse selection* was also a term of art in insurance. So I just imported them from insurance into economics. They have played a bigger role in financial economics than in medical economics.

How do you see the new work on ecological economics?
We have a lot to learn from standard economic analysis. There are areas that you can go into and see, without any great depth or theory, that what the world is doing is bad. Take water pricing in California. It is clear that the way it is being done is crazy; you don't need sophisticated theory. But these easy questions have not led to policy changes, so it is discouraging to discuss the more complex changes with much hope that it will improve policy. The interesting question is often the politics, not the economics. That's not totally true; we have made some progress on pollution control.

The broader question raised here is that we know in many cases the price system fails. The price system is a beautiful system on paper, and even in practice when it works. But the problem is what price do you put in when you don't have a price. We don't have good ways to get at that. The advantage of an observed price used in valuation is that we can be sure that that is something that someone actually is willing to give up.

We know that there are many cases where the price system doesn't work very well; problems are pervasive in the economy. One problem is that there's a lot that doesn't get covered by the simple price system. Or alternatively, you can put the question in quantitative terms. It's the same question in a different form. I was a little surprised that Norgaard said in his interview that he didn't want to discuss what the discount rate is; instead he wanted to discuss what each generation should get. In some sense these are the same questions.

It's not just the environment. The problem is, how do you determine the correct shadow prices? What one finds is that the answer is specific to the situation. There may be some fundamental sense in which the principles are identical, but the applications often take totally different forms, and they can be so different that the universal principles are not even helpful.

How about macro? Is that an area where we've gone beyond universal principles and can only pull out information from the data, guided loosely by theory, say as in the work of Chris Sims or David Hendry?

Well, I've got to tell you: I've never understood macro. What I mean by this is that my idea of understanding is having a model that captures what is going on. In macro we don't have that; instead we have empirical generalizations, and those generalizations tend to break down rather quickly. The question is, can you get some understanding of the empirical evidence from the models? One attempt has been to generate empirical work out of very simplistic models—essentially they are micro models blown up. I don't give much credence to those models. One of the things that microeconomics teaches you is that individuals are not alike. There is heterogeneity, and probably the most important heterogeneity here is heterogeneity of expectations. If we didn't have heterogeneity, there would be no trade. But developing an analytic model with heterogeneous agents is difficult.

Heterogeneity is closely tied to information and how information is diffused through the system. And it is also tied to individuals' limited capacity to process information. This is where complexity theory comes in. The original problems were complex enough, but now you're adding multiple additional levels of complexity to the point where it is beyond any real analytic capability. Time also fits in here, and Roy Radner (2001) and his students have been working on that issue. Think of the world as a computer. In these models you cannot have the right amount of information at the right time. It's infinitely costly. So even if you have a very simple information-processing theory, you have a problem that the information has to be processed, and that takes time.

It also leads to the infinite regress metaproblem—how long should I think about how long I should think about an issue?

That does bother me. I wrote a little essay (Arrow 2004) that made me decide that bounded rationality cannot be thought of as rationality with costly information processing. The optimal solution to the problem of deciding optimal information processing can be a harder problem than information processing alone.

Do you think Hayek was too optimistic about the price system as a conveyer of information?

Yes. I read that paper carefully a few years ago and think it is incoherent because he stresses the idea people can only know their local thing. He doesn't ever answer why the system's price conveys the correct global information. In the Walras/Pareto story you do wind up with the correct information—subject to the appropriate assumptions—but Hayek doesn't like that story. There are cases in game theory where local connections can actually cause a faster diffusion of ideas, and a faster convergence to Nash equilibrium than reactions to the population as a whole, but that's not in Hayek.

Many of our interviewees were trained as mathematicians, and clearly economics has become much more mathematical. Are you happy with the development as it has evolved?

Basically, yes. Whenever you mathematicize a subject, some people are going to get interested in mathematics, but who knows when some of this work will pay off? Both McCloskey (1997) and Blaug (2003) have recently said Arrow Debreu was a disaster for economics. But in a few years it led to an algorithm to solve general equilibrium problems, and that is a damn useful thing. I wouldn't like a great deal of resources of the profession going into pure math, but some are definitely worth it. Mathematics has been a great aid to clear thinking. There are problems that can only be expressed coherently in mathematics.

In the introduction we argue that for someone to be listened to in the profession that they must formulate the problem clearly, and that generally means mathematics. Given a clear mathematical formulation, someone can take what might be a heterodox view and be heard.

I'd emphasize the "clear" and not the "mathematical," although it is true for me that I generally turn to the equations to figure out precisely what is being said. But that is a personal taste. All I can say is that I'm pluralistic on this as in most other things. Essentially the argument had better be capable of being written down mathematically at some point. A lot of this empirical work now that is so common is very simple; there is no need to state it mathematically. But to do the statistics, you have to write it out.

Some people see a shift now in the math used in economics from a pure Hilbertian deductive approach to a more applied inductive approach.

Do you see the field of economics going that way?

Yes, but it's a change that is going on in mathematics too as far as I can make out. I never was convinced about the importance of the Bourbaki approaches. I was more applied; I worked on dynamic programming and inventory theory. Before I went to graduate school, I had studied to be an actuary, working one summer as an actuarial clerk, and it was one of the most educational periods of my life. I really learned a lot. I started taking some of the actuarial examinations because I didn't know how I was going to make a living. In 1939–40, making a living was very much on everyone's mind. I was thinking of being a high school teacher in mathematics; that was my dream. But there weren't any jobs. I went to graduate school because I had nothing else to do, and I came from a family where education was highly valued. But the idea of an academic career was not what I thought of myself as doing.

So you consider yourself mostly an applied mathematician?

Yes, I like pure mathematics and enjoy it, and I did want to set out what general competitive equilibrium was in the most general possible form. In proving an existence theorem, calculus would have only gotten in the way. But at the same time that I did that, I was also working on a paper on inventory theory. You use the mathematics that is appropriate to the problem you are working on.

In our introduction, we say that von Neumann was a forerunner in much of the developments that we believe are the current edge of economics. How aware were you of von Neumann's specific work?

Von Neumann is an absolute genius. Game theory is a reflection of that genius. But we didn't use anything in von Neumann-Morgenstern to prove existence of general competitive equilibrium. We knew von Neumann's work generally, but we derived our work from Nash. We knew there was this unresolved question about existence. There were German papers by Stackelberg, which I vaguely knew about since I had taken a year of German, saying that there were not general competitive equilibria. There was also this analysis by Schlesinger and Wald about the free goods problem, stating that you had to state what you mean by competitive equilibrium. In my work on general equilibrium, I was trying to answer these questions.

When I read Nash, I said to myself, "Maybe we can get existence of competitive equilibrium in this same way." The Nash equilibrium paper (Nash 1951) is just Cournot (1838) done right, so when I picked up Nash's paper, I said to myself, "Here's Cournot in abstract form." In his paper Nash refers to Kakutani (1941), which is just a simplification of von Neumann's fixed-point theorem, but the theorem is stated more clearly by Kakutani. I might add that von Neumann's growth paper is misguided in the sense that he does not need the fixed-point theorem for the theorems he proves in his 1937 paper (von Neumann 1937). All he needs is separating hyperplanes. It's trivial once you have the minmax theorem.

There is much in von Neumann's work. The reduction of very complicated situations to the normal form, which is mathematically easy, is something that makes everything very clear. Von Neumann and Morgenstern also had the idea of mixed strategies, although this idea is a little more dubious in economics. You can always get an existence theorem if you admit mixed strategies. Keynes had the beauty pageant, which was a mutual outguessing game.

Morgenstern had very pessimistic accounts of the possibility of forecasting, and he coined the Holmes-Moriarty problem, which was in Conan Doyle's "The Final Problem." If you admit mixed strategies, you can get rid of that, but I'm not sure that is a satisfactory solution.

If you come up with a strategic game—for example, one firm has entered and the other wants to enter—then how do they position themselves? The firms that enter should play mixed strategies. Most economists are very unhappy with that as an answer. So there is a question of what von Neumann actually contributed.

But there is also the complexity side of von Neumann's work.

Yes, I know Mirowski has this too. But I'm not sure what complexity theory has exactly done to economics. There is this literature about playing games by automata.

That is related to the development of virtual agents operating in virtual economies, and what we call agent-based modeling. How about Mirowski's work—what do you think of that?

While I haven't read much of his work, I do think that Mirowski is onto a very deep point—that there is an intrinsic conflict between the complexity point of view and all these sophisticated developments in information theory. But I don't think that this conflict has in fact played a major role in the development of economics. It's a logical conflict, but I'm not sure that it is historically significant. But it is quite true that von Neumann started both of these. His "Computer and Brain" lectures (von Neumann 1958), which were published posthumously, were a tour de force. I don't know what to do with it, but it was a terrifically brilliant insight.

Mirowski also mentions Alain Lewis, who directed you toward complexity.

Lewis was a very original thinker. He came from mathematical logic; for him complexity meant failure of recursive numerability. Mirowski quotes a letter from me, which he could because my material is on file at Duke and has public access. (I did read the citations to me and found there were a number of places where Mirowski was inaccurate about information about me—not negatively inaccurate but just inaccurate.) In that letter it seems that I am disapproving of the program, but all I was complaining about was that the definition that Lewis used didn't seem to work because something that struck me as very simple turned out to be one level up in the hierarchy of recursive innumerability. It seemed to me that if anyone described this as complex, it would not fit one's intuitive definition of complexity.

Let's conclude with a very general question: what do you consider to be the primary contributions in the last twenty-five years, and where do you see the profession going for the next twenty-five years?

Let's start with the question of where it has been; I think the biggest developments have been in how information is treated. It is pervasive, descending from Harsanyi's work on games with Bayesian players to practical applications—bank runs, and financial crises more generally, regulatory policy, the work that Jean-Jacques Laffont and Jean Tirole do. So it seems that the work on information is the most important. It's been the Magna Carta to a body of research.

There is also a change of tone in the work; there's a far greater amount of empirical work today. That is facilitated in part by more data and better computational technology, although the greater availability of data is partly endogenous since the users of data put pressure on the creation of more data. When I was young, I had occasion to fit an eight-variable regression. It took me eight hours with the best desk computer of that day, one that cost $600, which is the equivalent of at least $6,000 today. Today you enter such a problem into a small desktop, and the answer comes out. So obviously you are going to do a lot more empirical work since the cost has fallen so much.

As for prediction, I don't have much to say. Prediction is very difficult, especially for the future. This definitely fits in with the complexity theme of your book. I would not predict what is going to happen in the next twenty-five years. I had occasion many years ago to predict what was going to happen, and I said that theory had gone about as far as it would and that I thought that empirical work was the future of economics. Of course, this is just before the work on the core, and an enormous burst in theory over the next five years. Ever since then I've avoided predictions because the economics profession is a complex system in which you don't know where the next idea is coming from.

Kenneth Arrow

Professor (Emeritus) of Economics, Stanford University

INFORMATION ON THE WEB ABOUT KENNETH ARROW
http://www-econ.stanford.edu/faculty/arrow.html

EDUCATION
B.S., Social Science, City College of New York, 1940
M.A., Mathematics, Columbia University, 1941
Ph.D., Economics, Columbia University, 1949

SELECTED PUBLICATIONS
"On the Use of Winds in Flight Planning." *Journal of Meteorology* 6 (1949).
"Existence of an Equilibrium for a Competitive Economy," with Gerard
    Debreu. *Econometrica* 22 (1954).
"The Economic Implications of Learning by Doing." *Review of Economic
    Studies* 29 (1962).
General Competitive Analysis, with F. H. Hahn. Edinburgh: Oliver and
    Boyd, 1971.
"Limited Knowledge and Economic Analysis." *American Economic Review,*
    64 (1974).

SPECIAL HONORS AND EXPERIENCE
Also taught at University of Chicago, Harvard University, and Institute of
    Advanced Studies, Vienna
President, Econometric Society, 1956; Institute of Management Sciences,
    1963; and American Economic Association, 1973
John Bates Clark Medal of the American Economic Association, 1957
Economist on the staff of the U.S. Council of Economic Advisors, 1962
Honorary degrees of LL.D. from the University of Chicago, 1967, and the
    City University of New York, 1972, and that of Doctor of Social and
    Economic Sciences from the University of Vienna, 1971
Nobel Prize in Economics, 1972
Member Past President, National Academy of Sciences and American
    Philosophical Society
Fellow, American Academy of Arts and Sciences, Econometric Society,
    Institute of Mathematical Statistics, and American Statistical
    Association

CHAPTER 11

Paul A. Samuelson

Professor (Emeritus) of Economics, Massachusetts Institute of Economics

This interview was conducted by mail in May 2003. Paul read the introduction and earlier interviews and was kind enough to answer the following questions.

You are probably the person who is most responsible for shaping modern economics. Are you happy with the way it has turned out? How do you view new fruitful trends and view others as likely dead ends?

I hesitate to speak off the cuff about your last question. I am reminded that the great physicist Lord Rayleigh was asked early in the last century, "What do you think of quantum mechanics?" He replied, "You must not ask a scholar over sixty that question." Actually, this was excessive modesty since Max Planck's first breakthrough owed much to Rayleigh's investigations of black-body radiation's observable frequency distributions. I am well over sixty and feisty with pro and con judgments about new century trends in economics. However, research deadlines usurp my time for leisurely reflection. I go with A. E. Housman, the poet who wrote *A Shropshire Lad* in his spare time between his admired publications as a classic scholar. "Why did you not include item A in your collection of papers? Do you not think it good?" he was asked by a colleague. He replied, "I do think it good, but not good enough for me." Rather than compose evaluations that lack coherence and *detailed* understandings, I'll take a pass.

Where the influence of 1947 *Foundations* is concerned, one must understand that this 1937–1945 composition was exceedingly lucky in its timing. At that time it was still the case that so much of literary economics could still benefit from straightforward intermediate applied mathematics. That is why, in many diverse places around the globe, a baker's dozen of graduate students would meet to discuss and learn from this book, which was written largely in the latter 1930s, when I myself was a privileged Harvard Junior Fellow leisurely learning the tools that it contained.

For almost forty years the book went through successive printings that corrected its various typos but left its original text untouched. In 1983 I finally decided to enlarge it, strictly by adding compact analyses of the very many subsequent postwar theoretical developments: linear and nonlinear programming; Arrow-Debreu-McKenzie general equilibrium; post Heckscher-Ohlin and Jones trade theories, stochastic and intertemporal maximizing; modern finance theory a la Markowitz, Modigliani, Mandelbrot, Merton, Bachelier, Tobin, Sharpe, Fama; also many Ramsey and von Neumann goodies. In this effort completeness and not pedagogical verve was my goal.

The result: moderate sales and impact from what, objectively speaking, was a better book. Why? Presumptively because the end-of-century generation had by then been converted to the newer, more technical economics, and for whom learned journals and books had proliferated mightily to teach those willing to learn.

Foundations, *your long-time best-selling pattern-setting elementary* Economics, *and five (soon to be seven) volumes of* Collected Scientific Papers *have given you perhaps the reputation of Mr. Neoclassical Economics. Is that take right? And how do you feel about it?*

Mine is a more nuanced view. If the label *neoclassical* excludes the Keynesian abandonment of Marshallian-Wicksellian-Walrasian belief in Say's Law as a guarantor of quasi-full-employment equilibrium, then I am a heretic. Decades ago I initiated the popular notion of a *neoclassical synthesis.* Its two-word essence was that by use of non–Say's Law macro tools, a modern mixed economy could restore to relevance the microeconomic verities absent from Great

Depression or hyperinflation scenarios in economic history. My prescriptions and policy nostrums were not at all identical to Milton Friedman's monistic monetarism. But to "new classicist, rational expectationists" Robert Lucas or Tom Sargent, we might be lumped together as odd-couple bedfellows. (That would annoy *two* people!)

Bona fide neoclassicists—such as Sweden's Eli Heckscher or Gustav Cassel—were admirers of laissez-faire. In *Foundations,* I tirelessly stressed how empirical realities of technology and divided knowledge could vitiate Adam Smith's comfortable views on good-thing Invisible Hands. What I learned from Abram Bergson was how to distinguish between the efficiencies of (the infinite) Pareto Optima and the spread of distributive inequalities that they entailed. (My personal credo mandates: Never think about Pareto Optimality without at the same time contemplating differential effects on different peoples' well-being. Henry Simon tattooed my mind on the old Chicago Midway with the dictum: Any good cause can justify moves into realms of diminishing returns—which is why those moves need rational limiting.) When a Rawls or Bentham is persuasive, a good democracy can be justified in trading off some efficiency against the goal of some social harmony or equality. This is not a license for romantic utopianism that might in brute fact create horrendous and *gratuitous deadweight loss* as it misses the nice-sounding target of utopia.

Surely you have experienced some disappointments with real world trends and historical evolutions of economist tools and accomplishments?

Yes, and the day is not long enough to dig out all of them. Thus, I was more hopeful at age thirty that future statistical tools and techniques would pinpoint better understandings and forecasting. I knew that "Nature" (i.e., the economic history record) would not perform for us useful scatters of data like those achieved in the chemistry or physiology laboratory. However, early advances in multivariable regression techniques and identification were already in a degree useful. Still the best objective economists can be in disagreement, at the same time that both admit to limitations on their self-confidence about their best guesses.

On the macro front, we've done perhaps better than I had reason to guess half a century ago. *Quasi-micro* efficiency of securities markets exceeded my original guessings. However, macro *inefficiency* of aggregate stock market oscillations has also (slightly) exceeded my expectations for the new century. Net, though, my overall impression rebuts Tom Kuhn's relativisms in the history of science. In economics "later" generally is "better." Such a whig inference we are not free to believe in or to deny for personal subjective reasons.

When I sample novel proposals of today's brightest and best, my pulses rise but not yet wildly. Experience has taught: Give each new idea a friendly hearing. Expect most to fail. But better to be a bit gullible for the reason that overblown novelties will likely get cut down to size by future critical researchers. Overambitious claims are unlikely permanently to be taken seriously.

Experience early converted me to eclecticism. Try to be as eclectic as complex reality requires. But try not to be more eclectic than reality needs: an open mind can be an empty mind. Psychologically, I am averse to being wrong. Before Karl Popper recommended being your own best critic, I tried to capture for myself the fun of rebutting my own nominations. Nevertheless in the interest of being explorative, I've been willing to be occasionally wrong. ("That's big of you," Bob Solow says.) But what I hate most in life is to *stay wrong*.

It is not a paradox that I scrutinize most carefully the writings of contemporaries whose views differ systematically from mine. I can learn least from rereading expositions of buddies who concur with me. Most of us can learn least from "enemies." (When Keynes was resisting criticisms of his 1936 *General Theory* by Ralph Hawtrey in the years when the book was being written, those same exact arguments, if expressed by Keynes's protégé Richard Kahn, might well have seemed acceptable! That is why when I hope to convert an opponent out of what I believe to be a nonoptimal view, my devious mind seeks to plant the rebuttal into a mutual friend who will not raise the hackles that I might do.)

I might add in connection with this present book's efforts that in my experience *biography* of contemporaries does *usefully* help in understanding and testing their nominated novelties.

Paul A. Samuelson

Professor (Emeritus) of Economics, Massachusetts Institute of Economics

INFORMATION ON THE WEB ABOUT PAUL A. SAMUELSON
http://ideas.repec.org/e/psa57.html

EDUCATION
A.B. Economics, University of Chicago, 1935
Ph.D. Economics, Harvard University, 1941

SELECTED PUBLICATIONS
"A Note on the Pure Theory of Consumers' Behavior." *Economica,* February 1938.
"Interactions between the Multiplier Analysis and the Principle of Acceleration." *Review of Economics and Statistics,* May 1939.
Economics. 1st ed. New York: McGraw-Hill, 1948.
"The Pure Theory of Public Expenditure." *Review of Economics and Statistics,* November 1954.
Foundations of Economic Analysis. Cambridge: Harvard University Press, 1947; enlarged ed., 1983.
"An Exact Consumption-Loan Model of Interest with or without the Social Contrivance of Money." *Journal of Political Economy* 66 (1958).

SPECIAL HONORS AND EXPERIENCE
David A. Wells Award (best thesis, Harvard University), 1941
John Bates Clark Award, 1947
President, Econometric Society, 1953
President, American Economic Association, 1961
Albert Einstein Medal, 1970
Nobel Prize in Economics, 1970
Gold Scanno Prize in Economy, 1990
National Medal of Science, 1996
34 Honorary Degrees

Bibliography

Abreu, Dilip, and Ariel Rubinstein. 1988. "The Structure of Nash Equilibrium in Repeated Games with Finite Automata." *Econometrica* 56: 1259–82.

Aghion, P., R. Frydman, J. Stiglitz, and M. Woodford. 2002. *Knowledge, Information, and Expectations in Modern Macroeconomics: In Honor of Edmund S. Phelps*. Princeton: Princeton University Press.

Akerlof, George A. 1991. "Procrastination and Obedience." *American Economic Review, Papers and Proceedings* 81: 1–19.

Akerlof, George A., and Janet L. Yellen. 1988. "Fairness and Unemployment." *American Economic Review, Papers and Proceedings* 78: 44–49.

Albin, Peter S. 1998. *Barriers and Bounds to Rationality: Essays on Economic Complexity and Dynamics in Interactive Systems*. Edited by Duncan K. Foley. Princeton: Princeton University Press.

Albin, Peter S., and Duncan K. Foley. 1992. "Decentralized, Dispersed Exchange without an Auctioneer." *Journal of Economic Behavior and Organization* 18: 27–52.

Alchian, Armen A. 1950. "Uncertainty, Evolution and Economic Theory." *Journal of Political Economy* 58: 211–22.

Allen, R. G. D. 1938. *Mathematical Analysis for Economists*. London: Macmillan.

Allen, Todd M., and Christopher D. Carroll. 2001. "Individual Learning about Consumption." *Macroeconomic Dynamics* 5: 225–71.

Anderson, Philip W., Kenneth J. Arrow, and David Pines, eds. 1988. *The Economy as an Evolving Complex System*. Santa Fe Institute Studies in the Sciences of Complexity, vol. 3. Reading, MA: Addison-Wesley.

Arrow, Kenneth J. 1962. "The Economic Implications of Learning by Doing." *Review of Economic Studies* 29: 155–73.

———. 2004. "Is Bounded Rationality Unboundedly Rational: Some

Ruminations." In *Models of a Man: Essays in Memory of Herbert J. Simon,* edited by M. Augier and J. G. March. Cambridge: MIT Press.

Arrow, Kenneth J., and Gerard Debreu. 1954. "Existence of an Equilibrium for a Competitive Economy." *Econometrica* 22: 265–90.

Arthur, W. Brian. 1994. "Inductive Reasoning and Bounded Rationality." *American Economic Review, Papers and Proceedings* 84: 406–11.

Arthur, W. Brian, Steven N. Durlauf, and David A. Lane, eds. 1997a. *The Economy as an Evolving Complex System II.* Santa Fe Institute Studies in the Science of Complexity, vol. 27. Reading, MA: Addison-Wesley.

Arthur, W. Brian, John H. Holland, Blake LeBaron, Richard Palmer, and Paul Tayler. 1997b. "Asset Pricing under Endogenous Expectations in an Artificial Stock Market." In *The Economy as an Evolving Complex System II,* edited by W. Brian Arthur, Steven N. Durlauf, and David A. Lane, 15–44. Reading, MA: Addison-Wesley.

Aspromourgos, Tony. 1986. "On the Origin of the Term 'NeoClassical.'" *Cambridge Journal of Economics* 10 (30): 265–70.

Aumann, Robert. 1995. "Backward Induction and Common Knowledge of Rationality." *Games and Economic Behavior* 8: 6–19.

Axelrod, Robert. 1984. *The Evolution of Cooperation.* New York: Basic Books.

———. 1995. "The Convergence and Stability of Cultures: Local Convergence and Global Polarization." Santa Fe Institute Working Paper 95-03-028.

Axtell, Robert. 1999. "Endogenous Firms: Local Increasing Returns, Unstable Nash Equilibria and Power Law Distributions." Santa Fe Institute Working Paper 99-03-019.

———. 2000. "On the Complexity of Markets: 'Price Discovery' as Distributed Computation." Presented at Santa Fe Workshop on Financial Market Efficiency, May 2000.

———. 2001. "Zipf Distribution of U.S. Firm Sizes." *Science* 293: 1818–20.

Axtell, Robert, and Joshua M. Epstein. 1996. *Growing Artificial Societies: Social Science from the Bottom Up.* Washington, DC, and Cambridge: Brookings Institution and MIT Press.

———. 1999. "Coordination in Transient Social Networks: An Agent-Based Model of the Timing of Retirement." In *Behavioral Dimensions of Retirement Economics,* edited by Henry Aaron. New York and Washington, DC: Russell Sage and Brookings Institution.

Axtell, Robert, and Richard Florida. 2000. "The Evolution of the System of Cities: A Microeconomic Explanation of Zipf's Law." Mimeo, Brookings Institution and Carnegie-Mellon University.

Axtell, Robert, Robert Axelrod, Joshua M. Epstein, and Michael B. Cohen. 1996. "Aligning Simulation Models: A Case Study and Results." *Computational and Mathematical Organization Theory* 1: 123–41.

Axtell, Robert, Joshua Epstein, and H. Peyton Young. 2001. "The Emergence of Classes in a Multi-Agent Bargaining Model." In *Social Dynamics,* edited by Steven N. Durlauf and H. Peyton Young, 191–211. Cambridge: MIT Press.

Axtell, Robert, Joshua M. Epstein, Jeffrey S. Dean, George J. Gumerman, Alan C. Swedlund, Jason Harburger, Shuba Chakravartya, Ross Hammond, Jon Parker, and Miles Parker. 2002. "Population Growth and Collapse in a Multi-Agent Model of the Kayenta Anasazi in Long House Valley." *Proceedings of the National Academy of Sciences.* 99 (Supplement) 3: 7275–79.

Bak, Per. 1996. *How Nature Works: The Science of Self-Organized Criticality.* New York: Copernicus Press for Springer-Verlag.

Barkin, David. 1995. *Wealth, Poverty and Sustainable Development.* Washington, DC: Interamerican Council for Sustainable Agriculture.

Barnett, Harold J., and Chandler Morse. 1963. *Scarcity and Growth: The Economics of Natural Resource Availability.* Baltimore: Johns Hopkins University Press for Resources for the Future.

Bator, Francis, 1957. "The Simple Analytics of Welfare Maximization." *American Economic Review* 47: 22–49.

Becker, Gary S. 1961. *A Treatise on the Economics of the Family.* Chicago: University of Chicago Press.

Benhabib, Jess, and Richard H. Day. 1981. "Rational Choice and Erratic Behavior." *Review of Economic Studies* 48: 459–72.

Binmore, Ken. 1975. "An Example in Group Preference." *Journal of Economic Theory* 10: 377–85.

———. 1984. "Equilibria in Extensive Games." *Economic Journal* 95: 51–59.

———. 1987. "Modeling Rational Players I." *Economics and Philosophy* 3: 179–214.

———. 1989. "Social Contract: Harsanyi and Rawls." *Economic Journal* 99: 84–102.

———. 1990. *Essays on the Foundations of Game Theory.* Oxford: Basil Blackwell.

———. 1991. *Fun and Games.* Lexington, MA: D. C. Heath.

———. 1994. *Playing Fair.* Vol. 1 of *Game Theory and the Social Contract.* Cambridge: MIT Press.

———. 1996. "Introduction to the Essays of John Nash." In *Essays on Game Theory,* by John Nash. Cheltenham: Edward Elgar.

———. 1997. "Rationality and Backward Induction." *Journal of Economic Methodology* 4: 23–41.

———. 1998. *Just Playing.* Vol. 2 of *Game Theory and the Social Contract.* Cambridge: MIT Press.

———. 1999. "Why Experiment in Economics?" *Economic Journal* 109: F16–F24.

———. 2001. "The Breakdown of Social Contracts." In *Social Dynamics,* edited by Steven N. Durlauf and H. Peyton Young, 213–34. Cambridge: MIT Press.

Binmore, Ken, and Larry Samuelson. 1992. "Evolutionary Stability in Repeated Games with Finite Automata." *Journal of Economic Theory* 57: 278–305.

———. 1994. "Drift." *European Economic Review* 38: 851–67.

———. 1997. "Muddling Through: Noisy Equilibrium Selection." *Journal of Economic Theory* 74: 235–66.

———. 1999. "Equilibrium Selection and Evolutionary Drift." *Review of Economic Studies* 66: 363–94.

———. 2001. "Coordinated Action in the Electronic Mail Game." *Games and Economic Behavior* 35: 6–30.

Binmore, Ken, John Gale, and Larry Samuelson. 1995a. "Learning to be Imperfect: The Ultimatum Game." *Games and Economic Behavior* 8: 56–90.

Binmore, Ken, Larry Samuelson, and Richard Vaughan. 1995b. "Musical Chairs: Modeling Noisy Evolution." *Games and Economic Behavior* 11: 1–35.

Binmore, Ken, Avner Shaked, and John Sutton. 1985. "Testing Noncooperative Game Theory: A Preliminary Study." *American Economic Review* 75: 1178–80.

Blaug, Mark. 1998. "The Formalist Revolution or What Happened to Orthodox Economics after World War II." 98/10 Discussion Paper in Economics, University of Exeter (October).

———. 2003. "The Formalist Revolution of the 1950s." In *A Companion to the History of Economic Thought,* edited by Warren Samuels, Jeff Biddle, and John Davis. Oxford: Blackwell Publications.

Blume, L., and D. Easley. 1992. "Evolution and Market Behavior." *Journal of Economic Theory* 58: 9–40.

Bonabeau, Eric. 2002. "Predicting the Unpredictable." *Harvard Business Review* (March): 109–16.

Boulding, Kenneth E. 1981. *Evolutionary Economics.* Beverly Hills: Sage Publications.

Bowles, Samuel. 2004. *Microeconomics: Behavior, Institutions and Evolution.* Princeton: Princeton University Press.

Bowman, David, Deborah Minehard, and Matthew Rabin. 1999. "Loss Aversion in a Consumption-Savings Model." *Journal of Economic Behavior and Organization* 38: 155–78.

Boyd, Robert, and Peter J. Richerson. 1985. *Culture and the Evolutionary Process.* Chicago: University of Chicago Press.

Braverman, Harry. 1974. *Labor and Monopoly Capital: The Degradation of Work in the Twentieth Century.* New York: Monthly Press.

Brock, William A. 1974. "Money and Growth: The Case of Long Run Perfect Foresight." *International Economic Review* 15: 750–77.

———. 1975. "A Simple Perfect Foresight Model." *Journal of Monetary Economics* 1: 133–50.

———. 1977. "A Polluted Golden Age." In *Economics of Natural and Environmental Resources,* edited by Vernon Smith, 441–62. New York: Gordon and Breach.

———. 1986. "Distinguishing Random and Deterministic Systems." *Journal of Economic Theory* 40: 68–195.

———. 1993. "Pathways to Randomness in the Economy: Emergent Nonlinearity and Chaos in Economics and Finance." *Estudios Económicos* 8: 3–55.

———. 1997. "Asset Pricing Behavior in Complex Environments." In *The Economy as an Evolving Complex System II,* edited by W. Brian Arthur, Steven N. Durlauf, and David A. Lane, Santa Fe Institute Studies in the Sciences of Complexity, vol. 27, 385–423. Reading, MA: Addison-Wesley.

———. 1999. "Scaling in Economics: A Reader's Guide." *Industrial and Corporate Change* 8: 409–46.

———. 2000. "Some Santa Fe Scenery." In *The Complexity Vision and the Teaching of Economics,* edited by David C. Colander, 29–49. Cheltenham: Edward Elgar.

Brock, William A., and Edwin Burmeister. 1976. "Regular Economies and Conditions for Uniqueness of Steady States in Optimal Multisector Economic Models." *International Economic Review* 17: 105–20.

Brock, William A., and Steven N. Durlauf. 1999. "A Formal Model of Theory Choice in Science." *Economic Theory* 14: 113–30.

———. 2001a. "Discrete Choice with Social Interactions." *Review of Economic Studies* 68: 235–60.

———. 2001b. "Growth Economics and Reality." *World Bank Economic Review* 15: 229–72.

———. 2001c. "Interactions-Based Models." In *Handbook of Econometrics,* edited by James Heckman and Edward Leamer, vol. 5, 3297–3380. Amsterdam: Elsevier Science.

Brock, William A., and David S. Evans. 1986. *The Impact of Federal Regulations and Taxes on Business Formation, Dissolution, and Growth.* New York: Holmes and Myers.

Brock, William A., and David Gale. 1969. "Optimal Growth under Factor Augmenting Progress." *Journal of Economic Theory* 1: 229–43.

Brock, William A., and Cars H. Hommes. 1997. "A Rational Route to Randomness." *Econometrica* 65: 1059–95.

———. 1998. "Heterogeneous Beliefs and Routes to Chaos in a Simple Asset Pricing Model." *Journal of Economic Dynamics and Control* 22: 1235–74.

Brock, William A., and Blake LeBaron. 1996. "A Dynamic Structural Model for Stock Return Volatility and Trading Volume." *Review of Economics and Statistics* 78: 94–110.

Brock, William A., and D. Starret. Forthcoming. "Nonconvexities in Ecological Management Problems." *Environmental and Resource Economics.*

Brock, William A., and Russell G. Thompson. 1965. "Integrated Economic Structures: A New Approach." *Metroeconomica* 17: 131–51.

———. 1966. "Convex Solutions of Implicit Returns." *Mathematics Magazine* 39: 208–11.

Brock, William A., and A. Xepapadeas. 2002. "Optimal Ecosystem Management when Species Compete for Limiting Resources." *Journal of Environmental Economics and Management.* 44:189–220.

———. 2003. "Valuing Biodiversity from an Economic Perspective: A Unified Economic Ecological and Genetic Approach." *American Economic Revew* 93 (5): 1597–1614.

Brock, W., C. Hommes, and F. Wagener. Forthcoming. "Evolutionary Dynamics in Markets with Many Trader Types." *Journal of Mathematical Economics.*

Brock, William A., David Hsieh, and Blake LeBaron. 1991. *Nonlinear Dynamics, Chaos, and Instability: Statistical Theory and Evidence.* Cambridge: MIT Press.

Brock, William A., W. Davis Dechert, Blake LeBaron, and José Scheinkman. 1996. "A Test for Independence Based upon the Correlation Dimension." *Econometric Reviews* 15: 197–235.

Brown, Harrison. 1954. *The Challenge of Man's Future.* New York: Viking.

Carpenter, Steven, William A. Brock, and P. Hanson. 1999a. "Ecological and Social Dynamics in Simple Models of Ecosystem Management." *Conservation Ecology* 3 (2). Online at http://www.consecol.org/journal/vol3/iss2/art4.

Carpenter, Steven, Donald Ludwig, and William A. Brock. 1999b. "Management of Eutrophication for Lakes Subject to Potentially Irreversible Change." *Ecological Applications* 9: 751–71.

Charness, Gary, and Matthew Rabin. 2002. "Understanding Social Preferences with Simple Tests." *Quarterly Journal of Economics* 117: 817–69.

Chichilnisky, Graciela, Geoffrey W. Heal, and A. Beltratti. 1995. "The Green Golden Rule." *Economics Letters* 49: 175–79.

Clawson, Marion. 1950. *The Western Range Livestock Industry.* New York: McGraw-Hill.

Coase, R. H. 1960. "The Problem of Social Cost." *Journal of Law and Economics* 3: 1–44.

Colander, David C. 2000a. "The Death of Neoclassical Economics." *Journal of the History of Economic Thought* 22 (2): 127–43.

———. 2000b. "A Thumbnail Sketch of the History of Thought from a Complexity Perspective." In *Complexity and the History of Economic Thought,* edited by David C. Colander. New York: Routledge Publishers.

———, ed. 2000c. *Complexity Vision and the Teaching of Economics.* Cheltenham: Edward Elgar.

————. 2003. "Are Institutionalists an Endangered Species?" *Journal of Economic Issues*. 37, no. 1 (March): 111–22.

Conan Doyle, Arthur. 1893. "The Final Problem." In *The Memoirs of Sherlock Holmes*. London: Strand Magazine.

Costanza, Robert. 1997. *Frontiers in Ecological Economics: Transdisciplinary Essays by Robert Costanza*. Cheltenham: Edward Elgar.

Cournot, Augustin A. 1838. *Recherches sur les Principes Mathématiques de la Théorie des Richesses*. Paris: Hachette. Reprint, with English translation by Nathaniel F. Bacon, *Researches into the Mathematical Principles of the Theory of Wealth*, New York: Macmillan, 1897.

Daly, Herman E., ed. 1973. *Toward a Steady-State Economy*. San Francisco: W. H. Freeman.

Darwin, Charles. 1859. *On the Origin of Species by Means of Natural Selection or the Preservation of Favored Races in the Struggle for Life*. London: John Murray.

Dean, Jeffrey S., George J. Gumerman, Joshua M. Epstein, Robert Axtell, Alan C. Swedlund, Miles T. Parker, and Steven McCarroll. 1999. "Understanding Anasazi Culture Change through Agent-Based Modeling." In *Dynamics in Human and Primate Societies*, edited by T. Kohler and G. Gumerman. Oxford: Oxford University Press.

Debreu, Gerard. 1959. *Theory of Value, an Axiomatic Analysis of Economic Equilibrium*. New Haven: Yale University Press.

————. 1991. "The Mathematization of Economic Theory." *American Economic Review* 81: 1–7.

Duménil, Gérard. 1983. "Beyond the Transformation Riddle: A Labor Theory of Value." *Science and Society* 47: 427–50.

Easterlin, Richard A. 1995. "Will Raising the Incomes of All Increase the Happiness of All?" *Journal of Economic Behavior and Organization* 27: 35–47.

Ehrlich, Paul R. 1968. *The Population Bomb*. New York: Ballantine.

Ehrlich, Paul R., and Peter H. Raven. 1964. "Butterflies and Plants: A Study of Coevolution." *Evolution* 18: 586–608.

Ehrlich, Paul R., Anne H. Ehrlich, and John P. Holdren. 1977. *Ecoscience: Population, Resources, Environment*. San Francisco: W. H. Freeman.

Elster, Jon. 1992. *Local Justice*. New York: Russell Sage Foundation.

Ely, Richard T., and George S. Wehrwein. 1940. *Land Economics*. Madison: University of Wisconsin.

Engle, Robert F., and Duncan K. Foley. 1975. "An Asset Price Model of Aggregate Investment." *International Economic Review* 16: 625–47.

Faber, Malte, and John L. R. Proops. 1990. *Evolution, Time, Production and the Environment*. Heidelberg: Springer-Verlag.

Fama, Eugene F. 1970. "Efficient Capital Markets: A Review of Theory and Empirical Work." *Journal of Finance* 25 (2): 383–417.

Farrell, Joseph, and Matthew Rabin. 1996. "Cheap Talk." *Journal of Economic Perspectives* 10 (3): 103–18.

Fehr, Ernst, and Klaus M. Schmidt. 1999. "A Theory of Fairness, Competition, and Cooperation." *Quarterly Journal of Economics* 114 (3): 817–68.

Field, Alex. 2002. *Altruistically Inclined? The Behavioral Sciences, Evolutionary Theory, and the Origins of Reciprocity.* Ann Arbor: University of Michigan Press.

Foley, Duncan K. 1967. "Resource Allocation and the Public Sector." *Yale Economic Essays* 7: 43–98.

———. 1975a. "On Two Specifications of Asset Equilibrium in Macroeconomic Models." *Journal of Political Economy* 83: 303–24.

———. 1975b. "Problems vs. Conflicts: Economics and Ideology." *American Economic Review, Papers and Proceedings* 45: 231–36.

———. 1978. "State Expenditure from a Marxist Perspective." *Journal of Public Economics* 9: 221–38.

———. 1982a. "Realization and Accumulation in a Marxian Model of the Circuit of Capital." *Journal of Economic Theory* 28: 300–319.

———. 1982b. "The Value of Money, the Value of Labor Power and the Marxian Transformation Problem." *Review of Radical Political Economics* 14 (2): 5–19.

———. 1986a. "Liquidity-Profit Rate Cycles in a Capitalist Economy." *Journal of Economic Behavior and Organization* 8: 363–76.

———. 1986b. *Understanding Capital: Marx's Economic Theory.* Cambridge: Harvard University Press.

———. 1994. "A Statistical Equilibrium Theory of Markets." *Journal of Economic Theory* 62: 321–45.

———. 1996. "Statistical Equilibrium in a Simple Labor Market." *Metroeconomica* 47: 125–47.

———. 1999. "The Ins and Outs of Late Twentieth-Century Economics." In *Makers of Modern Economics IV*, edited by Arnold Heertje. Brookfield: Edward Elgar.

———. 2003. "General Equilibrium Theory." New School Working Paper, available at http://newschool.edu/het/profiles/foley.htm.

Foley, Duncan K., and Peter S. Albin. 2001. "The Co-evolution of Cooperation and Complexity in a Multi-player, Local-Interaction Prisoners' Dilemma." *Complexity* 6, no. 3: 54–63.

Foley, Duncan K., and Martin Hellwig. 1975. "Asset Management under Trading Uncertainty." *Review of Economic Studies* 42: 327–46.

Foley, Duncan K., and Thomas R. Michl. 1999. *Growth and Distribution.* Cambridge: Harvard University Press.

Foley, Duncan K., and Miguel Sidrauski. 1971. *Monetary and Fiscal Policy in a Growing Economy.* New York: Macmillan.

Foster, Dean, and H. Peyton Young. 1990. "Stochastic Evolutionary Game Dynamics." *Theoretical Population Biology* 38: 219–32.

Foster, John Bellamy. 2000. *Marx's Ecology: Materialism and Nature.* New York: Monthly Review Press.

Frank, Robert. 1978. "How Long Is a Spell of Unemployment?" *Econometrica* 46: 285–302.

———. 1984. "Are Workers Paid Their Marginal Products?" *American Economic Review* 74: 549–71.

———. 1985a. *Choosing the Right Pond: Human Behavior and the Quest for Status.* New York: Oxford University Press.

———. 1985b. "The Demand for Unobservable and Other Nonpositional Goods." *American Economic Review* 75: 101–16.

———. 1988. *Passions within Reason: The Strategic Role of the Emotions.* New York: W. W. Norton.

———. 1989a. "Honesty as an Evolutionarily Stable Strategy." *Behavioral and Brain Sciences* 12: 705–6.

———. 1989b. "If *Homo Economicus* Could Choose His Own Utility Function, Would He Want One with a Conscience? Reply to Harrington." *American Economic Review* 79. Reprinted in *Trust*, edited by Elias L. Khalil, Northampton, MA: Edward Elgar, 2003.

———. 1991a. *Microeconomics and Behavior.* 1st ed. New York: McGraw-Hill.

———. 1991b. "Positional Externalities." In *Strategy and Choice: Essays in Honor of Thomas C. Schelling*, edited by Richard Zeckhauser, 25–47. Cambridge: MIT Press.

———. 1996. "What Price the Moral High Ground?" *Southern Economic Journal* 63: 1–17.

———. 1998a. "Social Norms as Positional Arms Control Agreements." In *Values, Economics, and Organization*, edited by Louis Putterman and Avner Ben Ner. New York: Cambridge University Press.

———. 1998b. "Winner-Take-All Markets and Wage Discrimination." In *The New Institutionalism in Sociology*, edited by Mary Brinton and Victor Nee. New York: Russell Sage.

———. 1999. *Luxury Fever.* New York: Free Press.

———. 2000. "Progressive Taxation and the Incentive Problem." In *Does Atlas Shrug? The Economic Consequences of Taxing the Rich*, edited by Joel Slemrod. Cambridge, MA: Harvard University Press and Russell Sage Foundation.

———. 2002. "Willingness-to-Pay without Apology." Unpublished paper.

———. 2004. *What Price the Moral High Ground?* Princeton: Princeton University Press.

Frank, Robert, and B. Bernanke. 2001. *Principles of Economics.* New York: McGraw-Hill.

Frank, Robert, and Philip J. Cook. 1995. *The Winner-Take-All Society.* New York: Martin Kessler Books at the Free Press.

Frank, Robert, and Richard T. Freeman. 1978. *The Distributional Consequences of Direct Foreign Investment.* New York: Academic Press.

Frank, Robert, and Cass Sunstein. 2001. "Cost-Benefit Analysis and Relative Position." *University of Chicago Law Review* 68: 323–74.

Friedman, Milton, and Rose Friedman. 1979. *An Argument for Laissez Faire: Free to Choose.* New York: Harcourt, Brace, Jovanovich.

Gabaix, Xavier. 1999. "Zipf's Law for Cities: An Explanation." *Quarterly Journal of Economics* 114: 739–67.

Georgescu-Roegen, Nicholas. 1971. *The Entropy Law and the Economic Process.* Cambridge: Harvard University Press.

Gintis, Herbert. 1976. "The Nature of the Labor Exchange of the Theory of Capitalist Production." *Review of Radical Political Economics* 8 (2): 36–54. Reprint in *Radical Economics,* edited by Samuel Bowles and Richard C. Edwards, Schools of Thought in Economics, ed. Mark Blaug (Cheltenham: Edward Elgar, 1981).

———. 2000a. *Game Theory Evolving.* Princeton: Princeton University Press.

———. 2000b. "Strong Reciprocity and Human Sociality." *Journal of Theoretical Biology* 206: 169–79.

Gintis, Herbert, and Samuel Bowles. 1976. *Schooling in Capitalist America: Educational Reform and the Contradictions of Economic Life.* New York: Basic Books.

———. 1986. *Democracy and Capitalism: Property, Community, and the Contradictions of Modern Social Thought.* New York: Basic Books.

———. 1996a. "Productive Skills, Labor Discipline, and the Returns to Schooling." Paper prepared for the conference Meritocracy and Equality, University of Wisconsin.

———. 1996b. "Time Preference, Labor Discipline and Earnings: Explaining the Economic Return to Education." University of Massachusetts Working Paper.

Gintis, Herbert, and Tsuneo Ishikawa. 1987. "Wages, Work Discipline, and Unemployment." *Journal of Japanese and International Economies* 1: 195–228.

Gintis, Herbert, Joseph Henrich, Robert Boyd, Samuel Bowles, Colin Camerer, Ernst Fehr, and Richard McElreath. 2001a. "Cooperation, Reciprocity and Punishment in Fifteen Small-Scale Societies." *American Economic Review* 91: 73–78.

Gintis, Herbert, Eric Alden Smith, and Samuel Bowles. 2001b. "Costly Signaling and Cooperation." *Journal of Theoretical Biology* 213: 103–19.

Gintis, Herbert, Samuel Bowles, and Melissa Osborne. 2002. "The Determinants of Individual Earnings: Skills, Preferences, and Schooling." *Journal of Economic Literature* 39: 1137–76.

Gintis, Herbert, Samuel Bowles, Robert Boyd, and Ernst Fehr. 2004. *Moral*

Sentiments and Material Interests: On the Foundations of Cooperation in Economic Life. Cambridge: MIT Press.

Goleman, D. 1995. *Emotional Intelligence.* New York: Bantam Books.

Goodwin, Richard M. 1951. "The Nonlinear Accelerator and the Persistence of Business Cycles." *Econometrica* 19: 1–17.

Gowdy, John M. 1994. *Coevolutionary Economics: The Economy, Society, and Environment.* Boston: Kluwer Academic Publishers.

Gunderson, Lance H., and C. S. Holling, eds. 2002. *Panarchy: Understanding Transformations in Natural and Human Systems.* Washington, DC: Island Press.

Güth, Werner, R. Schmittberger, and B. Schwarze. 1982. "An Experimental Analysis of Ultimatum Bargaining." *Journal of Economic Behavior and Organization* 3: 367–88.

Hall, Darwin C., and Richard B. Norgaard. 1974. "Environmental Amenity Rights, Transactions Costs, and Technological Change." *Journal of Environmental Economics and Management* 1: 251–67.

Hansen, Lars Peter, and Thomas J. Sargent. 2000. "Wanting Robustness in Macroeconomics." Mimeo, available at ftp://zia.Stanford.edu/pub/sargent/webdocs/research/wanting.pdf.

Harberger, Arnold C. 1971. "Three Basic Postulates for Applied Welfare Economics." *Journal of Economic Literature* 9: 785–97.

Harcourt, Geoffrey C. 1972. *Some Cambridge Controversies in the Theory of Capital.* Cambridge: Cambridge University Press.

Harris, Donald J. 1978. *Capital Accumulation and Income Distribution.* Stanford: Stanford University Press.

Harsanyi, John. 1955. "Cardinal Welfare, Individualistic Ethics, and Interpersonal Comparisons of Utility." *Journal of Political Economy* 63: 309–21.

———. 1977. *Rational Behavior and Bargaining Equilibrium in Games and Social Situations.* Cambridge: Cambridge University Press.

Hart, Sergiu. 2002. "Evolutionary Dynamics and Backward Induction." *Games and Economic Behavior* 41: 227–64.

Hayek, Friedrich. 1945. "The Use of Knowledge in Society." *American Economic Review* 35: 519–30.

Hendry, David. 2000. *Econometrics: Alchemy or Science? Essays in Econometric Methodology.* Oxford and New York: Oxford University Press.

Hicks, J. R. 1939. *Value and Capital.* Oxford: Clarendon Press.

Hodgson, Geoffrey C. 1993. *Economics and Evolution: Bringing Life Back into Economics.* Ann Arbor: University of Michigan Press.

Horgan, John. 1997. *The End of Science: Facing the Limits of Knowledge in the Twilight of the Scientific Age.* New York: Broadway Books.

Hotelling, H. 1931. "The Economics of Exhaustible Resources." *Journal of Political Economy* 39: 137–75.

Housman, A. E. 1896. *A Shropshire Lad.* London: K. Paul, Trench, Treubner.

Howarth, Richard B., and Richard B. Norgaard. 1990. "Intergenerational Resource Rights, Efficiency, and Social Optimality." *Land Economics* 66: 1–11.

———. 1992. "Environmental Valuation under Sustainable Development." *American Economic Review* 82: 473–77.

———. 1993. "Intergenerational Transfers and the Social Discount Rate." *Environmental and Resource Economics* 3: 337–58.

Hurkens, Sjaak. 1995. "Learning by Forgetful Players." *Games and Economic Behavior* 11: 304–29.

Ijiri, Y., and Herbert A. Simon. 1964. "Business Firm Growth and Size." *American Economic Review* 54: 77–89.

———. 1977. *Skew Distributions and the Sizes of Business Firms.* New York: North-Holland.

Illich, Ivan. 1977. *The Right to Useful Unemployment and Its Professional Enemies.* London: Marian Boyars.

Jansson, Ann-Mari, ed. 1984. *Integration of Economy and Ecology: An Outlook for the Eighties, Proceedings from the Wallenberg Symposia.* Stockholm: Sundt Offset.

Jencks, Christopher S., M. Smith, H. Acland, M. J. Bane, D. Cohen, Herbert Gintis, B. Heyns, and S. Michelson. 1972. *Inequality: A Reassessment of the Effect of Family and Schooling in America.* New York: Basic Books.

Judd, Kenneth L. 1998. *Numerical Methods in Economics.* Cambridge: MIT Press.

Kahn, Alfred E. 1998. "Surprises of Airline Deregulation." *American Economic Review, Papers and Proceedings* 78 (2): 316–22.

Kahneman, Daniel, and Amos Tversky. 1988. "Rational Choice and the Framing of Decisions." In *Decision Making.* Cambridge: Cambridge University Press.

Kakutani, S. 1941. "A Generalization of Brouwer's Fixed Point Theorem." *Duke Mathematical Journal* 8: 457–59.

Kandori, Michihiro, George J. Mailath, and Rafael Rob. 1993. "Learning, Mutation, and Long-Run Equilibria in Games." *Econometrica* 61: 29–56.

Keynes, John M. 1936. *The General Theory of Employment, Interest and Money.* New York: Harcourt, Brace and World.

Koopmans, Tjalling C. 1957. *Three Essays on the State of Economic Science.* New York: McGraw-Hill.

Kremer, Michael. 2003. "Randomized Evaluations of Educational Programs in Developing Countries: Some Lessons." *American Economic Review, Papers and Proceedings* 93: 102–6.

Kreps, D., J. Roberts, P. Milgrom, and R. Wilson. 1982. "Rational Cooperation in the Finitely Repeated Prisoners' Dilemma." *Journal of Economic Theory* 27: 245–52.

Krugman, Paul. 1999. "The Role of Geography in Development." In *Annual*

World Bank Conference on Development Economics (1998), edited by Boris Pleskovic and Joseph Stiglitz, 89–125. Washington, DC: World Bank.

Kuhn, Thomas S. 1961. *The Structure of Scientific Revolutions.* Chicago: University of Chicago Press.

———. 1970. *The Structure of Scientific Revolutions.* Enlarged ed. Chicago: University of Chicago Press.

Kuran, Timur. 1995. *Private Truths, Public Lies—The Social Consequences of Preference Falsification.* Cambridge: Harvard University Press.

Laibson, David. 1994. "Essays in Hyperbolic Discounting." Ph.D. dissertation, MIT.

Lakatos, Imre. 1978. *The Methodology of Scientific Research Programmes: Philosophical Papers.* Vol. 1. Cambridge: Cambridge University Press.

Ledyard, John. 1995. "Public Goods." In *A Survey of Experimental Research,* edited by John Kagel and Alvin Roth. Princeton: Princeton University Press.

Lewis, Alain. 1979. "On the Formal Characteristics of Plausible Reasoning." Rand P-6462, Rand Corporation, Santa Monica, CA.

———. 1985. "Complex Structures and Composite Models—An Essay on Methodology." *Mathematical Social Sciences* 10: 211–46.

Littlewood, John E. 1986. *Littlewood's Miscellany.* Edited by Béla Bollobás. 1937; reprint, Cambridge: Cambridge University Press.

Locke, John. 1690. *An Essay Concerning Human Understanding.* Reprint, New York: Dover, 1959.

Lucas, Robert E. Jr. 1972. "Expectations and the Neutrality of Money." *Journal of Economic Theory* 4: 103–24.

———. 1987. *Models of Business Cycles.* New York: Blackwell.

Luce, R. Duncan, and Howard Raiffa. 1957. *Games and Decisions: Introduction and Critical Survey.* New York: John Wiley and Sons.

Lux, Thomas. 1998. "The Socio-Economic Dynamics of Speculative Markets: Interacting Agents, Chaos, and Fat Tailed Return Distributions." *Journal of Economic Behavior and Organization* 33: 143–65.

Mandelbrot, B. B. 1963. "The Variation of Certain Speculative Prices." *Journal of Business of the University of Chicago* 36: 394–419.

Manski, Charles F., and Daniel McFadden. 1981. *Structural Analysis of Discrete Data with Econometric Applications.* Cambridge: MIT Press.

Mantegna, Rosario N., and H. Eugene Stanley. 2000. *An Introduction to Econophysics: Correlations and Complexity in Finance.* Cambridge: Cambridge University Press.

Markowitz, Harry M. 1959. *Portfolio Selection: Efficient Diversification of Investments.* New York: John Wiley and Sons.

Marshall, Alfred. 1890. *Principles of Economics.* London: Macmillan.

Martinez-Allier, Juan, with Klaus Schlüpmann. 1987. *Ecological Economics: Energy, Environment and Society.* Oxford: Blackwell.

Marx, K. [1847] 1956. *The Poverty of Philosophy.* English ed. London: Lawrence and Wishart Press.

———. 1867. *Das Kapital.* Buch I. Hamburg: Verlag von Otto Meissner.

May, Robert M. 1973. *Complexity and Stability in Model Ecosystems.* Princeton: Princeton University Press.

Maynard Smith, John. 1982. *Evolution and the Theory of Games.* Cambridge: Cambridge University Press.

Maynard Smith, John, and G. R. Price. 1973. "The Logic of Animal Conflict." *Nature* 246: 15–18.

McCloskey, Deirdre. 1970. "Did Victorian Britain Fail?" *Economic History Review* 23 (December): 446–59.

———. 1973. *Economic Maturity and Entrepreneurial Decline: British Iron and Steel, 1870–1913.* Harvard Economic Studies. Cambridge: Harvard University Press.

———. 1981. *Enterprise and Trade in Victorian Britain: Essays in Historical Economics.* London: Allen and Unwin.

———. 1983. "The Rhetoric of Economics." *Journal of Economic Literature* 21: 482–517.

———. 1997. *The Vices of Economists; The Virtues of the Bourgeoisie.* Amsterdam and Ann Arbor: University of Amsterdam Press and University of Michigan Press.

McCloskey, Deirdre, and Stephen Ziliak. 1996. "The Standard Error of Regression." *Journal of Economic Literature* 34: 97–114.

———. Forthcoming. "The Misuse of Statistical Significance: Any Change in the 1990s?" *Journal of Socioeconomics.*

McCloskey, Donald [Deirdre] N. 1985. *The Rhetoric of Economics.* Madison: University of Wisconsin Press.

Medio, Alfredo. 1972. "Profits and Surplus Value: Appearance and Reality in Capitalist Production." In *A Critique of Economic Theory,* edited by E. K. Hunt and J. G. Schwartz. Harmondsworth: Penguin Books, 1972.

Merton, Miller H., and Franco Modigliani. 1958. "The Cost of Capital, Corporation Finance, and the Theory of Investment." *American Economic Review* 48: 261–97.

Milgrom, Paul. 1981. "An Axiomatic Characterization of Common Knowledge." *Econometrica* 49: 219–22.

Mill, John Stuart. 1929. *Principles of Political Economy with Some of Their Applications to Social Philosophy.* Ed. W. J. Ashley. London: Longmans, Green.

Mirowski, Philip. 1989. *More Heat Than Light: Economics as Social Physics, Physics as Nature's Economics.* Cambridge: Cambridge University Press.

———. 2002. *Machine Dreams: Economics Becomes a Cyborg Science.* Cambridge: Cambridge University Press.

Nash, John F., Jr. 1951. "Non-cooperative Games." *Annals of Mathematics* 54: 286–95.

———. 1996. *Essays on Game Theory.* Cheltenham: Edward Elgar.

Nelson, Richard R., and Sidney G. Winter. 1982. *An Evolutionary Theory of Economic Change.* Cambridge: Harvard University Press.

Newell, A., and Herbert A. Simon. 1971. "Human Problem Solving: The State of the Theory, 1970." *American Psychologist* 26: 145–59.

Norgaard, Richard B. 1968. "Streamflow, Fluctuation, Bar Roughness, and Bed Load Movement: A Hypothesis." *Water Resources Research* 4: 647–50.

———. 1971. "Streamflow and Sediment Deposition in the Lower Columbia." *Water Resources Research* 7 (October).

———. 1975. "Resource Scarcity and New Technology in U.S. Petroleum Development." *Natural Resources Journal* 15: 265–82.

———. 1976. "Integrating Economics and Pest Management." In *Integrated Pest Management,* edited by J. Lawrence Apple and Ray F. Smith. New York: Plenum Press.

———. 1981. "Sociosystem and Ecosystem Coevolution in the Amazon." *Journal of Environmental Economics and Management* 8: 238–54.

———. 1984a. "Coevolutionary Agricultural Development." *Economic Development and Cultural Change* 32: 525–46.

———. 1984b. "Coevolutionary Development Potential." *Land Economics* 62: 14–25.

———. 1984c. "Traditional Agricultural Knowledge: Past Performance, Future Prospects, and Institutional Implications." *American Journal of Agricultural Economics* 66: 874–78.

———. 1985. "Environmental Economics: An Evolutionary Critique and a Plea for Pluralism." *Journal of Environmental Economics and Management* 12: 382–94.

———. 1989. "The Case for Methodological Pluralism." *Ecological Economics* 1: 37–57.

———. 1994. *Development Betrayed: The End of Progress and a Coevolutionary Revisioning of the Future.* London and New York: Routledge.

———. 1995a. "Beyond Materialism: A Coevolutionary Reinterpretation of the Environmental Crisis." *Review of Social Economy* 53: 475–92.

———. 1995b. "Metaphors We Might Survive By." *Ecological Economics* 15: 129–31.

Norgaard, Richard B., and Michikazu Kojima. 2001. *Trade and Environmental Governance: Theory and the American Experience. Framing the Pacific in the 21st Century: Coexistence and Friction.* Edited by Daizaburo Yui and Yasuo Endo. Center for Pacific and American Studies. Tokyo: University of Tokyo.

O'Brien, Denis. 1998. "Four Detours." *Journal of Economic Methodology* 5, no. 1: 23–41.

O'Donoghue, Ted, and Matthew Rabin. 1999. "Doing it Now or Later." *American Economic Review* 89: 103–24.

————. 2001a. "Choice and Procrastination." *Quarterly Journal of Economics* 116: 160–212.

————. 2001b. "Risky Behavior among Youths: Some Issues from Behavioral Economics." In *Youthful Risky Behavior: An Economic Perspective,* edited by Jon Gruber, 1–28. Chicago: University of Chicago Press.

Phelps, Edmund S. 1994. *Structural Slumps: The Modern Equilibrium Theory of Unemployment, Interest and Assets.* Cambridge: Harvard University Press.

Rabin, Matthew. 1993. "Incorporating Fairness into Game Theory and Economics." *American Economic Review* 83: 1281–1302.

————. 1994a. "A Model of Pre-Game Communication." *Journal of Economic Theory* 63: 370–91.

————. 1994b. "Cognitive Dissonance and Social Change." *Journal of Economic Behavior and Organization* 23: 177–94.

————. 1998. "Psychology and Economics." *Journal of Economic Literature* 36: 11–46.

————. 2000. "Risk-Aversion and Expected Utility: A Calibration Theorem." *Econometrica* 68: 1281–92.

————. 2002. "Inference by Believers in the Law of Small Numbers." *Quarterly Journal of Economics* 117: 775–816.

————. 2003. "A Perspective on Psychology and Economics," Marshall Lecture. *European Economic Review* 46: 657–85.

Rabin, Matthew, and Joel Schrag. 1999. "First Impressions Matter: A Model of Confirmatory Bias." *Quarterly Journal of Economics* 114: 37–82.

Rabin, Matthew, and Richard Thaler. 2001a. "Anomalies: Risk Aversion." *Journal of Economic Perspectives* 15 (1): 219–32.

————. 2001b. "Risk Aversion." *Journal of Economic Perspectives* 15 (1): 219–232.

Radner, Roy. 2001. "Real-Time Decentralized Information Processing and Returns to Scale." *Economic Theory* 17, no. 3 (May): 497–544.

Ramsey, Frank P. 1928. "A Mathematical Theory of Saving." *Economic Journal* 38: 543–59.

Rawls, John. 1971. *A Theory of Justice.* Oxford: Oxford University Press.

Resnick, Stephen A., and Richard D. Wolff. 2002. *Class Theory and History. Capitalism and Communism in the USSR.* London: Routledge.

Rosser, J. Barkley, Jr. 1999. "On the Complexities of Complex Economic Dynamics." *Journal of Economic Perspectives* 13 (4): 169–92.

Roth, Alvin, and Ido Erev. 1995. "Learning in Extensive-Form Games: Experimental Data and Simple Dynamic Models in the Medium Term." *Games and Economic Behavior* 8: 164–212.

Roth, Alvin, and Marilda Sotomayor. 1990. *Two-Sided Matching.* Econometrica Society Monographs, 18. Cambridge: Cambridge University Press.

Rubin, I. I. 1972. *Essays on Marx's Theory of Value.* Detroit: Black and Red Press.

Rubinstein, Ariel. 1982. "Perfect Equilibria in a Bargaining Model." *Econometrica* 50: 97–109.

Rust, John. 1996. "Numerical Dynamic Programming in Economics." In *Handbook of Computational Economics,* edited by Hans M. Ammen, David A. Kendrick, and John Rust. Amsterdam: Elsevier.

Saez-Marti, Maria, and Jorgen Weibull. 1999. "Clever Agents in Young's Evolutionary Bargaining Model." *Journal of Economic Theory* 86: 268–79.

Salant, Steve. 2000. "Search Theory and Duration Data: A Theory of Sorts." *Quarterly Journal of Economics,* November 1976. Anthologized in *The Economics of Unemployment,* edited by P. N. Junakar, International Library of Critical Writings in Economics, Cheltenham: Edward Elgar.

Sally, David. 2001. "On Sympathy and Games." *Journal of Economic Behavior and Organization* 44: 1–30.

Salovey, P., and J. D. Mayer. 1990. "Emotional Intelligence." *Imagination, Cognition, and Personality* 9: 185–211.

Samuelson, Paul A. 1947. *Foundations of Economic Analysis.* Cambridge: Harvard University Press; enlarged ed., 1983.

———. 1948. *Economics, an Introductory Analysis.* 1st ed. New York: McGraw-Hill.

———. 1966–86. *Collected Scientific Papers.* Edited by J. Stiglitz. 5 vols. Cambridge, MA: MIT Press.

———. 1972. "Maximum Principles in Analytical Economics." *American Economic Review* 62: 249–62.

Sargent, Thomas J. 1993. *Bounded Rationality in Macroeconomics.* Oxford: Clarendon Press.

Savage, L. 1954. *The Foundations of Statistics.* New York: Wiley.

Scarf, Herbert. 1960. "Some Examples of Global Instability of Competitive Equilibrium." *International Economic Review* 1: 157–72.

———. 1973. *The Computation of Economic Equilibria.* New Haven: Yale University Press.

Schelling, Thomas C. 1960. *The Strategy of Conflict.* Cambridge: Harvard University Press.

———. 1971. "Dynamic Models of Segregation." *Journal of Mathematical Sociology* 1: 143–86.

———. 1978. *Micromotives and Macrobehavior.* New York: Norton.

Schlesinger, Karl. 1935. "Über die Produktionsgleichungen der Ökonomischen Wertlhehre." In *Ergebnisse eines mathematischen Kolloquiums, 1933–34, Heft 6,* edited by Karl Menger. Leipzig and Vienna: Franz Deuticke. (English translation, "On the Production Equations of Economic Value Theory." In *Precursors in Mathematical Economics,* edited by William J. Baumol and Stephen M. Goldfeld, LSE Series of Reprints of Scarce Works on Political Economy, no. 19. London, 1968.)

Scott, Anthony. 1955. *Natural Resources: The Economics of Conservation.* Toronto: University of Toronto.

Selten, Reinhard. 1975. "Reexamination of the Perfectness Concept for Points in Extensive Games." *International Journal of Game Theory* 4: 25–55.

———. 1980. "A Note on Evolutionary Stable Strategies in Asymmetric Animal Contests." *Journal of Theoretical Biology* 84: 93–101.

Sidrauski, Miguel. 1967. "Inflation and Economic Growth." *Journal of Political Economy* 75: 796–810.

———. 1969. "Rational Choice and Patterns of Growth." *Journal of Political Economy* 77: 575–85.

Simon, Herbert A. 1945. "Review of *Theory of Games and Economic Behavior* by J. von Neumann and O. Morgenstern." *American Journal of Sociology* 50: 558–60.

Sims, Chris. 1996. "Macroeconomics and Methodology." *Journal of Economic Perspectives* 10, no. 1 (winter): 105–20.

Smith, Adam. 1776. *An Inquiry into the Nature and Causes of the Wealth of Nations.* London: W. Strahan and T. Cadell.

———. 1790. *The Theory of Moral Sentiments.* Reprint, Indianapolis: Liberty Press, 1976.

Smith, Maynard. 1982. *Evolution and the Theory of Games.* Cambridge: University of Cambridge Press.

Smith, Vernon L. 1992. "Game Theory and Experimental Economics: Beginnings and Early." In "Toward a History of Game Theory," edited by E. Roy Weintraub. *History of Political Economy Annual Supplement,* 24: 241–82.

———. 1998. "The Two Faces of Adam Smith." *Southern Economic Journal* 65: 1–19.

Smith, Vernon L., Gerry L. Suchanek, and Arlington W. Williams. 1988. "Bubbles, Crashes, and Endogenous Expectations." *Econometrica* 56: 1119–51.

Stigler, George, and Gary Becker. 1977. "De Gustibus Non Est Disputandum." *American Economic Review* 67 (2): 76–90.

Stiglitz, Joseph, and Carl Shapiro. 1984. "Equilibrium Unemployment as a Worker Discipline Device." *American Economic Review* 74 (3): 433–44. Reprinted in *New Keynesian Economics,* edited by N. G. Mankiw and D. Romer, vol. 2, 123–42. Cambridge, MA: MIT Press, 1991. Also in *Macroeconomics and Imperfect Competition,* edited by Jean-Pascal Bénassy, 453–64. Cheltenham: Edward Elgar, 1995.

Streissler, Erich W. 1990. "The Influence of German Economics on the Work of Menger and Marshall." In *Carl Menger and His Legacy in Economics,* ed. Bruce J. Caldwell, *History of Political Economy Annual Supplement* 22: 31–68.

Strotz, Robert H. 1956. "Myopia and Inconsistency in Dynamic Utility Maximization." *Review of Economic Studies* 23: 165–80.

Sugden, Robert. 2001. "Ken Binmore's Evolutionary Social Theory." *Economic Journal* 111: F215–F245.

Thaler, Richard H. 1986. "The Psychology and Economics Conference Handbook" (commentary on papers by H. Simon, H. Einhorn, and R. Hogarth, as well as A. Tversky and D. Kahneman). *Journal of Business* 59: S279–84.

———. 1991. *Quasi Rational Economics.* New York: Russell Sage Foundation.

———. 2000. "From Homo Economicus to Homo Sapiens." *Journal of Economic Perspectives* 14 (1): 133–41.

Thaler, Richard H., A. Tversky, D. Kahneman, and Anna Schwartz. 1997. "The Effect of Myopia and Loss Aversion on Risk Taking: An Experimental Test." *Quarterly Journal of Economics* 112: 647–61.

Thom, René. 1975. *Structural Stability and Morphogenesis: An Outline of a Theory of Models.* Reading, MA: Benjamin.

Tirole, Jean, and Jean-Jacques Laffont. 1991. "Privatization and Incentives." *Journal of Law, Economics and Organization* 7: 84–105.

Varian, Hal R. 1992. *Microeconomic Analysis.* 3rd ed. New York: W. W. Norton.

Veblen, Thorstein. 1898. "Why Is Economics Not an Evolutionary Science?" *Quarterly Journal of Economics* 12: 373–97.

———. 1900. "Preconceptions of Economic Science." *Quarterly Journal of Economics* 14: 261.

von Neumann, John. 1937. "Uber ein Okonomischen Gleichungsststem." In *Ergebness eines Mathematishchen Kolloquiums,* edited by Karl Menger, 8: 1–9.

———. 1958. *The Computer and the Brain.* New Haven. Yale University Press.

von Neumann, John, completed by Arthur W. Burks. 1966. *Theory of Self Reproducing Automata.* Urbana: University of Illinois Press.

von Neumann, John, and Oskar Morgenstern. 1944. *Theory of Games and Economic Behavior.* Princeton: Princeton University Press.

von Stackelberg, H. 1938. "Probleme der Unvollkommenen Konkurrenz." *Weltwirtschaftliches Archiv* 48: 95.

Wald, Abraham. 1936. "Uber Einige Gleichungssysteme der Mathematischen Okonomie." *Zeitschrift Fur Nationalokonomie* 7: 637–70. Translated as "On Some Systems of Equations of Mathematical Economics," *Econometrica* 19 (1951): 368–403.

Waldrop, M. Mitchell. 1992. *Complexity: The Emerging Science at the Edge of Order and Chaos.* New York: Simon and Schuster.

Walker, Donald A. 1996. *Walras's Market Models.* Cambridge: Cambridge University Press.

Weintraub, Roy. 2002. *How Economics Became a Mathematical Science, 2002.* Durham: Duke University Press.

Weisbuch, Gerard, Alan Kirman, and Dorothea Herreiner. 2000. "Market Organization and Trading Relationships." *Economic Journal* 110: 411–36.

Weitzman, Martin. 2002. "Gamma Discounting." *American Economic Review* 91: 260–71.

Wolff, Edward. 1975. "The Rate of Surplus Value in Puerto Rico." *Journal of Political Economy* 83: 935–49.

Young, Allyn. 1928. "Increasing Returns and Economic Progress." *Economic Journal* 38: 527–42.

Young, H. Peyton. 1993a. "The Evolution of Conventions." *Econometrica* 61: 57–94.

———. 1993b. "An Evolutionary Model of Bargaining." *Journal of Economic Theory* 59: 145–68.

———. 1994. *Equity in Theory and Practice.* Princeton: Princeton University Press.

———. 1998. *Individual Strategy and Social Structure: An Evolutionary Theory of Institutions.* Princeton: Princeton University Press.

Young, H. Peyton, and Mary A. Burke. 2000. "Competition and Custom: A Case Study of Illinois Agriculture." *American Economic Review* 91: 559–73.

Index

behavioral economics, 1; and its best application, 151; and broader economic research, 127; and experiment limitations, 95; its first, second, and third waves, 147; and R. H. Frank, 22, 110; and D. Kahneman, 94; and the mainstream, 20; and M. Rabin, 22; and scarcity of offerings, 94; and shortcomings of term, 142; and V. Smith, 94; and type of graduate student, 151

behavioral economists, and overreaching, 52

behavioral science, and H. Gintis, 120–21

Beijer Institute, 173

Benhabib, Jess, and D. K. Foley, 204

Bentham, Jeremy, and justice, 273, 311

Bergson, Abram, and P. Samuelson, 311

Bergstrom, Ted, and what freshmen need to learn, 62

Best, Mike, and radical department at University of Massachusetts, 84

Bewley, Truman, and mainstream acceptance, 3

Bhagwati, Jagdish, and mainstream elite, 10

bifurcations, and D. K. Foley, 210

bifurcation theory, 173–74

Binmore, Kenneth G.: and Bayesian approach, 62, 63; and changing views, 14; and chaotic dynamics, 58–59; credentials, 76; and evolutionary game theory, 22, 99, 272; compared to R. Frank, 119; and game theory, 50–74; and his four political ideologies, 70; and how he became an economist, 49–51; and how he is seen by other professions, 68; and interaction with other disciplines, 22; and origin of his writing, 67; and M. Rabin, 138; and reception of his work, 66–67; and telecom auctions, 71–72

biodiversity, and economic value, 176–77

biography, and testing subjects' theories, 312

biologists, as good communicators and good listeners, 247–48

biology: and ecological economics, 226; and evolutionary game theory, 52–54; and influence on economics, 275

Bishop, Bob, and MIT teaching, 191

Black, Fischer, and D. McCloskey, 31

Blaug, Mark, 5; and Arrow/Debreu, 302

Blume, Larry, and Santa Fe Institute, 102–3

Bonabeau, Eric, and commercial application of agent-based modeling, 271

Booth, Wayne, and influence on D. McCloskey, 33–34

bootstrapping, 178

Boulding, Kenneth E., and evolution, 230

bounded rationality: and interdisciplinary economics, 296; and neoclassical economics, 19; and new work, 19, 56; and orthodoxy, 279–80

Bowles, Sam: assessed by R. H. Frank, 120; and J. Dunlop, 80; and game theory, 97–98; and H. Gintis, 79, 80–81, 83, 84, 85–86; and hiring at University of Massachusetts, 84–85; and influence on H. Gintis, 79, 80–81; and Marxism, 89; and Santa Fe Institute, 102–3; and tenure, 298

Boyd, Robert, and evolutionary game theory, 98

Braverman, Harry, and importance of skills, 81

Brewer, Michael, and R. B. Norgaard, 216

Brimmer, Andrew, and H. Gintis, 81–82

Brock, William A. ("Buz"): and BDS statistic, 162, 165; and changing views, 14; credentials, 182; and diversity of his work, 165–66; and his career in economics, 160–63, 164; and how he became an economist, 157–60; and new work, 46; and policy, 295; and work in complexity, 23

Brookings Institution, and computation, 269–70

Brower, David, and R. B. Norgaard, 215, 222

Coase, Ronald, and influence on R. H. Frank, 115, 116

coevolution, 203; and the arms race, 128; and complexity, 231; and decision making, 283; and development, 228–29; and fairness, 70; and institutionalists, 230; and public decision making, 234; with social organization, 234

coevolutionary approach: and R. B. Norgaard, 227–29; and its reception, 232

coevolutionary economics, and how it selects, 241, 242

coevolutionary theory: and alternative ways with economic issues, 240–41; and chaos theory, 231–32; and Marxist economists, 241; as part of economics, 229–30

cognitive models of real behavior, 258, 264

cognitive science: and economics, 284; and real behavior, 258, 264; and Henry Simon, 253–54

Cohen, David, and H. Gintis, 83

Cohen, Michael B., and replication of computational models, 261–62

Cold War, and shaping of economics, 207

communism: and its collapse, 204; and H. Gintis, 87–88

comparative advantage: and doing economics, 293; and trade agreements, 239

competition: and concentration, 125; and faster markets, 125; and its pervasiveness, 125

competitive environment, and warm-glow effect, 118

competitive equilibrium, and description of the economy, 298, 303–4

complex dynamic games, and M. Rabin, 151

complex environments, and imitation process, 264–65

complexity: and P. Albin, 204–5; and analytic capability, 301; and W. A. Brock, 23; and chaos, 265–66; and

defining rationality, 13; and D. K. Foley, 23; and knowing how the economy operates, 298–99; and its myriad definitions, 168; and the new work, 18; and positive theory, 293; and scaling, 257; and structuring of textbooks, 12; and tropical ecosystems, 228; and ways in which it is understood, 245

complexity issues, and D. K. Foley, 201–2

complexity theory: and economics, 304; and general equilibrium, 18; and model building, 17

complexity vision, and instability, 185

complex systems: and circuit of capital models, 204; and the economics profession, 2, 5, 306; and D. K. Foley's work with P. Albin, 205

computation, and R. Axtell's interest, 252, 253

computational economics, and P. Markowski, 269

computationally intensive techniques, 178

computational power: and its improvement, 305–6; and increasing capacity, 283; and its increasing importance, 281

computation price, and changes in standard, 163

computer network, and K. G. Binmore, 54

computer programming, and D. K. Foley, 186

computer science, vs. psychology, 141

computer simulations: and model building, 17, 18; and prediction, 294; and J. von Neumann, 19

computer technology, and economics, 45

computing, and complexity, 293–94

computing power: and its advances, 279–80; and how to harness it, 284–85

computing time, and effect of its cheapness, 178

Conard, Joe, and D. K. Foley, 183, 184

Duesenberry, James, and influence on H. Gintis, 78, 82, 83, 84

Duménil, Gérard, and monetary approach, 199

Dunlop, John: and S. Bowles, 80; and socialization at Harvard, 91–92

Dupuit, Jules, and neoclassical evolution, 15–16

Durlauf, Steve: and W. A. Brock, 166–68, 171–72, 178; and Santa Fe Institute, 102–3

Earth Island Institute, and D. Brower, 222

Easterlin, Richard, and relative reference work, 152–53

Eckstein, Otto, as D. McCloskey's teacher, 28

eclecticism, and P. Samuelson, 312

ecological economics, 172–73; and K. Arrow, 300–301; characterized, 223, 224–25; and R. Costanza, 222; and its future, 225–26; and interrelation of nature/economy, 18; and natural resource economics, 223–24; and R. Norgaard, 23

Ecological Economics, and R. B. Norgaard, 222

ecological systems: and social systems, 225; and tensions with environmental economists, 224

econometric work, and empirical proof, 18

econometrics: Bayesian, 38; and W. A. Brock, 23; as empirical method, 45; and D. K. Foley's disillusion, 184; and R. H. Frank, 108; and R. B. Norgaard, 221–22; vs. theory, 32

economic actors, and globally optimal decisions, 264

economic decisions, and why they are made, 278

economics: and cognitive science, 284; and developments in past twenty-five years, 305–6; and difference from the 1940s, 291–92; and diversity, 296; as engineering, 59; and its future, 73, 74, 100, 130–32, 152–54, 180–81, 210, 211–12, 225–26, 249, 269, 283, 285–87; and history of theory, 291–92; and how to define, 211–12; how working in other fields helps an economist, 247; and incremental improvements, 149; and language, 42–43; and its links to other fields, 103; and mathematics, 31; and its most important developments, 73; radical, 79; and significance testing, 36–37, 44; as social science, 28–29; and threats from other disciplines, 211

economics of information, 252

economics profession: and centralization of power, 209; as complex system, 306; and its hierarchical organization, 187–88; and opening it to other disciplines, 246; and openness to new ideas, 130; and what it rewards, 221–22

economics schools, compared to business schools, 121

economic theory, and auction theory, 59

economic understanding, and policy debates, 249

economists: from abroad, 21–22; and access to government, 243; and boundaries of the profession, 1–2; as broadly cultivated individuals, 29; and physicists, 225

economy, and dynamic steady state, 267–68

econophysics: and mathematical identity, 295; and its models, 269

econophysics movement, 167–69

edge, of economics, 2, 3; and W. A. Brock, 177; and Center on Social and Economic Dynamics, 270; and its four different aspects, 22–24; and its history, 14–18; and those who work there, 9–14, 18–24

Edgeworth, Francis, and modern economics, 206

education: and European budgets, 235; and wages, 80–81

educational theory, and H. Gintis, 80–81

Edwards, Richard: and H. Gintis, 79, 82; and University of Massachusetts, 85

efficiency: as first goal of policy, 128–29; and government waste, 131–32; and neoclassical economics, 241; vs. social equity, 311; and sustainability, 238

efficiency wages, 211

Ehrenberg, Ron, and radical department at University of Massachusetts, 84

Ehrlich, Paul, 227–28, 230–31

eigenvalues, 173

El Ferol model, and agent-based modeling, 261

elite, and who's in it, 297–98

Ely, Richard T., and natural resource economics, 223–24

empirical arguments, and dominant strategy, 256

empirical credibility, and models, 265

empirical economics, as practiced by M. Rabin, 143

empirical evidence, and its value, 119

empirical work: and W. A. Brock, 23; and its cost, 306; and increasing importance, 305–6; and D. McCloskey, 32–33

endowment effect, 147–48, 149, 151

Engerman, Stan: and W. A. Brock, 160; and D. McCloskey, 32

engineering, and D. K. Foley, 186

Engle, Bob, and D. K. Foley, 195

enlightened self-interest, and economics' change to, 1

environmental economics: characterized, 223; and opposing forces, 221; as standard economics course, 219–20

environmental economists: and name-brand universities, 219; and tensions with ecological economists, 224

environmental epistemology, characterized, 232–33

environmental issues, and R. B. Norgaard, 215–18

environmental justice: and environmental economics, 234; and equity issues, 238

Environmental Protection Agency: and environmental economics, 223; and R. B. Norgaard, 238

Epstein, Joshua: and agent-based modeling, 256; and R. Axtell, 257, 264; and commercial applications of agent-based modeling, 271; and interdisciplinary credentials, 270; and orthodoxy, 279; and replication of computational models, 261–62

equilibria, multiple, 54–55

equilibrium: and aggregate steady state, 279–80; and W. A. Brock, 23; and economics' adherence to, 1, 2, 3–4; and evolutionarily stable strategies, 274; and how it works, 64–65; and trial-and-error adjustment, 52; undesirable, 174–75

equilibrium assumption, and game theory, 280–81

equilibrium theory: and public goods, 186; and its triumph, 63–64

equity theory, and economics, 143

ethics, and D. McCloskey's research, 42

evolution, of D. K. Foley's work, 204–5

evolutionary drift, and layers, 56

evolutionary economics: and relation to other concepts, 203; and its tenets, 279

evolutionary game theory, 1, 17, 22; and K. G. Binmore, 272; and edge of economics, 22; and integration of institutions in the analysis, 18; and H. P. Young, 23, 271–88

evolutionary model, and its dynamics, 174

evolutionary processes: and historical development, 273; and new work, 19

evolutionary stable strategies (ESS), and K. G. Binmore, 55

evolutionary theory, and ecological theory, 176–77

evolving ideas, and economics, 2–5

evolving preferences, and convergence, 259–60

experimental economics, 1; and changing behavior, 65–66; and the eco-

nomics of psychology, 144–46; and
empirical work, 18; and funding, 209;
and H. Gintis, 77–104; and the mainstream, 19, 20; and proper controls,
63–64; and rejection of traditional
economics, 145; and Henry Simon,
254; and structuring of textbooks, 12
experiments: controlled, 94–95; and M.
Rabin, 147
externalities: and W. A. Brock, 160–61;
and R. H. Frank, 116; and market-oriented ways of correcting, 161

Faber, Malte, and ecological economics,
223
fairness, 118, 119, 120; and behavioral
models, 54; and K. G. Binmore's theories, 68; and coevolution, 70; and E.
Fehr, 98; and D. K. Foley, 187; and its
evolutionary origin, 65–66, 272–73;
and future of labor economics, 152;
and games, 151; and leadership, 71;
and monetary components, 145; and
public decisions, 129; and reciprocity,
151; and selecting equilibria, 132; and
social preferences, 150
fallacy of division, 255
Farrell, Joe, and M. Rabin, 139, 140
federal policy, vs. solutions from communities, 230
Fehr, Ernst, and influence on experimental economics, 98
Fei, John, and D. K. Foley, 185
Feldman, Marcus, and stochastic stability, 275
feminism, and economics, 40–41
feminists, and heterodoxy, 9
Field, Alex, 43
financial crises, and recent developments in economics, 305
financial economics: and K. Arrow, 300;
and engineering discipline, 61
financial markets: and agent-based
modeling, 277; and computer power,
284; and T. Lux, 282; and Santa Fe
Institute, 295
first welfare theorem, and alternate terminology, 264

Fisher, Irving, and modern economics,
207
fish market, and A. Marshall, 286–87
Florida, Richard, at Carnegie Mellon
Public Policy School, 252
Fogel, Robert: and W. A. Brock, 160;
and D. McCloskey, 31, 32
Foley, Duncan K.: and K. Arrow,
297–98; and changing views, 14; and
the complexity revolution, 203; credentials, 213; and his crises at MIT,
192–93; and cutting edge, 198–99; and
H. Gintis, 86–87; and feelings of iso-
lation, 193–94; and how he became
an economist, 183–87, 188–89, 193–94,
201; and the mainstream, 23; and
pacifism, 188; and unifying vision,
192; and work in complexity, 23; and
his work on Marxian economics,
198–99
Foley/Sidrauski model, 195
Ford Foundation, and R. B. Norgaard,
218, 227
formalism: vs. interdisciplinary/multi-
disciplinary approach, 133–34; and its
problems, 116
fossil hydrocarbons, and their exhaus-
tion, 226
Foster, Dean, and perturbed dynamical
systems, 274
Fourier analysis, 186
Frank, Robert H.: and behavioral economics, 22, 110; and career choices,
115–16; credentials, 135; and distribution issues, 113–14; and experimental
economics, 99; and explanation of
the new work, 21; and how he
became an economist, 107–8; and
new work, 46; and Peace Corps, 108,
113–14; and personal choices, 108, 109,
111; and popularization, 22, 115–16;
and his publications, 110; and relative
reference work, 152–53; and Santa Fe
Institute, 124–25; and spread of his
ideas, 18, 122; and teaching career,
107, 108–9, 121
Freeman, Harold, and D. K. Foley,
193

of Massachusetts, 84; as social
activist, 77–80, 81, 83; and tenure,
298; and what he cares about, 87, 90
global changes, 2
global issues, and distribution, 243–44
Gödel's theorem: and common knowledge, 59–60; and perfect rationality,
61–62
gold, 14–15
Goleman, Daniel, and popularizing
others' work, 122–23
Goodwin, Richard M., and D. K. Foley,
201, 204
Gordon, David, assessed by R. H.
Frank, 120
government intervention, and
agricultural economics,
220
Gowdy, John, and R. B. Norgaard, 232
graduate economics, and the way it is
taught, 92–93
graduate programs, their homogenization, 210
graduate students, and agent-based
modeling, 270
Graham, Carol, and interdisciplinary
credentials, 270
greed, and economics' adherence to, 1,
3–4
Griliches, Zvi, and H. Gintis, 82
Gunderson, Lance H., and ecological
economics, 173
Gurley, Jack, and Marxian economics,
196
Gustafson, Eric, as D. McCloskey's
teacher, 28
Güth, Werner, and ultimatum game
theory, 53–54

Haberler, Gottfried, and influence on
H. Gintis, 79
Hall, Robert: and Axtell/Epstein retirement model, 264; and R. H. Frank,
109
Hamilton, William, and game theory,
272
Hansen, Alvin, and economists of the
1940s, 29

Hansen, Lars Peter: and Knightian
uncertainty, 13; and rational expectations, 202
Harberger, Al, and D. McCloskey, 31
Harberger, Arnold: and market decisions, 237–38; and R. B. Norgaard,
219
Harris, Don, and Marxian economics,
196–97
Harris, Lawrence, and London School
of Economics' efforts to fire him, 189
Harrison, Bennett, and R. Axtell, 252
Harsanyi, John: and game theory, 305;
and game theory/biology, 53; and
interpersonal comparison of utility,
67
Hart, Oliver, and M. Rabin, 138
Harvard University, and H. Gintis's
experience there, 82–84
Hayek, Friedrich, and the price system,
302
Heckman, James: and his important
work, 21; and statistical significance,
45
Heilbroner, Robert, and influence on
D. McCloskey, 27
Hellwig, Martin, and D. K. Foley, 195
Hendry, David, and work in macroeconomics, 301
Herreiner, Dorothea, and dynamics of
markets, 286
heterodox, and H. Gintis's objection to
the characterization, 103
heterodoxy, 6, 8; and ecological economics, 224; in Europe, 44; and
funding difficulties, 14; vs. orthodoxy, 9, 296
heterodoxy/orthodoxy, and W. A.
Brock, 163
heterogeneity: and mainstream, 279–80;
and microeconomics, 301; and orthodoxy, 279–80
Hicks, John, 7
Hildenbrand, and large-economy limits, 179
hiring, and criteria for, 165
Hirshman, Albert O., and H. Gintis,
82–84

Hobsbawm, Eric, and D. McCloskey, 30

Hodgson, Geoffrey C.: and coevolution, 230; and ecological economics, 223; and Marx's labor theory of value, 85; and R. B. Norgaard, 232

Holdren, John, and R. B. Norgaard, 227–28

Holland, John, and Santa Fe conferences, 263

Holling, C. S. ("Buzz"), and ecological economics, 173

Holling's Frustration, 174

Hommes, Cars, and W. A. Brock, 178

homodox, defined by H. Gintis, 91

homogeneous agents, and heterodoxy, 279–80

Horgan, John, and agent-based modeling, 265

Hotelling, Harold: and allocation of resources, 235; and mathematical economics, 291; and modern economics, 206

Howarth, Richard, and R. B. Norgaard, 235, 238

Hume, David, and balance of payments, 15

hyperbolic discounting, 145–46; and core macro, 152

ideas: and acceptance by the elite, 4, 5; and their dissemination, 11–13

ideology, and D. K. Foley, 195

Illich, Ivan, and importance of skills, 81

imperfect competition: and K. Arrow, 299; and game theory, 292

impossibility theorem, and K. G. Binmore, 50

inclusion, and economics, 101–2

income equality, 237

inefficiencies, and policy, 131

infinite possibilities, and simplicity, 258–59

information: as a commodity, 299–300; and heterogeneity, 301; increasing, 125; and its treatment, 305–6

informational economics, as important change, 152

innovation, vs. technical competence, 297

insider/outsider behavior, 96

Institute for Advanced Study, and H. Gintis, 82, 85–86

institutional economics, and computer power, 285

institutionalist economists, and ecological economics, 223

institutions, and their design, 285–87

integer programming, 185

interacting particle systems, 169

interconnectedness, 232–33

interdisciplinary economics, 25n. 10

interdisciplinary programs, and agent-based modeling, 276–77

interest rate, 235–37

International Society for Ecological Economics (ISEE), 222

interviewees, rationale in choosing, 20–24

invisible hand, and competition, 125

invisible hand theorem, and swarm intelligence, 264

Iowa, University of, and D. McCloskey, 33–34, 35–36, 43

Ishikawa, Tsuneo, and H. Gintis, 86

Ising models, 169

Jansson, Ann-Mari, 222

Japanese auction, and K. G. Binmore, 71–72

Jencks, Christopher S. ("Sandy"), and H. Gintis, 83

Jevons, William Stanley, and evolution of neoclassical economics, 15, 16

job market, and M. Rabin, 132

jobs: and connections, 193–95; and getting hired, 5, 94

Johnson, Harry, and R. B. Norgaard, 217

Jones, Ron, and W. A. Brock, 160

Journal of Economic Perspectives, and formalistic scientific models, 134

journals: cutting edge, 209, 210; and economics education, 310; and D. K. Foley, 198–99; and keeping up, 297; mainstream, and editorial shortcom-

ings, 199; and publication in
agent-based modeling, 270–71; and
the respect they command, 115
Jovanovic, Boyan, and R. Axtell's firms
model, 268
Judd, Ken, and numerical economics,
281–82

Kahn, Fred, and R. H. Frank, 110
Kahneman, Daniel: and game theory,
94; and innovation, 130; and rational
choice framework, 116–17
Kandori, Michihiro, and game theory,
57, 58
Kant, Immanuel, and K. G. Binmore,
68
Kasen, Carl, and economists of the
1940s, 29
Kennedy, Joan Taylor, and market theory, 41
Keynes, John Maynard: and critics of
The General Theory, 312; and game
theory, 304; and the macroeconomic
revolution, 16–17; and market clearing, 101; and recognition, 292
Keynesian Cross, and D. K. Foley, 183
Keynesian economics, and New School
for Social Research, 206
Keynesian model, 17
Kirman, Alan: and dynamics of mar-
kets, 286; and large-economy limits,
179
Klein, Lawrence, and large-scale econo-
metrics, 270
Klemperer, Paul, and British telecom
auctions, 71–72
Knightian uncertainty, 13
Koopmans, Tjalling C.: and D. K. Foley,
186, 298; and modern economics,
207–8
Kremer, Michael, and data collection,
103–4
Kreps, D. P., 252; and game theory, 97
Krueger, Alan, and his important work,
21
Krueger, Anne, and mainstream elite,
10
Krugman, Paul: and geographical con-

siderations in economics, 32, 35; and
mainstream acceptance, 3
Kuhn, Thomas: and economics'
modification of paradigm shift, 4, 12;
and P. Samuelson, 312
Kuhn-Tucker-type theorems, 185
Kuran, Timur, and explosive change,
132

labor, and economics at University of
Massachusetts, 85
labor market, and price of moral satisfaction, 128
Laffont, Jean-Jacques, and empirical
work, 305
LaGrange multiplier, 170–71
Laibson, David: and behavioral economics, 94; and hyperbolic discounting, 145; and improving savings
behavior, 153
laissez-faire, and neoclassicists, 311
Lakatos, Imre, 4
lake game model, and catastrophe theory model, 173
lakes, and stable states, 174–75
language: and its power, 187; and same
terms with different meanings, 248
Lave, Lester, and R. Axtell, 252–53
Leamer, Ed, and testing, 39
learning, and different strategies, 185
LeBaron, Blake: and agent-based simulations, 178, 179; and financial markets, 277, 282; and rational expecta-
tions/realistic regimes, 265
Ledyard, John, and private provision of
public goods, 65–66
Le Grand, Julian, and M. Rabin, 138
Leontief, Wassily: and H. Gintis, 83–84;
and modern economics, 206
Lerner, Lange, and K. Arrow, 299
Levenstein, Chuck, and H. Gintis, 78
Levitt, Steve, and data collection, 103–4
Levy, Frank, and acceptance at different
schools, 127–28
Lewis, Alain, and complexity theory,
305
Lewis, David, and common knowledge,
60

linear programming, 207; and P. Samuelson, 310

Lipman, Bart, and R. Axtell, 252

Litan, Bob, and interdisciplinary support, 270

Lloyd, Seth, and complexity definitions, 168

local changes, 2

Locke, John, and H. Gintis, 88–89

London School of Economics, and M. Rabin, 138

loss aversion, and continuity, 148–49

Lucas, Robert E., Jr.: and the importance of tools for economics, 260; and invisible hand theorem, 264; and D. McCloskey, 31; and new work, 46; and rational expectations, 202; and P. Samuelson, 311; and his writing, 35–36

Luce, R. Duncan, and game theory, 97

Lux, Thomas: and financial markets, 282; and nonnormal distribution, 267

MacArthur Foundation: and funding, 257; and H. Gintis, 92

MacEwan, Arthur, and H. Gintis, 79

macroeconomic dynamics, and suboptimal outcomes, 264–65

macroeconomics: and agent specification, 285; and its models, 301–2; and P. Samuelson's assessment, 311–12

Mailath, George J., and game theory, 57, 58

mainstream: and agent-based modeling, 270; and agent-level equilibrium, 255–56; and behavioral economics, 127; and bounded rationality, 279–80; and change, 4–5, 16, 17, 18, 19, 37; and coevolutionary approach, 231–32; and its composition, 3; and dynamic change, 4–5; and experimental economics, 19; and D. K. Foley, 23; and government policymaking, 238; and heterogeneity, 279–80; and its meaning, 5–6, 9; and its membership, 94, 270; and R. B. Norgaard, 221–22; vs. orthodox, 8; and pragmatic design,

286; and M. Rabin, 151; and rapid change, 16–18; and social networks, 279–80

mainstream change, and strong economists, 240

mainstream journals, and editorial shortcomings, 199

Maler, Karl-Göran, and ecological economics, 173

Malthus, Thomas: and J. M. Keynes, 16; and Adam Smith, 15

Mandelbrot, B. B.: and D. K. Foley, 206; and stock market price fluctuations, 267

Manhattan Project for large-scale software, 262

Manski, Charles F., and W. A. Brock, 166

Mantegna, Rosario N., and nonnormal distribution, 267

marginalist revolution, 7

Marglin, Steve: and lack of knowledge, 95; and his radical direction, 196

market, and feminism, 40–41

market equilibrium, and money, 195

market failure, and buying and selling labor, 85

market power, and its abuse, 62

markets, 100–101; and their design, 286–87; and efficiency, 19; and environmental problems, 220; and the lack of self-control, 153; and what freshmen need to learn, 62

Markov chains, 275

Marschak, Jacob, and modern economics, 207

Marshall, Alfred, 7; and ecology, 225; and evolution of neoclassical economics, 15; and J. M. Keynes, 16–17; and modern economics, 206

Martinez-Allier, Juan, and R. B. Norgaard, 222–23

Marx, Karl, 8; and labor theory of value, 85, 86

Marxian economics: and D. K. Foley, 86–87, 192, 196–97, 198–99, 200–201,

204; formally elaborated, 197; and funding, 209

Marxian theory, and profit opportunities, 120

Marxism: and Arrow/Debreu, 87; and distribution, 244; and game theory, 97–98; and H. Gintis, 22, 78, 85, 86, 87–89, 90–91

Marxist economics, and New School for Social Research, 206

Marxist economists: and ecological economics, 223; in the 1970s, 30

Marxists, and heterodoxy, 9

Mason, Ed, and economists of the 1940s, 29

materialism, and environmental problems, 244

mathematical economics, and coevolution with computer technology, 234

mathematical modeling, and policy, 187

mathematics: and the advantages of its training, 73; and K. G. Binmore, 49–50; and W. A. Brock, 157–58; and computers, 181; departments, and game theory, 283; and economics, 30, 31; and economists' training, 302; and D. K. Foley, 183; and R. H. Frank's career, 107–8; and H. Gintis, 77; inductive vs. deductive in economics, 302–3; and R. B. Norgaard, 215, 217; as preparation for economics, 158–59, 161–62; and Howard Raiffa, 79; and the University of Chicago, 161

Maxis Entertainment, and games, 263

May, Robert, and complexity, 228

McCloskey, Deirdre: and applied economics, 30; and Arrow/Debreu, 302; and Aunt Deirdre persona, 41; and challenge to mainstream, 18; and changing views, 14; characterizes herself, 34; and Chicago School, 30–32, 33–34, 44; classmate of H. Gintis, 79; credentials, 47; and empirical work, 32–33; and gender-crossing, 29–30, 34, 39–41; and E. Hobsbawn, 30; and influence on M. Rabin, 143–44; and

Iowa, University of, 33–34, 35–36, 43; and political issues of the 1960s, 29; and postmodernist influence, 22; and rhetorical work, 33–34, 35; and rhetoric in economics, 244; and socialism, 29, 30; and Stanford University, 31, 32; teachers who influenced her, 27–28; and University of Illinois at Chicago, 43–44; why she is an economist, 27

McCloskey, Donald. *See* McCloskey, Deirdre

McFadden, Daniel: and W. A. Brock, 163, 166; and R. H. Frank, 109

McGovern, George, and W. A. Brock, 163

McRae, Greg, and R. Axtell, 253

Medio, Alfredo, and Marx's labor theory of value, 85

Menger, Carl, and evolution of neoclassical economics, 15, 16

mercantilism, as precursor of classical economics, 14–15

metaphor, and communication with the public, 244–45

meteorology, and theory, 293–94

methodological change, and edge of economics, 22

Meyer, John, as D. McCloskey's teacher, 28

Michelson, Stephan, and H. Gintis, 79

microeconomic equilibrium, and complex systems, 193–94

Milgrom, J. Roberts, and game theory, 97

Milgrom, Paul, and common knowledge, 60

Mill, John Stuart, and Adam Smith, 15

Miller, John, and R. Axtell, 257

Miller, Merton, and D. McCloskey, 31

minimum wage, and unemployment, 36

Minsky, Marvin, and artificial intelligence, 131

Mirowski, Philip: and R. Axtell's work, 269; and complexity theory, 304–5; on economics and related disciplines, 207; and neoclassical theory, 205

MIT: as best graduate school for M. Rabin, 138–39; and D. K. Foley, 189–93; and offerings in graduate education, 94; and the study of psychology, 141; and Walrasian orthodoxy, 191

Mitchell, Wesley, and dominance in economics, 291–92

mixed strategies, and J. von Neumann, 304

model: agent-based, 1, 23; of the human actor, 94; Keynesian, 12, 17; rational expectations, 17; standard, 19

model building: and complexity, 17; and computer simulations, 17, 18; and the mainstream, 17; and nonlinear dynamics, 20

modeling, and alternative methodologies, 10–11

models: and ecologists, 223; and policy decisions, 239–40; and protective barriers, 178–79; and their simplification, 145; and their usefulness, 149

modern economics, and how it evolved, 206

modified evolutionary stable strategies (MESS), described, 55–56

monetary policy, and D. K. Foley, 186

money: and formulation of an impossible problem, 192, 195; its function and power, 101; and irrational behavior, 150; and the Keynesian model, 17; and Marxism, 198–99; and M. Sidrauski's work, 190; and a synthetic view, 195–96; and whether it matters, 145

money illusion, and future economics, 152

Monsanto, and Bt corn, 177

Moore's Law, 186

moral hazard, and K. Arrow, 300

moral voice, and D. McCloskey, 41–42

Morgenstern, Oscar: and K. G. Binmore, 50–51; and competitive equilibrium, 303; and game theory, 304

Morse, Chandler, and R. B. Norgaard, 217–18

Mott, Tracy, and D. K. Foley, 196

Mullainathan, Sendhil: and behavioral economics, 94; and data collection, 103–4; and demand for behavioral economics, 127

multiagent models, of organizations, 285

multiagent systems, and purposeful behavior, 263

multidisciplinary economics, 25n. 10

multidisciplinary programs, and their value, 248

multiple equilibria: and K. Arrow, 186; and W. A. Brock's strategy, 162, 163; and the complexity vision, 185; and the evidence, 163

multiple ways of thinking, 225

multivariable regression techniques, and early advances, 311

Mun, Thomas, and balance of payments, 15

Mundell, Robert, and Alfred Marshall, 247

Musgrave, Richard, and D. K. Foley, 198

Myerson, Roger, and bargaining theory, 51

Nagel, Ernest, and "as if" arguments, 253

Nash, John: and K. G. Binmore, 51–53, 54–55, 56–57, 64; and competitive equilibrium, 303–4; and A. Cournot, 303–4; and mixed strategy equilibria, 280–81

Nash equilibria, and social regularities, 255

Nash equilibrium model, 280–81

National Academy of Science, and interdisciplinary scholarship, 238

National Science Foundation, and funding, 9

natural resource economics, and ecological economics, 223–24

Nelson, John, and influence on D. McCloskey, 34

Nelson, Richard R., and evolution, 230

neoclassical approach, espoused by R. H. Frank, 116–17

neoclassical economics, 2, 5, 6, 7–8; and

K. Arrow's education, 292; and its Chicago branch, 8; and conspiracy to protect, 68; and its evolution, 15; and financial economic theory, 19; as considered by H. Gintis, 80, 89; and its methodological approach, 143–44; and R. B. Norgaard, 239; and its Paretian-Pigovian branch, 8; and its quality, 233; and where it works, 64

neoclassical model: and its critics, 240; and economists' use of it, 226–27; and fairness, 119; and skewed distribution, 267

neoclassical paradigm, and ecological economics, 224

neoclassical synthesis, and P. Samuelson, 310–11

neoclassical theory: and D. K. Foley, 184; and human behavior, 95; and physics, 205; and power-law distribution, 206

neoclassicism, and the future of economics, 269

new assumptions, vs. surprising results from old assumptions, 140

Newberry, and his trucking study, 161

New Classical rational expectations model, 13, 17

new economics, 1

Newell, A., and complex information processing, 253–54

New School for Social Research, and D. K. Foley, 206

nonlinear dynamical systems, and their usefulness, 266

nonlinear dynamics: and general equilibrium, 18; and the mainstream, 20; and model building, 20

nonlinear programming, and P. Samuelson, 310

nonlinear techniques, and W. A. Brock, 23

Norgaard, Richard B.: and K. Arrow, 23; and H. J. Barnett, 217–18; and Bayesian econometrics, 221–22; and M. Brewer, 216; and H. Brown, 216; and constructive dissent, 240; and cost-benefit analysis, 128; and his

current research, 245; and H. Daly, 216; and P. Diamond, 216; and discount rate, 300; and *Ecological Economics,* 221–22; and Environmental Protection Agency, 223, 238; and Ford Foundation, 218, 227; and M. Friedman, 217; and Arnold Harberger, 232; and J. Holdren, 227–28; and R. Howarth, 235, 238; and how he became an economist, 215–20; and H. Johnson, 217; and mainstream, 221–22; and J. Martinez-Allier, 222–23; and mathematics, 215, 217; and C. Morse, 217–18; and neoclassical economics, 2, 5, 6, 7–8; and new ecological economics, 23; and Santa Fe Institute, 13; and T. W. Shultz, 218–19; and Sierra Club, 215–16; and M. Smith, 231; and G. Tolley, 219; and University of Chicago, 217–19

normal economists, and evidence, 177–78

norms, and problem solving, 124

North, Douglas, and D. McCloskey, 41

no-trade theorem, and econophysics, 269

Notre Dame University, 43

numerical economics, and computational economists, 281–82

Oaxaco, Ron, and radical department at University of Massachusetts, 84

object-oriented programming, and agents, 260–61

O'Brien, Denis, and K. Arrow, 299

O'Laughlin, Bridget, and D. K. Foley, 196

Old Institutionalists, and heterodoxy, 9

optimal habitat design, and economists, 180

organizational science, 285

originality, and the edge of economics, 3–4

orthodoxy: and its acceptance of variance, 3; and basic tenets, 279; compared to heterodoxy, 9, 296; vs. mainstream, 8, 9; and its meaning, 5, 6; in modern economics, 209–10;

Prisoners' Dilemma, and R. Axelrod, 71, 271

probability theory, and K. G. Binmore, 50

production theory, and undergraduate teaching, 92–93

programming, linear and nonlinear, 185

progress, in economics, 312

promotion, in academia, 127–28, 188

Proops, John L. R., and ecological economics, 223

Proposition 13 (California), and education, 132

proto-neoclassicals, 15

psychological economics, 17–18; and its development, 296; as important change, 152; and teaching the subject, 151; and treatment of rationality, 18

psychologists, and pressure on economics, 211

psychology: and economics, 143; and M. Rabin's study, 131–32

publication, 11, 188; and W. A. Brock, 165; and its difficulty, 270–71; and R. H. Frank, 114–15, 122; in good journals, 130; and perturbed dynamical systems, 273–74, 275; preferred media, 123; and its professional value, 123; vs. pursuit of new ideas, 194

purposeful behavior, and economics' change to, 1

quality control, in economics, 249

Quesnay, François, and Adam Smith, 15

Rabin, Matthew: and behavioral economics, 22; credentials, 155; and experimental economics, 99; and formal modeling of fairness, 119–20; and how he became an economist, 137–38; and innovation, 130; and interdisciplinary interests, 131–32; and interest rate, 236; and psychology in economics, 73; and risk aversion, 69; and spread of his ideas, 122

radicalization, and Vietnam War, 192–93

radical vision, and understanding people, 153–54

Radner, Roy, and the problem of time, 301

Rafael, Rob, and game theory, 57, 58

Raiffa, Howard: and game theory, 97; and influence on H. Gintis, 79

Ramsey, Frank, and discount rates, 145–46

RAND Corporation, and modern economics, 207

Rapping, Leonard, 13; and University of Massachusetts, 85

rational agents, and aggregate rationality, 277–78

rational behavior, and economic thinking, 292

rational choice: and D. Kahneman, 115–17; and the prescriptive decisions, 131

rational choice model, and its interpretation, 116–17

rational expectations: and W. A. Brock, 163, 166; and D. K. Foley, 202; and its interpretation, 116–17; and the no-trade theorem, 269; and orthodoxy, 210; and realistic regimes, 265; and its replacement, 211; revolution, 12–13, 17; and P. Samuelson, 311

rationality: as basic tenet of orthodoxy, 279–80; and economics' adherence to, 1, 3–4

rational outcome, when individuals are not rational, 264

Raven, Peter, and coevolution, 228, 230–31

Rawls, John: and K. G. Binmore, 67–68; and justice, 273, 311; and "veil of ignorance," 236

real mainstream, and optimization exercises, 120

real world, and paying a price, 166

redistribution, and efficiency, 130

redistribution of rights, and efficiency questions, 234

regulation, and messing up the economy, 126

regulatory policy, and recent developments in economics, 305

renewable energy, 226

RePast, program system for system models, 262

researchers, youthful and older, 22–23

Resilience Alliance, 173, 174–75, 176

Resnick, Rick, and University of Massachusetts, 85

Resnick, Steve, and postmodernism, 90

resource scarcity, and R. Howarth, 235

retirement model, and computational approach, 264

Review of Radical Political Economy (RRPE): and D. K. Foley, 198; and H. Gintis, 81

rhetoric, and D. McCloskey, 33–34, 35, 37–38

Ricardo, David: and J. M. Keynes, 16; and Adam Smith, 15

Richerson, Peter J., and evolutionary game theory, 98

rights, and future generations, 236–38

Rose, Hugh, and W. A. Brock, 160

Rosen, Sherwin: and W. A. Brock, 160; and R. H. Frank, 123

Roth, Alvin: and game theory, 94; and matching markets, 286; and revealed preference theory, 65–66

Rothenburg, Tom, and R. H. Frank, 109

Rubin, I. I., and Marxism, 87

Rubinstein, Ariel: and bargaining theory, 51, 52, 53; and bounded rationality, 56; and unique equilibrium, 60

Rust, John, and numerical economics, 281–82

Sahlins, Marshall, and Prickly Paradigm Pamphlets, 41

Salant, Steve, and R. H. Frank, 110

Salovey, Peter, and emotional intelligence, 122

Samuelson, Larry: and coordinated action, 60; and modified evolutionary stable strategies, 55, 56–58; and Santa Fe Institute, 102–3; and the ultimatum game, 66

Samuelson, Paul A., 7; and being

wrong, 312; and A. Bergson, 311; and bifurcation, 173–74; credentials, 313; discusses his *Foundations,* 310; and M. Friedman, 311; and influence of his textbook on H. Gintis, 78; and judging new trends, 309–10; and R. Lucas, 311; and mainstream elite, 10; and D. McCloskey's characterization, 37, 43, 44; at MIT, 189, 191; and neoclassical synthesis, 310–11; and new ideas, 312; and physics, 205; and RAND Corporation, 207; and rational expectations, 311; and his reflections on change, 21; and T. Sargent, 311; and Herbert Simon, 311; and A. Smith, 311

Sandburg, Lars, as D. McCloskey's teacher, 28

sandslide models, 169–70, 171

Santa Fe Institute, 13; and its approach to economics, 102; and K. Arrow, 294–95; and R. Axtell, 257; and W. A. Brock, 166; and R. H. Frank, 124–25; and getting better at economics, 205; and new ways of thinking, 19–20; and R. B. Norgaard, 231; and relation of two complementary approaches, 169–71; and T. Sargent, 19; and work in complexity, 23

Sargent, Thomas, 13; classmate of H. Gintis, 79; and his important work, 21; and loss of faith in rational expectations, 19; and the no-trade theorem, 269; and rational expectations, 202; and P. Samuelson, 311

Savage, L., and consistency, 62–63

scaling laws, 168–71; and econophysicists, 269; and exponents in power relations, 266; and relevance for economics, 267–68

scarcity, and natural resources, 218

Scarf, Herbert, and D. K. Foley, 184, 185

Schelling, Thomas C.: and agent-based modeling, 269; and evolutionary dynamics, 257; and game theory, 140, 141; and influence on R. H. Frank, 116; and mainstream acceptance, 3; and mainstream elite, 10; and opera-

tion at the edge, 287; and parsimonious representation, 257–58
Scholes, Myron, and D. McCloskey, 31
Schultz, George, and D. McCloskey, 31
Scott, Anthony, and natural resource economics, 223–24
self-interest, and its interpretation, 150
self-organized criticality, 266
Seltein, Reinhard: and Bayesian approach, 62; and game theory, 52, 53
Sen, Amartya, and mainstream elite, 10
Sen, Chiranjib, and D. K. Foley, 196
Sen, Gita, and D. K. Foley, 196
Shakel, Avner, and Nash bargaining solution, 52, 53–54
Shannon indices, 176
Shell, Karl, and MIT, 191
"shoulds," and economics, 236
Shultz, T. W., and R. B. Norgaard, 218–19
Sidrauski, Martha, murder in Argentina, 190
Sidrauski, Miguel: and D. K. Foley, 189, 190; and rational expectations, 202
Sierra Club, and R. B. Norgaard, 215–16
signaling problem, and R. Axtell, 256
significance testing: and economics, 36–38, 44; and empirical method, 45
SimCity, as game without social science content, 263
Simon, Henry, and P. Samuelson, 311
Simon, Herbert: and R. Axtell, 23, 254, 266; at Carnegie Mellon, 253, 264; and characterization as economist, 252; and complex information processing, 253–54; and complexity, 293; and R. D. Luce, 268; and O. Morgenstern, 268; and skewed distributions, 268; and sociology, 285; and U-shaped cost curve, 267; and vindication of his views, 287–88; and J. von Neumann, 268
Sims, Chris, and work in macroeconomics, 301
Smith, Adam: and complexity, 168; and instability, 185; as mainstream economist, 15; and myopic agents, 264; and

philosophy of ethics, 42; and P. Samuelson, 311
Smith, Eric, and physics' relation to economics, 205
Smith, Maynard: and agent-based modeling, 265; and evolutionarily stable strategies, 274; and game theory, 52, 53, 55, 98, 272; and R. B. Norgaard, 231
Smith, Vernon: and bargaining, 52; and behavioral economics, 94; and data sharing, 145; and difference in experimental methods, 144; and experimenting, 98; and radical department at University of Massachusetts, 84
Smithies, Arthur: and the CIA, 82; and H. Gintis's Ph.D. dissertation, 81; as D. McCloskey's teacher, 28
smoking, and government policy, 126
Smolensky, Eugene, and M. Rabin, 137–38
socialism: and K. Arrow, 299; and its downfall, 89–90; and D. McCloskey, 29, 30, 39
socialization theory, and internalization of norms, 101–2
social networks, 279–80
social psychology, and experimental economics, 96
social science: and its components, 73, 74; and controlled experiments, 80; and politics, 96–97; and its tensions, 93–94
social theory, and D. K. Foley, 192
social welfare function, and political process, 241–42
sociologists, and pressure on economics, 211–12
software, and simulation, 284
Solow, Robert: and his influence, 36; and mainstream elite, 10; and MIT pressure, 189; and MIT teaching, 191; and problem solving, 192; and RAND Corporation, 207; and P. Samuelson, 312; and truth, 35
Sonnenschein, Hugo, and radical department at University of Massachusetts, 84

ulations, 178; and the SymBioSys platform, 263

testing, 36–39, 44, 147; and controlled experiments, 80

tests, and rhetoric, 37–38

textbooks: and K. G. Binmore's in math, 50; and dissemination of new ideas, 11–13; and economists' faulty choices, 92; and the standard principles book, 62

Thaler, Richard: and acceptance of new ideas, 117; and R. H. Frank, 110; and improving savings behavior, 153; and incorporation of more realistic models, 152; and innovation, 130; and mainstream elite, 10; and postanomalies behavioral economics, 147; and risk aversion, 69; and term "behavioral economics," 142

theory: and adaptation, 178–79; and evidence, 80

Thom, René, and catastrophe theory, 173

Thompson, Gary, and R. Axtell, 252–53

Thompson, Russell, and influence on W. A. Brock, 158

Thompson, Sandy, and D. K. Foley, 196

Tilman-type model, 176

time, and information processing, 301

Tirole, Jean, and empirical work, 305

Tobin, James, and D. K. Foley, 185

Tobin tax, 179

Tolley, George, and R. B. Norgaard, 219

tools, and their importance in development of economics, 260

tradable permits, 220, 223, 234

transdisciplinary economics, 18, 25n. 10

transdisciplinary work, and K. Arrow, 299

truth: and H. Gintis, 87, 91; and D. McCloskey, 35, 42; and science, 158; and R. Solow, 35; and teaching undergraduate economics, 92–93

turf protection, and the philosophy of science, 171–72

turnpike growth theory, 185

Tversky, A.: and acceptance of new ideas, 117; and innovation, 130

two-person zero-sum game, 203, 208

ultimatum games, and confusion, 150–51

uncertainty: and honest reporting, 177–78; and its true level, 175–76

unemployment, and minimum wage, 36

unexpected utility theory, and its disappearance, 64

union movement, and its relevance, 90

Union of Radical Political Economy (URPE), and H. Gintis, 81

University of California at Berkeley: and its economics department, 142; and R. H. Frank's career, 108–9

University of Chicago: and W. A. Brock, 161, 164; and R. B. Norgaard, 217–19

University of Illinois at Chicago, and D. McCloskey, 43–44

University of Iowa, and D. McCloskey, 33–34, 35–36, 43

University of Massachusetts, and H. Gintis's radical department, 84–85

University of Rochester, and W. A. Brock, 160, 161

University of Wisconsin, and W. A. Brock, 164

utility maximization, 149–50

utility theory economics, and classical thermodynamics, 205

values, and models, 232–33

Varian, Hal R., 152; and his micro textbook, 147–48

Vaughan, Richard, and game theory, 58

Veblen, Thorstein, 8; and complexity, 293; and evolution, 230

Veblenian institutionalist approach, 203

Vietnam War, 50, 79, 82; and academic freedom, 189; and American imperialism, 196; and career choices, 188–89; and emotional political issues, 196; and general equilibrium economics, 187; and D. McCloskey,